THE VIRUS TOUCH

EXPERIMENTAL FUTURES: Technological Lives, Scientific Arts, Anthropological Voices

A series edited by Michael M. J. Fischer and Joseph Dumit

THE VIRUS TOUCH

Theorizing Epidemic Media

BISHNUPRIYA GHOSH

Duke University Press *Durham and London* 2023

Printed in the United States of America on acid-free paper ∞
Designed by Courtney Leigh Richardson
Typeset in Portrait and IBM Plex Mono
by Westchester Publishing Services

Library of Congress Cataloging-in-Publication Data
Names: Ghosh, Bishnupriya, author.
Title: The virus touch : theorizing epidemic media / Bishnupriya Ghosh.
Other titles: Experimental futures.
Description: Durham : Duke University Press, 2023. | Series: Experimental futures | Includes bibliographical references and index.
Identifiers: LCCN 2022040234 (print)
LCCN 2022040235 (ebook)
ISBN 9781478019213 (paperback)
ISBN 9781478016571 (hardcover)
ISBN 9781478023845 (ebook)
Subjects: LCSH: Epidemics in mass media. | COVID-19 (Disease) in mass media. | AIDS (Disease) in mass media. | Pandemics—Social aspects. | Health risk communication. | BISAC: SOCIAL SCIENCE / Media Studies
Classification: LCC P96.E63 G46 2023 (print) | LCC P96.E63 (ebook) | DDC 306.4/61—dc23/eng/20230113
LC record available at https://lccn.loc.gov/2022040234
LC ebook record available at https://lccn.loc.gov/2022040235

Cover art: Luke Jerram, *Past, Present, Future.* Triptych of smallpox, untitled future mutation, and HIV. 25 × 18 cm, 21 cm, and 23 cm. Courtesy of the artist.

Contents

Illustrations

FIGURES

PLATES

Abbreviations

ACTG	AIDS Clinical Trials Group
ART	antiretroviral therapy
ARV	antiretroviral
BCI	Barro Colorado Island
CDC	Centers for Disease Control and Prevention
cDNA	complementary DNA
CFAR	Centers for AIDS Research
CHEETAH	Center for the Structural Biology of Cellular Host Elements in Egress, Trafficking, and Assembly of HIV
CNICS	the CFAR Network of Integrated Clinical Systems
DRC	Democratic Republic of the Congo
DSN	disease surveillance network
EID	emerging infectious disease
Env-DATA	Environmental-Data Automated Track Annotation
EVL	Electronic Visualization Laboratory
FDA	US Food and Drug Administration
GIS	geographic information system
GVFI	Global Viral Forecasting Initiative
HIVE	HIV Interactions in Viral Evolution
HMP	Human Microbiome Project

HST	Humsafar Trust
HVTN	HIV Vaccine Trials Network
IAC	International AIDS Conference
IUCN	International Union for the Conservation of Nature
JAMA	*Journal of the American Medical Association*
LDMS	Laboratory Data Management System
MSF	Médecins Sans Frontières
MSM	men who have sex with men
NACO	National AIDS Control Organization (India)
NCSA	National Center for Supercomputing Applications
NEA	National Endowment for the Arts
NIH	National Institutes of Health
NHP	nonhuman primate
PBMC	peripheral blood mononuclear cell
PCBs	polychlorinated biphenyls
PCR	polymerase chain reaction
PEP	postexposure prophylaxis
PEPFAR	US President's Emergency Plan for AIDS Relief
PLHIV	people living with HIV
PPE	personal protective equipment
PrEP	pre-exposure prophylaxis
RT-PCR	reverse transcription polymerase chain reaction
SAIC	School of the Art Institute of Chicago
SIGGRAPH	Special Interest Group on Computer Graphics and Interactive Techniques
SIV	simian immunodeficiency viruses
TG	transgender
TMV	tobacco mosaic virus
WHO	World Health Organization

Acknowledgments

Those who potentiated this hydra-headed book are legion. Those we lost to the HIV/AIDS pandemic and those who lived on provided the impetus before writing began in 2005. Since then, the debts assume concrete form: there are research clusters and institutions, colleagues and friends, solidarities and alliances whose engagements shape its form. The first investigations began as a modest contribution to a quarter-long research cluster, Speculative Globalities (2009), hosted in Irvine by the University of California Humanities Research Institute: Bhaskar Sarkar, Rita Raley, Cesare Casarino, Colin Milburn, Geeta Patel, Sudipta Sen, and Aimee Bahng were the first fellow travelers in theorizing speculative media. Thinking-feeling with other research enclaves has followed: Risk@ Humanities at the Society for the Humanities, Cornell University (2012–13); Speculative Futures (Critical Issues in America, 2011–12) at the University of California, Santa Barbara; Breakfast Club II, Santa Barbara (2019–present); and the Colby Summer Institute in the Environmental Humanities (2021). When I have presented parts of this work in lectures and conferences, my interlocutors have enriched the project. In particular, I recall discussions at the Thought of AIDS (Brown University), the World Picture Conferences, Rendering the Visible (Georgia State University), 4S, and the Society for Cinema and Media Studies meetings, as well at the University of California, Santa Cruz; the University of Washington; Columbia University; the University of Cape Town (AIDS and Society Research Unit); the University of Pennsylvania (Cinema and Media Studies); the University of Applied Arts (Vienna); and the University of California, Irvine. Most of all, my colleagues and graduate students across departments at the University of California, Santa Barbara, have been my intellectual life support in general. For this project, in particular, I have to call out Christopher Walker, Rahul Mukherjee, Lindsay Thomas, Megan Fernandes,

Joshua Neves, Lisa Han, Jeff Schieble, Nicole Starosielski, Melody Jue, Stephanie LeMenager, Alan Liu, Greg Siegel, Alenda Chang, Janet Walker, Constance Penley, Roger Friedland, Simonetta Falasca-Zamponi, Rich Kaplan, Catherine Nesci, Elisabeth Weber, Mayfair Yang, Russell Samolsky, Teresa Shewry, Paul Amar, Uttathya Chattopadhyaya, Debanuj Dasgupta, Surojit Kayal, Maile Young, Pujita Guha, Somak Mukherjee, Miguel Fuentes, Christina Guirguis, and Carolina Arias.

Across academic networks, there are those who have inspired, sharpening nascent thoughts and mature arguments: there is much I owe Anjali Arondekar, Lucy M. Burns, Alexandra Juhasz, Lucas Hilderbrand, Chandan Reddy, Conerly Casey, Madhushree Datta, Kaushik Sunder Rajan, Kirsten Ostherr, Priscilla Wald, Nanna Heidenreich, Alessandra Raengo, Angelo Restivo, Jennifer Barker, Renate Ferro, Vinzenz Hediger, Priya Jaikumar, Elizabeth Freeman, Rafico Ruiz, Radhika Govindrajan, John Durham Peters, Stacy Alaimo, Imre Szeman, Meghan Sutherland, Brian Price, Michael Warner, Cindy Patton, Hannah Landecker, Alec Nading, Pooja Rangan, Eileen Joy, Deirdre Joy, David Laishram, Chaoba Thiyam, and Debashree Mukherjee. For those who quietly provided institutional backing in time, thought, and resources, no book could be complete without you. A special thanks to David Theo Goldberg (University of California Humanities Institute), Timothy Murray (Society for the Humanities), Mark Juergensmeyer (Orfalea Center for Global and International Studies), and David Marshall (executive vice-chancellor, University of California, Santa Barbara). My editor, Courtney Berger at Duke University Press, kept faith with the project over fifteen years, offering critical insight and invaluable editorial guidance along the way—always with the graceful touch that directs without hampering creative energies. A big thanks to Somak Mukherjee, Lisa Lawley, and Sandra Korn for putting together the manuscript's many moving parts. This would have been a much lesser book without the incisive reviews from the two external reviewers at Duke University Press.

The generosity of practitioners, interviewees, and guides at the research sites for this book deserves special mention: Robert Coombs, Joan Dragavon, Erin Goecker, and Nina Kim (Clinical Retrovirus Lab, University of Washington); Vivek Anand, Santosh Karamba, and Urmi Jadhav (Humsafar Trust, Mumbai); Rebecca Hodes (AIDS and Society Research Unit, University of Cape Town), Fanelwa Gwashu and Anna Grimsrud (Médecins Sans Frontières, Cape Town); Janet Iwasa (Animation Lab, University of Utah); David S. Goodsell, Arthur Olson, and Stefano Forli (Center for Computational Structural Biology, Scripps Research); Melinda Rostal, Noam Ross, and Anne Laudisoit (EcoHealth Alliance); and Roland Kays (North Carolina State University). I thank those who threaded the needle, putting me in touch with these sites and hosting me across the world: Avijit Mukul Kishore, Diedre Joy, Somayeh Dodge, Kyle Croft, Swaha and Surojit Shome, Afzal Shah, Tufan Ghosh, Oinam Doren, Chaoba Thiyam, David Lashiram, and Suhair Solomon.

The font was always love and loss. Many are gone, but your imprints mark these pages. For those in my life living on with pandemics, with the difficulty of survival, this is written in solidarity. And always my coconspirator in large, dark rooms of moving forms and quieter environs of moving thoughts, Bhaskar Sarkar, as we continue to continue, without your touch the experiential fabric of this book would not exist.

INTRODUCTION

Epidemic Media

We are not alone. Once, that iconic observation compelled fantasies of alien invasions and red planets. Now it discloses microbes that make up the human. The total weight of the microorganisms in the human body is as little as two hundred grams, we learn from the Human Microbiome Project (HMP), even as microbial cells outnumber human cells ten to one.[1] Placing these findings in histories of the biosphere, popular science writer Dorion Sagan radically decenters the Anthropos: we arrive at a distributed figure that Stefan Helmreich pithily anoints as *Homo microbis*.[2] With research on the microbiome comes a "new biology," argues Rodney Dietert, in which humans are multispecies "superorganisms" and not a single species at all.[3] Ed Yong offers a more poetic capture: minus human cells, a "ghostly microbial shimmer" remains around a "vanished animal core."[4] If the HMP illuminates an ever-swarming biobody in the more-than-human Anthropocene, then it also establishes microbes as beneficial allies in ensuring human health.[5] Against the ecological tide, however, alarm at microbial abundance surfaces iteratively during acute infectious disease emergencies. In proliferating stories of infection and entropy, pathogenic microbes emerge as malevolent antagonists; among them, *pathogenic viruses* command the lion's share of attention. In every flu season and every viral outbreak, alarm turns to fear, fueling a warlike stance against these proverbial enemies.

This book is devoted to how the extreme situation of a global viral pandemic compels a recalibration of multispecies politics. Since the late twentieth century, acute infectious disease epidemics have been recast as unfolding ecological disturbances ("emerging infectious disease," or EID, events) in a reconfiguration I characterize as the *current epidemic episteme*. Such viral emergences grab our attention at the phase of extensive community transmission that health experts transcribe as a global public health emergency. Putting species extinction on the table, the recognition sends scientists hurtling back to where it all began, to origins, to changing multispecies distributions. As Sagan notes, if the planetary swarm of life, growing, eating, and merging into itself, always posed the problem of "crowd control," acute infectious disease epidemics force a new reckoning.[6] Then it becomes all too easy to revert to the anthropocentric fear and loathing of microbes as germs despite knowledge of "our" microbial shimmer. *The Virus Touch* analyzes how we make sense of the concert of microbial abundance and host loss in the epidemic episteme. Immanent to the logic of infection, multispecies relations habitually surface during infectious diseases emergences as organizing nodes for plotting targeted interventions into individual bodies, populations, and disease milieus. At the current juncture, this structuring node is the multispecies relation between SARS-CoV-2 and its human hosts. Such multispecies relations, sometimes characterized as "novel" (as in *the novel coronavirus*), *appear* to us medially as image and number, milieu and movement. Infection may be experienced in the fever and the fret, but it is not intelligible as such without technical mediation. We read PCR (polymerase chain reaction) results; we watch the curve. Spiky orbs become indelible cultural icons; creative images of lung damage proliferate. Enter epidemic media.

My study of epidemic media across epistemic settings—from laboratories to clinics to forests—affords an understanding of how epidemic media actualize multispecies relations so as to measure, assess, and locate harms. Mobilizing (what Hans-Jörg Rheinberger named) "epistemic objects" such as viruses and hosts, epidemic media set in motion research agendas, institutional action, and public policy.[7] Such media can compound or dislodge harmful habits of targeted industrial interventions such as the shortsighted overuse of antibiotics or toxic pesticides in the post–World War II period; this is all the more reason to analyze their making/unfolding in concrete locations. But how exactly do epidemic media inscribe infection? What epistemic objects enable targeted interventions into fluctuating multispecies relations? One might begin with epidemic media as enactments of epistemic cuts in dynamic multispecies assemblies. There is mastery in the mediatic objectification of *one* multispecies relation plucked out from the living processes and relations of the biogeological churn. Yet, as we shall see, ongoing challenges to that media-technological mastery ultimately activate another kind of knowledge altogether: a sensuous apprehension of multispecies entanglements that implode all organismic boundaries. Epidemic media compel thinking-feeling one's molecules stretching intensively ("in" here) and extensively ("out" there), emplacing us in the experiential intensities of multispecies entanglement. They also alert us to varying harm and loss, since epidemic eventfulness is qualitatively different for communities made vulnerable by long-term socioeconomic inequities, willed biopolitical neglect, or exponentially high levels of chemical harms. Studying the media situation, I argue, attunes us to these multiplicities, recasting the (universalized) global health emergency in terms of living differentially "altered lives," as Michelle Murphy characterizes it, in the slow violence of planetary disrepair.[8]

This book began many moons ago with the last great pandemic in recent history: the long-wave HIV pandemic that closed out the twentieth century.[9] That global pandemic remains the historical archive for my reflections on epidemic media. Writing during the present COVID-19 crisis that stilled all life as we knew it in March 2020, I found my generational experience of HIV/AIDS suddenly historical in the flash of a spillover event. The cataclysmic COVID-19 transformed all frames of reference as stark differences emerged between the two global plagues. But the viral emergence of HIV remained a touchstone for theorizing epidemic media because of all those historical lessons learned (or ignored)—everything from deadly zoonotic spillovers, to population segregation, to pharma capitalism. Even as the scramble to manage the COVID-19 pandemic overshadows ongoing HIV/AIDS epidemic interventions, even as popular imaginaries of COVID-19 harken back to the 1918 influenza pandemic that claimed 56 million lives, and even as the biomedical solution for COVID-19 remains the obverse of HIV therapies (the HIV vaccine is as yet unapproved, and there are but few antivirals for COVID-19), the scientific-technological knowledge practices that made HIV/AIDS hyperendemic offer rich opportunities for "living otherwise" (as Murphy suggests) with global pandemics, for moving beyond the short sight of health emergencies. Epidemic media are the engine for these knowledge practices as they inscribe, store, and transmit multispecies relations *and* tweak, alter, and modify them. I approach those knowledge practices in the long shadow of the collective traumas that are the HIV/AIDS and COVID-19 global pandemics. For many, these historical experiences are rent with enduring losses, flashing insights, and accumulating effects, generationally and personally. As a media scholar located in the Anglo-American academy, I live between the United States and India, nations with high death tolls in both global pandemics. This situation lends historical urgency to the questions I pose about epidemic media. Navigating the media storms around HIV/AIDS and COVID-19 has led me to ask: What can "epidemic media" as a research concept offer for living with pandemics? Conversely, what are the implications of a comprehensive epidemic media theory for media studies?

Now epidemics come in all shapes and sizes. Scholars across disciplines criticize the positioning of acute infectious disease emergences as *the* universal health emergencies at the cost of ongoing epidemics, some invisible (as in the case of chemical toxicities), some slow (as in the case of global metabolic disorders), and others chronic (as in malaria, tuberculosis, or dengue emergences in the Global South).[10] As Elizabeth Povinelli writes, the constitution of such universal events is an assertion of political power privileging the biosphere over the colonial sphere, in which ancestral catastrophes have been ongoing for centuries.[11] In keeping with this line of thought, I articulate the two spheres throughout the book: the deep timescales and nonhuman agencies of the biosphere appear and recede alongside the accelerating dispossession, (inter)generational trauma, and anthropogenic violence of the colonial sphere. This interrogation of acute infectious disease emergences as universal catastrophes informs and directs the multispecies politics of health in *The Virus Touch*. It compels a historical look at previous viral storms at a time when COVID-19 appears as a one-of-a-kind experience, a vertiginous rupture irrevocably changing all that came before. The centrality of the HIV/AIDS global pandemic in this book effects a conceptual displacement from the present, reminding us of all-but-forgotten historical lessons. The point is not to trace the uncanny familiarities between the two global pandemics—the widening health inequities, the uneven global distributions of biomedical panacea, the phobic myths of mysterious origins, the ever-mutating virus pointing the way to hyperendemicity, and all that feels like history's return as farce—but to probe a logic that structures both. That logic is *distribution*: the sharing of resources between parasite and host (biological), within populations (social), and across living systems (ecological).[12] What constitutes the health emergency is a multispecies relation—once the

HIV-human relation, now the SARS-CoV-2–human relation—whose distributive logic structures the complexities and multiplicities of global pandemics. Analyzing processes of mediation that materialized that multispecies relation for the HIV/AIDS pandemic not only provides a beginning for living with COVID-19 but also installs a new memory for pandemics to come.

Life, Returning

Since the late twentieth-century viral storms, each EID event has refocused attention on "life," again, despite all the debates over what life has come to mean. Life becomes immanently valuable as a particular configuration of matter during epidemics precisely because new processes and relations challenge that configuration. As a cultural shorthand, life appears as a time span one leaves behind as losses mount; life is palpable in shortness of breath, cascading fevers, and mounting fatigue; life is enmeshed in the tangle of tests, needles, tubes, and cylinders; life is a bat in the recesses of the blue planet, or a sick animal in a wet market. As life wanes (for the animal/plant host) and flourishes (for microbes), epidemic media render multispecies relationalities as distributions calculable in escalating viremia (in individuals) and in the R_0 or reproductive rate (in populations). *An epidemic emerges.* From the Latin root *emergere* ("to come forth"), and the later French *émergence* (an "unforeseen occurrence"), emergence signifies something that *appears* and something that is *new* or unprecedented.[13] "Emergent life," argue Nigel Clark and Myra Hird, confronts us continually, often in unpredictable microontologies, but only some ontological disturbances galvanize political action.[14] The acute infectious disease event is one such disturbance: its recognition motivates the remaking of multispecies relations constitutive of life. This remaking institutes what Isabelle Stengers characterizes as "reciprocal capture": microbe and human/animal/plant emerge with each other.[15] To differentiate species may well seem counterintuitive to the process-relational ontologies of planetary processes, as environmental theorists note.[16] Life, after all, continually unfolds; its relational unfurling and its endemic processualities are recalcitrant to stabilizing configurations such as distinct species. But in the epidemic episteme of acute infectious disease emergence, distinctions between the species, virus and host, are *immanent*: that is, the epistemological distinction is constructed as such to elaborate infection as fluctuating relations between two discrete entities. Following multispecies theorists, I understand these species distinctions as not "natural" but arising from motivated scientific-cultural performances. Viral epidemics are occasions for marshaling "the virus" as epistemic object: as a particle, as code, and as an organism suddenly lifelike in its actions. At first glance, the pursuit of "the virus" in *The Virus Touch* seems to tarry in the deadening world of objects. But as in the case of Thom Van Dooren's snails, viruses in this book operate as portals into "giant networks" of biotic and geologic relations and processes.[17] Viruses' process-relational ontologies are biogeological because this is *nonlife* that undertakes *lifelike* activities—sensing (irritability) and replicating (reproduction). A bit of nucleic acid (with a protein coat and no cell walls), these obligate parasites "come alive" relationally; as border objects, they relocate their hosts in the planetary biogeological churn.

Despite these entangled materialities, the knowledge practices of the epidemic episteme render virus and host as the central biological participants in a struggle over resources, thereby motivating the search for viable "solutions" to balance (microbial) abundance and (human/animal/plant) loss. Industrial-technological fixes such as therapies and vaccines often constitute premier biomedical solutions. The biomedical triumph of the HIV antiretrovirals, for instance, turned exigent life into a manageable condition; so, too, with COVID-19 vaccines and experimental therapies. Those who survive HIV or COVID-19 have submitted to the technological governance of life. That governance plots a trajectory toward health as deliverable outcome; in turn, health as structuring horizon motivates the study of specific biological targets (antigens, cells, antibodies) to "correct" pathogenic multispecies distributions. In the persistent shadow of the current pandemic, we tend toward health in our bodies, our pods, our communities. For viruses, too, viable hosts are necessary, since these parasites rely on host resources to metabolize and to multiply. Hence, health in the epidemic episteme is an intricate multispecies game and not merely a human medical concern. If nothing else, the HIV/AIDS pandemic taught us these plain truths: we know health is a moving target that orients and reorients knowledge practices seeking to meddle in life. At this early juncture in the book, we can say that "life" under epidemic exigencies takes shape as distinct forms (host and microbe), as unfolding change (life spans), and as multispecies distributions (evolving relations) across domains of action.

If epidemics force a revaluation of "life," this particular configuration of matter or specific mode of organization is offset from "nonlife." There is a rich body of scholarship that questions the life/nonlife boundary and its devastating social and ecological consequences. The wariness is well founded, but there is no escaping the fact that global pandemics are historical thresholds when the specificity of life flashes up again and again. Anyone who has struggled not to die has inevitably instituted the life/nonlife binary as exigency—sometimes against the grain of their environmental politics. Many of us ward off radical entropy with recourse to vaccines and therapies. This larger imperative toward anthropocentric survival mandates probing how life is epistemologically constituted *precisely* to take stock of valuing life over nonlife and human lives over nonhuman ones in emergency situations. In this regard, the virus is a particularly productive site *because* it crosses the border between life and nonlife. Once viruses assume parasitic relations, life becomes precarious for both virus and host. Confronted by potential loss, distinctive elements such as cells, genes, or proteins appear as iconic forms of life. They acquire significance as "lively materialities" that impinge on the media practices that seek to compose them in biotechnical forms. Later in the chapter, I pause on differential notations of life—the "lively," the "biological," and the "vital." But at the outset, let us stay with the incessant appearances of life in the epidemic episteme.

Notations of life surface amid epidemic agon because we confront massive species losses. (Some will remember musings on an "extinction-level event" in the early days of COVID-19.) When the species under potential erasure is *human*, the struggle for life can amount to narrow technological fixes engineered to provide "human health" as deliverable good. An anthropocentric myopia that privileges human health exclusively undercuts "structural one health" that constellates human, animal, and ecosystem health as historical necessity. Enshrined in the twenty-first-century principles of "planetary health," this ecological orientation has gained credence after the EID events of the late twentieth century.[18] To reckon with life at its most precarious is to address the "threatening ecologies," as the curators of the *Feral Atlas* put it, of the more-than-human Anthropocene.[19] Without this long view, global pandemics will be "our" perpetual planetary futures. Epidemics are one among many ongoing planetary crises: they disclose precarious life on a precarious planet. At the same time, epidemic histories illuminate all the ways in which the most anthropocentric of concerns, human health, has always been an unevenly distributed good. Think of the pharma wars of the HIV/AIDS pandemic or COVID-19 vaccine capitalism. Hence, a multispecies politics must necessarily address histories of race, colonialism, and capitalism that institute difference within new multispecies assemblies. No epidemic is intelligible without feedback effects between structural forces (racism, capitalism, and colonialism, for instance) and evolving molecular relationalities, as the burgeoning conversations on "molecular colonialisms" reveal.[20] Indebted to these conceptual turns, *The Virus Touch* crosshatches the study of interlocking *bio*technological, *bio*medical, and *bio*geographic interventions into new multispecies relations. The noticeable emphasis on the "bio" marks life as governed, becoming *bios*, and situates knowledge configurations in the multiform biosciences central to securing life. The upshot is a transdisciplinary endeavor that articulates the biosciences with media studies to make the case for epidemic media as environmental media.

The epidemic episteme reconfigures life as form, process, and relation, and, perhaps most crucially, as mediation. Understanding the processes of mediation is critical to surviving perpetual pandemics, I argue, at least for those who are not in the space race to leave a damaged planet. To analyze epidemic media is to grapple with how we capture, manipulate, and sometimes fabricate life at its most exigent. The media question is fundamental to epidemics because of the microscopic character of microbial multispecies assemblies. How often do we hear of an "invisible enemy" since SARS-CoV-2 entered the scene? How often have we watched a curve to understand fluctuating infections within host populations? As submicroscopic particles, viruses are perceptible in their technical mediation. Even as virus-human relations manifesting as disease emergence harkens back to ancient plagues, and even as microbiology in the mid-nineteenth century instituted microbial life-forms as epistemic objects, the media-technological or machinic capture of the virus arrives at a later stage, in 1938, with its optical appearance. One hundred to five hundred times smaller than bacteria, these microbes had passed through Louis Pasteur's porcelain filters for bacteria and remained invisible under the ordinary light microscope. It took the electron microscope to render the virus technically legible as epistemic object. Media histories such as these dot *The Virus Touch*. They disclose a will to more precise, more efficient, more extensive machinic capture. But, as always, mediation is mutually transformative: as Rey Chow explains it, media-technological "capture" is ever a medial entanglement with machine, animal, human, and the environment.[21] Following this line of thought, I argue that multisensory attunements to multispecies relationalities always supplement technical-aesthetic object-making. Such mediatic matters are the focal point of this book. What media materialize biotechnical forms of life in the epidemic episteme? What processes of mediation detect and compose, alter and fabricate, life? How does understanding these processes illuminate their world-making force?

The Media Question

Contemporary expansions of the media concept provide a starting point for what epidemic media are and what they can do. "Epidemic media" in *The Virus Touch* is a capacious rubric for much more than the proverbial contagion fare of films and television shows, pulp fiction, and literary works.[22] My study of epidemic media attends to life unfolding as process-relational ontologies, to life as always becoming. To bring into focus a singular "multispecies relation" is to enact an "epistemic cut" that privileges and selects, differentiates and stabilizes, particular objects, rendering them intelligible within (what Michael Foucault once named) the "order of things."[23] To emphasize such object-making as a "cut" is to call attention to the backcloth, to dynamic surrounds that remain in rack focus. As living processes and relations appear as *forms of life*, technical-aesthetic mediation is more than a representational moment, for the differential human, animal, and machinic agencies of making/doing/enacting complicate any objective mastery. These lively materialities activate a sensuous relation to the nonhuman world. Before I turn to media theories that inform the concept of epidemic media, let me elaborate the claim by way of an example from the COVID-19 experience.

We have become anxiously aware of the air/water within us, exiting the "molar" body (the self-contained, unified, organic body rendered distinct from the environment) as droplets (of respiratory mucous), then drying as aerosolized particulates, drifting in the air between us.[24] In these processes, a vital medium (respiratory mucus) transmutes into an elemental one (droplets and particles in air); both media are life-sustaining environments for microbes and humans. *Vital* designates medial substances like blood and saliva, urine, or feces that cannot survive for long *as such* outside their site of origin; their situatedness marks their finitude.[25] But as we shall see, vital media are danger zones for infection because they are immensely transitive; they *extend* well beyond their site of production. Extensive media environments as the surrounding milieu are familiar to environmental media studies, but as Joshua Neves writes, it is time indeed to think of media intensions.[26] This is especially crucial for configuring "infection environments," which are both intensive and extensive. Every COVID-19 test quantifies individuated multispecies distributions (the basis of positive or negative results), offering a snapshot of the intensive environment. Every public health advisory aims to measure and manage the air extending between us. We come understand these infection technicities over time, even as living with acute infection around us remains a visceral and affective experience. The notion of *epidemic intensity* encompasses all these infection modalities of pandemic time. Etymologically, *intensity* signifies an extreme stretching tight: these days, as we breathe, we feel the molecular stretch of particular surrounds (a body, a room, a county, the globe) with dangerous air rushing *into* our lungs as we seek *out* oxygen from our surrounds. Infection's risk environment spreads out but does not dissipate; epidemic intensity is a piling on, an accumulation. When scientific images, for example, render air/breath calculable, epidemic intensities appear in their technical valence:

as measures for gaseous and particulate concentrations, including magnitude, degree, direction, and level of dilution. Despite this seeming neutrality, epidemic intensities are deeply subjective. In the domain of feeling, intensity is the thickening, layering, and bundling of sensations/affects; it is a term that translates qualitative perceptions of energetic forces between things into subjective experience. In this regard, epidemic intensities are experiences of stretching tight, centripetally and centrifugally, in infection environments. Scientific, artistic, and popular media make epidemic intensities sensible, composing breath scattering into the air, infusing air into breath. Something latent, something imperceptible moves between us: we understand it informationally; we sense it affectively.

That the endemic transitivity of air/breath has transformed the medium into *the* risk environment for the COVID-19 epidemic experience is evident in diverse technical mediations. In the early days of COVID-19, there were several scientific visualizations of the distance that sneezes travel (six feet and over). Process-relational ontologies of the sneeze found transcription in animations, such as one published on the online platform of the *Journal of the American Medical Association* (JAMA) in March 2020 (figure I.1).[27] As this scientific visualization inscribed the scattering of the vital medium into air, respiratory mucus appeared in droplet form as lively media carrying "active" viruses enfolded in the elemental medium of air. The visualization articulates the transition of a vital medium into an elemental one, spelling danger in the composite. We find such visualizations of infection environments across COVID-19 epidemic media made in diverse epistemic settings, from basic science laboratories and art studios. For example, artist Pato Hebert's visual inscription of his own breath dissipating into air from the "Trying to Catch Your Breath" series (2008) took on a new life *after* he contracted COVID early in the pandemic. The photographs documenting his breathing complement the *JAMA* visualization, albeit sans measurement (figure I.2).[28] In Hebert's rendition, breath/air takes technical-aesthetic form as a dissipative unfurling visually stilled at the moment of exhalation. I return to Hebert later in the book and, more importantly, to media practices like these that attempt partial connections (as Isabelle Stengers describes them) between scientific and cultural "findings."[29] In such epidemic media practices, we find "modern practitioners" engaged in negotiating their often-differing visions of the world. They are the media makers featured in this book.

This brief illustration intimates how epidemic media direct our actions: the *JAMA* visualization, for instance, can serve to dictate the social conduct of life, informing public health advisories on physical distancing precautions. In this

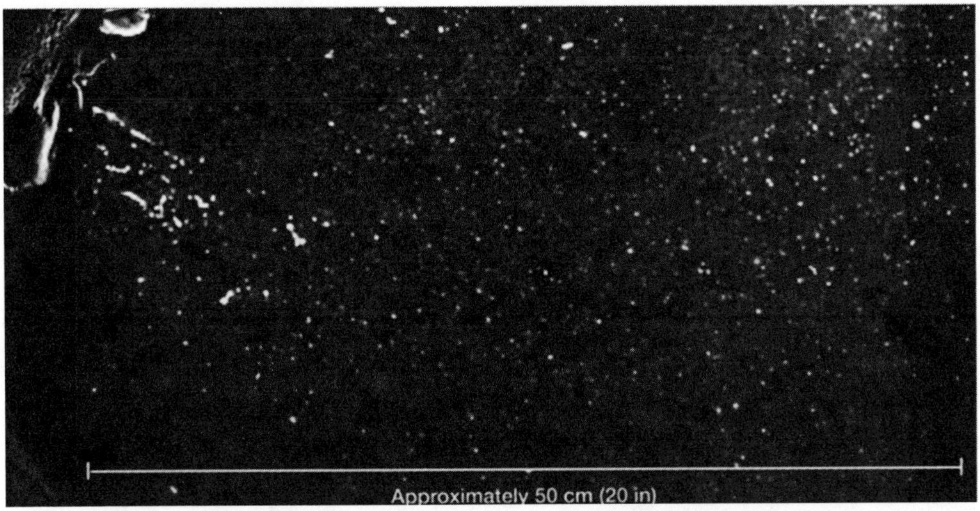

Figure I.1. Visualization of a sneeze, 2020. Source: Video illustration in Bourouiba, "Gas Clouds Demonstrate Their Ability to Travel Great Distances."

regard, epidemic media are world-making, as Adrian Ivakhiv suggests: as media "draw and hold things together," they enact the "worlding of things."[30] Beyond representational forms, looking closely at processes of mediation requires scrutiny of more than apparatuses and devices or technical media (print, photochemical, electronic). It requires understanding the physical processes, the interactions between "things"—light and fluids, in this instance—that have differential agencies and are mutually transformative. The relatively simple examples offered above emphasize what is commonplace to environmental media studies: media in/as environment compels thinking beyond the media-technological situation. Situated in environmental media studies, *The Virus Touch* engages the modern science of the virus alongside its media histories to study process-relational ontologies and their inscription, encoding, and composition as media environments.

Among the modern sciences, the geological has held pride of place in the crucible of climate catastrophes. But facing a pandemic activates a shift of gears, bringing *biogeological processes* into sharper focus. For the past fifty years at least, substantially dislodging biology's (so-called) anthropocentrism, the multiform biosciences have developed varying conceptual frameworks for rearticulating the biological with planetary processes; as we shall see, the turn to multispecies studies arises within this turn. More centrally, historians of the biosciences have underscored the need to study the impact of bioscience research on planetary damage. Hannah Landecker's writings on the articulation of the metabolic

Figure I.2. Pato Hebert, untitled, from the series *Trying to Catch Your Breath*, 2008. Archival pigment print, 10 × 13⅓ in. Credit: Pato Hebert.

sciences, industrialized agriculture, food systems, and planetary health, for example, exemplify such material histories.[31] Adopting the chemical gaze as a method, in historicizing metabolism, Landecker tracks "enzymatic and energetic conversions between different kinds of matter" to show how biological targets made and unmade in basic science laboratories and how industrial research units "carry forward" industrial products into living systems.[32] Drawing inspiration from her insistence on the planetary location of the biosciences, my study of epidemic media foregrounds the biological and technological hinge in the making/doing/enacting of epidemic media. How do media practices materialize biotechnical forms to ready them as targets of intervention? What are the planetary impacts of this constitution? To ask such a question is to think the biosciences and media studies together in their conjoined planetary world-making.

The qualifier *biotechnical* in *The Virus Touch* is an analytic for inextricable biological and technological processes that emphasizes their respective material specificities. Epidemic media are biotechnical forms—an image, a number, a milieu, a movement—that materialize otherwise imperceptible processes and relations. In this respect, they are representations constrained by their settings, by the media practices that give them form. More often than not, epidemic media are *experimental* representations, reflexive and improvisatory, that gesture toward their own provisional nature. When the effort is to detect and compose a *novel* multispecies relation, the representation is necessarily, and often explicitly, conjectural or speculative. Machinic inscriptions often run up against accelerating viral changes (mutations becoming variants, for example) or the new complexities of multicellular organization (which of "our" proteins help the viral spike protein to fuse to "our" cells).[33] Such lively materialities find coding/transcription over time in bioscience research—but only *over time*. Media entanglements in furiously accelerated pandemic time motivate my exploration of epidemic media's forms and technologies. There is the urgent push for better probes, new software, and smaller cameras as media-technological processes unfold *with* lively materialities; not all of the latter, nonhuman agencies erupting in unpredictable events, are fully legible as *biological* processes. Sometimes liveliness registers as disruptive excesses, as strong affects. An animal spotting a camera trap alters its route and subsequently dislodges the camera; a vital medium poses haptic danger despite controlled safety precautions. Too much noise or disturbance, error or redundancy, scuttles efforts at efficient machinic capture. These differential agencies, animal and machinic, underwrite the speculative orientation of epidemic media's biotechnical forms.

My observations of epidemic media practices commence with *sense perceptions* of lively materialities as the not yet comprehensible, as the partially known.[34] The most abstract epidemic medium turns out to be irreducibly sensuousness. This sensuousness may arise from direct sense data, but not exclusively. Epidemic experiences reconstitute those perceptions as another kind of knowledge: an awareness of casual relatedness and processual flux between discrete entities that current environmental thought transcribes as *entanglement*. Too often a vague buzzword, *entanglement* has a range of critical modalities (as in Karen Barad, Donna Haraway, and Rey Chow) relevant to *The Virus Touch* that I turn to in the following pages. Here, Rey Chow's elaboration is most pertinent: media entanglement, suggests Chow, is the intuitive feeling for "mysterious connections" to media-technologically captured entities (animals, humans, minerals, or plants) even when *their* desires and motivations, actions and relations, remain obscure. These intuitions supplement the "active relation" that "contains, detains, and retains" its epistemic object in acts of mastery.[35] Media technologies like microscopes or camera traps might seek to establish “enmeshments and linkages” between humans, animals, or machines, but in fact they afford an awareness of the “voidings and uncoverings that hold things together.”[36] As media technological practices enfold sensory data, feelings, thoughts, and intuitions, they initiate a phenomenological awareness of entanglement. A coagulating *epidemic intensity* surfaces. In the midst of epidemics, no one is spared from this intensity, this “flux of participation,” as ecologist philosopher David Abram describes it, and all the more in confronting radical uncertainty.[37] As modern practitioners struggle to objectively transcribe “life” as process and relation, they act with urgency, facing the pressing need to make intelligible radical uncertainties. The consequent speculative orientation of epidemic media gestures toward another space beyond the institutional settings of media practices—to inextricable multispecies entanglements. This sensuous knowledge accompanying objective mastery has implications for the “worlding of things” that I explore in the chapters.

It should be clear from these opening remarks that *The Virus Touch* traverses science and technology studies and environmental media studies to articulate the conceptual rubric of epidemic media. All too often, the articulation of the biosciences with media studies ends up as biomedia studies, with tangential implications for environmental media theory. My aim is to center the study of biological and technological processes in environmental media studies. What follows is the research framework that is the backbone of epidemic media theory.

ENVIRONMENTAL MEDIA

In the cross-disciplinary terrain of environmental media studies, media include “life-sustaining” elemental media rife with human and nonhuman signals as well as the media-technological practices that render them readable. A few years ago, John Durham Peters’s monumental study of the four elements (in the Western sciences) reverberated as the field of elemental media studies.[38] Scholars turned to industrial histories of an elemental medium (e.g., Yuriko Furuhata on air); to mutual transformations of elemental media and media infrastructures (e.g., Nicole Starosielski on underwater cables); to mediatic transcriptions of risk signals (e.g., Rahul Mukherjee on electromagnetic transmissions); and to rethinking media theory in terms of specific elemental media (e.g., Stefan Helmreich and Melody Jue on ocean contexts).[39] There is excellent scholarship on the many conjunctures of media + environment: on the deleterious dimensions of media *in* the environment (from sonic booms to toxic e-waste); on how media scale between local events (a flood, a storm) and planetary processes (sea-level rise); on how media record and track ecological relations and processes, readying them as environments in need of intervention; and what media can do to slow down, redirect, and even thwart ongoing planetary damage. In all these accounts, mediatic processes compose what we understand as the "environment." Throughout the book I analyze the making of *infection's media environments* in biotechnical forms. One classic example is the "interaction domain" whose processes shape viral particles entering host cells. Molecular visualizations zoom into viral protein assemblies—a wiggling viral spike protein reaching toward host cells—as they fuse with cellular membranes. The environment, in this case, is the extracellular fluid that transports viral particles at the interface with cell membranes. Conformational changes in that environment are crucial for viral proteins to begin their journey into cells; both host and virus are participants in the drama. The interaction domain vibrates with the form of life transcribed as the viral particle; the media-technological practices of scientific visualizations inscribe viral unfolding in molecular-scale "events" for scientific insights into unknown parameters. Here, as in other instances, biotechnical forms and media environments are not figure and ground but are configured as assemblages. Besides the interaction domain, there are the "interior milieu" and "biogeographic regions" in subsequent chapters: these are the media environments for quantified viral ratios in vital media (x number of particles in y milliliters of blood) or for animal movement patterns in biodiverse habitats. Taken together, these media-technologically rendered forms offer a comprehensive account of viral infection's nested risk environments.

What is the upshot of considering these different life-form–environment assemblages together in this book? Infection as a fluctuating multispecies relation occupies *extensive* planetary space. But to understand how infection travels from cross-species transmission into host individuals and populations requires a multiscalar analytics attentive to the specificity of media environments. The life-form–environment assemblages throughout the book afford a fractal view of the unfolding multispecies relation: that is, each assemblage is a fraction of the infection story, distinct from but resonant with what happens at another scale. This fractal multiscalar perspective positions infectious disease epidemics as biological-social-ecological catastrophes emerging both intensively and extensively. Epidemiological studies lead the way in such transcription of infection across institutional domains: infection is at once medical/clinical, social/industrial, and geological/atmospheric. Animal/human feces release bacterial swarms into the soil; mosquitoes breeding in standing water convey parasites between bodies. These disease vectors highlight the transitivity of infection. We know quantifying county or district fecal waste is one epidemiological method for assessing COVID-19 community infection rates: media-technological practices inscribe vital traces folded into elemental media to materialize infection's environments as "risk environments" and to render harms calculable.[40] This complex picture can be grasped as fractal cameos that locate readers in the individual host (interaction domains), between hosts (the milieu), and, finally, between species (biogeographic regions). The point is most clearly developed in chapter 3's tracking of excorporated blood stored outside its site of origin. The biomedical goal of managing infection in individuals and populations necessarily "cuts" the vital medium into discrete "interior milieus," which are filed as blood samples, blood data, and blood pictures. The interior milieu points centripetally inward, but as the chapter demonstrates, each composition is constantly displaced centrifugally so that the vital medium comes to embody the greater disease milieu. In this way, *The Virus Touch* analyzes and elaborates infection's environments as epidemic media.

Finally, this book is in conversation with one disciplinary enclave in environmental media studies that stays with forms of life: the theory and practice of multispecies studies. As Helmreich writes, multispecies talk, especially regarding the *human* microbiome, is a "strange back-to-biology move" at a point when decentering anthropocentrism is urgent.[41] As we see in the next chapter, the new biosciences are hardly invested in either classical biological individuality or organic forms of life. Biology is indisputably "more than biological" today.[42] This decentering of anthropocentrism is formative to the heterogeneous field that is animal studies, one that includes multispecies theory and practice. While some strains in animal studies veer toward large, charismatic animals, multispecies inquiries analyze fungal, bacterial, and viral assemblies as teeming life grown into each other, their commingling imploding species boundaries. Two strains in these enclaves are intellectual settings for the study of epidemic media. The first is "microbial media" theory and practice. Artistic "multispecies spectacles" range from transgenic phantasmagoria (e.g., the Critical Art Ensemble's cultivation of *E. coli* bacteria) to self-ethnographies of infection (e.g., Caitlin Berrigan's experimental assemblage of HIV and the common weed), while theorists (e.g., Stefan Helmreich, Heather Paxson, Celia Lowe, Nigel Clark and Myra Hird, among others) rethink the multispecies politics of microbial media.[43] These critical-creative endeavors are salient to my study in their attention to the medial enactments of multispecies relationalities. Second, there is robust inquiry into disappearing animal species (extinction studies) and habitat fragmentation (biodiversity studies), and these inform my focus on zones of virulence. *The Virus Touch* engages animal hosts as lively media, as multispecies forms of transport carrying microbes over distances; their changing movements create new conditions for pathogenicity. Writings in animal studies such as Ursula Heise's *Imagining Extinction* and Frédéric

Keck's *Avian Reservoirs* shape these explorations of animal hosts. Their critical methods tracing the collaborations between biologists and veterinarians, naturalists and local buffs, big-data analysts and computer programmers that produce multisite field data and software programs inspire my research into media-technological inscriptions of zones of virulence. Chapter 4 directly addresses the multispecies question, pursuing animal-tracking media for sensing animal movements. Assembled into spatial forms, these tracking data are the basis for composing zones of virulence as threatening ecologies. As the curators of the *Feral Atlas* argue, pathogenic multispecies assemblies are organic and nonorganic relationalities—the nondesigned consequences of imperial and industrial infrastructure.[44] Such a focus on anthropogenic drivers obviates the depoliticized emphasis on evolutionary phylogenies that dominate natural histories of mutating viruses. Social and ecological histories of the colonial sphere become critical to understanding cross-species infection and the establishment of viral strains that go pandemic. In all these ways, environmental media theory and practice are the conceptual apparatus for my pursuit of epidemic media across the chapters. As they materialize biotechnical forms and media environments, epidemic media articulate pandemics as social-ecological catastrophes.

MEDIA AND THE BIOSCIENCES

My location of the biosciences in environmental media studies points toward science laboratories as some of the main settings for making epidemic media. Scholarship in science and technology studies has a formidable oeuvre on "what happens in the lab." Bruno Latour and Steve Woolgar's *Laboratory Life* (1979), documenting material techniques at the Salk Institute for Biological Studies, sets standards early in the game; Hans-Jörg Rheinberger's and Karin Knorr Cetina's elaborations of the material construction of "epistemic things" in science laboratories are other critical influences in this area of study.[45] One could multiply these histories, but here I select a few insights that shape my inquiries into experimental epidemic media in laboratories. Latour and Woolgar examine scientific facts as material performances and underscore their historical construction. "A substance could not be said to exist," they note, "without a particular configuration of apparatuses"; after all, one cannot run a viral bioassay without an "inscription device" such as a PCR machine.[46] Each inscription can be subject to a variety of interpretations before scientific facts come to stay. When an interpretation becomes "fact," it "loses all temporal qualification and becomes incorporated into a large body of knowledge drawn upon by others."[47] This insistence on making epistemic objects (and, consequently, facts) as situated material performances is crucially important given the provisional character of epidemic media. To some degree, this provisionality arises from the sheer novelty of the problem at hand, its radical uncertainty. But beyond this general condition, there are scientists who eschew universalizing claims proven within the constraints of *one* scientific practice for negotiated understandings that make partial connections with other sciences. These "modern practitioners," according to Stengers, are willing to work across the discordant landscapes of modern science, willing to negotiate competing visions of the world.[48] We find them making epidemic media in three labs that craft the novel multispecies relation as image, number, milieu, and movement: a computational structural biology lab that images virus macromolecules, a clinical medicine lab that inscribes and stores blood samples, and two forests segmented for study as the "living laboratories" of the world. While the latter are not quite of the same order as the basic science laboratories, Latour reminds us that forests, too, materialize as such within scientific practices. Following two scientists, a botanist and a pedologist (specializing in soil science) into the Amazon, Latour describes how one sees the trees, and the other the soil; how the pedocomparator (a square box for soil-sample collection) as instrument, for example, transforms and orders what we come to know about the forest.[49]

Drawing on his two-year stint at the Salk Institute, Latour notes that naturalized techniques in laboratories appear *as* material construction at moments of failure or breakdown. As we shall see, the scientists, artists, computer programmers, and technicians who appear in this book all put pressure on the media-technological limits of what their apparatuses and devices can deliver; pushing boundaries, they call for new tool kits for imaging living systems, for more sophisticated PCR machines, for better motion-sensor technologies. In recognizing the limitations of machinic inscription/transcription, they reflexively convey a distributed sense of what exceeds machinic capture. The "traceability" of reference that hangs around material substances, in Latour's (1999) analysis of the Amazon forest, registers as noise, as partial or unclean data, indexing the difference between form and matter. The ontological question returns as lively materialities that proliferate at the edges of scientific practices. We find such instances of affective force in the many accounts of lively disturbances that surface in the book; the clearest examples are to be found in chapters 3 and 4 on vital media and animal movements. At the Clinical Retrovirus Laboratory, one of my research sites, I observed repeated evocations of "clean data" (meeting standards that other research facilities could trust) and intimations of "dirty" excesses scuttling precise inscription; and in interviews with Roland Kays about his remote-tracking experiments on Barro Colorado Island, disruptive vegetal movements in tropical forests were a formidable challenge to differentiating animal movements. This sense of *supplementary* noise is endemic to epistemic cuts invested in bringing clarity to some phenomena at the cost of others. Attending to mediation—the makings/doings/enacting in laboratories—illuminates these medial actions as material performances. Mediation highlights the labor that enacts scientific findings and, ultimately, facts. Woolgar and Latour characterize these labors as "slow practical craftwork" thickly entangled in (what Karen Barad names) agential objects, apparatuses, and practices, a point to which I return shortly.[50]

Barad, Stengers, and Latour all hint at *discordances* between scientific practices, which, in turn, constrain media-technological practices in laboratory settings. Armed with a specific purpose, every scientific practice relies on particular apparatuses and devices to mediate its epistemic objects.[51] A structural biologist will have optical-computational technologies for the study of molecular structures; a geneticist pursuing genomic fingerprints will have a PCR machine. Epidemic media are intelligibility machines that make epistemic objects cohere within the constraints of scientific practices. And yet most experimental scientific endeavors are open to the *limits* of their own scientific practices and rely on evolving collaborations. The movement between scientific practices is most clearly plotted in chapter 2, where I track the making of the HIV-1 macromolecule through long-term and contingent collaborations among scientists, artists, and creative industries. The epidemic media that they make together accommodate competing visions of the world, pressing up against the limits of scientific practices. As modern practitioners, the scientists featured in this book collaborate with artists, software writers, health-care workers, and local animal experts, among others, and I track their making/doing/enacting of epidemic media in each chapter. Together, these modern practitioners make partial connections around specific epistemic objects—like the air between us—participating in making "a world of many worlds," as Marisol de la Cadena and Mario Blaser suggest, inclusive of humans and nonhumans.[52] Such "ontological politics," notes Stengers, are critical to environmental thought and action.[53]

BIOTECHNICAL FORMS

A domain of inquiry critically salient to making scientific images is biomedia studies, a field of theory and practice that informed the start of my inquiries into epidemic media. Taking the biosciences as the epistemic setting, in his landmark book *Biomedia*, media theorist Eugene Thacker set an agenda for studying interlocking biological and technological processes at the biodigital interface.[54] There is excellent scholarship on this interface inspired by the conjunctions of cybernetics and biology in the mid-twentieth century, one in which the gene becomes the definitive substrate of life.[55] In subsequent alliances between new materialism and new media, processes of extraction implicated in the modification and alteration of life come under scrutiny. If new media design and build "life itself," molecule by molecule, and if biological substrates are subject to the same kind of flattening, reproduction, and patenting as are CDs, DVDs, and cassettes, it is time to evaluate how we study biological and technological processes as they transform each other.[56] Throwing down the gauntlet in *Life after New Media*, Sarah Kember and Joanna Zylinska, following Henri Bergson's account of life, define life as processual flux appearing as "life itself" in epistemic cuts that still the flow.[57] Studying viruses in an agar plate under the electron microscope, for example, involves multiple medial actions, ranging from preparing appropriate samples to setting the electron probe for precise detection. Quantifying viable viral particles in a demarcated time-space, as we shall see in chapter 3, enacts a cut that readies one unfolding multispecies relation for targeted therapy. Representations, in this regard, are one part of biotechnological interventions in life's processes and relations. Kember and Zylinska's epistemic cut is most relevant in my discussion of biotechnical forms confronting "lively" temporal excess in chapter 2. The radical incompletion of the -morphic image, I argue, opens to what is as yet to be medially graspable and exemplifies an encounter with speeding viral temporalities.

Each chapter stages a dramatic encounter between lively materialities and biotechnical forms, even as different theorists diverge on what "life" is and can become. Analyzing simulations of living systems from a mechanist perspective, for example, Manuel DeLanda places models of living systems on a "synthetic-biologic" continuum but argues that ultimately what is not known can be mathematically theorized; conversely, in her account of scientific enchantments with "excitable" molecules, Natasha Myers argues for the irreducible liveliness of matter.[58] Still others, like Jennifer Gabrys, suggest that the biological organization of matter is "anterior" to its media-technological capture; therefore, emergent life-forms on a computationally programmed earth are "organism-machine-milieu" assemblages.[59] Whether it is the preparation of biological samples for optical inscription, or protein modelers twisting and turning with their 3D models, or vegetal interferences disrupting animal motion detection, notations such as these designate lively actions that exceed machinic inscription/transcription despite faster microprocessual capabilities, despite the theoretical power of infinite simulations. My attention to tangible media (live cell cultures, for instance) and material performances (of laboratory procedures and techniques, for example) underscores the "lively materiality" of epidemic media. When they disrupt or confound planned outcomes, such materialities are often perceived as excesses to be weeded out; nevertheless, they also invoke curiosity, even wonder. This affective charge is indicated in the qualifier *lively*.[60]

An insistence on lively materiality bucks a history that reduces the virus to its molecular constitution as code. We know this cultural history well in the celebration of virus*like* behaviors or uncontainable virality that thwarts all attempts at social or political control. The virus is feted for its uncontrollable informatic cutting, pasting, and multiplying (the meme); for its simple microprocessuality (the homegrown machine); for its bottom-up, hydra-headed, acentered organization (the swarm or brood); and for its ability to set in motion a series of sudden and unpredictable effects (contagion). In these capacities it is something of a cultural analogue for informational and social systems. Jussi Parikka's early *Digital Contagions* references HIV as a cultural figure for understanding the behaviors of computer bugs, worms, and viruses; in the 1980s, informatic contagion would be known as "computer AIDS." Of course, Parikka's later conception of medianatures, an attunement to machinic-geological continuities, probes media materialities beyond tropological capture; but the notion of informatic virality remains resonant in the study of new media.[61] In a different intonation, Tony Sampson's *Virality* extends the model of network contagion to rethink microsocialities and the capacity for social transformation. Both Parikka and Sampson see contagion not as a fearsome force but as an open-ended system that enables a jump cut to something qualitatively new.

In a fascinating reflection on curves and simulations, Sampson and Parikka argue that such data visualizations are *the* "epidemic image" for the COVID-19 experience because of their microprocessuality: they are capable of changing with new inputs coming in every day from a massive operational matrix.[62] Everything from human behavior to health-care provision to viral mutations impacts the curve, contouring it in feedback loops. By contrast, the image of SARS-CoV-2 as spiky orb may well be ubiquitous, but it has limited capacity, argue Sampson and Parikka; the viral image is a stable configuration that captures the epidemic only at molecular scale. In this regard, the image seems less capable of keeping up with the fast-moving landscape than the moving curve. There is no doubt that watching the curve—a mathematical form that has come to stay since the early twentieth century—has become a fundamental media experience in unfolding pandemics. Moving curves keep abreast of pandemics as a dynamic multitemporal emergences. And yet, the viral image is a significant competitor as *the* iconic epidemic image: a constant reminder of the immanent multispecies relation that galvanized a qualitative multitemporal shift. As Kirsten Ostherr noted in an interview on COVID-19, the heightened anxieties in the early days of the pandemic were fueled in part by not being able to locate the microbial agent responsible for the shift.[63] Externalizing a microbial agent as epistemic object, the viral image was the pandemic punctum; in this regard, visualizing data in the viral image is a fierce competitor to the curve. As classic disease emergences, pandemics make us feel our internal environments intensely—our cells and microbes, mucous and lungs. The viral image gestures inward, as we feel molecular in constant tests, and outward to what lies in planetary matrices; perceptually, it overwhelms other technical mediations, settling as the cultural icon of a pandemic. More importantly, scientific viral images are anything but stable: their very functionality lies in their malleable, constantly editable, dynamic and speculative capacities. Biotechnical images keep abreast of fast-paced research, as we shall see in chapter 2, and they intuitively entertain scientific hunches in confrontations with the radically unknown. That unknown inheres in the biotic qualities of the multispecies relations that keep changing, as we know from the current confrontations with wily variants. At the biodigital interface of the postgenomic era, then, the viral image returns us to the multidimensional problem of life that biology poses; it exemplifies an integrative approach to the biological complexity of living systems. Chapter 2's discussion of structural biology as it interfaces with genomic research resituates informatic understandings of viruses (the virus as code) in the expanding frame of the multiform biosciences.

Beyond both curve and image, as I have suggested, infection environments are ubiquitously palpable during epidemics. Bristling and active, vital and elemental media require constant negotiation at every scale, as we see with managing breath/air during COVID-19. Machinic inscriptions render these media intelligible in biotechnical forms as the surrounds are cut out from dynamic biogeological processes. The exhausting uncertainties of pandemic situations, however, make us deeply aware of living processes and relations that are not as yet fully comprehensible. At the biological and technological fold, these "lively materialities" are all too apprehensible, affecting us daily, as we know from sense perceptions of uncontrollable viral variants—uncontrollable in part because they are only partially known. As media-technologies inscribe infection environments, medial entanglements sharpen awareness of lively materialities. This general awareness is keener still when the biotechnical processing involves tangible media: technologically fabricated cell cultures, blood samples, agar preparations, animal models, all that sustains biotic relations so that they can be stabilized for study. Following Myers, "tangible media" in *The Virus Touch* refers to this "wetware," visceral in modality; volumetric and tactile, such tangible media are critical to the constitution of biological targets.[64]

This discussion of biotechnical forms gestures toward what lies beyond machinic capture as the biosciences, armed with new technologies, explore the "limits of life."[65] On the way, life expands as theoretical object. But what does this imply for making/doing/enacting epidemic media? Accompanying biotechnical intelligibility, lively materialities are referential traces of what lies beyond. Registering on the perceptual sensorium, these materialities activate another kind of knowledge—a multisensory "knowing" that troubles abstraction. In every instance of biotechnical forms, "life," manifest in multisensory media-technological processes, exceeds machinic inscription and aesthetic composition.

MULTISENSORY MEDIATIONS

Epidemic media enact multispecies distributions: they are rife with human, animal, and machinic signals, some bristling below conscious awareness, some escaping human perceptual registers altogether. Take, for example, our immune system, the focal point of HIV epidemic media. Research on HIV has extensively traced how the virus attacks the CD4 or T-cells, which are the "intelligence units" in the immune system, in that they recognize pathogenic attacks and send instructions to other cells (often called the foot soldiers) to attack pathogens. All the vaccine talk of the COVID-19 era is about installing a memory of SARS-CoV-2 in our immune systems. Perception, then, is a cognitive process that regulates the emerging-with nonorganic and organic matter. Immune systems have memories, as do muscular and nervous systems; volumes have been written about the sentience of living systems. It is amid mounting ecological damage that we tune in to these intelligences, consciously installing, as Stengers maintains, a "new memory."[66] The smoke in our nostrils, she argues, has become ontological evidence of snowballing damage, bringing home the causal interrelatedness of planetary existence.

The example of immune system memories locates the human senses in a perceptual complex. As one register, the human sensorium is our conduit to direct sensuous experiences. And it is this sensorium that epidemic media organize in their machinic compositions. Inscribing a new vital relation, each composition invokes some senses and "partitions away" others as supplementary; intelligibility comes at a price.[67] Intelligibility connotes the normative governance of multiple intelligences, if we follow Michel Foucault's evocative phrase "grid of intelligibility," the system of elements by which we order and classify process-relational ontologies.[68] An extracting, distilling, classifying, and composing is underway in the making of epistemic objects, abstracting different kinds of matter as image, number, milieu, and movement. But confronted with lively materialities that do not fit, making/doing/enacting epidemic media is equally a dispersion into the sensorium. Supplementary sense data may compel intuitions or hunches, or they might just irritate. More importantly, they open to an awareness of animal-machinic perception unfolding together and therein of nonhuman agencies, of our entangled materiality.

In posthumanist studies, the perceptive capacities of all living forms are testament to nonhuman agencies. We hear of "smart" bugs, of "extrasensory" plant sentience, of animal "intelligence." This robust scholarship provides the broader intellectual context for new materialist and environmental media theorists, who, in turn, examine mediatic traces of nonhuman intelligence in communicative signals—from whale songs and bird flight patterns to plant movements and microbial chatter. The scholarship on vast, untapped perceptual worlds teeming with indiscernible signals compels new analytics, histories, and theories. Throughout the book, theorists of life-forms and living systems underscore the sensing of forces and relations as the open spatiality of life. Some see perception as the unfurling of the body into its milieu. Knowledge is sensory immersion in a phenomenological milieu: one organism senses possibilities in the milieu, as we know from Jakob Uexküll's example of a tick intuiting the warm blood of a mammal.[69] Active relationalities in the environment bristle, becoming sensory knowledge; lively materialities affect medial acts of mastery. In this phenomenological domain, one influential thinker is David Abram, whose study of magicians/healers in *The Spell of the Sensuous* theorizes the craftwork of "throwing" the senses beyond what is immediately given.[70] As intermediaries between human communities and the larger ecological field of animals, plants, and landforms, Abram's version of "modern practitioners" render the hidden dimensions of the sensible world directly sensuous; they focus on the malleability of perception to yield a constantly emergent world. Although Abram opposes direct experience to machinic mediation, and although subjective illusion (of magic) is not the craft of epidemic media, ongoing technological and aesthetic experiments among scientists, artists, and activists, among others, reveal a commensurate immersion in techniques of perception. The modern practitioners of epidemic media, intent on perceiving a new multispecies relation, are caught in the "flux of participation," in the vortex of human and nonhuman intelligences.[71] The "touch" in this book's title, then, signifies much more than the haptic sense or indeed pure sense data alone. It encapsulates another kind of knowing based on experience, one that medially entangles as/in the environment.

The craftwork of epidemic media renders the processualities of life *sensible*. Natasha Myers (*Rendering Life Molecular*) invokes "tangible media," and

Inga Pollmann (*Cinematic Vitalism*) "vital media," in their respective takes on machinic engagements with lively matter; theorists of immersive media like Oliver Grau (*Virtual Art*) highlight the medial experiences of "being with" living systems. These renditions of sensuousness proliferate in the book. Then there are those media scholars who approach lively materiality in terms of media-technological limitations. An abundance of signals is the "noise" of lively milieus that challenges the effective computation of animal motion-sensing data. Such "parasitic" noise, as Greg Siegel notes, is endemic to the signal, in that it is a part of the "contrapuntal matrix" from which information must be extracted.[72] As I illustrate in chapter 4, movement ecology scholars address such interference with a range of techniques such as object segmentation and deep-learning classifications. Still others explore critical media practices that push against technological limits. In every case, the making of biotechnical forms is confronted with technical difficulties, which stimulate further media-technological innovation and aesthetic experiments—new apparatuses, devices, and tool kits, new practices and designs. Epidemic media practices reflexively become media theory attentive to lively materialities. In all these respects, a theoretical curiosity opens epidemic media to untapped fluctuations and complexities, unruly spatialities and unexpected agencies, and perceptual complexes. Epidemic media render life intelligible as it ingests, digests, excretes, expands, grows, or shrinks. In them, we come to know only a sliver of human and nonhuman signals, for "Nature," as Victor Frankenstein once learned, does not yield "her secrets" easily.

Life, Emerging

Back in 2008, one of the starting points for *The Virus Touch* was the rise of new materialism as a media theory insistent about process-relational ontologies.[73] Early in the twenty-first century, a number of critical approaches coalesced as new materialism, crafting distinctions between "life" as an ontological force and "life itself" as its extraction. Jane Bennett's *Vibrant Matter* and William Connolly's *The Fragility of Things* are often regarded as posthumanist works that question the distinction of the human within its material environment. They challenge any separation of human matter as more vibrant than other configurations; the emphasis falls on how matter *moves* and *morphs* in new assemblies. New materialism includes many strains of thought that I will not rehearse here. What is compelling about the turn is its questioning of the anthropocentric focus on *human* life plucked from its environment. Against human mastery over ecological domains come theories of nonhuman agencies and entangled materialities. Of these, entanglement remains a key concept in my study of epidemic media, but the term's vertiginous intellectual migrations makes it imperative to specify how it operates in the following pages.

A range of critics locate "entanglement" as a theory that understands matter as a group of particles that come into view in their relation *with each other*. In the physical sciences, the point is to consider the quantum state of the whole. As Karen Barad argues in *Meeting the Universe Halfway*, theories of entanglement position groups of matter as *intra-active agents* that transform each other. Their complementarity articulates coming into being (the *ontos*) with knowledge production (the *episteme*). After Niels Bohr, Barad calls for an "onto-epistemology" that grasps the "agential realism" of matter. Realism is no longer preoccupied with correspondences between representation and reality but with the practices/doings/actions, as Myers describes them, that *perform* epistemic objects.[74] To track entanglement is to expose the mastery of the knowing subject over an epistemic object as an illusion. The environment, in this account, is hardly inert or passive: nonliving matter has intentions and motives, claims and actions. Entanglement foregrounds material agencies in making worlds; in their coming into being, the world is always emergent. Barad's emphasis on scientific-technological material performances returns us to Adrian Ivakhiv's medial "worlding of things."

Writing for *The Multispecies Salon*, Barad expands these observations to one life-form's entanglement in its material environment. The brittle star, she explains, is a creature without a brain whose entire morphology (skeletal and nervous structures) *is* an optical system. To perceive/know is its very "mode of being," for there is no separation between the subject and an external world.[75] In this regard, the brittle star exemplifies knowing as onto-epistemological process. Barad's elaboration of this life-form is illuminating for thinking about multispecies entanglements emergent in epidemic media. Epidemic media, as I have suggested, institute epistemic cuts in biotechnical forms: these transcribe signals in visual or numerical terms, most of the time, cutting into living processes and composing them as forms of life. But as intra-active performances, these media enfold distributed sense data that are supplementary in that they are irrelevant to the task at hand. A haptic sense of blood's transitivity, for example, is simply irrelevant to quantifying the viral load. But Barad's theories suggest these "supplementary" sensations, affects, and intuitions may indeed open to entangled modes of being—to emerging-with matter as *another kind of knowing*. In the epidemic episteme, we come to "know" multispecies relations in technically and aesthetically composed biotechnical forms; we objectify virus and host as distinct entities in the grid of (biological) intelligibility.[76]

While attempting to weed out media-technological distractions—the "blurry traces, sibilant transmissions, unruly corporealities," writes Siegel—epidemic media open to what Brian Larkin has named "the material conditions of existence for media."[77] But they also intuit something else. Crafting epidemic media *accentuates* sensuous medial entanglement because of the experiential intensity of the epidemic situation, the furious accelerated time of crisis. Epidemic intensities are deeply visceral: there is trouble "in here" and "out there," breaching all constructed boundaries. In this scene, viscerally materializing biological-geological processes as epistemic objects and navigating tangible media (blood samples to feces) only deepens the awareness of multispecies entanglements. Modern practitioners caught in the flux of participation find themselves in a vortex of lively affects.

In sum, epidemic media are material performances that institute a new multispecies relation by imposing temporal cuts, spatial boundaries, and fractal configurations. Struggling with what remains unintelligible—pushing for more data, more precision, more accuracy—epidemic media are reflexive about their conjectural, provisional nature. Openly speculative, they court the apprehensible. Yet curiosity and wonder are tempered by urgencies: the need to produce biotechnological or biomedical solutions to stem host losses. This is epidemic media's instrumental yoke, one that is often expressed as a warlike stance toward perilous microbes. As we shall see in the next chapter, such a stance has yielded deadly consequences. The point is that epidemic media have always directed how we live with pandemics by attempting to fix multispecies distributions. In this regard, their material construction of epistemic objects extracts and isolates biological targets from processes and relations, then compounds the problem by iteratively folding those targets into problem-solving exercises aimed at producing viable industrial solutions.[78] Pesticides and antibiotics—the DDT strategy, as Stengers names it—that have generated microbial drug resistances and cancerous conditions are historical evidence of why the material construction of biological targets matters.[79] In epidemic media, isolated microbes appear as exterminable targets. But if epidemic media also open to sensuous entanglements, they can possibly recast the myopic view that ends in a biotechnological fix (in vaccines and drugs). We could begin to know "our" multispecies entanglements and to emplace "our" precarious life in a precarious planet. The heuristic separation of "life" and "techne" in *The Virus Touch* illuminates the limitations of media-technological inscription: biological processes outpace machinic capture even as "we" race to modify a new multispecies relation. Put simply, even though we'd rather turn our backs on pathogenic germs, exterminating them when we can, *we have no option but to emerge with them*. The radical uncertainty of new pathogenic emergences just reinforces the issue. Under epidemic conditions, "life" is, once again, "untamed ontology," as Michel Foucault named it, and we become deeply aware of its *qualitative difference* from technological processes.[80] Epidemic histories tell us it is not always possible to calculate all outcomes to life's unfoldings. If all outcomes were indeed calculable, after the first SARS outbreak, why was COVID-19 a black swan event?

These contours of epidemic media set in motion the "biological" (the *episteme*) and the "lively" (the *ontos*) in *The Virus Touch*. Biology codes process-relational ontologies, but unprecedented qualitative shifts call for another notation. When epidemics emerge, a qualitative shift in multispecies relationalities is already underway, for the most part without our knowledge. The virus has jumped, infection has spread, and then the shift becomes sensible as a crisis at the phase of extensive community transmission. Catching this qualitative shift in evolving multispecies relations at a particular moment of history, epidemic media enact reciprocal capture: they render spiraling viral replication (viremia) and deteriorating host conditions (disease) intelligible. Ongoing multispecies relationalities materialize as "life" in biotechnical forms. In the intra-action of objects, practices, and apparatuses, "life" becomes *bios*, to be governed—but not entirely. The remainder is the lively materialities pulling the knowing subject into an affective vortex. Liveliness indexes material conditions of the media-technological situation, including affective and sensory perceptions that index that other space of multispecies entanglements; liveliness as noise obviates objective mastery, spurring curiosity. As new multispecies relations materialize in biotechnical forms, their untamed ontologies challenge and excite the experimental ethos. Throwing the senses toward the nonhuman world, epidemic media entangle us in multispecies relations when they feel most difficult.

Theorizing Epidemic Media

The Virus Touch theorizes epidemic media as processes of mediation that render multispecies relationalities sensible so as to manage them during, or, even better, before the next epidemic. These media materialize in scientific practices, artistic compositions, and activist inscriptions. In epistemic cuts, epidemic media render one novel relation—the one responsible for the qualitative shift—intelligible, readying it for targeted interventions. They materialize biotechnical forms as image, number, milieu, and movement. Yet, as medial actions tangle with lively materialities, the processes of mediation—that is, epidemic media as making/acting/doing—activate a distributed sense of interlocking living systems. This is especially salient for perceiving multispecies entanglements. There is no getting past dwelling with viruses, with sharing accommodations on the blue planet. This open promise of epidemic media is inherent in the research concepts that animate the chapters on specific biotechnical forms: the "-morphic image," the "sensible medium," and the "multispecies kinesthetic." Predictably, the keen sense of lively materialities motivates engagements with media-technologies. Epidemic media are critical practice: they recognize the inherent difficulties of rendering human, animal, and machinic signals intelligible. They are constantly evolving, pushing media-technological boundaries, recomposing the times, spaces, and agencies of the more-than-human Anthropocene. Materializing not just new multispecies relations but also media environments, epidemic media operate as theoretical tools for contemplating what media can do in an epidemic. As they disperse the mastery of the knowing subject, partially dislodging warlike stances toward difficult kin, epidemic media train the analytic gaze on mediation as prehension, as a grasping, meddling, interfering in life's process-relational ontologies. This orientation alerts us to media's world-making capacities: Will epidemic media deliver specific technological fixes? Will they attune us to multispecies relationalities? Smart media, they neither foreclose possibilities nor pretend we can wish away the virus touch. They enable us to recognize epidemics already here, and epidemics to come—or, should we say, epidemics that *will* come—as productive sites for a renewed multispecies politics as survival strategy. The long game marks the intentional politics of this book: I elaborate a "multispecies politics of health" in the following pages, knowing that both "multispecies" and "health" continue to be thorny problems in environmental studies.

Unfolding this argument, the book commences with a historical chapter on the epidemic episteme, followed by three chapters on research concepts familiar to media studies: image, medium, and movement. Even as these concepts arise in specific media histories, it is in their articulation together that one can understand how life comes to be reconstituted in the epidemic episteme. A comprehensive epidemic media theory is in order, I argue, one that constellates a range of media practices that inscribe, store, and transmit a new multispecies relation. The brief conclusion draws out the theoretical and disciplinary implications of analyzing epidemic media.

Chapter 1 lays historical ground for the current epidemic episteme. That episteme harkens back to the late twentieth-century viral emergences that recast global public health crises as ecological catastrophes. With this turn, four decades of research on HIV-human multispecies relations came to shape epidemic media as we know them. This is why the living archives of the previous global pandemic are critical for understanding our new encounter with SARS-CoV-2. The EID outbreaks since the early 1980s set the new agenda in two ways. First, a reckoning with precarious life means a recalibrated multispecies politics; and, second, this politics implies that a rethinking of health across differential epidemic experiences is in the cards, once again. Arguably, all modern pandemics have been crucibles for reengaging health for individuals, populations, and species; yet, the massive overhaul of health during the HIV/AIDS pandemic was a watershed, as health expanded to the care of life, to health as global commons, and to structural one health. This chapter articulates a multispecies politics of health as the condition of possibility for unfolding medial actions that attempt to inscribe, store, and transmit life.

Chapter 2 presents classic instances of epidemic media instrumentally oriented toward machinic capture that nevertheless emplace scientists and artists in living systems. Following media practices of molecular visualization that make "scientific images," the chapter focuses on collaborations between artists and scientists, biotech and creative industries, in three locations: at the Center for Computational Structural Biology at the Scripps Research, San Diego; in the Chicago-based (art)n collective; and in the media practices of cell biologist and scientific animator Janet Iwasa (based at the University of Utah's Animation Lab). The *-morphic image* as critical practice animates the chapter's study of epidemic media. -Morphic images in the epidemic episteme have specific goals: to ensure health is conceived as altered molecular relationalities and delivered as biotechnological solutions. As such, these are malleable, speculative images that integrate multiple data streams to keep abreast of lively fluctuations (expressed as viral mutations). In this functionality, the -morphic image is one stop in turning data into flesh. The emphasis on visible form embeds these scientific images in cultural histories that transcode them, despite the imperative toward greater mathematical realism—toward more precision, more accuracy, more faithfulness to data. That imperative inevitably leads to preoccupations with tools and techniques, image production and image experience; circling mediation as prehension, the -morph returns as technique. As with other epidemic media, as the machinic drive encounters lively materialities, the -morphic image appears incomplete, imperfect (as suggested by the suffix form). Exploratory media-technological experiments engaging more than the visual sense afford multisensory experiences and attune viewers/users to lively temporalities.

Chapter 3 turns to mediatic processes that clinically translate a vital medium into frozen blood samples (for refrigeration), blood data (for the databases), and blood pictures (for clinical points of care) and thereby organize time-spaces of infection as serial snapshots. These are the blood files that denature and fabricate, quantify and transcribe blood. Analyzing transmuted vital media as infection's milieu, I track the circulation of blood files in the global biomedical infrastructures of "managed HIV." I start with blood-specimen processing at the University of Washington's Clinical Retrovirus Laboratory, then examine blood samples stored in the Centers for AIDS Research (CFAR) biorepositories and blood data stored in the CFAR Network of Integrated Clinical Systems (CNICS) databases, and end up at three points of care: Seattle's Madison HIV Clinic, Mumbai's Sanjeevani clinic, and the "original" HIV adherence club in Khayelitsha, Cape Town. The chapter explores epistemic cuts that compose blood as specific "interior milieus" to enable the clinical control of the transitive medium. And yet the lively materiality of blood disperses this milieu beyond individuals and demographic aggregates. As interior milieus unfurl into disease milieus and further into global hot spots, blood emerges as an extensive infection environment. At every site, blood in biotechnical forms tangles with the knowing subject, heightening the sense of multispecies entanglements.

Chapter 4 examines processes of mediation that differentiate particular animal hosts from their milieu (swaying grasses, leafy vibrations, diverse animal forms), aesthetically recompose them as organism-environment assemblages, and then locate them in spatial forms of planetary habitation (maps and atlases). These mediatic processes ultimately produce the "multispecies kinesthetic" as the basis for controlling zoonotic spillovers. As a figure immanent to the epidemic episteme, the animal host is center stage, assuming biotechnical form as a lively medium for the transport of microbes. Entering the "living laboratories" of tropical forests, I follow wildlife biologist and epidemiologist Anne Laudisoit's "walk with the chimpanzees" in the Ituri highlands of the Democratic Republic of the Congo (DRC) and Uganda, and zoologist Roland Kays's experiments at the Smithsonian Tropical Research Institute's Biological Station on Barro Colorado Island. Their multispecies kinesthetic employs geospatial technologies (radio collars, camera traps, and thermal sensors) and techniques (walking the transect to object segmentation) to detect wild primates (the reservoirs for HIV) in threatened habitats. I close with signal and noise from tracking media that materialize in two different geospatial forms: EcoHealth Alliance's zoonotic surveillance maps and the open-ended *Feral Atlas* project. Knowing multispecies distributions in animal-host media appears provisional, conjectural, as lively traces surface and disappear, as noisy forests create disturbances. In such dissolving differentiations, the sensuousness of organism-environment assemblages haunts epidemic media, once more; in the distribution of the senses, multispecies entanglements become apprehensible.

In the brief conclusion, I turn to the implications of studying epidemic media for media studies more generally, remaining aware of the difficulty of "theory in an epidemic." Turning to specific interventions and critical method, I argue that epidemic media are crucial for installing a new memory of epidemics as biological, social, and ecological catastrophes. Such a new memory, and the critical discordance that accompanies it, is crucial for living otherwise with perpetual pandemics.

The orientation toward mediation eschews understanding biotechnical forms as exclusively shaped by the biological sciences. There is no doubt that mediatic processes that elucidate blood data or viral entry are crucial interventions that alter and modify "biological substances" as they materialize in scientific settings. And yet the media histories of epidemic media provide a more complex view. They show how image making, record keeping, and motion sensing are fundamentally collaborative endeavors that constellate media makers and scientists, formal and informal expertise: biologists hook up with moviemakers to simulate possible outcomes; clinical medicine labs rely on grassroots communities to ensure drug adherence; eco-epidemiologists solicit information and data inputs from local experts and citizen-scientists. We come to experience how modern practitioners accommodate worlds within their worlds, a transformative thinking-feeling that moves beyond the imposition of universal reason. Epidemic media, in these stories, are intensely collaborative, articulating skills and talents, institutions and industries, agents and actors. The focus on collaborations defines the mixed research methods of this book: historical-archival digging, semistructured interviews at multiple sites, short-term participant observation, and critical-interpretive media analysis. I hope to bring into the same critical space epidemic media made in institutional settings (accruing value as expertise) and those made in informal ones. The scientific practices of molecular visualization, clinical translation, and animal movement tracking all evidence robust negotiations of knowledge practice across epistemic settings. Their pursuit opens readers of this book to the living archives of epidemic media that span everything from marvelous virus crystals in sweltering caves to homespun art-science long forgotten in a garage.

To think of multispecies relations during a global pandemic is to approach the problem from an extreme situation, in the thick temporality of epidemics. The environmental thrust of *The Virus Touch* challenges the myopic call for expensive technological solutions. If ecology has installed a new kind of memory for revaluating "unintentional processes" of the past that led to harm ("the DDT strategy") we should know by now that anthropocentric survival strategies are misguided. Recognizing the biological, social, and ecological dimensions of novel multispecies distributions is but a first step toward this new memory. Under these circumstances, how do we approach aggressive parasites? The ones that threaten social paradigms of kinship? How shall we live with them? Will we persist in the failing war on germs? As carriers of biological-social-ecological memory, epidemic media emplace us in interlocking milieus. Sometimes that milieu is but six feet in distance; at others, it stretches to dark caves in Yunnan province. Along these stretches, intensely, we feel the virus touch.

ONE

THE EPIDEMIC EPISTEME

Health as Multispecies Politics

The pictures don't lie, even as historians debate the evidentiary truths they disclose. These famous pictographs complied in the Codex Florentine and the Codex Aubin visually narrate smallpox deaths in sixteenth-century central Mexico when three smallpox epidemics wiped out half of the Indigenous Nahua populations. While there is some dissension on the exact extent of the devastation, most scholars agree that smallpox eradicated Indigenous populations at a scale unimaginable for Europeans of the time.[1] The Florentine Codex records progressive vital decline from smallpox, a disease for which there was no Indigenous term (see figure 1.1). The deteriorating vital conditions in individual bodies and in infected populations were mostly named *cocoliztli* (illness, great plague, or pestilence), with a few references to *çahautl* (translated as the French *variole*) in the Indigenous historian Chimalpalin's notations of

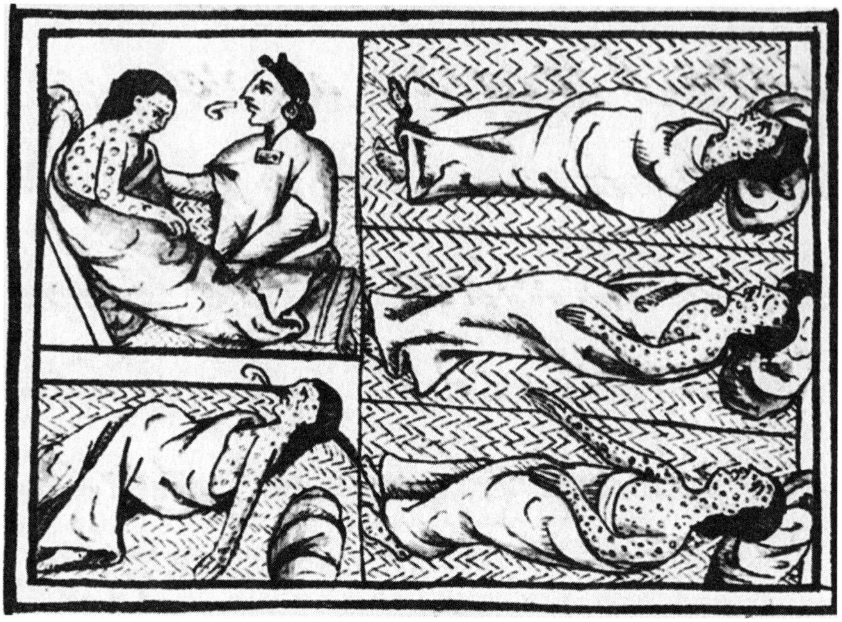

Figure 1.1. Pictograph of smallpox outbreak, Mexico. Source: Unknown (possibly Nahua) artist, collected by Bernardino de Sahagún, Codex Florentine (1540–85).

the new plague.[2] The medium of transmission, the pus from pustules, makes appearance in the recurring Spanish term *pegar* ("stick" or "adhere"). The pictographic and etymological records intimate viral emergence: something radically new that was not the Spanish invader but an unseen agent that would change the course of global history.

Historians proverbially grapple with the extent of the military and civilian damage caused by smallpox outbreaks in sixteenth-century Mexico's central valley and therein the role of that demographic catastrophe in ensuring Spanish victories. Apocryphal stories of a Black slave, Francisco Egnía, as the human vector, mythic tales of biblical plagues and weakened warriors, recorded testimonies of personal losses (some from Nahau rulers), and eyewitness accounts of paralyzed populations abound in the Spanish chronicles. The most comprehensive chronicle, the Franciscan monk Bernardino de Sahagún's monumental *General History of the Things of New Spain* (completed 1555–85), underscores the historical significance of the *first* smallpox epidemic (1519–20) to the Spanish conquest; contemporary historians note that the second and third epidemics (1545 and 1576) were far more devastating.[3] In the *General History*,

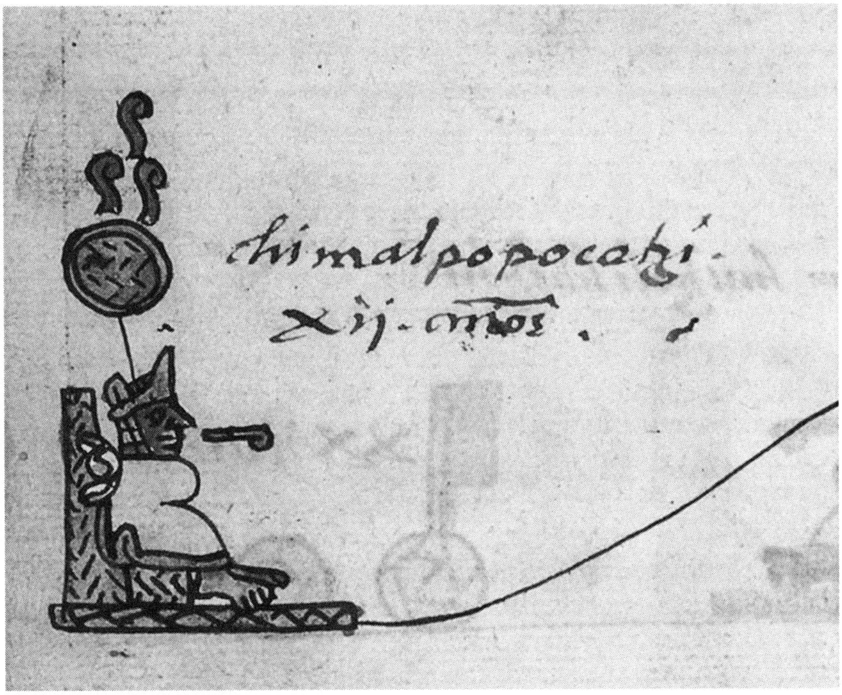

Figure 1.2. Pictograph of Cuitláhuac's death. Source: Unknown artist, collected by Fray Diego Durán, Codex Aubin (1576; pub. 1867).

we find an interpretive synthesis of the Florentine smallpox pictograph that firmly links the smallpox epidemics to civilizational decline (figure 1.1). The point comes into sharper focus in the pictographic record of the Aztec ruler Cuitláhuac's death from smallpox in December 1520, compiled in the Codex Aubin (figure 1.2). Cuitláhuac ruled for only forty days after his brother Moctezuma's demise, and his death provoked a renewed Spanish attack on the city of Tenochtitlán, the Aztec capital. The pictograph visualizes the king surrounded by tiny globes (*ampollas*) that were the symbol for smallpox (according to Mexican historian, Manuel Orozco y Berra[4]). Cuitláhuac's death from smallpox finds no mention in Hernán Cortés's account of his victory. Historians suggest this sleight of hand reflects that it was far more politically efficacious to claim that the Spanish military killed Cuitláhuac than to attribute his death to a nonhuman "victor," the virus. After all, the great valor of Cuitláhuac, as "the lord who ejected us from Mexico," posed a real threat to the Spanish army.[5] The Nahuatl pictograph, however, mourns the hero, the great king outflanked not by human enemies but by a natural calamity.[6] Medical, biological, botanical, geological, and meteorological data in these sixteenth-century compendia are marshaled for a natural history of the Aztec kingdom's fall to the Spanish invaders. Spain had three smallpox epidemics before the sixteenth century, in AD 1393, 1407, and 1420, but these epidemics did not bring as many fatalities as the one that attacked the Amerindians in AD 1520.[7] Evolutionary geneticists argue that the *Variola* strain emergent in central Mexico proved to be more virulent in this population because of the genetic homogeneity of the Amerindians. Others foreground a drought in the central valley, which galvanized *Variola* movement from dying rodents to humans as new hosts. These political and natural histories frame the smallpox epidemics in sixteenth-century Mexico as a crisis event, at once a political emergency and an evolutionary fluctuation. The tension between the two histories underscores not only the technical-aesthetic appearance of the epidemic in visual, oral (transcribed), and print media but also the purposeful interpretations of pus and pustule, body and population, valley and rodent, in the practices of history. Together, the Spanish and Nahuatl chronicles, heroic poems, codices, glossaries, and dictionaries offer a snapshot of a demographic catastrophe almost a century before smallpox would turn virulent in Europe and motivate the first modern public health interventions in a spatialized disease milieu.[8]

The *Variola* story is a fitting start for this chapter because it contextualizes modern epidemic epistemes that once sought to wrest human health from the clutches of global pathogenic agents. As we shall see, we have come a long way since then. By the late twentieth century, infectious disease emergences constituted as epidemics came to be understood as complex biological, social, and ecological crisis events that remake the world. Such recognition of a complex multitemporal event surfaces in the social and natural histories of smallpox in the Codex Florentine and Codex Aubin; these historical inscriptions further situate infectious disease emergence as part and parcel of colonial invasions. Starting this chapter with Indigenous notations of smallpox outbreaks frames the story of how the modern Western sciences came to constitute *Variola* emergences as epidemics. The history of the late twentieth-century shift toward an ecological understanding of epidemics positions them as biospheric catastrophes, arriving continually, but the smallpox episodes in sixteenth-century Mexico index the ancestral catastrophes of the colonial sphere. Burgeoning scholarship in decolonial and postcolonial studies attentive to ancestral catastrophes (pace Elizabeth Povinelli) and to anticolonial contestations of imperial public health (as David Arnold has demonstrated vis-à-vis smallpox campaigns) makes the case that infectious disease emergences have long been understood as planetary unfoldings in Indigenous epistemologies.[9]

This scholarship establishes a "future anterior" to what I characterize as the "current epidemic episteme."[10] The current epidemic episteme that recognizes infectious disease emergence as a nonlinear, multitemporal event and that proposes the mitigation of anthropogenic damage constitutive of threatening ecologies is late to the table. Health is the structuring horizon in this episteme: if health was once isolable as medically deliverable, in the past four decades, it has become increasingly clear that without animal and ecosystem health, "we" will have no option but to iteratively confront deadly pathogenicity. A bitter pill to swallow, this turn to planetary health has come neither easily nor willingly. And amid global health emergencies like COVID-19, it is all too quickly set aside. But sans the long view on anthropogenic activities that create conditions of pathogenicity, viral emergences will always appear "suddenly," as if out of the blue, catching us unawares. Hence, it is critically important to chart how modern global institutions like the World Health Organization (WHO) came to institute "structural one health" as a core principle for pandemic management.

To claim a paradigm shift that understands infectious disease emergence as ecological catastrophe is to situate universalized global health emergencies within the historical arc of colonial-modern medicine and public health commencing in the eighteenth century. The very constitution of global viral pandemics *as crisis events* takes us back to modern biopolitics, germ theory, and imperial medical technologies, complex histories that precede the post–World War II American-led institution of global public health. If the late twentieth-century paradigm shift privileged biospheric thought enshrined as "facing Gaia," those living with ancestral catastrophes present alternative readings: anthropogenic damage arising from the possession of land, soil, water, air, animals, and plants *as property* that instituted epistemic divisions between humans and the earth, goes the argument, has been endemic to the colonial sphere for centuries. A multispecies politics that rearticulates "health" within and between species, in this chapter, situates infectious disease emergence in the biosphere but refuses the occlusion of ongoing colonial dispossession. The histories of molecular colonialism, of place-based planetary disrepair, tell us how new infectious diseases are deadlier for those living with intergenerational, often deepening, harms. In tracking uneven socioeconomic distributions of health, the colonial sphere continues to haunt the biosphere.

The agonistic *Variola*-human multispecies relation of ancient lineage sets the stage through a historical look at how we came to the present pass—to the age of recurring viral storms. Epidemic histories tell us that *Variola*-human relations harken back to ancient times. We find notations in the Athenian plague histories and archaeological research on Egyptian mummies.[11] But this virus assumes greater historical significance because of its centrality to the modern Western sciences. The control of *Variola* motivated the first successful biomedical advances against viral diseases and the first modern public health campaigns. Smallpox eradication is often cited as the triumph of modern science over ancient pathogens: it was smallpox management that launched the modern epidemic episteme that prioritized human health above all else. It would take another book for these *Variola* stories. Of Edward Jenner's experiments with serum from cowpox (caused by the vaccinia virus, named after its host, *vacca*, Latin for "cow") for cutaneous insertion in human subjects as prevention for smallpox.[12] Of the eighteenth-century smallpox inoculation campaigns that institutionalized medical intervention on a mass scale, demarcating demographic differentials, identifying and classifying populations into risk groups. Of the WHO's triumph in eradicating smallpox in 1978 (approved by the World Health Assembly in 1980), which remains the gold standard for viral epidemic management. Of the ecological persistence of poxviruses (the "viral cousins," monkeypox and cowpox) in the wild that still emerge in human populations, as in the case of the 2022 monkeypox outbreaks.[13] If, post-1978, the only live attenuated forms of *Variola* remain frozen at the Centers for Disease Control and Prevention (CDC) in Atlanta, Georgia, and at the State Research Center for Virology and Biotechnology (VECTOR) in Novosibirsk, Siberia, the "demon in the freezer" (to recall Richard Preston's evocative moniker) still fuels thrilling tales of espionage, lab leaks, and deadly bioweaponry.[14] In other words, the *Variola*-human relation continues to emerge even after the early 1980s, when other explosive viral outbreaks—Ebola and HIV, notably—claimed pride of place in global history.

In all these smallpox stories, we find echoes of the Codex Florentine and Codex Aubin. *Variola* is inextricable from wars, laying waste to great armies and populations. *Variola* is positioned as the enemy in the "war on germs" fought in the latter half of the twentieth century. This warlike stance is at stake in rethinking health in the more-than-human Anthropocene. Against the dawning realization that "we" humans have lost the war on germs comes a perception of health as a moving target whose goals lie beyond medical advances. Now HIV is hyperendemic because 67 percent of HIV-infected people are on antiretroviral therapies (ARTs), while others still struggle for access.[15] And SARS-CoV-2 is tending toward endemicity. We don't seem to be winning this "war," even as human activities continue to generate the conditions for future emerging infectious disease (EID) events. Instead of pitting humans against viruses, then, epidemics call for a well-crafted multispecies politics that continues to decenter the human while addressing differential vulnerabilities within human communities. Such an orientation emplaces precarious life *in* an increasingly precarious planet.

This chapter lays historical ground for the current epidemic episteme. This episteme is embedded in the history of modern Western sciences, whose knowledge practices dominate health emergencies. Health emergencies might compel us to rethink health in expansive ways, yet epidemic intensities often obscure ecological lessons of the past. We return to the fear and loathing of germs, to warlike stances against the invisible enemy. But if we situate infectious disease emergences historically, then we open to a new memory: a recasting of epidemics as biological, social, and ecological crises. The new memory proceeds unevenly, along different temporalities, global and planetary; geological and industrial, biological and political forces move at different speeds and scales. Massive traumas—the floods and fires, industrial accidents and pandemics—are triggers for new memory. This chapter takes the ontological force of viral emergences in the late twentieth century as a threshold that recasts knowledge configurations of infectious disease epidemics: the "current epidemic episteme" I explore in this chapter begins there. Given both the promise of "*Homo microbis*" ("we" cannot do without microbes) and the peril of pathogenic microbes ("we" are under potential erasure), the sudden emergence of deadly pathogens in the early 1980s compelled a recalibrated multispecies politics articulated within the structuring horizon of health. The HIV/AIDS pandemic was a watershed event because it forced new reckonings with viral emergences *and* with global health crises. Four decades of HIV/AIDS has motivated complex expansions of health: health as care, health as global public commons, and health as structural one health. Simultaneously, the biological HIV-human relation has set the stage for understanding multispecies relations with deadly pathogens more than any other virus in the past four decades (including Ebola). On the one hand, then, the book illuminates the current epidemic episteme with a focus on HIV/AIDS emergence. On the other, the current epidemic episteme acquires its historical distinction from the other virus histories that surface in *The Virus Touch*. Those stories disperse as new memories; each commands its own archive. The virus stories purposively scatter how to know a pandemic because these are frustratingly multileveled events that are not amenable to linear causal accounts. Rather, as new memory, the virus stories track a deepening awareness of multispecies entanglements and of the relatedness of human and nonhuman agencies. Perhaps the coherence of the HIV/AIDS story and the dissipation of virus histories will enable the plotting of myriad trails for the unfolding COVID-19 experience, connecting the frightening experience of breathing trouble to distant multispecies encounters in the planet's recesses.

Centering the HIV/AIDS global pandemic in this way heeds Michelle Murphy's call to think "life otherwise." Writing about chemical relations, Murphy argues that the drift of PCBs (polychlorinated biphenyls), hormones, and soils maybe analyzed at molecular scales, but these assemblies are constituted by structural relations. Some bodies bear more PCBs depending on which neighborhood they live in; one could just as well argue that some bodies are less capable of handling SARS-CoV-2 because of long-term inequities in health-care provision. Thinking of social and political structures rather than molecules exclusively, maintains Murphy, alerts us to extensive and entangled relations, to the "inter-generational and looping temporalities" of chemical infection.[16] Murphy's conception of the altered lives attends not only to the ongoing violence of late industrial capitalism that no one can escape but also to the everyday surviving of vulnerable communities that, despite daily depredations and scant resources, pursue "life otherwise." If we transpose Murphy's iconic PCBs with iconic viral pathogens, the HIV/AIDS politics of survival in the past decades serves as one exemplar of living otherwise. At times performed in spectacular forms, HIV/AIDS activism played a critical role in forging the current epidemic episteme as protracted negotiations among multiple stakeholders reconstituted the global pandemic's eventfulness as well as its locations of injury. The battles over health not only exemplify successful negotiations among modern practitioners intensely engaged in therapies, clinical protocols, care affordances, and health policies but bring to the fore stories of "life otherwise" that interrupt a global history of universal scientific and technological progress.

Arguably, no pathogen other than HIV has commanded such prolonged attention not only as an epistemic object for the biosciences—at least before SARS-CoV-2—but also as a site for rethinking health. The following chapters bear out this claim across distributed sites of inquiry. One of the reasons for the historical significance of the HIV/AIDS pandemic is its materialization *over* four decades. It is a long-wave pandemic that is now regarded as *hyper*endemic, with increasingly large numbers of people living with AIDS accessing ARTs and struggling to stay on them. Staying undetectable is quotidian for all on ARTs, but, as ever, for those with scarce resources (medicines, yes, but also nutrition, housing, and transport), altered life can be intensely precarious. As the global history of HIV/AIDS goes, HIV burst on the public health scene as early as 1969 in many accounts (some disputed), but there is general agreement that the first recorded case was in 1981.[17] The first International AIDS Conference (IAC), held in Atlanta in 1985, hosted by the CDC and the WHO, recognized a global health crisis, but it was not until 1992 (the IAC in Amsterdam) that a global strategy materialized to address it.[18] Histories of HIV/AIDS indicate why infectious disease emergences have come to overwrite commonplace understandings of epidemics. We know that global infrastructural connectivity turned HIV's emergence in human populations into a geographically extensive infectious disease. As the extensive time-spaces of infection grew, global institutions came to constitute the infectious disease emergence as a *synchronous* experience even as that experience was starkly different in intensities and complexities across the world. The differences tell us global synchronicity does not imply universality, as pandemics emerge unevenly across global regions, while global institutions struggle for a common strategy. The production of global synchronicity sets in motion a classic pandemic calculus (of morbidity and mortality) that plots viral emergence as a global health crisis, a decisive turning point with a before and after, with origins, peaks, and wanes. Amid widely shared pandemic situations such as HIV emergence, new *pathogenic* multispecies relations become immanent (as we know from the commonplace nicknames *corona* or *the rona* for SARS-CoV-2). Subsequently, therapies and prophylactics also become commonplace, even where they are contested. This experiential synchronicity of infectious disease health emergencies makes them the iconic instance of epidemics (as opposed to the more localized opioid or gun violence epidemics).

For many health activists, the global turn to infectious disease health emergencies in the early 1980s meant the derailment of other global health agendas, most notably those enshrined in the "Health for All" agenda of the Alma-Ata Declaration in 1978.[19] As sensational events, infectious disease emergences, they argue, obscure other health emergencies, including slow violent epidemics such as obesity, (environmental) cancers, tuberculosis, and malaria.[20] (Ironically, the new scare of COVID-19 partially derailed ongoing clinical research/trials on the HIV vaccine.[21]) But as HIV/AIDS activism engaged vigorously with racial, class, and geopolitical inequities, the problematic of acute versus chronic health emergencies met partial redress in the critique of long-term health affordances and provision. The subsequent battles over health—health care and infrastructures, pharma distributions and patents—have had lasting impacts beyond the pandemic paradigm. Refusing the "end-of-AIDS" narrative, recent scholarship on "AIDS time" in the shadow of COVID-19 undertakes curatorial care work for HIV/AIDS activist histories. Alexandra Juhasz and Theodore Kerr's *We Are Having This Conversation Now* insists on the timeliness of speaking/acting about HIV infection: their textual performance of the nonlinear looping "times" of the AIDS crisis seeks to "trigger" community-based interactions among writers, educators, media makers, activists, and friends in present COVID time. As an "archival ethnography" of 1908s and early 1990s HIV/AIDS activism, Marika Cifor's *Viral Cultures* pushes for a "vital nostalgia" that can repoliticize AIDS after HIV infection has become a privately lived chronic condition in the post-retroviral era.[22] These works scuttle attempts to forge a linear history of AIDS: one that unfolds as the four-decade evolution from the panic of early AIDS to the post-1995 pharmacological triumph to the projected "end of AIDS."[23] As of 2019, 25.4 million HIV-infected people worldwide (67 percent) access ARTs, while 12.6 million are still waiting.[24] We have learned to live with HIV because of pharmacological interventions of epic significance to my generation, which had sustained grievous losses. When new ARV designs for managing HIV/AIDS (and later, PEP and PrEP) became scalable to diverse populations, the AIDS pandemic became a success story of biomedical triumphalism.[25] This global history of AIDS plotted around medical breakthroughs occludes the massive distributed labor of staying undetectable and preventing "loss to follow" (nonadherence to ARTs). The many stories of managed HIV in *The Virus Touch* attend to these occlusions, to the uneven epidemic intensities in AIDS time across the world.

Scientific research continues to probe HIV mutations, establishing multispecies differentiations, while social systems organize pharmacological dispensation across populations. The fact that we now "live with" HIV places a technologically managed multispecies relation at the front and center of the epidemic episteme. That management relies on processes of mediation that continue to render intelligible the multispecies relation. With four decades of research on HIV-human relations still emergent, the pandemic media archives are extensive. In all these ways, *this* virus touch is historically the most *mediated* biological, social, and ecological event. Hence, it is a particularly fecund site for research on epidemic media.

Beyond the robust media archives, HIV emergence alongside the Marburg virus, hantavirus, and the Ebola virus in the early 1980s situates us, historically, in a paradigm shift. On the one hand, these "outbreaks," as Priscilla Wald has described them, impelled an ecological orientation toward microbial life from planetary recesses crossing into new host populations.[26] As scientists gathered around EID events and their zoonotic agents, by 1989, Joshua Lederberg, the scientist who coined the term *microbiome,* christened pathogenic viruses as the single biggest threat to human dominance of the planet.[27] Indeed, the literature on animal reservoirs tells us that viruses live in opportunistic tolerance in some hosts, causing little trouble, until changing conditions create new conditions for cross-host transmission. On the other hand, for decades, public health experts struggled with extensive community transmission, which is the second phase of an EID event. Responsible for 40.1 million deaths from AIDS (range 33.6–48.6) and 38.4 million people living with HIV worldwide (range 33.9–43.8) by the end of 2021, according to WHO statistics, HIV/AIDS raged as a deadly global pandemic until the 1995 Federal Drug Administration (FDA) approval of ARTs for widespread use turned the tide.[28] As the story of "managed HIV" goes, acute infections stabilized as chronic conditions individually lived in the privacy of the doctor's office. But to get there, we learned much about the socioeconomic distributions that divide, segregate, and sort a single species even as we press on with the urgent task of living as multispecies. In all these ways, the long-wave global pandemic birthed a complex epidemic episteme that came to stay.

But why an epidemic "episteme"? Following Michel Foucault, I understand an episteme to be a historical configuration of knowledge that defines the conditions of possibility for all other knowledge practices. First defining *episteme* in *The Order of Things* (1966), Foucault suggested in subsequent writings that several epistemes may coexist in historical time. Without rehearsing extant understandings, my mobilization of the term is an attempt to mark a paradigm shift in thinking infectious disease emergences. Foucault's episteme is most often compared to Thomas Kuhn's much-discussed notion of the paradigm as a knowledge configuration in *The Structure of Scientific Revolutions* (1962). But where the paradigm is a conscious exemplar of a disciplinary matrix, the episteme can function as an epistemological unconscious: epistemes work as orderly structures that underlie scientific knowledge but that might remain invisible. The paradigm shift activated by the EID in the 1980s reverberated across the human sciences, but it also settled in a wider public consciousness. In part, this wider consciousness was driven by HIV-affected communities that routinely engaged in deliberations over scientific findings; amid epidemic intensities, both scientific and larger public cultures were rife with anxieties and fears, desires and prohibitions, despite claims to neutrality. Remarkable interventions into evolving HIV science from scholars like Cindy Patton, Paula Treichler, and Steven Epstein have shown how science was indeed a cultural complex.[29] For all these reasons, I characterize the paradigm shift in conceptualizing disease emergence as an epistemic break in the modern health sciences with far-reaching implications for research agendas, institutional change, and public policy.

The paradigm shift evolved into a distinctive epidemic episteme partly because of the vigorous role of science journalism in disseminating scientific findings. Pulitzer Prize–winning science journalist Laurie Garrett's writings in *Newsday* (published as *The Coming Plague* in hardcover in 1994) and Richard

Preston's reports on global hotspots (famously "Crisis in the Hot Zone," published in the *New Yorker* in 1992) brought home to wider publics the deadly effects of human incursions into dark caves and arboreal canopies.[30] Garrett's book remained on the *New York Times* best-seller list for nineteen weeks before its paperback edition appeared in 1995, while Preston's report on Zaire Ebola virus became the blueprint for his best-selling nonfictional *The Hot Zone* (1994).[31] Importantly, these journalistic accounts contributed to the environmental perception that the anthropogenic drivers of disease emergence, including inroads into animal habitats, played a critical role in viral crossings into human populations. Such science journalism would inspire fictional works, producing endless contagion fare in screen cultures. With the SARS and Ebola outbreaks in the early 2000s, bats would come to stay in popular imaginaries as "dangerous" viral reservoirs. It was not as if these mammals were dangerous in themselves; they continue to be recognized as important ecological actors, eating insects and pollinating plants. But disruptions that alter their foraging habits, inciting them to move beyond their home ranges, raised possibilities for zoonotic spillovers. Science journalism continues to serve as a public warning system in both nonfictional accounts and fictional scenario building. Scientists such as Peter Daszak and Jonathan Epstein of EcoHealth Alliance, one of the institutions I explore further, were media celebrities during the early months of COVID-19; they were constantly on CNN, bringing news of bats in China's Yunnan province as the reservoir hosts for coronaviruses.[32] Others, such as celebrity epidemiologist Larry Brilliant, who played a key role in the WHO programs for the eradication of smallpox in the early 1970s, have become consultants for fictionalized accounts of spillover events.[33] Steven Soderbergh's screenwriter for the prescient *Contagion* (2011), Scott Burns, consulted Brilliant on the scientific facts surrounding bats as reservoirs and pigs as intermediate hosts. Inspired by the 2002–4 SARS epidemic, the fictional virus in *Contagion* (named MEV-1) was depicted as transmitted via aerosolized respiratory droplets; no wonder the film was on constant replay on television channels in the early days of COVID-19. This nexus of science journalists and celebrity scientists made the case for zoonotic spillovers as ecological disturbances, emphasizing cross-species transmission, and located the spillover as anterior to the phase of extensive community transmission.[34]

The emergence of HIV birthed a formidable knowledge domain that composed global and planetary time-spaces of infection.[35] One of the most enduring compositions organizes the long-wave epidemic timeline around 1995 as a turning point, when pharmacological solutions became available in resource-rich contexts. Since then, the biomedical imperative has been to innovate biotechnological solutions to living with HIV. Scientists dream of precision medicine in taming viruses so that one can potentially live with low levels of once deadly pathogens; new frontiers in wiping out HIV reservoirs project a "cure."[36] Although credit accrues to singular figures and singular research enclaves, scientific collaborations and institutional partnerships back such experimental technological solutions. The point is a particularly touchy issue for the HIV/AIDS pandemic since the struggles over the ownership of illness and health, solutions and models, initiatives and policies, have been fierce since the late 1980s. In the early years, Cindy Patton's *Inventing AIDS* was a landmark publication that underscored occlusions in a motivated scientific enterprise.[37] The book represents the many contributions of feminist and queer activists and theorists who fought the macabre politics of "letting die" disposable populations.[38] The call for a citizen science questioned depoliticized relations between microbes and therapeutic agents. The story of how both science policy and a participatory therapeutic citizenship demanded better funding for research and better delivery systems is well documented. What is compelling about the social histories of the HIV/AIDS pandemic is the creative collaborations and multisectoral alliances at the center of the success story. Like no other, "managed HIV" continues to be a massively distributed enterprise in present AIDS time.

That enterprise would transform the location of health as the purview of medical research and practice alone. Health as the care of exigent life during epidemics appears as craft, practice, and knowledge production. The expansion of the medical humanities into the health humanities exemplifies this rethinking of health. Pressing beyond medical research and practice, the health humanities emphasize care practices *as* knowledge production, muddying episteme and techne, theory and applied skills.[39] Wellness regimes incorporate care as craft; social medicine extends care practices beyond clinical settings. On the ground, the creative practices of care in the HIV/AIDS pandemic led the way against the deathly indifference of the Ronald Reagan government. Institutional medical knowledge was regularly reviewed, assessed, and evaluated against communal knowledge practices. As Cifor notes, HIV/AIDS activists not only invested in communal knowledge practices, but also lovingly curated them as a viable health commons. Health came to be a negotiated *horizon* for constituting the baseline for medical decisions, clinical practices, and public health policies; those negotiations involved many contingent collaborations between doctors and patients, for sure, and among state officials, drug companies, hospital administrators, clinicians, biomedical technicians, public health workers, caregivers, activists, counselors, and affected communities.[40] This would have a lasting impact on HIV/AIDS health care well past the antiretroviral turn: in a constantly emergent zone of contestation, health would become "public culture."[41]

These social histories further highlight the distributive calculus that underwrites *public health*, for health in the early AIDS era was avowedly *not* a public good. Both the politics of letting die and the pharma wars, replaying like a bad movie during COVID-19, are ample evidence of this abiding fact. Once the virus was identified, there was talk of a HIV vaccine on the scale of the Manhattan Project. When Margaret Heckler announced the development of a diagnostic test for HIV at a press conference (April 23, 1984), she expressed hope that an AIDS vaccine would be ready soon.[42] That never materialized. Instead, HIV/AIDS became a chronic condition in the post-ARV era, and prophylaxis came in the form of pills (PEP and PrEP launched globally in 2015). The HIV vaccine research made it possible, however, for COVID-19 vaccines to make the cut in record time; quixotically, two years *after* the COVID-19 outbreaks, mRNA technologies hold promise for a HIV vaccine successful in animal models. For a generation like mine that watched and waited, fought and endured losses, the cry to mobilize a Manhattan Project–like effort for the COVID-19 vaccines felt surreal. In all these ways, HIV/AIDS haunts COVID-19 as a collective historical experience. Living with one foot in India, in March 2020, I watched with horror as a million migrants walked home after a botched lockdown; in April 2021 the health-care infrastructure under the Narendra Modi–Amit Shah government collapsed as the delta variant ravaged the subcontinent. For Indian Americans unable to fly back, civil-society mobilizations—oxygen acquisition, food deliveries, home-care provision—were the only affirmative glimmer as people scrambled to make do in the face of deathly indifference. Of course, COVID-19 is also the first "digital pandemic," as my students note; it was possible to mobilize faster because of technological affordances and connectivity.[43] But apart from this distinction, both global pandemics saw distributed endeavors that made public health a collective enterprise. These social histories make it imperative to account for historical differences *within* species in any attempt to rethink health; no multispecies politics can afford to elide them as they distribute life within and across host populations. In other words, "life otherwise" in pandemic situations mandates accounting for the structuring force of racism, capitalism, and colonialism on molecular processes and relations.

In the ongoing COVID-19 episodes, health-care workers were on the front lines with scientists in managing this new multispecies relation; these were not just doctors but nurses, paramedics, and hospital staff who struggled to keep a species alive. Other distributed forms of collective enterprise mushroomed, from mask-making cottage industries to communal kitchens. They ring a bell, reminding us of the food pantries and hospices, clean-needle exchanges and buyer's clubs, of the HIV/AIDS pandemic. This, too, is a multispecies politics, this adjusting to newly active multispecies relationalities. The HIV/AIDS pandemic has taught us to gather, archive, and curate such histories: all those situated local networks as well as international collaborations and partnerships, alliances and solidarities that effectively amplified collective epidemic intelligence, pooled resources, and shared knowledge and practices of care across epidemic situations. In my interviews and visits to a selection of local outfits in Seattle, Mumbai, and Cape Town, it was clear they had little time and fewer funds to archive their pasts. A part of the effort in *The Virus Touch* is to circulate their epidemic media and therein to constellate a "living archive"—partial, open-ended, constantly accumulating—for pandemics to come. The archaeology of HIV/AIDS epidemic media in *The Virus Touch*, then, is a situated generational reflection.[44] Not only images, voices, and writings but blood, heartbeats, molecules, DNA, microscopes, computer programs, drones, radio collars, and more proliferate in this living archive.

The Epidemic Crisis Event

The yawning COVID-19 crisis makes the historical turn to pandemics past particularly urgent. In *Anti-crisis*, Janet Roitman notes that crises as turning points present remarkable opportunities for reconstituting the past. With the financial crisis of 2008 and its aftermath as her case in point, Roitman bypasses the blame game to think of the political work of crisis. To recognize a crisis is an epistemological moment in the second order of knowledge. For instance, I may experience ill health and feel my symptoms *before* I abstract them as a threshold in an underlying disease. My perception will spur thought about how this critical phase came to be: What had I missed? Where was I negligent? This reconstruction of the past, almost inevitably a critique of the past, also galvanizes a new future: I must act differently from now on. Crisis is not "intrinsic to the system," says Roitman, but "a distinction that produces meaning."[45] If we understand crisis events in this way, then we gain a deeper understanding of the political will to constitute particular epidemics in universalizing terms as global health emergencies. It has taken decades to constellate the varying intensities of the HIV/AIDS "global health crisis" across the world; the results indicate how the crisis event lands differently for those communities enduring multiple catastrophes for generations.[46] To think about how the crisis is experientially different, how its eventfulness is understood, is not to deny the ontological force of infectious disease emergences such as HIV/AIDS and

COVID-19. The geographic extension of both pandemics underwrites massive collective tragedies, still unfolding. Rather, to pause on the *recognition of crisis* as an epistemological moment highlights the politics of plotting pandemics, of organizing the many pasts, presents, and futures. With both COVID-19 and HIV/AIDS, there is no simple answer as to origins, for example, whether those origins are the first medical cases or the first cross-species transmission. Keeping in mind these challenges, we can ask: What can the errors and failures, successes and triumphs, of pandemic plots teach us about the COVID-19 crisis experience? Can studies of past pandemics produce meaningful accounts of what we missed *before* this outbreak? *The Virus Touch* turns to how we came to live with HIV in order to gather our present scattered perceptions of the COVID-19 pandemic.

There is no question that COVID-19 places us in a global and planetary crisis, one that registers as a *new* event. How many times do we hear the term *unprecedented* these days? As the etymological cousin of *emergency*, *emergence* is, in this instance, a novel multispecies relation that could logically spell potential species extinction, even as virologists and epidemiologists assure us that this, too, will pass.[47] We arrive every so often at such crises (a term that once signified a turning point in disease progression) when populations constitutive of a species are under threat.[48] Such radical disturbances are "epidemics," hailing from the Greek *epidemios*, meaning "a condition against the *demos*," first used in Homer.[49] In this book, *epidemic* is the generic term for a widespread disease incidence at a given time, while the *pandemic* typically takes global form and meets specific criteria (designated by the National Institutes of Health [NIH]) such as wide geographic extension, minimal population immunity, and contagiousness.[50] As I have noted earlier, infectious disease emergences tend to overwrite the general term because of spectacular instances of *extensive* infection topologies and large-scale *accelerated* entropy; both create conditions for the recognition of a synchronous global crisis event and shared traumatic experiences. While the definition of the epidemic suggests an anthropocentric perspective on the crisis event ("against the *demos*"), histories of science indicate otherwise. The virus was first identified as a genre of microbe that attacked *plant* life: in 1892 the "poison" that was destroying tobacco leaves came to be understood as the source of a radical disturbance in farmed life-forms. Since then, the biological actions of such parasitic microbes have been a matter of global concern. The difficulty of encountering emergence is its unfolding across orders of association. What happens at one level might not have direct causality for or a positive correlation with what happens at another. As a nonlinear occurrence, an emergence boggles the mind, as we know from juggling all we have come to know about the COVID-19 pandemic.

Preventing such crisis events mandates a multipronged approach, even as emergences are notoriously difficult to predict. We know this from futile attempts to stabilize the exact coordinates of a spillover event and from previous mistakes about the "patient zero" as the "origin" of community transmission.[51] For COVID-19, we hear of possible contagion from horseshoe bats via intermediate hosts into human populations. Warnings of such latent spillovers haunt us. As scholars of all cloths rush to make sense of the unprecedented event, accusations about what "we knew" abound. Sometimes it is that sidelined intelligence report; at other times, it is existing scientific findings. As if in rack focus, these reports oscillate between the particular and the general: there are virologists, such Shi Zhengli, who had identified massive coronavirus reservoirs in the bat caves of Guangdong, Guangxi, and Yunnan, and there are a legion of disease-surveillance experts who place the blame for radical ecological disturbances squarely on anthropogenic drivers such as unregulated wildlife trade across borders, livestock farming, industrial agriculture, deforestation, mineral extraction, and transportation infrastructure.[52] Others pursue ideologically motivated conspiracy theories: the Wuhan lab leak theory, to which I return in the closing chapter, has already gained steam, soaking up anger and distress. Along with the growing sense of an unhomely planet comes the recognition of intensified global connections that make possible interspecies contact and community transmission. As SARS-CoV-2 interactions with humans turn deadlier still, burgeoning literatures diagnose and predict the global impacts of the COVID-19 pandemic. The diagnosis is socioeconomic and political: the failing health infrastructures, the disrupted supply chains, the biopolitical purge of dispensable populations, the stunning vacuum in global leadership. The litany mounts for an ongoing event too new for retrospection and too complex for diagnosis in medias res. The daunting multiplicity of "What is to be done?" is the best evidence of a multileveled nonlinear emergence that is a global pandemic. No wonder there is a call to reboot: to enact civilizational transformation in everything from personal hygiene to social contact to global supply chains necessary to manage the virus touch.

The jury is still out on the COVID-19 pandemic. But the management of the HIV/AIDS pandemic is superbly documented. We have learned to live with HIV—to live as multispecies—after massive social trauma that shored up congeries of disposable humans and challenged the unitary notion of the human in universalizing discourses of planetary disturbance.[53] That trauma is a matter of historical record and, in certain parts of the world, is still continuing. It has also taught us a great deal about the possibilities and limits of scientific-technological achievements. Human efforts that disable frenetic viral replication teach the body to live with new pathogens: how to recognize and attack them. But we might remember *there has never been a cure for viruses*—never that eureka moment equivalent to the discovery of penicillin that enabled the eradication of bacteria (that is, until some bacteria became drug resistant). After 1995 human hosts can live as multispecies *because of* the biomedical modifications we call the antiretrovirals (ARVs). While this is no doubt a landmark, the nature of the virus dictated the timeline of therapy. It takes HIV about a year to achieve the scale of cellular entropy that Ebola accomplishes in ten days; therefore, ARVs for HIV have more time to act within the body. This is all to say that the distinctive temporality of a pathogen continues to dictate normative epidemic mitigation. One day, we will live with SARS-CoV-2, but the new virus will dictate the timeline, posing a tough reply to the plaintive query "When will this be over?" This is why, historically, major global viruses—variola (smallpox), HIV (AIDS), and SARS-CoV-2 (COVID-19)—have had very different trajectories of management.

The period known as early AIDS reset the warlike stance of the modern epidemic episteme. The resurgence of deadly viruses in the early 1980s was a watershed moment for the war on germs that had gathered momentum since the mass manufacture of penicillin during World War II. The US antimalarial program that launched an attack on the "third enemy," the *Anopheles* mosquito (as the disease vector), was inextricable from military mobilization. "Atomic bombs, jets and rockets, radar and penicillin," were critical aspects of wartime research and development; the Office of Malaria Control in War Areas was established in 1942, evolving into the Centers for Disease Control and Prevention in the postwar years.[54] It is no wonder that emergency biomedicine—once for the AIDS vaccine, now for COVID-19—gets formulated as a Manhattan Project–like endeavor. Melinda Cooper's *Life as Surplus* (2008) traces how the post–World War II war on germs was derailed in the early 1980s; other scholars variously track the unintended consequences of the age of "wreckers and exterminators" hellbent on eradicating pests and pathogens.[55] These are not wholesale attacks on pharmaceutical therapies and prophylactics: the eradication of smallpox, the polio vaccine successes, and HIV/AIDS ARTs are undeniably beneficial in the balance. But the point is to approach eradication with caution, looking ahead to microbial agencies that combat chemical interventions. Relating the 2022 monkeypox outbreaks to the victory over smallpox, some scientists now speculate that the eradication of the one virus might well have opened the door to others filling the ecological niche.[56] The deadly SARS-CoV-2 delta variant was a reminder that wily viruses unable to flourish in vaccinated bodies will evolve in the unvaccinated as their petri dish. Back in the early 1980s, viral outbreaks brought home these hard facts about microbial agencies in no uncertain terms. Right after the WHO recorded the last case of smallpox in 1978, deadly pathogens were back with a bang.[57] Perhaps the hubris of actually eradicating an ancient pathogen without proverbial therapies, perhaps the militarized approach to exterminating germs, had much to do with the *shock* of "sudden" viral scares in the early 1980s. Panic over future EID events alongside melancholia over the lost war on germs spawned an ecological perspective: disease emergence became a multitemporal event as scientists sought out the phylogenetic histories and the anthropogenic drivers of pathogenic emergence. The introduction of a new course in infectious diseases at the CDC in 1985, argues Melinda Cooper, serves as one marker for crossing into the age of "viral storms."[58] The aforementioned best seller, Garrett's *The Coming Plague* (1994), capturing deliberations at the now-famous 1989 Emerging Viruses conference of the National Institute of Allergy and Infectious Diseases and the National Institutes of Health at Washington, DC, was the tipping point for public panic. The very next year, the CDC launched its *Emerging Infectious Diseases* journal. Since those decades, the virus as proverbial bioinformatic agent (rewriting human DNA code, hitching a ride on human cellular resources, replicating and multiplying) has morphed into an ecological threat—a prehistoric species whose evolutionary resilience terrifies and awes its human other. The ontological status of the virus as living-in-obligation to other living organisms has made it something of a biological exemplar, even a model from which we are learning to learn, eschewing the century-old antagonism toward this pathogen as an indubitable enemy of the human.

The ecological prognosis is clear: viruses will continue to emerge from disturbed habitats, hitching a ride into host populations through global supply chains and human traffic. They will become perceptible as *novel* multispecies associations once community transmission accelerates. Then we will develop viral load tests for therapeutic intervention or SIR (susceptible-infectious-recovered) models that articulate virulence/lethality with the basic reproductive rate (R_0) of the novel virus.[59] Once again, a new multispecies relation will become manageable but possibly at high costs. Consider the present struggle to anticipate what SARS-CoV-2 will do—how it will mutate, how it will act, what its long-term impacts will be—in the midst of a furious scramble for tests, drugs, and vaccines. Were we disinclined to repeat this history, the EID literature of the past four decades could be our guide: it teaches us not to disconnect human health from environmental reason. After the 2003 Ebola outbreak, that reason was enshrined in the WHO's One Health program, which articulated human health (public health) with animal health (veterinary expertise) and ecosystem health (biodiversity/conservation).[60] Meanwhile, in 2015, the Rockefeller Foundation and *Lancet* launched a movement toward "planetary health" as the new imperative.[61] By 2018 Disease X with pandemic potential had become a top research priority for the WHO.

This understanding of epidemics as ecological crises situates "health" within environmental studies. Health is no longer *only* a medical or public health concern; it is much more. It is a multiform horizon for abating potential species extinction; it involves meddling in multispecies distributions but not as wrecker and exterminator. Structural one health is a new science that tracks disease emergence along "multispecies circuits," notes Celia Lowe, denaturalizing "evolutionary niches within which infections arise and become deadly."[62] This orientation recasts disease emergence as a natural and social disturbance. Epidemics force us to think from the point of the pathological: when life surfaces as exigent, the immediate task may be to find technological solutions, to specify disease entities and their microbial causes. But the search for causes takes us into the geohistories of microbes lying deep within the earth's crust. We are plunged into therapeutic and prophylactic actions as well as into environmental excursions back to animal hosts and biogeological matrices. Disease emergence expands as biological and ecological event.

Viral Emergence

One of the earliest histories of disease emergence underscores the linear causalities of germ theory as a foundational moment in how we understand virus-host relations today. As microbiology probed microbial presences, solidifying as a differentiated branch of biology in the mid-nineteenth century, multisymptom diseases such as syphilis, notes historical epistemologist Ludwik Fleck, came to be constructed primarily as biological events. Preceding Thomas Kuhn's *The Structure of Scientific Revolutions* (1962) but not widely circulated until 1976, Fleck's *Genesis and Development of a Scientific Fact* (1935) presents the thoroughfare between disease concepts and evidence that mutually defines both.[63] This thoroughfare regularly marginalizes—keeps secret, unseen, inadmissible, or exceptional—whatever appears to contradict standardized definitions. Tracing the history of syphilis, Fleck notes the slippages around the concept ever since its first emergence in the fifteenth century: the causes and treatments for syphilis were part mystical-ethical (resulting from the movement of stars or from carnal excess) and part empirical-therapeutic (treatable with mercury). The debate on whether or not one could characterize the syndrome that included sores, dementia, and progressive paralysis *as* a disease entity raged through centuries before germ theory established a single cause, the *Spirochaeta pallida* bacterium. Fleck's treatise underscores the historicity of science and therein the fabrication of plastic scientific objects that harden into fact over time; he exemplifies a host of historical epistemologists who saw the sciences as always provisional and open-ended—always seeking to overcome their past.[64] Even as systemized scientific vade mecums (for general experts) followed linear disease causalities, establishing *Spirochaeta pallida* as the cause of syphilis, the difficulties of identifying one particular form of this parasite livened discussions in journal science (for researchers). Tracking debates over what appears as scientific fact shores up protracted negotiations among multiple expert "thought communities." This historical reading of how disease entities are constructed reveals how multispecies relationalities came to be plotted exclusively along single trajectories: only as a pathogen destroying host resources, only as an undisturbed crystal awakening from dormancy, only as a macromolecule commandeering (host) cellular actions. But if one attends to what any one account occludes, one opens to the "fuzziness" of the epistemic object (to recall Hans-Jörg Rheinberger) that migrates across domains of study.[65] Then the disease entity reappears as disease emergence.

This fuzziness is intrinsic to the emergence of the virus in the biosciences. A microbe that takes its name from the Latin for poison or other noxious liquids, the first identified virus, the tobacco mosaic virus (TMV), appeared as a disease entity in Dutch scientist Adolf Mayer's studies (1876–79): evidence took the form of an enzyme-like sap mottling tobacco leaves. Mayer characterized the sap as a biochemical agent, seeping, leaking, and spreading into host-plant populations. As a novel multispecies relation came into view, Mayer's observations suggested the enfolding of the virus in the medium that sustained it; the virus was always already relational. By then another kind of science, microbiology, had paved the way for isolating organisms from their multispecies relationalities. In 1876, Robert Koch proved specific microbes caused specific diseases, enshrining proof in the four causative criteria.[66] As the pillars of nineteenth-century germ theory, these criteria established direct causality between a microbe and a host, cause and symptom. Just a few years later, in 1892, the Russian microbiologist Dmitri Ivanovsky made the topological observation that a toxin, a noxious "contagious living fluid, was causing a wildfire" in tobacco plants, and identified the causative agent as a "filterable" virus.[67] Soon after, in 1898, Dutch botanist and microbiologist Martinus Beijernick named the toxin *virus*.[68] And so appeared the first identified virus, the tobacco mosaic virus, whose ability to bring economic ruin motivated further research. Filtering the sap from diseased tobacco plants, Beijernick found that he could infect other plants with the same fluid: the toxin was transmissible. The cause of these biotic processes, he surmised, was something lively, a "flame in a substance."[69] For immunologists, the flame illuminated the condition of the host, its state of illness or health, its vulnerabilities and defenses. Within a year of the TMV discovery, foot-and-mouth disease became the first viral infection observed in animals, quickly followed by yellow fever as the first among humans. By the turn of the twentieth century, there was a growing ecological perception that these microbes became pathogenic when they skipped the species barrier: for instance, measles (paramyxovirus) in humans was tracked to distemper in dogs. This well-documented history situates the virus-host relation within the biosciences and the modern enterprises of virology, immunology, and epidemiology.

Among these enterprises, virology was late to the table. When Thomas Rivers definitively established the virus as an obligate parasite in *Filterable Viruses* (1928), there was momentum for its mediatic capture.[70] The first micrographs of the TMV appeared almost a decade later, disclosing thin, needlelike structures enfolded in cellular media (figure 1.3). As these discoveries motivated research on virus morphologies, virological classifications began in earnest until cracking the code of life redirected energies to genomic investigations.

These media histories surface throughout the book, framing my study of epidemic media. With virology came fierce debates over the ontological status of the virus. In 1929 a professor of pathology at the University of London would evocatively characterize the virus as a thing that rises between a brick and a sunflower: "Our general notion of the structure of the universe leads us therefore to expect that we might well meet with things which are not so alive as the sunflower and not so dead as a brick, and the phenomena that we study under the heading 'filterable viruses' suggest that we now have sight of some of this intermediate group."[71] Writing in *Nature*, the researcher defined the virus as an "intermediate" organism, dead and alive.[72] The rumination was not unusual for the time, as vigorous debates over the distinction of living things raged throughout the twentieth century. One of the most influential definitions came in the mid-twentieth century with physicist Erwin Schrödinger's lasting distinction in *What Is Life?* (1944), a book based on public lectures delivered in 1943.[73] As opposed to crystals, Schrödinger maintained that living things (aperiodic crystals) were defined by their capacity for self-regeneration (to grow, repair, and reproduce), which enabled their struggle against dissipative

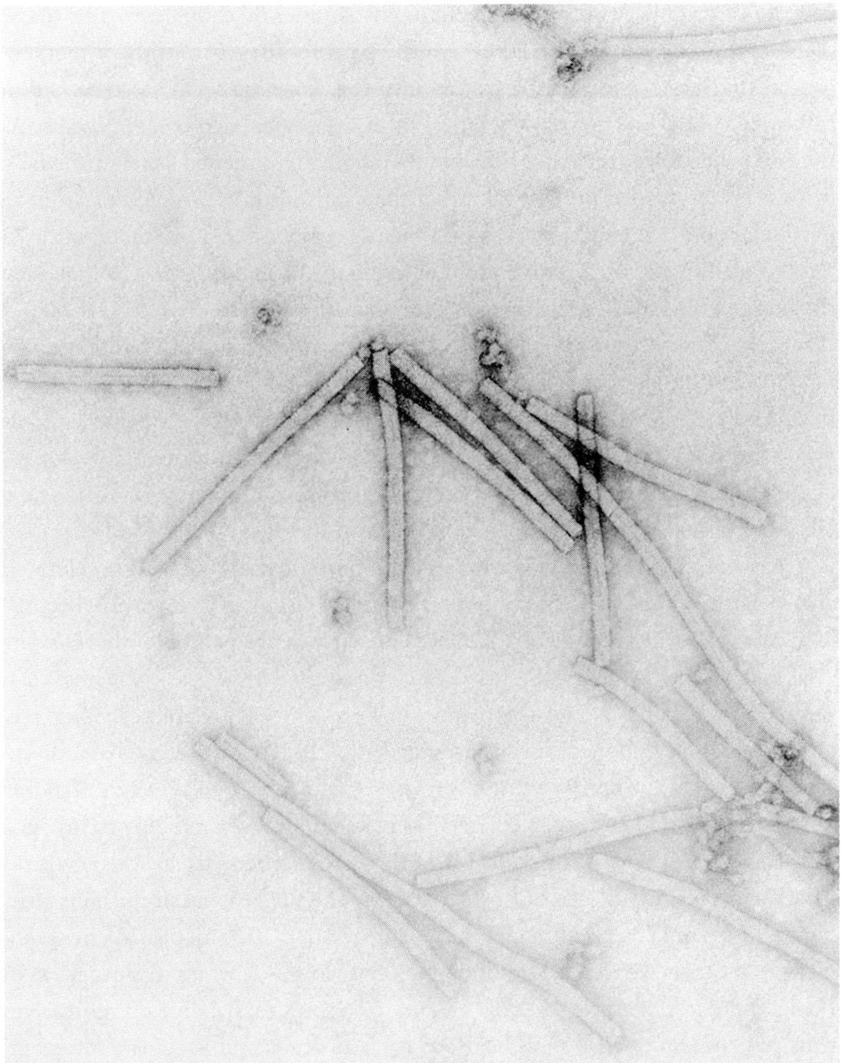

Figure 1.3. Tobacco mosaic virus (TMV) particles negative-stained with heavy metal under transmission electron microscopy (TEM), 1939. Magnified 160,000×. Source: Unknown creator. Credit: USDA Agricultural Research Service.

entropy. Reproduction (genetic instructions) and metabolism (conversion of resources) were soon recognized as the pillars of life that imposed contingent order, stalling dissipation; a third capacity, irritability, signaled the capacity of living things to adapt to changing relationalities. The scientific fortunes of reproduction and metabolism would take different paths, notes Hannah Landecker, with the former holding pride of place for most of the twentieth century (the century of the gene). But as environmental thought turned to the planetary distribution of resources, in the past decades, the study of metabolism as the "conversion of the world" into the "somatic self" has returned in full force.[74] Life was constantly emergent as biological-ecological process. As the two procedures (reproduction and metabolism) hardened as scientific fact, life was understood as processual rather than substantial. If *procedure* signifies a particular conduct of actions, the presence of reproduction and metabolism as twin procedures of life became proof of living forms and systems.[75] What were the implications of these distinctions for viral ontologies?

Under certain circumstances, dormant viruses exhibit irritability: they share information in "quorum sensing" that influences microbial group behavior.[76] In this regard, they perceive their living milieu, modifying their behavior to fit new conditions and initiating new relations when viable hosts come along—literally, when a bat, a primate, an insect, or a human crosses their path. As they detect densities of populations in an environment, they coordinate their response. There is not only intensifying microbial communication but also accelerated changes in viral informatic actions and chemical circuits. Then viruses become lifelike in the will to multiply. But because viruses are parasites, there is one drawback to their generative telos: they can stay alive insofar as their hosts can share resources and the host continues to regenerate its resources. They rely on the metabolic labors of hosts, jumping from host to host on media and vectors; sans locomotion, they must always find the means to hitch a ride. Trouble arises when there is serious depletion of host resources, a radical disturbance that can spell species extinction for both. As Lederberg once noted, viruses have no interest in killing the hosts that serve them; the ideal situation is ameliorated virulence.[77] Historically, hosts survive depleting parasitic encroachments over time when the rate of depletion is slow. But when it is quick, as in Ebola, there is little time to find a balance of resources. Balance often involves consistent technological modifications such as drugs and vaccines; for example, we take the new influenza vaccine every year and sometimes take boosters. In this biological-medical history, the virus acquires relevance as a *biological* object when it exhibits lifelike actions. Other histories, however, locate it as biogeological matter lying dormant, baked into the earth's crust. Over the course of the twentieth century, Schrödinger's distinctions prompted inquiry into the many pasts of the virus. Was it one of the first organisms (a pre-Luca cell) in a four-billion-year-old primordial soup? Was it a relic with primitive RNA? Was it once autonomous? A fugitive from the host genes? When did viruses degenerate into parasitic lifestyles?

In the years to come, as biologists rethought what life was and what it could be, viruses came to be incorporated as *limit forms of life*. As Stefan Helmreich writes in "What Was Life?," the opening chapter of *Sounding the Limits of Life*, since the late 1980s, life as the theoretical object of biology has been "bursting out of the box," so to speak, transforming normative conceptions.[78] He exemplifies these transformations in three ventures: the decoupling of life from carbon instantiation by scientists working on artificial life, research into extremophiles whose elasticity is not grounded in organic chemistry, and the study of biosignatures by astrobiologists who situate earthly life in cosmic ecologies. In the context of these biosciences, the viruses, hovering between life and nonlife, come to occupy the "fourth domain of life."[79] There are ongoing efforts to decode the viral genome (the Global Virome Project), but the scale and complexity of the task are daunting. Around 631,000 to 827,000 viruses can infect humans, and 99 percent of the estimated 1.5 million mammalian and waterfowl viruses remain unknown.[80] The size of the problem aside, a bristling virosphere is now widely recognized, and this has substantial implications for global pandemics to come. It is not just the *Homo microbis* that shimmers with microbial matter but the entire biosphere.

Such biospheric thought is not new; it predates the viral outbreaks of the early 1980s. Famously, microbiologist Lynn Margulis drew attention to the role viral RNA plays as biota (the totality of living organisms) that act within the biosphere (an adaptive control system that maintains the earth's homeostasis) to regulate the earth's chemical composition, surface pH, and climate.[81] As Margulis joined atmospheric chemist James Lovelock's speculative "Gaia thesis" (written as a series of journal articles, 1972–74), microbes took center stage in the biological, geological, and chemical disturbances that gave rise to the earth as a planet hospitable to life-forms.[82] Facing Gaia discloses viral emergences to be biospheric events harkening back to ancient histories of the blue planet. Writing with Dorion Sagan, Margulis would reformulate life as emergent symbiosis in *What Is Life?* As a series of biotic mergers on a crowded planet, symbiogenesis was intrinsic to life, argue Margulis and Sagan, a riotous commingling of organisms, constant "hypersex," as Helmreich characterizes it, that calls into question classical forms of biological individuality.[83] These claims have gained credence over time with the deepening of symbiotic perspectives across the biosciences. Botanists record rhizobia, mycorrhizae, and endophytic fungi; metagenomics illuminates hereditary symbiosis that challenges the one-genome/one-organism doctrine; and the immune "self" turns out be created by the resident microbiome.[84] Pushing back into evolutionary time, biologists identify ancient viruses in the human metagenome, vastly outnumbering human and bacterial cells. Celia Lowe writes about syncytin, a viral gene that codes for a protein made in the placenta, as a contributor to the "evolutionary emergence of mammals"; and Dorion Sagan (2013) notes that bacteria and humans share as many as forty genes.[85] Indeed, we have been multispecies from the beginnings of life. These theories motivate multispecies research into microbial geohistories. Writing in *The Multispecies Salon*, Eben Kirksey, Nicholas Shapiro, and Maria Brodine foreground astrobiologist Penelope Boston's research on radioactive landscapes, in which microbes, including viruses, survive.[86] Microbial communities trapped in hot and abyssal caves endure nuclear winters, waiting to reintroduce their banked genes at a later point in the earth's history (plate 1).[87] As the living dead, the virus lives in the huge air bubbles trapped in caves; with melting permafrost, long-frozen viruses surface with deadly consequences.[88] A Cthulhu-like thing, as Donna Haraway puts it, the virus is always already there in the planet's geological matrix.[89]

These inseparable biological and ecological dimensions of virus-host relations have congealed since the late twentieth century as evidence of planetary disrepair mounts. We have come to locate potential viral emergences in the "patchy ecologies" of the more-than-human Anthropocene.[90] As all eyes turn to Gaia, we are reminded of the intellectual histories that sought to unthink anthropocentrism. Margulis's claims resurface, bringing back RNA viruses as critical actors in the evolution of the biosphere and not just as germs slated for extermination. Her insights inspire others who imagine life otherwise, as we shall see in the closing discussion on symbiosis. Of course, she is not the only proponent of the ecological view on germs that precedes the early 1980s; there are many others. Two mid-twentieth-century biologists, Georges Canguilhem and René Dubos, are salient to the expansive view of disease emergences that I pursue in *The Virus Touch*. In the thick of the mid-twentieth-century war on germs, they sought to resituate health at the biological-ecological nexus. Together, Canguilhem, Dubos, and Margulis afford pathways into biology's epistemological pasts, and their theories are increasingly significant to the current epidemic episteme. One might consider their works as countercurrents written in the crucible of the war on germs, opening up a different history for multispecies politics. As we shall see in the following pages, there has been a return to all three after the late twentieth-century infectious disease emergences.

As a doctor and historian of science, Canguilhem thought of life from the point of the pathological—from the spiraling deaths of World War II. A pacifist forced to join the French Resistance, Canguilhem's writings on biology, medicine, and health have gained greater purchase in the past three decades because of their attention to the continuous mediation of living being by its milieu. In his mid-twentieth-century treatise *Knowledge of Life* (1952), Canguilhem defined the process of living as the enactment of precarious and contingent compromises with the milieu as the sustainable medium for living being. Canguilhem focused on the dynamic feedback between living being and its milieu as an ongoing creative process, both preservative (seeking equilibrium) and creative (making new norms), and for him, life was a cognitive process, a knowledge of active relationalities. This knowledge enables the constant changing of "vital norms," a process that becomes urgent when radical disturbances arise. Such disturbances can be a novel multispecies relation that living being encounters as ill health; in turn, these disturbances motivate the making of new vital norms. If COVID-19 has taught us anything, it is the making of new norms at every level, and hence the return to Canguilhem in seminars, conferences, and reading groups. We find a similar emphasis on life as emergent active relationalities in microbiologist, philanthropist, and philosopher of science René Dubos's writings in the mid-twentieth century. His *Mirage of Health* (1959) warns of a biomedical triumphalism that divorces the biological sciences from the social sciences and environmental expertise. As such, he eschews linear etiologies of disease causation for a greater comprehension of "nature" as not idyllic utopia but an unseen world of permanent struggle. As Melinda Cooper reads Dubos, we no longer have to mobilize against dangerous life-forms but against emergence itself.[91] In the new science of structural one health, Dubos's observations of biological-ecological health come to roost as a survival strategy. With them, health returns as an environmental imperative.

These intellectual histories make greater sense than ever before amid the recognition of planetary disrepair in the past decades. Focusing on anthropogenic change has made the Anthropocene a household word in these discussions.[92] As an epochal definition, the term has met with vigorous debate, not least owing to the sense that many vulnerable communities have lived with extensive and deepening planetary damage for centuries. And yet it is also the case that the scale and intensity of planetary disasters have increased exponentially. In the many efforts at periodization, the great accelerations of the 1950s are one significant threshold for the intensifications of industrial capitalisms in general, and for technoindustrial solutions to health in particular (including the mass manufacture of pharmaceuticals and pesticides). More than periodization, however, in this book, the Anthropocene (alongside its competitors) marks a mode of thought: the recognition of destructive anthropogenic actions motivated by a deep-seated modern anthropocentrism that mines and extracts, depletes and damages ecologies, perhaps irrevocably. Pandemics arising in "threatening ecologies" rival climate disasters in their catastrophic proportions.

Disease emergence turns out be a radical disturbance that we cannot live with. We may experience that disturbance socially as failing health, as precarious life, but Anthropocene thought compels the situating of disturbances in a precarious planet. In a memorable phrase, Anna Lowenhaupt Tsing captures planetary damage as ruin. "Ruins are now our gardens," she muses, in her pursuit of matsutake mushrooms from forests to restaurants; living in those "blasted ruins" sets in motion complex goals.[93] It is not only a matter of criticizing, containing, and eliminating anthropogenic practices and the regimes that support them (such as fossil-fuel economies) but also a matter of figuring out what is to be done. This deepening sense of historical urgency galvanizes present environmental knowledge practices.[94] The "most promising oasis of natural plenty requires massive intervention," notes Tsing.[95] Which ones are worthy of targeted intervention? A political question: the pandemic plot thickens.

The Global Pandemic

The story so far has highlighted the biological and ecological orientation toward health under pandemic conditions that mandates a multispecies politics. Such an orientation might all too easily unify each species at the interface of one immanent multispecies relation. This unification makes little sense after genomic research into the messiness of natural classifications. Moreover, multispecies theorists argue that since naturally occurring variations vastly exceed our knowledge systems, species are best understood as scientifically and culturally performed. What, then, does it mean to perform a unified "we"—meaning all humans—in the face of an emergency? After all, historical differences within the species belie the fact that we all confront the same exigency. As emergencies, pandemics lay bare structural inequities that cast a shadow over *shared* species self-interest. In the worst manifestations, the historically vulnerable become dispensable, reduced to bare life, much like intrusive microbes; they appear too abundant, placing too many demands on ever-shrinking resources.

The core *social* logic of the HIV/AIDS pandemic in its early years revealed how a zoonotic spillover became a "disaster" because of its social distributions, its biopolitics of letting die. That Ronald Reagan mentioned the AIDS crisis only after a nine-year-old hemophiliac was infected from a blood transfusion is not forgotten; by then, thousands had perished in the United States.[96] During COVID-19, the willingness to cull vulnerable populations was on display, once more, across the globe. The governor of Texas asked the elderly to "sacrifice" themselves; in Delhi thousands of migrant labors made a deadly trek back to villages during a lockdown designed to protect those with homes; some nations reported horror stories of health-care workers having to choose between patients, leaning toward potential survivors as ventilator supplies thinned. We will have to live with the consequences of these calculative dispensations. In such scenes of pandemic emergency, the illusion of shared species self-interest wavers. The historically vulnerable continue to struggle in the patchy Anthropocene, losing homes, livelihoods, and health. To understand epidemics as emergences is to situate them as not only as biological and ecological events but also as social and economic crises. This demands cross-disciplinary engagements that do not sit easily together. For instance, this section on the socioeconomic distributions of health might sit uncomfortably, for some, in a chapter devoted to *multispecies politics,* since the latter are often of biospheric concern. But the discomfort is precisely the hinge between the biosphere and the colonial sphere. At that hinge, I read global pandemics as crisis events whose varying intensities expose the uneven impacts of anthropogenic actions on human populations *and* on other species.[97]

My guide for instituting historical difference in the story of disease emergence is medical anthropologist Paul Farmer, whose oeuvre abounds in stories of the structural violence that has accompanied the modern plagues. No account of EIDs, Farmer argues, could ignore social forces such as poverty and inequality. These "biosocial realities" called for a dynamic, systemic, and critical approach that crosses clinical medicine with social theory.[98] His insistence returns us to epidemiology's beginnings as a demographic science that approached health from its imminent decline: the mortality and morbidity tables of the Black Death provided data for the birth of modern epidemiology. Farmer's point is that death does not distribute evenly across the species even though the virus may appear as the great leveler—an equal-opportunity pathogen. Attending to structural inequality, then, recasts occlusions and obfuscations arising from the global hierarchies of racial capitalism as they frame global health crises. The EID events of the early 1980s are, for Farmer, evidence of how health, illness, and death are unevenly distributed under pandemic conditions.

The story of Ebola Zaire emergence in 1976, for instance, argues Farmer, is equally the story of the Democratic Republic of Congo's Mobutu regime, which shaped medical practices at the Mission Hospital (the locus of the outbreak).[99] Similarly, US-Haiti racial geographies underwrote early racist epidemiological accounts of AIDS as a Haitian disease (tracked to the twenty-six-year-old refugee Solange Éliodor in 1982) that could well be the outcome of "strange voodoo practices."[100] Farmer's observations on these viral emergences reverberate in Donald Trump's racialized account of SARS-CoV-2 as the "Chinese virus." More importantly, the comorbidities such as hypertension among African Americans as the vital condition that turned COVID-19 deadly speaks to Farmer's greater point about the centrality of *structural inequality* to pandemics—that is, the underlying lack of access to adequate health care, drug therapies, and food security that distributes death. In the South African HIV epidemic, Farmer demonstrates how tuberculosis had been a durable plague among the poor and how infection with *Mycobacterium tuberculosis* came to be a major coinfection for vulnerable HIV-infected communities.[101] Of the 11.8 million HIV-infected people worldwide in 1992, 4.6 million were coinfected with this bacterium.[102] In the United States, significant outbreaks of multidrug-resistant tuberculosis were reported in homeless shelters, prisons, and medical facilities from Washington, DC, to San Francisco; similar trends were found in Latin American countries and the Soviet Union. The "new tuberculosis," argues Farmer, had everything to do with poorly nourished bodies, noncompliance with drugs, and expensive therapies. Those who could ill afford four to five drugs over twenty-four months were likely to develop multidrug-resistant tuberculosis as a deadly comorbidity. Farmer reconstitutes biological-ecological events as social processes, which ultimately leads to criticisms of resource distribution. *Infections and Inequalities* is a monumental volume dotted with stories of how individual agents live altered lives, trying to address the structural conditions that place them in grave danger.

Just after the biomedical triumph of the ARTs, it seemed scientifically and technologically possible to intervene in molecular human and viral relationalities. But it soon became clear that this biomedical intervention came at a price. Histories of global capitalism made landfall as the mythic HIV/AIDS pharma wars. The pandemic transformed into a global public health crisis in which persistent geopolitical imbalances rooted in histories of colonialism and racial capitalism sorted and segregated host populations, *distributing health* across the world. Medical anthropologists such as Melinda Cooper and Kaushik Sunder Rajan took note of value distributions that shaped illness, survival, and death; their scholarship tracked, more generally, an uneven global bioeconomy in which the regions of the Global South continued to play handmaiden to biomedical research institutions of the Global North.[103] More recently, physician-anthropologist Eugene T. Richardson has argued global public health "manages (as a profession) and maintains (as an academic discipline) global health inequity" whereby Global North institutions retain their cultural-economic hegemony.[104] Paul Farmer introduces Richardson's *Epidemic Illusions* as one of the most salient critiques of the public health's coloniality. Evidence of Richardson's critique harks back to the dramatic days of HIV discovery. Memorably, when Luc Montagnier of the Pasteur Institute accepted the Nobel Prize as joint recipient for the discovery of the virus causing AIDS in 1984, he noted his own debt to early scientific findings and raw materials from African contexts even as his own research unit accrued credit for the scientific advance.[105] Montagnier's criticism of the perception that scientific breakthroughs flow unidirectionally *from* the Global North (typically, Europe, North America, and Japan) *to* the resource-poor Global South still holds today.[106] Scientific-technological solutions (products, expertise, protocols, models) continue to arrive from the Global North, and raw materials (from wet samples to genetic data) from the Global South. Pockets of disadvantaged or disenfranchised HIV-affected communities *still* await the humanitarian largesse of global institutions despite coordinated efforts at global rollouts by targeted programs such as the United States President's Emergency Plan for AIDS Relief (PEPFAR) or global organizations like Médecins Sans Frontières.[107] Yet the geopolitical distributions of health in the HIV/AIDS global pandemic are not always organized along the north–south historical axis, given persistent racial and capitalist divisions *within* the Global South. Gowri Vijayakumar, for one, examines the geopolitical jockeying among state and nonstate actors in the 1990s after an agglomeration of agencies, programs, and donors (pithily characterized as "the global AIDS field") descended on India in anticipation of a pandemic explosion; not only did the new HIV/AIDS funding outstrip that for all other needs, including malaria (the number-one killer at the time), but the Indian crisis was consistently racially pitted against the worsening one in sub-Saharan Africa.[108] These fractures have been reopened by COVID-19 vaccine capitalism: resource-poor nation-states await vaccine dispensations, once again, even as new actors in the present multipolar globalization leverage vaccine distribution for soft power. Global public health continues to remain fraught as unrelenting historical differences persist within the smooth space of global flows.

One corrective to these geopolitical imbalances came in the form of the participatory solidarities of the HIV/AIDS era that claimed public health as global commons. South Africa's famous Treatment Action Campaign led the way in insisting that global health could be operationalized only by undoing abiding geopolitical stratifications, political and economic. This was one among many responses to the corporatization of global health. By the mid-1980s, cascading global health emergencies had already focused attention on the problem of acute communicable diseases.[109] But the neoliberal economic overdrive of the period exacerbated the crisis because of unregulated expensive new biomedical solutions: the open market was seen as the arbiter of their equitable distribution.[110] The pharma wars of the HIV/AIDS epidemic proved that public health governance had become a corporate biocapitalist enterprise.[111] At the time, South Africa was the nation with the largest population of HIV-infected people (6.8 million) after the first reported case in 1982.[112] But because of the (now-famous) AIDS denialism, the nation had seen a slow rollout of ARVs at mass scale; as a consequence, scholars estimate, almost 330,000 lost their lives.[113] Against this backdrop South Africa's Treatment Action Committee sued Thabo Mbeki's government for preventing access to nevirapine, in one of the bitterest pharma wars in modern times.[114] Volumes such as Nicoli Nattrass's classic *The AIDS Conspiracy: Science Fights Back* have been written about South Africa's management of the HIV/AIDS epidemic to rectify skewed histories that recast denialism in terms of cultural difference.[115] The focus on denialism obscured the estimated 11 million African lives lost because of the expense, and therefore inaccessibility, of ARTs. In the fight over distributing health, activists all over the world and pharmaceutical giants like Cipla (producing cheap generics) joined the Treatment Action Campaign's pharma wars in orchestrated transnational collaborations and partnerships, alliances and solidarities.[116]

It might be remembered that India and South Africa were nations with some of the highest statistical incidences of HIV infection; hence, my HIV/AIDS archives span the United States, South Africa, and India to relationally track global public health inequities in *The Virus Touch*. It is notable that India and South Africa once more joined hands to present a proposal to waive COVID-19 vaccine intellectual property rights to the World Trade Organization in December 2020.[117] Arguing that only 2 percent of the 700 million doses of COVID-19 vaccines worldwide had reached low-income countries, these member nations warned of a replay of needless losses documented in the post-ARV HIV/AIDS era. Such a focus on *national* epidemic histories is roundly criticized by those who rightly point to the implosion of individuals, communities, and nation-states in the face of microbial threats. What difference do geopolitical negotiations make when microbes do not abide by borders? We understand this all too keenly during COVID-19 as national travel bans and COVID tests at borders fail to stem the landing of new variants on every shore. Microbial movements destabilize the individualist and communal autonomies that underwrite biosecurity measures.[118] There is rich scholarship in this area, ranging from biosecurity studies to microbial international relations. Anthropologists like Andrew Lakoff write about the pervasive "generic biological threat" that haunts national biosecurity regimes and funds a "vital systems preparedness"; political scientists like Stefanie Fishel call for a new vocabulary to rethink the body politic in relation to "microbial states."[119] These works critique territory-based political forms (citizen, nation, globe) that are conceptually inadequate to imagining emergent multispecies assemblies. Their preoccupations address an overemphasis on molar borders that obscures sprawling multispecies relationalities. I approach the problematic from the other side, as it were. Within the greater story of a biological-social-ecological catastrophe, I attend to the role that nation-states, global corporations, and international institutions play in distributing life and death unevenly across the world.

The Planetary Catastrophe

If the HIV/AIDS pharma wars teach us anything, it is to focus on the distributive logic of multispecies relationalities unfolding at the phase of global community transmission. That logic makes it incumbent to think the "globe" and the "planet" together, despite the historical and conceptual differences between them. The discomfort has been addressed across environmental thought but perhaps most historically in Dipesh Chakrabarty's "The Planet: An Emergent Humanist Category" (2019).[120] While *the globe*, *the earth*, and *the planet* are sometimes used interchangeably, Chakrabarty argues that they have very different histories in relation to *human* life. The globe is eminently a human category constituted by human institutions and technology, while the earth is that "critical zone" crucial for the maintenance of life. A near-surface layer—from the "tops of the trees to deepest groundwater"—the earth is where most geomorphological activity unfolds, and it the most recognizable, trackable, and manageable part of the planet.[121] The relations between the *earth* and the *globe* are most salient to *The Virus Touch* in locating the EID events or potential zoonotic spillovers in biogeographic regions. The planet, according to Chakrabarty, historically arrives later—after accelerated anthropogenic damage. As the earth and globe strain against each other, their relations are upended by the unhomely eruptions of the planet (from climate change disasters to interplanetary phenomena). In the closing decades of the twentieth century, such eruptions escalate as climate refugees from low-lying deltas become perpetual migrants and polar bears starve in disappearing habitats. At these junctures, the planet surfaces in the deep earth, rising as the molten lava and dissolving icebergs, confounding global histories.[122] Against this backdrop, natural histories of multicellular life date microbes in the oceans and the earth's crust to three billion years. By contrast, our human-animal multicellular ancestors are about 700 million years old. Evolutionary histories of viruses point to geological and astronomical distributions of multicellular life that are jolting to the human sense of the globe. These histories rush at us in EID events driven by anthropogenic change. Throwing down the gauntlet, environmental thinkers such as Bruno Latour and William Connolly situate multicellular life at deep planetary timescales.[123] With Gaia, the fates of humans, plants, and animals are no longer separable: we are all in it together.

For Chakrabarty and others, global human histories obscure histories of anthropogenic change in which the planet confronts us with breakdowns and failures. Epidemic histories present countless instances of this recurrent nightmare. Sonia Shah's prescient *Pandemic*, for example, follows the story of the *Vibrio cholerae* bacterium, which famously traveled from the Bengal mangroves to London in the bodies of British soldiers.[124] Shah's history unravels the interlocking processes of disease emergence: how the bacterium lived symbiotically with crustacean copepods in the mangroves; how the clearing of the mangroves for rice planting, after the British East India Company set up colonial shop, activated the jump across the species barrier; how the 1817 Jessore monsoons enabled a spillover of copepod-rich waters into homes and wells; and how the crowded ships back to England fostered ideal conditions for the bacterium to speed through host populations.[125] The subsequent cholera outbreak in London led to John Snow's famous 1854 map—the first in modern epidemiology—tracing infection back to a single source, a water pump. Disease emergence assumed a spatial form that would become normative in times to come. By the close of the twentieth century, cartographies of infection were ubiquitous, later evolving into real-time disease-surveillance maps.[126]

The cholera story is but one story of colonialism as a historical force behind epidemic crises as anthropogenic disasters. Those histories take us back to early modern expansions, beginning with the European incursions into the Americas. This chapter's first story, about the sixteenth-century smallpox outbreaks in central Mexico, institutes this historical frame, highlighting colonial expansions as extinction events for Indigenous populations. Extinction as global and planetary history emerges in decolonial scholarship as Indigenous scholars refute the colonial animal-human species classifications that underwrite colonial-modern anthropocentrism. Writing about northern Australia, Deborah Bird Rose, for instance, documents the "double death" of animals and Aboriginal Australians as an ongoing extinction event that draws attention to the entangled histories and futures of living systems.[127] In *Wild Dog Dreaming*, Rose writes: "How to engage in world making across species? How to work toward world making that enhances the lives of others? And how to do this in the time of extinctions, knowing, as we must, that we are living amidst the ruination of others?"[128] Her incitement to making kin begins with colonial dispossession as ancestral catastrophes continue to unfold around us. Postcolonial historians, meanwhile, track bottom-up Indigenous ecological conceptions of health whose origins disappear in their colonial translation and appropriation into imperial public health: for example, writing about one British civil surgeon's campaign (1907–18) to domesticate cats as animal technologies for stemming plague outbreaks, Projit Bihari Mukharji traces the preventive initiative back to a small village in western India.[129] One could multiply these decolonial and postcolonial histories. My greater point is that Indigenous cosmologies offer vast repertoires of what the modern environmental sciences characterize as biospheric thought. Now that extinction seems imminent even for the most privileged, we all embrace the planet eschatologically as Gaia. Sometimes on parallel tracks, and sometimes articulated together, such epidemic histories install a new memory for living with pandemics.

Tracing the late twentieth-century ecologically oriented epidemic episteme, I have argued that the epistemological pursuit of multispecies relationalities situates us at global and planetary time-spaces of infection. Qualitative shifts in multispecies relationalities are unpredictable: there are volumes written on why we did not see this (our current predicament) coming. Unless we make structural changes to anthropocentric activities, the only prediction possible is that the modern plagues will be constant. And yet their prognoses and diagnoses have remained on the back burner of environmental knowledge practices. *The Virus Touch* is a reorientation: it focuses on multispecies relations that we must learn to navigate better. Feeling, understanding, and acting on multispecies relationalities requires a calibrated environmental politics as smart multicellular survival. This is especially difficult when emergent multispecies relationalities are constituted as health emergencies; typically, this extensive phase of community transmission puts tracking conditions of pathogenicity on the back burner. We are at a thorny pass: What does a multispecies politics entail amid emergencies? How do we live with flourishing pathogenic microbes?

A Multispecies Politics of Health

Multispecies studies constitutes one strain in the large heterogeneous field that is animal studies today. It shares with animal studies interrelated concerns about "making kin," about material entanglements, about species extinctions. Multispecies scholarship seeks to redirect attention from large, charismatic animals, domestic (like dogs) and wild (like tigers), to often-unlikable, sometimes pathogenic life-forms that muddy differential taxa between animals and plants, biological and geological strata. If conservationists, activists, and academics have devoted considerable energy to nonhuman suffering, insisting on an ethics of "being with" all creaturely life, multispecies ethnographers, biologists, and artists join hands to probe, and sometimes interrupt, scientific regimes that manage and produce interspecies boundaries and species distributions. Among them, Heather Paxson's "microbiopolitics" is salient to "being with" pathogenic microbes in the epidemic episteme. Paxson's writings on the modern craft of artisanal cheese making espouses a post-Pasteurism that "moves beyond an antiseptic attitude to embrace mold and bacteria as potential friends and allies."[130] Looking back to pasteurization, Paxson underscores the deep anthropocentrism that continues to accompany human relations with microbial agents of infection and digestion, one that arises in nineteenth-century germ theory and its corollary sanitation regimes. Critical reflections on these scientific histories are not *anti*-Pasteurist, she cautions, since dairy farming and cheese making include parsing "good" and "bad" microbes, but a rethinking of hygienic orthodoxies. With infection as its loci, the epidemic episteme has deep roots in the same antiseptic ethos: we see this again in the current hygienic rituals of masking and sanitizing to abate COVID-19 infection. The point is not to evacuate hygienic measures but to mitigate paranoid attempts at securitizing infection's time-spaces so as to externalize microbial agents. Paxson's caution rings true when microbial agents are emergent as pathogens. Then, the orientation toward mutualism wavers, and a different multispecies engagement is in the making.

In the past decade, sociologists, biologists, and geographers of microbial emergence have addressed the problem by questioning an overenthusiastic embrace of multispecies flourishing. As Franklin Ginn, Uli Beisel, and Maan Barua write in a special issue of *Environmental Humanities*, the abundance of "awkward creatures" such as pests, parasites, and pathogens makes multispecies "togetherness" difficult when "vulnerability is in the making and death is at hand."[131] Pondering the messiness of vermicomposting, of modulating the poison (sting) and the gift (honey) among beekeepers, and of eliminating damaging laccase in wine making, the coeditors elucidate the *differential vulnerabilities* in multispecies assemblies. As species entangle and knot together, some collectives prosper at the cost of others. This is the epidemic situation: an extreme condition of microbial abundance that radically stymies the flourishing of plant, animal, or human host populations. The most vulnerable in these populations face accelerated extinction, as we have witnessed in both the HIV/AIDS and COVID-19 pandemics. The epidemic episteme makes clear differential vulnerabilities operating among and between species. Quite apart from the ethical gesture of "being with" all creaturely life, we are faced with entanglement as a *problem*. How we navigate this problem can be a return to unthought anthropocentrism, but that is the very stance that got us to this sorry pass in the first place. A recalibration of entanglement is in order: the search for new ways of "being alongside" life-forms that are difficult kin. But what does this imply?

Reflecting on "Abundance in the Anthropocene," Eva Giraud, Eleanor Hadley Kershaw, Richard Helliwell, and Gregory Hollin call attention to anthropogenic "affordances" that generate microbial abundance.[132] Processes of ocean acidification that produce abundant jellyfish; insecticide infrastructures that enable resistant bedbugs; antibiotics that generate bacteria resistant to antimicrobials; colonial mines, railroad beds, reserves, and plantations that tip endemic hookworm infection into diseases in tropical and subtropical colonies: these are affordances that call for dismantling existing industrial regimes and pausing technological interventions that create known conditions for pathogenicity. Natural and social histories of entanglement present overwhelming evidence of such ecologically unsound structures and processes that reconfigure multispecies relationalities in ways that catapult beneficial mutualism or absent relations into difficult copresence. Writing about three emergences of the hookworm as parasite, ghost, and mutualist, Jamie Lorimer, for instance, shows how one life-form can become pathologically excessive, or totally absent, or potentially beneficial.[133] Such histories set the agenda for a multispecies politics of reentanglement.[134] The extreme situation of an infectious disease emergence forces a new reckoning with making kin from the point of potential death.

Donna Haraway's remarkable oeuvre on "making kin" provides a baseline for a microbiopolitics of epidemics when immanent multispecies relations call for intervention—for "living artfully" in the Chthulucene. In *Staying with the Trouble*, Haraway elaborates "living artfully" as the creative process that recognizes the copresence of ancient Cthulhu always already in planetary matrices.[135] As health emergencies, epidemics call for managing this copresence, often with techne. Biomedical remedies such as drugs, vaccines, and therapies are immediate responses that mitigate loss. This might involve killing microbes ad nauseam, as was the case in the war on germs. In other instances, blocking or thwarting microbial abundance, as the ARVs do for HIV replication, also manages copresence. Prophylactics such as COVID-19 vaccines or PEP/PrEP for HIV transform the vital conditions of the host so as to make them less beneficial for microbial flourishing; public health measures preventing viral transport between hosts (like social distancing protocols) mitigate the conditions for mass infection. All these actions govern parasitic distributions amid health emergencies. As I argue in the ensuing chapters, epidemic media enable such governance by rendering multispecies distributions intelligible in image, number, milieu, and movement. Life appears as life itself, an epistemic cut that prepares a new multispecies relation for artful technological intervention. The question haunting this book is: How can epidemic media enact reentanglement amid epidemic intensities? Can these media orient us to larger stakes beyond the immediate health emergency?

Haraway's arts of living prompt us to think about creative processes beyond the immediate extermination of pathogenic microbial agents. The environmental imperative is to place epidemics in the deep temporality of the Chthulucene. Returning to Lynn Margulis, Haraway articulates multispecies entanglement as a creative process: a sympoiesis that "unfurls" self-regeneration as a "being with" others.[136] The call is backed by the turn to biological symbiosis, as I have noted elsewhere, which challenges classical models of individual organisms (autopoietic regeneration).[137] Symbiosis in parasitic relations is a gradually derived state: a transition from pathogenesis to opportunistic tolerance or mutually beneficial relations that includes a stable, managed partitioning of resources.[138] One of the foremost theorists of symbiosis, Angela Douglas, notes that one partner, usually the host, takes control of resource distribution over time, imposing sanctions and controlling transmissions for both partners. Both develop novel capacities (a lateral, not hereditary, transfer of properties) in order to live with the other.[139] Less virulent parasites are at a selective advantage; they can work toward mutualist futurities. But with aggressive pathogenic viruses, the situation is somewhat different. Symbiosis must be actively pursued as "artfully" as possible. Ecologically oriented epidemic histories are guides to artful living with flourishing awkward creatures; they tell us that wholesale eradication, a radically anthropocentric disentanglement, has only exacerbated the problem of microbial abundance. After the lesson of the late twentieth-century viral emergences, we are faced with an *imperfect* "symbiotic agreement" (as Isabelle Stengers names it) that *reentangles* with microbes not by wrecking and exterminating but by interrupting and dismantling known anthropogenic threats that instigate pathogenicity.[140]

Reentanglement, then, proposes a multispecies politics that enfolds judicious biomedical technofixes alongside long-term environmental solutions. Living with endemic infection is one form of reentanglement, a "making together" with technological enhancement: the creative process of adhering to HIV therapies is a case in point. Reentanglement in planetary disturbances might include everything from environmental policy (e.g., policing illegal wildlife trade or halting deforestation) to the technological repair of living systems (e.g., engaging in underwater farming to restore coral reefs)—all interventions in the threatening ecologies of the more-than-human Anthropocene. This mandates a multipronged strategy across domains of expertise, hence the historical need for modern practitioners who can settle for tactical compromises around common targets. Ensuring measured distances, redistributing vital resources, and understanding technological repair work at all scales—individual bodies, populations, multispecies relations, living systems—modern practitioners perform a symbiotic multispecies politics. That politics renews the natural and social contract of "being with" other species and with one's own.

As a shared horizon, health *concretizes* the symbiotic agreement: its historical situatedness sets specific goals and agendas for a multispecies politics. In epidemic situations when life is exigent, what health should be is hotly contested, as we see in both the HIV/AIDS and the COVID-19 pandemics. Arguably, all modern pandemics have been crucibles for rethinking and restructuring health for individuals, populations, and species. Health is not the purview of medicine alone; it must include the care of life in therapies and wellness regimes, in housing and food security. Health cannot be left to the free market's vicissitudes but must become a global commons. Health cannot be constrained to human health; it must be crosshatched with animal and ecosystem health. Health is at once a complex multiform *horizon* for multispecies cohabitation and a concrete public good toward which we strive. In other words, health structures the ethical call to symbiotic agreements as a *situated place-based politics*. With each epidemic we learn more about what is to be done about health. Moving toward symbiosis ups the ante: health must be renegotiated as deliverable in renewing social and natural contracts. In all these ways, health is a reentanglement with flourishing microbial life, a living otherwise with pandemics whose conditions continue to unfold around us. It conjures and concretizes the multispecies politics of the current epidemic episteme.

I have made the case for a qualitative change in our approach to epidemics as health emergencies since the early 1980s. Setting in motion a new epidemic episteme, this approach understands EIDs as biological, social, and ecological crisis events. Viral emergences, in particular, force a reckoning with planetary damage and therein a new multispecies politics. That politics organizes the renewal of social and natural contracts around health as deliverable commons, global and planetary. Epidemic media render such renewal possible since processes of mediation make multispecies relations intelligible. Beyond intelligibility, in every chapter, biotechnical forms reentangle "us" in the biogeological churn. Life emerges as geomorphic activity, an unfurling sympoiesis with others in image, number, milieu, and movement.

Coda: Human Lingering

Anticipating the three chapters that follow, I close this chapter on the epidemic episteme with two artistic performances from the HIV/AIDS and COVID-19 pandemics. Built around health, they are of a different order from multispecies spectacles. The artworks here address practices of health as the inhabitation of global and planetary commons. Invoking different collectivities, they urge us toward a multispecies politics. The first of these is famous in the annals of HIV/AIDS epidemic media, and it resonates in the context of COVID-19 vaccine capitalism. Daniel Goldstein's post-ARV engagements with global HIV-affected communities seem ever more relevant to rethinking public health today. In 2006, when the director of the Art and Global Health Department at the University of California, Los Angeles, asked Goldstein to make a piece for the international art exhibition *Make Art/Stop AIDS*, Goldstein returned to the hanging assemblages he had made early in his career. In collaboration with John Kapellas, he created three hanging figures made of syringes and HIV medicine bottles that made public the precarious and collective experience of living with these chronic technological modifications. As the exhibition traveled to South Africa, this artwork, titled *Medicine Man*, generated a buzz. When the Durban Art Gallery invited Goldstein to create a *Medicine Man* specifically for South Africa, he worked with local assistants and the Umcebo Trust to create a figure titled the *Invisible Man* with small, brightly colored spindle shapes covered in brilliant glass beadwork. Along with a number of syringes, these spindles surrounded the figure. The six colors of the spindles represented the six major side effects of the drugs being used in South Africa (plate 2). The finished figure, hovering over a white disk on the floor, had the side effects of the drugs spelled out around the perimeter in the same bright colors as the beaded spindles (plate 3). People living with HIV who visited the exhibit were encouraged to write their own side effects on the white disk with crayons; others who had contributed their medicine bottles chose to leave their names unredacted, in bravura acts of public disclosure. By the end of the first exhibition, the disk was completely covered in writing, testifying to lives altered by HIV/AIDS. In this incorporation of drugs, needles, and personal data, the communal *Homo microbis* was a "ghostly shimmer" hanging from the ceiling; a spectral human, the dispersive figure was a social composite reconstituted with the very technologies (needles and drugs) that probed and modified it. The moniker for the series, *Medicine Men*, highlighted self-directed personal and communal care, while the international co-production curated HIV knowledge practices across borders. In all these ways, the *Medicine Men* series exemplified the distributed health commons of the HIV/AIDS pandemic.

The second is emergent COVID-19 epidemic media—emergent not only historically but also technologically, because these photographs of personal protective equipment (PPE) strewn in Elysian Park, Los Angeles, from Pato Hebert's "Lingering" series, were reprinted on silkscreens for an installation at the Pitzer College Art Galleries in early 2022. Hebert is a COVID-19 long-hauler who contracted the disease in March 2020. Like many of my generation, he approaches the new pandemic from the historical experience of HIV/AIDS: first as a sex-positive harm-reduction organizer in San Francisco; then as an artist and educator in Los Angeles's HIV/AIDS queer communities of color, involved in AIDS Project Los Angeles; and currently in his work with MPact Global Action that advocates for the health rights of global communities of men who have sex with men (MSM). A faculty member at New York University's Tisch School of the Arts, Hebert divides his time between the coasts. When COVID-19 burst on the scene, his spot of green in the middle of bustling Los Angeles afforded tranquil repose from the indoors on his daily walks. Elysian Park had been marshaled as a COVID-19 testing site—one of the first in the city. Walking to increase his breath and stamina, Hebert found his local environs had transformed: his eye fell repeatedly on PPE nested in soil, grass, brambles, and weeds (plates 4–6). Snapping pictures on his iPhone, he began to document the material ecology of an urban pandemic.[141] In solitude, the PPE popped vividly as traces of absent others in the surrounds; in my interview with Hebert, he noted the loss of the horizon, the sky, as his gaze locked onto terrestrial minutiae.[142] A few years ago, Hebert had created the "Oscillator" series, featuring a human form wandering in Elysian Park, reflecting its environs, catching light and shade.[143] Both "Lingering" and "Oscillator" are situated media embedded in the Los Angeles quotidian, but they are also ecological cosmologies that engage human and nonhuman collectives. To be sure, the constellation of signs in "Lingering" (beyond PPE) gather vital traces of social scattering in the COVID-19 health emergency. They are equally vibrant scenes of the corporeal isolation that Hebert experienced during the COVID lockdowns. The color-treated ground of the image *distributes* the figures in the foreground: they seem caught in particulate matter. Sensuous entanglement arises from Hebert's deliberative abstractions, fabrications, and artifice. In "Oscillator," the human form disintegrates into the environment, recalling the *Medicine Men* series; it is nothing but its environment. But in "Lingering" the human form is absent altogether, as is the imperceptible virus. And yet viral matter proliferates its industrial traces in the city park. In these photographs "we" are truly multispecies, enmeshed in the natural-industrial fabric of urban life. In the interview, Hebert intimated that he "wanted to make space for the virus to emerge," and it does, in its inimitable, invisible way, enfolded in PPE.

I try to make sense of new assemblies in the emergent practices of health and well-being during COVID-19. I try not to crave the somatic commons of urban bustle. Hebert's Elysian Park recalls the huge Maidan of my childhood, a green smack in the center of Kolkata always tagged as "the lungs of Calcutta." I follow my friends seeking out green lungs in their COVID-19 long haul. I try to rethink health while living with two global pandemics.

TWO

THE -MORPHIC IMAGE

Visualizing the Virus

The drawings in figures 2.1 and 2.2 anticipate the optical capture of the virus under the electron microscope in 1938. Published to animate Vilhelm Ellermann and Olaf Bang's findings on the cellular abnormalities arising from viral infection, these 1908 illustrations are an early attempt at visualizing experimental outcomes: the results of transferring infectious material into chicken bone marrow cells via injection. While studying bacterial infections, Bang and Ellermann discovered "filterable agents" that could cause cancer, yet the scientific community largely ignored the significance of their experiments at the University of Copenhagen until the mid-twentieth century.[1] The late acknowledgment followed Peyton Rous's Nobel Prize win in 1966, half a century after he had published papers on transmissible sarcomas (1910–11).[2] Despite the growing fame of his experiment with the iconic Plymouth Rock hen at the Rockefeller

Figure 2.1. Vilhelm Ellermann and Olaf Bang's drawings of chicken bone marrow, 1909. Source: Ellermann and Bang, "Experimentelle Leukämie bei Hühnern. II."

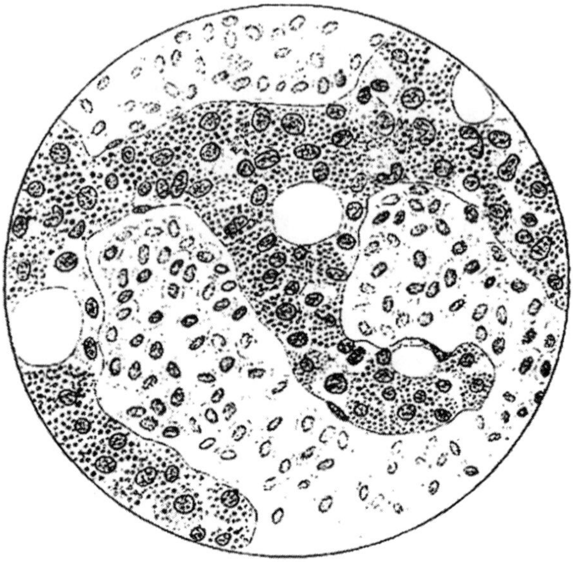

Figure 2.2. Vilhelm Ellermann and Olaf Bang's drawings of chicken bone marrow with sarcoma, 1909. Source: Ellermann and Bang, "Experimentelle Leukämie bei Hühnern."

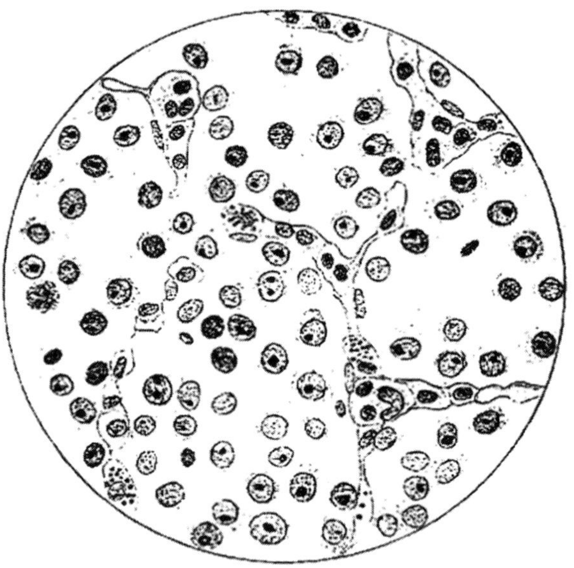

Institute in New York, Rous acknowledged in his Nobel Prize lecture that Bang and Ellermann had beaten him to it. This tale of international cooperation places a multispecies relation at center stage: the virus emerges as flourishing "infectious material" visualized in these two-dimensional portraits of cellular dynamics. The visualization anticipates the emergence of the virus as a visible form in biotechnical images later in the century. The preoccupation with visible form persists in the -morphic image well after the shift from analog to digital inscription. The -morphic image is the subject of the chapter: I trace its vicissitudes in the late twentieth to early twenty-first century media-technological practices of molecular visualization that enact digital images of viral macromolecules.

The 1908 drawings sequence a temporal cellular event: they visualize infection as a disturbance in the normal processes of cellular metabolism. The two images of normal and leukemic cells invite the scientist to reconstruct the past and present of the cell in order to comprehend the extent of the damage. Such temporal distinctions between the normal (past) and the pathological (present) of technically augmented or cultured cells obtain in most symptomatic readings, but in the case of the virus, "seeing" the cellular event almost always involves seeing a *relation*. This is especially so for viruses that live in obligation to their hosts as lively media; isolating viral particles for scientific experiments relies on the effective preparation of the medium that sustains them. In the 1908 portraits, that medium is mammalian cells, which, as Hannah Landecker notes, were "cultured" as technologies in the early twentieth century.[3] Interrelated scientific and technological histories of visualizing the virus, from these early decades of the twentieth century into the twenty-first century, always feature a dynamic biological relation. The viral particle-host milieu assemblage constitutes the epistemic object. As "the virus" disaggregates into active particles observed in their drift in extracellular fluids, their entry into host cells, their bloom and blast, in contemporary animations, the orientation toward *morphḗ* (Greek for "form") expressive in the image endures well into our data-rich postgenomic present. This chapter's beginning with early twentieth-century scientific images highlights this continuity. The reason for the persistence of images, I argue, lies in their efficacies in turning data into flesh.

This chapter elaborates the concert of biological and technological processes in the making/enacting of biotechnical images. Exemplary biomedia, these scientific images are crucial for researching and developing biotechnological solutions in epidemic time. The most studied viruses in the twentieth century—first the tobacco mosaic virus (TMV) and then HIV—acquire immanent value because of their pathogenic impacts, their abundance that generates vital loss in plant and human populations. Through such model organisms, the biosciences approach a general problem. How to enact more precise machinic capture of changing multispecies relations while remaining aware of their lively flux? The suffix form, the *-morphic* gestures toward an imperfect, ever-evolving biotechnical form attuned to temporal excess. This attunement in image making motivates a reflexive turn to media capacities, aesthetic grammars, and image experiences—in short, to mediation as prehension, a grasping, meddling in life itself. As multisensory biotechnical images abound, collaborations among artistic, industrial, and scientific image makers surface in the media history of molecular visualization. In that history, modern practitioners of different cloths perform an ontological politics, negotiating competing visions of the worlds they study.

There could be many starting points for this long view on visual inscriptions of viral macromolecules. But keeping in mind the identification of viruses as distinctive microbial agents in 1892, the late nineteenth century's romance with the relationship between form and vitality is most relevant here. If the sequential 1908 drawings aspired to depict a cellular event, fulfillment came just a year later with the appearance of Julius Ries's famous microcinematography featuring the life of a sea urchin.[4] Microcinematography afforded new possibilities for the machinic observation of growth and reproduction; early experiments with the cinematic image imbricated the medium in scientific histories of the period. As James Cahill reminds us in his exploration of Jean Painlevé's "non-human" cinema, research laboratories in the natural sciences (such as the Marey Institute) served as incubators for the developing cinematic apparatuses.[5] Étienne Marey's famous diagrams were early explorations of the cinematic apparatus: the aim was to observe how (and to what extent) the camera could mediate vital motion, to "see" life-forms in action and therein come to "know" life as unfolding activity.[6] If early scientific cinema experimented with technical capacities and aesthetic propensities for the sequential capture of life as activity, animation presented an alternative in its very artifice. Memorably, reflecting on his drawings, Soviet filmmaker and theorist Sergei Eisenstein argued that cartoon animation (in characters such as in Mickey Mouse) was "plasmatic" in representing the contoured movement of forms; animation could exhibit the fluid dynamics of primal protoplasm.[7] His remarks plot a trajectory between the 1908 sketches and the digital animations of the present, and accentuate the coevolution of the life sciences and media technologies in the making of scientific images. Anticipating their digital counterparts, the 1908 sketches can be regarded as experimental storyboards signaling the aesthetic vivification of a hypothesis based on existing data. To begin here is to emphasize media histories of continuities, joining recent conversations in cinema studies (e.g., Cahill's *Zoological Surrealism*), in new media studies (e.g., Adam Nocek's *Molecular Capture*), and in science and technology studies (e.g., Natasha Myers's *Rendering Life Molecular* and Philip Thurtle's *Biology in the Grid*).

Digital images in current molecular visualizations retain the push toward realism—toward more data, greater resolution, more precision—while harvesting the productive artifice of plasmatic images, morphing and elastic. One might say that morphing is an attribute of digital images in general. But in the domain of scientific images that inscribe biological processes and living systems, *-morphic* (as suffix) marks the radical incompletion of visible form, its imperfection, in speculating on multispecies relations. Digital images of virus macromolecules are exemplary instances of -morphic scientific images because they occupy a tensioned space between techne and life. As image makers collaborate on pushing the boundaries of technical mediation, the -morphic references cultural technique, the craftwork of media practices in research laboratories that transforms matter into "material substance."[8] In visiting laboratories working on computational images of viruses, I was hyperaware of this craftwork and of my inexperience at "knowing" what I was "seeing" on computer monitors equipped with headgear for the 3D image experience. The throbbing molecules in Brownian motion at the Olson Lab, at Scripps Research, San Diego, simply appeared simply as tiny colliding particles through which I could zoom with a click. Only under Arthur Olson and David Goodsell's patient guidance did I come to appreciate them as the physical trembling of vibrant matter.

This chapter pursues the -morphic as the governing attribute of virus images in scientific (life science laboratories) and artistic (art galleries/museums) settings. It unfolds around three stories about visualizing the HIV-1 macromolecule. The Olson Lab is the location for one of these stories and is important to *The Virus Touch* because this unit, once named the Molecular Graphics Lab at Scripps Research, San Diego, has been making editable 3D images of the HIV-1 macromolecule for a number of years. Its chief biologist, Arthur Olson, is a pioneer in the computer graphics foundational to molecular visualization (his papers date to 1979). Founded in 1981, the "Olson Lab" (as it is nicknamed) was recalibrated as the Center for Computational Structural Biology in 2018. Sourcing its data from molecular biologists (studying gene transcriptions), biochemists (studying chemical interactions), and structural biologists (studying protein assemblies), the Olson Lab continues to build integrative crowdsourced models of the macromolecule HIV-1 as well as to produce software for scalable 3D models. The second story unfolds around the (art)n collective, famous for immersive 3D images patented as the "PHSCologram technology"—the term PHSCologram stands for a combination of photography, holography, sculpture, and computer graphics. Trained in sculpture at the Art Institute of Chicago, Ellen Sandor founded the collective in 1983 and experimented with analog 3D images before developing digital processing of the PHSCologram s in the 1990s. The (art)n collective has historical significance as the makers of one of the first computer-generated images of the HIV macromolecule in 1987. They would continue to visualize viruses in numerous collaborations with scientists across the world, including Arthur Olson and David Goodsell at the Olson Lab. My third story is a little more complex: it involves the "molecular movies" in which digital images made for scientific research interface with those made for larger media cultures of scientific edutainment. I thread my discussion through Janet Iwasa's molecular animations at the Animation Lab at the University of Utah, based on a series of interviews and correspondence with her since 2013. Iwasa's molecular animations visualize molecular events for the scientific community (to use in testing competing hypotheses), as well as for broader citizen-science publics (gamer communities, students, online gallery goers).

One of the surprises in researching these sites were the crisscrossing paths of the major players. Arthur Olson's HIVE (HIV Interactions in Viral Evolution) Center is a sister center to the Center for the Structural Biology of Cellular Host Elements in Egress, Trafficking, and Assembly of HIV (CHEETAH), which is one of the institutional collaborators with Iwasa's Animation Lab; Graham Johnson, who developed cellPACK while a postdoc at the Olson Lab, inspired Iwasa; and Ellen Sandor worked with both Olson and Goodsell in her art-science projects. I had not started with these connections; they emerged in my visits and conversations with various actors at my research sites. The connections showed highly collaborative ventures spanning decades that visualized *just one virus macromolecule*: HIV-1. These are instantiations of "partial connections," to recall Isabelle Stengers, made in the pursuit of a common goal.[9] Before moving deeper into these sites, however, I pause on the -morphic image as a research concept and offer a brief account of molecular visualization as a scientific-cultural media practice to set the stage.

The -morphic Image

The two-dimensional space of the 1908 drawings demarcates the cell, the basic unit of analysis since the inception of biology in the 1800s, and the timescale of the cellular event.[10] Much has changed since the mid-twentieth-century advent of molecular biology: life is understood as a series of actions unfolds as molecular-cellular events within complex living systems that buck any imposition of linear causalities. As we shall see, genetic mutation, biochemical change, and protein assemblies together emerge in -morphic digital images of the late twentieth to early twenty-first centuries. Molecular visualizations model such actions based on experimental data (such as a micrograph) and mathematical calculations (such as genomic codes). The first features empirical observations of *what exists*, while the latter calculates probable outcomes of *what might be*. Both imperatives are implicit in the 1908 drawings, but the observational mode in them is weighted toward what verifiable data could deliver in the heyday of experimental biology. A hundred years later, the trend leans heavily toward theoretical biology, with faster and faster microprocessing capabilities allowing computer simulations of probable interactions in living systems. Present collaborations among biologists, artists, computer scientists, and media makers are full of promise: infinite possibilities arise for mapping vital forms, for reconfiguring their contours, for moving across their dimensions. Media technologies seem more equipped than ever before to accurately inscribe and simulate the biological complexity of living systems in their endless flux.

Unlike in cinema, however, where several frames are sequentially edited to produce the image, synthetic media and algorithmic logics materialize dynamic forms whose contours are infinitely malleable. Mathematical calculations render biological data into the structural elements of an image; these elements, such as the spike on a viral orb, remain modular as specific details of the constitutive elements undergo change. Those changes arise from recalculations of the key points that selectively contour the image plane. To pick a simple example, think of a nose whose contours are mapped along key points, as we see in common image morphs. As new data emerge, recalculations produce a shift in these points, spatially rearticulating the difference as a morph; as the first image begins to transform into a second one, we "see" change. The cultural technique of the morph in computer animation illuminates this transition. All digital images morph, but a slowed-down transition catches the change as fluid distortion. Pausing on the mathematical bases of the morph indicates efficacies of digital inscription: lively fluctuations can be constantly *recalculated* in morphing images whose contours stretch and flex, expand and contract. Further, the capacity to fabricate by rewriting code allows digital images to hypothesize structural details where there are insufficient or missing data and therein to speculate on what remains partially known. At the same time, the editable image is eminently "realistic" when faithful to accurately transcribed data; it is bound to a mathematical realism. Digital microprocessualities present the illusion of keeping abreast of lively flux, of catching up with life's unfoldings, of moving toward more perfect machinic inscription as "capture." In the domain of these scientific digital images, *capture* refers to mathematical precision in accounting for lively microprocesses. Now more than ever before, it seems possible to render infinitesimal changes mathematically calculable with exactitude and to correct errors continually: this is the mathematical realism of theoretical biology. As scientists source multiple data streams to build editable models of living systems, the -morphic image flashes up as a totality in the universe of particles and waves. On interactive platforms, scientists can not only reconfigure structural details based on new data but also move *in* and *with* the matter that they seek to understand in order to intervene in vital actions.

In this story of the constant morph, why focus on the virus's *image*? What is its purchase in the media-technological inscription of life as activity? At first glance, the morphological imperative may seem counterintuitive to keeping up with lively fluctuations and interactions. Form stills life as activity, capturing snapshots of unfolding events. So, what is the scientific purchase of images? Why the continued investment in molecular visualization?

The purchase lies in the functionality of digital images to make large data sets cohere as a single insight. Even as microprocessual capacities allow real-time calculations to modify structural details, the image enacts what statistician and artist Edward Tufte characterizes as "de-quantification."[11] The -morphic image is made from data inputs from varied sources: for example, from X-ray crystallography and electron microscopy alongside genomic codes. Making images articulates "wet" processes such as purifying proteins (for X-ray crystallography) and preparing samples (for electron microscopy) with "dry" ones such as writing algorithms for rendering images. These processes of technical mediation materialize malleable, and ideally scalable, images, "emergent wholes," as Manuel DeLanda (2011) describes them, that present probable outcomes of interactions within living systems.[12] DeLanda's notation of the "emergent" highlights the dynamism of -morphic images, while "wholes" accentuates them as provisional flashes of totality. The latter places digital images within what we already know. As Vilém Flusser's account of digital images suggests, to organize dispersed particles and waves *into* an image is to "envision" or to imagine a shape that draws on scientific-cultural images.[13] This dimension of digital images references existing image banks and thereby cultural histories of visible forms. Emphasizing envisioning as an imaginative act, Philip Thurtle situates digital images within scientific-cultural histories that identify and classify life-forms: life appears paradigmatically "in the grid."[14] Understood this way, molecular visualizations of scientific images cannot be disarticulated from cultural histories of visible form. New recalculations from emergent data might tweak specific structural details, varying and recombining them, rendering them in modified images. But historically identifiable structures based on morphological histories are durable templates—stick-like (TMV), orb-like (HIV, SARS-CoV-2), or hook-like (Ebola). Following Lev Manovich on the historical relationship between analog and digital media, one might say the computational image undergoes a "transcoding" that places it in larger cultural systems even as scientific images eschew overt aesthetics as distortions that might impede accurate data transcriptions.[15] The -morphic image surfaces in tensioned space, in negotiations of aesthetic artifice and mathematical realism.

My emphasis on scientific-cultural histories embeds the future-oriented, speculative -morphic images within existing image and structural data banks. Makers of scientific images routinely draw on the Protein Data Bank (a repository founded in 1971), for example, for three-dimensional structural data on large biological molecules. Over time, widely accepted visible forms based on this structural data become points of common scientific reference. In the hands of master illustrators, stable encodings of visible forms consolidate underlying aesthetic grammars; consequently, as we shall see, some aesthetic patterns become shared vocabulary. Such common vocabulary signals the embedding of scientific images in cultural histories of visible forms. The -morphic image indexes extant scientific-cultural forms as well as the ways they have unfolded over time. As lively microprocessualities speed ahead of their machinic inscription, image makers return to their materials—to better tools and skills, to new procedures and techniques. They question the media capacities as well as the perceptual systems, human and machinic, of image-making. In this regard, the -morphic image is an ongoing encounter with life, science, and media.

To think the image in this way closes the institutional distance among science laboratories, media industries, and art galleries. This is not to elide significant differences in how the -morphic image operates in these settings. There are clear distinctions between digital images made for public circulation and those made for scientific research. Scientists mobilizing experimental data habitually constrain the plasticity of the digital image. Artists, however, are less concerned with native data files than they are with the image experience. Despite these differences I track the desire for visible forms across institutional settings and their epistemic cultures. Across these settings, the -morphic image makes data cohere even as the editable image processes volumes of new data coming in from fast-paced scientific research. The imperfect—morphic image rushes to keep abreast of incoming data. This infinitely unfinished quality constitutes its very value as scientific image.

Figure 2.3. Still from Janet Iwasa's HIV *Life Cycle* animation, 2018. Source: Iwasa, HIV *Life Cycle*.

Visualizing HIV

We encounter an ominous spiked orb almost on a daily basis in reportage on the COVID-19 pandemic. Those spikes attach with ease to the ACE2 receptors of human respiratory cells, we are told, enabling a deadly viral takeover of host resources. But we've heard this story before: SARS-CoV-2 does to respiratory cells what HIV once did to the CD4 cells of the immune system. The proverbial accompaniments to every pandemic are the scientific visualizations of virus macromolecules in host environments found in edutainment, video games, and citizen-science media. These images place us in a "molecular fantastic"—of the same order as Akira Lippit's twentieth-century "optical fantastic"—where macromolecular orbs circle and encounter each other in what resembles intergalactic space.[16] They fill us with wonder, in forgetfulness of the structural data they transcribe. Figure 2.3 presents the HIV-1 RNA molecule approaching the cellular membrane of a human CD4 cell in a scientific animation by Janet Iwasa. Made on Autodesk's Maya platform, the animation represents one genre of molecular visualization dubbed the "molecular movies," stemming from collaborations among academic researchers, biotech corporations, and digital animators.[17]

I have explored Iwasa's scientific animations elsewhere, and I return to her oeuvre in scientific images later in the discussion.[18] But I begin with her molecular animation made as public pedagogy to introduce the most common image experience of the HIV-1 macromolecule. In science fairs and classrooms, in online edutainment and galleries, such animations have brought home a sense of distributed subjectivity as viral macromolecules always appear in relation to the hosts they occupy. A protein-lipid combo, the submicroscopic particle unenclosed by a membrane emerges *with* the vital medium in which it lives—that is, in volumetric host cellular or extracellular fluid media. The intergalactic voyage emplaces viewers in the relational worlds of multispecies encounters. As John Armitage notes of the SARS-CoV-2 orb, this emplacement scales human hosts to the submicroscopic particles, displacing and objectifying "us" as the interactive domain or the media environment for the virus to thrive. This undercuts anthropocentric orientations, as "we" are forced to "position ourselves differently toward the world, taking up perhaps a new multispecies position."[19] Armitage's call to think what virus images do during epidemics indicates how scientific images intensify an awareness of embodied relations. "Our" multispecies entanglements surface as deeply intimate as we turn toward these internal environments, jolting any sense of morphological autonomy as the signature of biological individuality. Epidemic exigencies place us in living systems where we experience the virus touch as embodied, dispersed vibrant matter.

Epidemic exigencies might motivate desires for new image experiences in digital entertainments for public pedagogy. But those exigencies in urgent, accelerated epidemic time, also make -morphic scientific images a historical necessity in the biosciences, as HIV research has shown. There are over ninety genetic mutations of HIV-1 (including secondary mutations indicating drug resistance) documented in Stanford University's famous database that drives *continued visualizations* of the virus macromolecule.[20] The *biotechnical image* is one stop on the long road to keeping up with lively fluctuations. Genetic mutations in viruses are quotidian mistakes in editing gene instructions during viral replication; not all mutations are necessarily consequential. When one or more mutations coalesce in a variant, changing virus efficiencies, then the variant mandates classification (typically marked by a letter in the Greek alphabet). Classified variants can sometimes instigate a qualitative shift in the multispecies relation, as we are learning with SARS-CoV-2's delta and omicron variants. Mutation speak is one modality of lively viral temporalities that open new horizons for research. If we take a page from HIV research, then the role digital images play in keeping up with mutations becomes clearer.

The HIV-1 subtype is well researched, but keeping up with its mutations is a challenge. The smart bug evolves alongside the drugs that stem its virulent actions. There are as many as thirty-odd drugs on the market that block viral actions in vivo at four levels: preventing entry into the cells and then interfering in the three catalytic actions of the enzymes (reverse transcriptase, integrase, and protease). One story of drug-resistant mutation concerns reverse transcriptase, which is an enzyme (a special kind of protein) that catalyzes HIV replication. It does so by wrapping its arms around viral cDNA—a complementary DNA strand produced during replication—at "active sites" or grooves in the viral biomolecular structure. One of the most effective ways to block reverse transcriptase actions is to insert a drug molecule into the site: the preferred drugs are nevirapine, tenofovir, and zidovudine (all nonnucleoside reverse transcriptase inhibitors). But genetic mutations of HIV-1 scuttle this biomedical strategy (specifically, the K101E, K103N, and GP190E mutations). The changed genetic codes instruct HIV proteins to fold differently, altering the protein assemblies at the active site. The "K" mutations block the site, and the "G" mutation bulks it up, so that the nevirapine molecule no longer fits the groove. Without the drug molecule, HIV-1 can continue to make its cDNA, replicate, and take over the host cell. This short illustration indicates why it is necessary to *visualize* what happens at the active site. The image that envisions the changing biomolecular elements at the site draws on genomic and biophysical data, in this example. Cast in Manuel DeLanda's terms, these data index very different "biological possibility spaces," and they command specialized branches of study.[21] But neither can be ignored to address the mutation challenge. Therefore, molecular visualizations of virus images are necessarily collaborative, articulating different "possibility spaces" and therein traversing disciplinary boundaries between scientific practices.

Since new drug molecules must be designed, envisioning the constitutive elements of the overall biomolecular structure is an ongoing research agenda. Mutating viruses materialize *fluctuating relations* that outpace emergent data streams. Keeping up with mutations becoming variants is an urgent challenge in epidemic time. All hands are on deck to assess what new variants can do, as is clear from investigations of the "furin cleavage" site for SARS-CoV-2 catalytic actions (see conclusion, note 1). This state of affairs begs the question: What is the role of -morphic images in media-technological inscriptions of virus-host relations?

In search of answers, I travel on well-trodden ground in new materialist theories of life and techne. Theorists such as Eugene Thacker, Sarah Kember and Johanna Zylinska, Natasha Myers, and Philip Thurtle, among others, have variously explored how media not only represent but also build life molecule by molecule.[22] I develop my study, here, turning to these theorists now and then, in tracking decades of building HIV-1 molecules. The long-term investment in modeling HIV makes this microbe particularly significant in analyzing how images mediate *virus-human* relations. In the biosciences, TMV long held sway in virological research as the "model organism," or an epistemic object whose study can be generalized. It was the first to be discovered, to be identified as a virus, and to be crystallized for optical observation. These endeavors are inextricable from epidemic time: after all, concern with TMV arose from economic losses in tobacco plants during the late nineteenth-century tobacco mosaic disease epidemics. In the 1950s, TMV surfaced as the model for the biochemical study of relations between nucleic acids and proteins; a few decades later, it became the target of genetic engineering for strengthening plant resilience.[23] No other virus rivals TMV's stature as model organism other than HIV—at least until now. Amid viruses that burst onto the scene in the emerging infectious diseases outbreaks of the late twentieth century, Ebola was the first to be optically rendered in the Center for Disease Control's chief virologist Fredrick A. Murphy's micrograph made in 1976 (based on the Ebola Zaire and Ebola Sudan strains).[24] Sporting the pastoral look of a shepherd's staff, the micrograph roused scientific and popular curiosity. Murphy went on to colorize the image, enhancing the "dark beauty" within which lay unimaginable power. A few years later, the HIV/AIDS epidemic dominated scientific attention, turning the spiked orb into the iconic image of a virus. In May 1983 one of the first images of HIV appeared in *Science* as an electron micrograph made from sections of an original lymph node biopsy.[25] Rendered at Luc Montagnier's laboratory, the indexical image was the pandemic punctum as one of the first visual traces of the microbial agent. Montagnier would return to it twenty-five years later in a public lecture to the World Foundation for AIDS Prevention and Research in December 2008 (figure 2.4).[26] For the first time, in 1983, the viral particle appeared as an orb with a dense conical core, a graphic trace that would become iconic. We see it later in this chapter, for example: plate 14 shows the computational construction of the HIV "mesh" to be "filled" with ingredients drawn from incoming data. The historical micrograph became the historical basis for computational images to come, its blurriness acting as noise and activating further investigation. Since then, HIV has occupied an unusual place in virological research. In *The Machinery of Life*, David Goodsell, whose scientific illustrations are foundational to modeling HIV, suggested that this virus is the best understood of any organism, while a star among molecular animators, Janet Iwasa, noted (in one of our exchanges) that four decades of research on HIV has made it a model system for the study of viruses.

This brief history of visualizing viruses indicates how epidemic exigencies drive research on viruses. The biotechnical image as attunement to visible

Figure 2.4. HIV micrograph, 1983. Source: Françoise Barré-Sinoussi's Lab Notebook, Institut Pasteur.

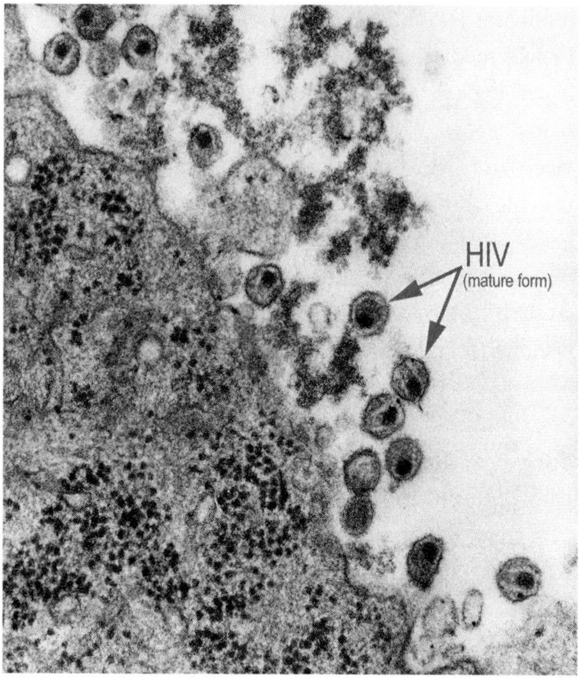

form is biomedia for turning data into flesh. To make such a claim is to track the continuities rather than disjuncture between early morphological studies and the genomic decoding of viruses. The focus on *morphḗ* as form harks back to biotechnical images made under the electron microscope in the age optical hegemony. Digital images in the current data-rich postgenomic era that model probable outcomes of data integration, modifying and tweaking living systems, may appear radically different from those early micrographs. And yet, in building editable virus macromolecules, the morphological persists as imperative. In this chapter the -morphic signals three modalities of visualization. First, *morphic* as a qualifier simply refers to the *visible forms* of biomolecular structures; second, *to morph* as a verb calls attention to the constantly evolving *techniques of visual inscription*; and, last, *-morphic* in suffix form connotes an *unfinished image* that attempts to keep up with biological complexity and dynamism. These attributes suggest -morphic images are more than just instrumental, closely tied as they are to biotechnological research and development. They can be experientially potent amid epidemic intensities, and when immersive, they can mobilize visual-haptic perceptions of "being with" living systems, entangling image-makers in difficult multispecies relations.

The ongoing effort to visualize HIV-human emergence has sparked new technologies and platforms, new methods and practices. Digital inscription mandates inventing tools, writing code, and refining protocols, to be sure. But the imperfection of the -morphic image further turns prehension into a site of inquiry: What kinds of images afford understandings of lively fluctuations? What kinds of images disclose the limits of visual intelligibility? Can images open viewers/users to perceptions beyond the visible? The affordances of digital media technologies allow the mapping of infinite probabilities, and beyond prediction, they can further enable viewers/users to inhabit the image space of the living systems they scrutinize. Three-dimensional images are particularly alluring because they activate thickly layered experiences, emplacing viewers/users in multisensory environments. Not all digital images of HIV macromolecules pursued here are in 3D. But more than one interviewee expressed a preference for them, often in full realization of the virtual illusion that 3D generates. Before I turn to specific instances, it is important to distinguish two different kinds of 3D images of the HIV macromolecule. Some 3D images are processed in the visual cortex: two offset images stimulating two eyes are combined in the visual cortex to give an illusion of depth, even as, strictly speaking, the images are in 2D. This kind of 3D images demands active prehension in donning headsets: viewers/users are intensely aware of their wiring in human-machinic perceptual systems. These 3D images are of a different order from "'true' 3D images" in which an *object* exhibits depth cues. Holograms, for one, are photographic recordings of interference patterns that reproduce a 3D light field. Here the detection and composition of objects into 3D images are optical and computational, before their processing in the visual cortex. The PHSCologram of the (art)n collective are experiments in this latter mode of 3D imaging. Both kinds of images, however, stimulate depth perception, enabling a volumetric emplacement of users/viewers within dimensional image space.

Toward Molecular Visualization

In this chapter, I unpack the "emergence" of the HIV-1 macromolecule as epistemic object in scientific settings and on public platforms. Following Bruno Latour's articulation of "the historicity of emergence," an emergence implies the coming together of multiple agents—hosts and viruses, scientists and clinicians, laboratories and technologies.[27] Asking if microbes existed before Louis Pasteur's successful "ferments" of 1858, Latour insists on recounting the material conditions that made microbes intelligible at Pasteur's laboratory in

Lille.[28] Bacteria existed in ferments before Pasteur, to be sure, but they were also transformed, becoming microbes, in the ferments. A network of flasks, laboratories, bacteria, and the scientist, among other material agents, emerges together in this early moment of microbiology. Such historicity reverses cause-and-effect formulations: microbes are not the causal agents in the ferments but the *effects* of this network of elements. This reading of historicity informs my tracking of a nonlinear course toward the digital HIV-1 macromolecule in the media-technological practices of molecular visualization. The image flashes up within networks of scientists, artists, commercial applications, display sites, tools, techniques, and institutions; short histories of these actors accompany my perusal of the emergences. The upshot is an interested trajectory toward the -morphic image made and remade at the intersection of bioscience research (salient to the virus as epistemic object) and media-technological developments (impacting its material construction).

The first visual appearance of a virus macromolecule (TMV) comes with electron microscopy.[29] The powerful beams of the electron microscope—different from its sibling, the light microscope—had resolution powers 250 times greater than the optical microscope and magnification power up to 2 million times the object's size, as opposed to 500 to 1,500 times in optical systems.[30] The charged electron beam made it possible to determine intracellular structural details of the viral submicroscopic particles; the shorter wavelength of the electron microscope enabled higher resolutions of submicroscopic particles, even as the electron beams touched crystallized viral particles, probing and moving them for study. The credit for the first micrograph of TMV goes to physicist Ernst Ruska and electrical engineer Max Knoll.[31] For the first time, the virion—a nucleic acid strip with an outer coat of protein, the capsid—was clearly visible in the needlelike biophysical structure of TMV. Shortly thereafter, as the diversity of viruses became known, a membrane of lipids (an envelope) surfaced in some. Electron imaging initiated morphological studies that identified physical attributes of different viruses. And so began the task of classifying viruses, with a deepening appreciation of structural mechanisms and dynamic interactions. This was the high age of visible forms. With advances in electron scanning later in the century, it became possible to reconstruct biomolecular structures in their three dimensions (3D tomography), resolved at atomic scale. Visual preoccupations were supplanted, however, with the mid-twentieth-century interest in the gene as the gauge of biological specificity.[32] For viruses, this break in how to define "life" meant a turn toward the biochemistry of their gene expression until, subsequently, the confluence of the information sciences and molecular biology in the 1970s articulated life as information.

Amid new alliances among physicists, chemists, biologists, and engineers, biological specificity became code, and the virus became a bioinformatic agent. This also meant a shift in emphasis from the study of biomolecular structures to that of informatic substrates, opening the door to potential manipulations of genetic code. The capacity to build life meant an inevitable lean toward theoretical biology. Infinite probabilities for designing biomolecules accentuated the speculative axes of the -morphic image. The turn to genetic code meant viruses would be identified not by their morphologies but by their genomic fingerprints. As theorists such as Eugene Thacker have noted, the extraction and manipulation of the genetic code had wide commercial implications that fueled the rise of biotech industries specializing in biological products.[33] In HIV therapy, for one, the fact that zinc scissors can cut and snip DNA unveiled the possibility of new, if expensive, gene medicine. Products such as Cal-1, developed at Cal-Tech, seek to modify human genetic instructions for making the CCR5 receptor cells where the HIV-1 virion docks. The idea is to produce a mutation, the CCR5-Δ32, that "jams the door knob" and makes the cellular receptor inhospitable to the virion. Edgier experiments such as "cleaning up" DNA to produce genetically modified babies—as was the case of the Chinese twins with modified CCR5 receptors resistant to HIV—have raised hackles over the bioethics of such technological interventions.[34] Changing "life" at its very inception seems a bridge too far even though it follows the same logic as gene therapy.

Such experiments have been the subject of feminist science studies engaged in "debiologizing biological facts" and in exploring the ethical implications of mechanizing life. Of course, one could date the mechanization of life back to Jacob Loeb's experiments in artificial parthenogenesis of sea urchins (chemical fertilization without spermatozoa) as early as 1899.[35] But it would take almost a century to realize the implications of Loeb's experiments at industrial scales. Stem cell science, regenerative medicine, and tissue engineering in the late twentieth and early twenty-first centuries have irrevocably blurred the distinctions between living and nonliving, organic and nonorganic matter. In *Making Sense of Life*, Evelyn Fox Keller, for one, argued that developments such as turning differentiated cells back into their pluripotent states "dissolved" the biological itself since cellular differentiation is life's progress. Others such as Sarah Franklin called for a socially embedded understanding of the "artificial" or mechanized development of living or organic matter. In *Biological Relatives*, Franklin maintains that the ambivalent experience of in vitro fertilization technologies—their immense promise (control over reproduction), bodily difficulties, and proverbial disappointments—makes it a fecund site for rethinking biology.[36] One of the promises of mechanized biology is the capacity to reset relations and to make strange kin—unclassifiable, chimerical. In the gene-edited twins, we have a stellar example of resetting biological relations between virus and human in a conspicuous disentanglement from a difficult multispecies relation.

In the last decades of the twentieth century, systems biology pushed for a more multidimensional approach to biology after the gene-centrism of the 1980s and 1990s. As the successor to genomics, systems biology repositioned genomic data as one part of the network constitutive of living systems; running perturbations in living systems at multiple levels, systems biologists emphasized data integration across the biological practices. Structural, biochemical, and genetic data could be thought together in their nonlinear interactions. In some respects, systems biology's speculative force was not amenable to industrial applications, leading some scientists to wryly christen it "low input, high throughput, no output biology."[37] The "no output" meant the discipline's practitioners were less and less "servants of the machine," as Stengers designates them, not instrumentally yoked to producing commercially viable biotechnologies.[38] Rather, the focus was studying the multidimensional problems that biology poses.[39] These histories of the biosciences and their corollary media-technological practices resonate in the making of -morphic images that digitally process lively fluctuations. Dynamic and malleable, speculative and contingent, the -morphic image is a staple in research on the virus. As described in HIV research, the study of biomolecular structures is epidemic media with instrumental goals (such as new drug designs); here is a clear trajectory between media practices and therapeutic interventions. But this does not foreclose the speculative orientation to pursue what was not yet known or to predict ongoing changes—genetic mutations to protein folds—impacting structural elements. Progress can be slow in envisioning biomolecular structures even when the macromolecule is a relatively simple one. The HIV macromolecule has eight structural proteins, but it took decades to stabilize the biomolecular structure of a single element. The "HIV trimer" remained on the most wanted list of protein macromolecules for decades, until the scientific community finally agreed on its definitive crystalline structure in 2013.

These histories span material practices in computer graphics, bioscience research, and virtual art. Molecular visualizations deliver an expanded moving image on a synthetic-biological continuum. As virtual images afford immersive enchantments, users become image makers. I turn to three collaborations to explore specific dimensions of the -morphic image: the technical-aesthetic rendering of visible forms (*morphḗ*), experiments with the tools and techniques of the image experience (*the morph*), and synthetic-biological mediations of lively fluctuations (*morphing*).

Morphḗ *in Janet Iwasa's Molecular Movies*

As one genre of molecular visualizations, animated scientific images featuring unfolding molecular events enhance and redesign existing data for presentation, collaboration, and, increasingly, the exploration of a scientific hunch. A closer look at what animated images *do* sets the stage for the speculative character of the -morphic image. The protagonist in this story of collaborations is Janet Iwasa, a cell biologist who doubles as a digital animator. Her oeuvre illustrates the embeddedness of the -morphic image in scientific-cultural histories. As Iwasa notes, her early interest in microscopy soon gave way to a fascination with "realistic animations" at the University of California, San Francisco.[40] There she encountered Graham Johnson's kinesin animation (while he was a fellow there) and was inspired to think of what 2D or 3D images *set in motion* could achieve. A cell biologist trained in studying dynamic processes, Iwasa developed an interest in animating "molecular events," attended several science-visualization meetings, and took a crash course in the advanced animation software Maya, developed by Pixar. In my exchanges with Iwasa, she explained that "scientific animators" are a new breed whose disciplinary training in the biosciences can vary from cell biology to biochemistry to structural biology.[41] All this would come to roost in the many collaborative ventures that followed. For Iwasa as a digital animator, her collaborations are often project driven, articulated as temporary partnerships within and between diverse institutions.

One of these partnerships flourished at the Harvard Medical School, when Iwasa took a position in the Department of Cell Biology. There she met Gaël McGill, who directed the Center for Molecular and Cellular Dynamics. As a scientist who straddles what was once traditionally the media arts (image compositing, special effects, storyboarding) and once traditionally lab-based scientific research, McGill had created opportunities for scientific professionals to share their research in open online communities. She founded Digizyme, a company that hosts a directory of molecular and cell animations, and collaborated on building "Molecular Maya," a free software tool kit for programming animation that streamlines and modifies Pixar's Maya.[42] As I discuss elsewhere, Iwasa and McGill soon collaborated on "Dengue Virus Entry" (showcased on the https://clarafi.com platform).[43] Drawing structural biologist Stephen

Harrison into the collaboration, McGill and Iwasa would craft a molecular movie of the dengue virus that articulated the 3D architecture of molecules (structural biology) and their dynamic functions in the cellular context (cell biology) concurrently. The idea was that the conjugation of cell biology and structural biology would produce a fuller picture of molecular events than either one could achieve within their respective disciplinary contexts. As Harrison maintained, new technologies such as "super resolution microscopes," "new image-analysis software," and more "flexible fluorescence tagging" made possible such an integrated approach to the physiological dynamism of cells.[44] Since physiological signals are "transient, contingent, and complex," these new imaging technologies allowed greater insight into the *morphing* structures of individual molecular machines.[45] This promise fuels the drive for -morphic images appearing and fading at molecular and cellular timescales. Interactive platforms like Molecular Maya allow scientists to present incipient hypotheses from their specific disciplinary enclaves to the larger scientific community. In this regard, McGill suggests scientific animations are not necessarily "the end of the process" but "can inform discovery."[46] The -morphic image materializes reasoned conjecture faithful to existing data structures. But it also presents incipient hypotheses about aspects of lively processes that are not yet fully known—that is, they are not empirically verifiable.[47] Such images are efficacious *because* they speculative: they think in the vicinity of the unknown.

Speculative methods foreground the provisional nature of scientific insights. Such conjectural reason is most apparent at the edges of scientific practice. As Isabelle Stengers argues in "Life and Artifice: The Faces of Emergence," any scientific object stabilizes only in relation to its emergence in other practices.[48] The fulsome term *water*, for instance, can emerge as an element composed of hydrogen and oxygen molecules *and* as a solvent; the first designates a physical actor, the second, a chemical one. To think both together involves negotiations between scientific practices, and sometimes between competing visions of the world. We can see the relevance of such emergence to speculating on the lively fluctuations of virus-host relations. The -morphic image emerges between different scientific practices such as structural biology, genomic studies, and cell biology. Here modern practitioners make many worlds cohere in the image. Collaborations articulate a fuzzy epistemic object as image makers recognize not only the constraints of each practice but the provisional nature of scientific insights produced at the interstices. A speculative method underwrites the -morphic image, appearing and dissolving, dissipating and cohering, across biological spaces of possibility. In this regard, the -morphic image harvests the microprocessual capacities of the digital medium to the fullest extent.

The McGill-Iwasa-Harrison collaboration exemplifies open-ended knowledge practices of molecular visualization in which no single figure has full control of the -morphic image. In the simplest sequence, scientists provide data from diverse sources such as from light microscopy with charged-coupled device (CCD) cameras, Cyro-EM (cyro-electron microscopy), and X-ray crystallography. An animator then carries out numerous aspects of image processing: they can code sampled 2D surfaces (a single-plane image or tomogram) into numerical values (bits of information), or they can render those bits into images; they can create the "scene file," which includes information on the geometry, viewpoint, texture, lighting, and shading of the virtual scene; or they can script algorithms to calculate the final outputs for the image. There is also wide variance in how information is rendered as image. For 3D images, compositing involves rendering tilted 2D surfaces on a 3D vector field; by contrast, direct volume rendering arrays 3D data in voxels instead of pixels, skipping the 2D to 3D conversion. Once digital assets are made from existing structural data, animators generate storyboards and put the images in motion following well-known filmmaking conventions. While visual models representing "molecular interactions, movement, structure and localization" are staples in cell biology, maintains Iwasa, animations temporalize these models by sequencing lively processes as a series of *molecular events*.[49] As such they provide insights about dynamic interactions that might not be readily legible in the models alone.[50]

The animator can enter the collaboration at multiple points in the process as they undertake different tasks such as sampling, coding, rendering, storyboarding, motion capture, and postproducing sound (voice-over and/or music). For her *Clathrin-Mediated Endocytosis* animation, for instance, Iwasa generated storyboards from discussions *with* an expert in the field (Tomas Kirchhausen at Harvard Medical School), which involved researching databases for already available data sets and reading relevant papers.[51] For the "Dengue Virus Entry" animation, the storyboards were provided to Iwasa, who then rendered out the frames and created the digital assets. Since the latter was not pitched at researchers but prepared for a public platform, Boston's WGBH, Iwasa's film was postprocessed (adding sound, motion through video capture, and additional effects) at the XVIVO design company, known for the award-winning animation *The Inner Life of the Cell* (2006).[52] The company XVIVO exemplifies numerous outfits that bring together animators, medical illustrators, and interactive designers to create animations of lively processes. The mushrooming of such companies indexes the industrial boom in new optical-computational technologies.[53] Such a nexus of actors represents the willingness of researchers to harvest participatory energies and technological innovations beyond the rarified enclaves of their science laboratories. One of the most famous examples of distributed research is the 2008 breakthrough on the HIV enzyme protease structure by gamers playing *Fold It* who had responded to a challenge from the University of Washington's virology labs.[54] Such instances can be multiplied. They bear out claims by scholars such as Colin Milburn and Alenda Chang, among others, that the lines between scientific research and industrial entertainment are more blurred today than ever before.[55] This is especially the case for scientific animations and 3D immersive media.

Iwasa represents scientist-animators working at the intersections of scientific research, biotech, and creative industries. She makes animations for scientists testing competing hypotheses as well as for scientific edutainment; both function as science communication but with one difference. Some critics of scientific visualizations caution against overly expressive animations that guide interpretations of original data; they also worry about incorrect samplings of original data. They underscore the National Science Foundation's data management stipulations to store original data in native file formats.[56] As Adam Nocek notes, seamless movements through Cartesian space, colors, distinctive shapes, and clear edges are often regarded as unnecessarily distracting, even distortions of experimental data.[57] This call for accuracy demands mathematical realism in the making of -morphic images. While highlighting this need for accuracy, Iwasa notes how speculative images visualizing a scientific hunch internal to an unfolding hypothesis can remain faithful to data but also fill in the blanks with calculated sequences. Probabilistic calculations habitually constrain aesthetic possibilities in the making of scientific images. But in public-oriented projects, such as Iwasa's *HIV Life Cycle*, there is greater artistic license since the point is to make data comprehensible *and* attractive to wider audiences; maintaining native file formats is not the primary issue.[58] In our exchanges, she explained the error bar for edutainment animation is far greater, since the inclination toward coding for expressive design elements can rival coding for sampling accuracies.[59]

These debates over artistic license, however, do not mean freedom from aesthetic constraints. Quite the contrary. Animators follow well-trodden traditions of scientific illustrations as well as techniques of measurements (density, scale, dimension) for proper technical-aesthetic compositions. One of Iwasa's large-scale public-oriented projects is the molecular animation of the HIV life cycle, drawn from two decades of structural data. The animation was a collaboration between Iwasa's lab and CHEETAH, and it was funded by the National Institute of General Medical Sciences. Launched on the website Science of HIV, the animation includes voice-over narration and a musical score by cellist and composer Joshua Roman.[60] The animation plunges viewers into familiar intergalactic voyages: as the HIV-1 viral particles approach the surfaces of the CD4 cells, we notice the aesthetic grammar that distinguishes proteins belonging to the virus (in red) from those belonging to the cellular membrane proteins (in yellow). Zooming into the molecular events of proteins folding between two surfaces, the animation offers a visually coded account of these molecular machines as they collide, separate, and adhere. The proteins wriggle and twist, making possible the fusing of the viral particle into the CD4 cell (plates 7 and 8). The same aesthetic grammar informs *Clathrin-Mediated Endocytosis*, which is Iwasa's personal favorite because the visualization captures molecules in Brownian motion. Iwasa's aesthetic choices ensure clarity and precision; they enact optical consistency to build common reference. As such, her aesthetic grammar transcodes the -morphic image, embedding it in scientific-cultural histories.

The point is elaborated in Edward Tufte's *Envisioning Information*, where he argues that "color is a natural quantifier" that *captures* variations in the smallest degree and orchestrates a symphony. Color brings to information, he continues, "an incredible fineness of distinction, at a precision comparable to measurement."[61] Color in information design can label (viral proteins versus cellular proteins), measure (signaling depth, for instance), represent or imitate reality (oceans as blue, meadows as green), or enliven and decorate. Both labeling and enlivening come into play in Iwasa's animation, indicating the aesthetic qualities of her images. Enlivening is evident in color and motion, narration and musical scores. For instance, both *HIV Life Cycle* and *Clathrin-Mediated Endocytosis* are set to scores dominated by string instruments that underscore the buzzing of molecules in motion. Such sound design accentuates the immersive experience, attuning viewers to (what Myers denotes as) uncontainable "excitable matter."[62] Although the animation organizes the visual sense into the aesthetic field, the liveliness of vibrant matter registers in sound and motion. These artistic enhancements often reference time-honored aesthetic practices that ensure optical consistency. This is evident in the Science of HIV website's citation of David Goodsell's famous watercolor illustrations.[63] Goodsell's legendary illustrations magnify atomic structures of macromolecules to scale specifications and develop a color-coding system consistent throughout his oeuvre. These cultural techniques have set the standards for aesthetic coding to come. The iterative emphasis on color codes and gradients, among other design elements, for illustrators and animators indicates an *aesthetic grammar* at work despite the touted wild west of artistic license. The aesthetic grammar can be personalized for early-career animators like Iwasa (who notes she prefers red for proteins whenever possible) or congealed into aesthetic tradition for veterans like David Goodsell. Whichever the case, *grammar* indicates the embedded language, or *langue* (to recall Ferdinand de Saussure), of scientific images that institutes them as a common reference.[64]

This anchoring in aesthetic conventions underscores the importance of "optical consistency," as Bruno Latour characterizes it, in making the new widely acceptable. "If you wish to go out of *your* way and come back heavily equipped so as to force others to go out of *their* ways, the main problem to solve is that of *mobilization*."[65] Latour is speaking of drawings (such as sketches and diagrams) that carry "immobile" grammars, so to speak, intended to impart the optical consistency necessary for "others to go out of *their* ways." Such consistency is especially urgent for the speculative image that entertains a scientific hunch. In other words, even as the aesthetic question may seem tangential to scientists preoccupied with visualizing data, it is crucial in order for -morphic images to gain scientific authority. Optical consistency creates the common reference necessary for entertaining conjectures. Goodsell's stature as an illustrator generates such consistency, making his images the basis for many aesthetic compositions. References to his mastery in scientific and artistic circles indicate the pivotal role of the aesthetic in the making of scientific images.

In my interview with Ellen Sandor of the (art)n collective, she characterized Goodsell as the Rembrandt of molecular visualization, an observation that points to histories of art-science-tech collaborations that initiated, accompanied, or preceded the development of virtual 3D images in scientific visualizations. I turn to one such collaboration with its genesis in the art studio and not in the bioscience lab: the imaging of viral macromolecules by the (art)n collective, which Sandor founded in 1983. In the making of virtual art, the question of what images can do returns but not entirely in the service of scientific research. It is more fundamentally aesthetic: What *is* the "image" in the new image spaces of virtual art? More specifically, what kind of experience does the 3D image afford at the user interface? In the larger context of the book, how do these immersive images foster sensuous experiences of multispecies entanglements?

Morph as Mediation: The (art)n Collective's Immersive Media

The (art)n collective exemplifies lasting art-science-tech collaborations spanning decades that include a flexible cast of participants as well as the dexterous capacity to move with technological and aesthetic change. It is also lasting in its impact. The (art)n collective's patented technology of the PHSCologram from the 1980s is widely considered a precursor to immersive media.[66] The collective's early association and collaborations with the Electronic Visualization Laboratory (EVL) of the University of Illinois Chicago and the National Center for Supercomputing Applications (NCSA) at the University of Illinois, Urbana-Champaign locate the PHSColograms as inspiration for the Cave Automatic Virtual Environment (CAVE) developed at the EVL. The PHSColograms are artistic forms that constellate photography, holography, sculpture, and later, computer graphics. When the first PHSColograms were exhibited in 1983, Sandor recounts how early developers of computer graphics at the EVL predicted that one day the volumetric displays would "go digital" as 3D visualization media. At the time, Sandor notes that she had no idea what that meant.[67] The 1983 exhibit was a tribute to artists and had little to do with scientific images. Recognizing (art)n's artistic and technological contributions, when the CAVE was displayed at the 1992 SIGGRAPH (Special Interest Group on Computer Graphics and Interactive Techniques) conference in Chicago, forty PHSColograms were displayed on the exterior walls to prepare viewers for the experience to come and to acknowledge their contribution to scientific immersive media.[68] The (art)n collective would go on to make sculptures, videos, PHSColograms, games, and virtual reality in the years that followed. They approached the 3D image as virtual art: What were the dimensional potentialities of optical (and, later, computational) images, if one were to think beyond one media genre? As self-declared "radical empiricists," Sandor told me, (art)n invested in the virtual image, the image *to come*, with aesthetic and technical experiments. This included building a large wooden camera run along a horizontal track for the first analog PHSColograms, which shot a single image from nine different angles, in a "real-garage art process," as Sandor named it.[69] The point was to imagine and experiment with what 3D images could do in multisensory image spaces, a question that drives what came to be known as immersive media. In this regard, the -morphic image places prehension under construction in grasping at lively fluctuations. Mediation as prehension is the agenda in the many experiments with immersive image experiences that try to facilitate "being with" living systems.

There is vast art historical scholarship on immersive media, especially in thinking about the embodied illusion of 3D images. In one rich account, Oliver Grau places contemporary 3D images as virtual art in a long history that ranges from frescoed spaces to panoramas, stereoscopic television, and IMAX cinema, to name just a few critical junctures.[70] Gaining institutional ground in the 1980s, video, computer graphics, and animation came to constitute contemporary virtual art, and with this came the intensification of the immersive experience. Viewable on monitors, display consoles, or physical surrounds with projection capabilities, 3D images commonly rely on stereoscopic vision to enfold viewers within the image space so as to create a visual illusion. A scattering of particles and waves excites the viewer's visual cortex to produce visual-spatial effects: that is, two 2D images are resolved for 3D effect in the brain in an "an illusory address to the senses."[71] When the images are of living systems and it becomes computationally possible to tinker with those systems, as is the case in telepresence or genetic art, notes Grau, virtual art becomes an active "being there" within living systems. The "object" and its machinic "capture" are less significant than exploring the human-machinic perceptual complex that underlies the tweaking, altering, and modifying of life itself. The question of medial entanglement dominates media-technological experimentation. As early experiments with image capacities, the PHSCologram imagined viewer experience as critical to living "in" matter as the collective became more and more engaged in collaborative scientific visualizations. Mathematical calculations became increasingly central to building immersive media. But the driving motor remained the embodied inhabitation of image spaces. No doubt Sandor's training as a sculptor at the School of the Art Institute of Chicago (SAIC) had much to do with the collective's preoccupation with volumetric displays. In my June 2020 interview with Sandor, she more than once insisted on the collective's inclination to make "physical things" and "hard-copy" 3D images shot on film stock. In their installations the PHSCologram were mounted in light boxes, sometimes arranged on the wall, sometimes freestanding, so that viewers could circle the glowing vibrant images.

As the HIV/AIDS epidemic decimated friends and colleagues in the mid-1980s, the collective turned to scientific visualizations of living matter. Sandor noted her fascination with Arthur Olson's early physical models and videos of the poliovirus as inspiration for (art)n's virus visualizations, starting with the HIV macromolecule in 1987 (*AIDS Virus*, first edition). Soon an exhibit in 1989–90, *Visualizing the Invisible*, featured a section on 3D images of viruses (the exhibit is now viewable online).[72] In the "bright, colorful, lively abstraction," as they described it, (art)n placed a then-novel living organism, HIV, in proximity to viewers fearful and curious about it.[73] Amid the heightened epidemic intensities of the pre-ARV era, the image experience situated viewers "within" infection topologies, sensuously entangling them with difficult kin. Thus began artistic collaborations on visualizing viral molecules: the virus PHSCologram traveled with the "Science in Depth" show (1991–92), which showed at venues such as the NASA Ames Research Center and the Association for Computer Machinery SIGGRAPH, and the "A Look in Depth" show on 3D imaging, coordinated by the Boston Museum of Science (1989–91). The (art)n collective's many collaborations positioned their technical and aesthetic experiments at the intersection of multimedia art, computer graphics, and the biosciences. At that nexus lay the dimensional study of images.

On the scientific front, the dimensional study of biomolecular structures had evolved into molecular visualization practices. That time-honored history dates back to the early twentieth century, when Max von Lau and William Bragg ran X-rays through protein crystals. The process would later become X-ray crystallography, which involves purifying and crystallizing proteins and then studying X-ray diffraction patterns (scattered shadows) to glean their structure. Natasha Myers's ethnography of protein crystallography details the history of this practice, so I will not belabor it here.[74] Rather, the point is to plot a trajectory from early dimensional experiments to molecular graphics. In 1958 John Kendrew won the Nobel Prize for X-ray crystallography with molecular biologist Max Perutz, who was known for building physical models; famously, Perutz took twenty-two years to build the physical structure of hemoglobin. By the 1960s, optical and computational techniques began to converge in early computer graphics as researchers sought to assign numerical values to X-ray diffraction patterns and then back-calculate the location of atoms in the molecular structure. There are apocryphal stories of a monochrome oscilloscope nicknamed "the Kluge," part of MIT's Project MAC (Mathematics and Computation), which produced the first interactive molecular graphics. Enabling researchers to rotate the molecular structure in "3D effect," the Electronic Systems Display console could be manipulated with a trackball and a light pen. And so was born the first virtual graphic of a macromolecule in a scientific collaboration between molecular biologist Cyrus Levinthal and X-ray crystallographer C. David Barry. In a six-minute 16mm film *Proteins* (1966), short peptide chains were subject to energy-minimization algorithms that produced simulations of potential conformational changes.[75] Presenting his pitch for a speculative visual-numerical science, Levinthal mused in the *Scientific American* (1966) that it was "too early to evaluate the usefulness of the man-computer combination in solving real problems of molecular biology" but that "it does seem likely, however, that only with this combination can the investigator use his 'chemical insight' in an effective way."[76] The rest is history, as we know from exponential advances in molecular modeling software and imaging technologies. It is no accident that Arthur Olson was trained in X-ray crystallography, a practice that continues to contribute structural data for 3D models. By 1971 the atomic coordinates of known proteins were made public in the open-access database, the Protein Data Bank, which currently archives over 160,000 structures.[77] The Molecular Graphics Society was formed in 1982 and launched a journal for research on molecular visualization in 1983.

The (art)n collective was formed that same year with a core group from the School of the Art Institute of Chicago or SAIC (Sandor had graduated from there in 1975). A year earlier, Sandor had made a commissioned 3D image of financial markets in the form of a large backlit poster. This stimulated her interest in 3D images and the desire to push aesthetic and technical frontiers. The first PHSCologram were labor-intensive: shot on Kodak film, nine exposures (which took forty-five minutes each to develop) were interleaved to form a single image. A device placed in front of the image, a barrier strip, which looks like a vertical venetian blind, integrated the blurry overlapping images and brought them into sharp focus. No clunky headgear was necessary for viewing 3D images in this genre of autostereograms. But things would change when the collective began to collaborate with Donna Cox, a pathbreaking figure in immersive media who ran the Advanced Visualization Lab at the NCSA.[78] The collaboration strengthened ties among the SAIC, the NCSA, and the EVL. Dan Sandin, a video and computer graphics artist at the EVL, became a member of the collective.[79] Cox was trained in visual art: she was studying color perception when she became interested in visual mathematics. In 1986 (art)n collaborated with Cox and the EVL on Romboy homotopies, which gave visual life to mathematical abstractions. Together they made the 4D image *The Etruscan Venus* (11 × 14 in.), experimenting with volume and depth perception.[80] This was the first "scientific" PHSCologram, so to speak, based on mathematical calculations. Soon the PHSCologram were no longer shot using purely analog means but by using computer camera images (images shot off the computer screen); mathematical calculations of the distance between the interleaved images became more precise, and the exposure time dwindled to fifteen minutes per image. By 1987 Sandin's student Stephan Meyers had entered the collaboration, writing software for the PHSCologram. Soon it became possible to computationally process and interleave as many as sixty-four images for viewing with barrier-screen technology. The coedited volume *New Media Futures* documents the intersecting histories of these collaborations, with each actor changing what the image could do, each version of the PHSCologram experimenting with new aesthetic and technical capacities.[81] In this regard, the PHSCologram were emergent in their "creative" movement forward, working with an intuitive sense of images as immersive media. They embody the -morphic as evolving media-technological practice, as deep engagement with the technicity of mediation.

Such intuitions would have historical urgency in the visualization of viruses. Amid the emerging infectious diseases outbreaks of the early 1980s, (art)n turned their attention to making multispecies relations palpable in 3D installations. The 1989–90 exhibit displayed stunningly designed images of *Papilloma* (third edition), *Herpes*, *Human Rhinovirus*, the *AIDS Virus* (third edition), and *Adenovirus* to the viewing public. The edition numbers indicate the collective had been making 3D images of viruses before the exhibit; and they would continue to make them long after. The visual sculpture of *AIDS Virus* (as it was called then) was mounted as the centerpiece of a plexiglass cross sculpture (96 × 60 in.) titled *Messiah* (plate 9) for the 1989–90 exhibit. The sculpture was produced in-house at (art)n, unlike the later art-science-tech collaborations on 3D images of viruses. Behind and around the glowing HIV orb was the colorized CAT scan of patient "Messiah," who had died from AIDS-related complications at the Cook County Hospital.[82] By the time it was exhibited separately in a plexiglass box in 1989 (third edition), scientific images of HIV-1, blurry and ill-defined as they were, were coming into public circulation. The most famous among these was HIV budding out of a cell on the cover of the *Scientific American* in 1988.[83] But optical-computational accuracy with regard to the HIV macromolecular structures was not possible yet. In my interview with Sandor, she noted that the 1989 image was 85 percent accurate—but that was not what drove the making of the image.

Like many images of the time, this was mourning work: "We felt compelled to visualize our confusion and sorrow," said the collective in its artist statement.[84] Inscriptions of "hope," "chance," and "death" accompanied the *AIDS Virus* image mounted on the cross. In years to come, this PHSCologram would circle the globe and acquire international fame.[85] With an intensified epidemic experience, these glowing images fostered a deepening awareness of multispecies entanglements. The historical urgency to visualize the strange beauty of viruses would persist beyond the 1989–90 exhibit. In 2014 Sandor collaborated with Luke Tamm at the Center for Membrane Biology at the University of Virginia to make a glowing red "Ebola" (30 × 30 in.) reminiscent of the hemorrhagic fever associated with this viral infection (plate 10). Animation made it possible for the 3D images of viruses vibrate: to "keep them alive," as Sandor explained in our conversation, intensifying the multisensory experience of "being with" a living system.

The anchoring of the virus macromolecule "in" an optically indexical medical image (the CAT scan) rendered a multispecies relation sensible. At the time, the image would hurt amid epidemic intensities. But that was the point of "tough art," noted Sandor when I interviewed her, art that visualized the "beautiful stranger" that had come to stay.[86] The point was not to aestheticize as distant abstraction but to present scientific findings on "our" multispecies entanglements as image experiences. The colorized medical image would be repeated in the scan of a mammogram that accompanied the PHSCologram of the *Papilloma Virus*. In the making of virus images, Sandor started to collaborate with David Goodsell and Arthur Olson at Scripps Research on several pieces, including the early *Adenovirus* and *Poliovirus* and, later, *Nanoscape II: Viral Assembly* (1999), featuring the outer layer of the HIV viral capsid (plate 11). By this time the PHSColograms had begun to draw on various kinds of scientific data, including X-ray crystallography, MRI, mammogram, CT and PET scans, and other imaging techniques. The collective created in-house 3D images from data (as in the case of *AIDS Virus*), or they received multiple rendered views from scientists before translating the rendered images into the PHSCologram medium.[87] When we get to *Nanoscape II*, it is clear that the 3D images probe atomic structures more intensely, drawing on extensive research on the HIV-1 macromolecule. The image interleaves sixty copies each of four distinct protein subunits of the HIV viral capsid, which self-assemble to form the spherical particle. The 1983 blurry electron micrograph from the Pasteur Institute had blossomed in color and form over sixteen years.

The primary imperative for the radical empiricists at (art)n was to push the technical and aesthetic boundaries that separated different media, bringing sculptural volume to photographic images and optical complexity to physical models. -Morphic images enfolded different media-technological practices in a constant experiment with mediation as prehension. These volumetric images drew the attention of scientists (like Arthur Olson) and computer graphics artists (Dan Sandin) invested in structural and topographical forms as the story of this collaboration demonstrates. As one commentator in the *New Art Examiner* indicated, “Their works of art operate very much like scientific theories. Scientific theories are dispassionate deductions about the real world. But when passion is factored into the equation, very powerful works of art are created from structurally very similar intellectual systems.”[88] In her ethnography of protein modelers, Myers demonstrates how immersive experiences enchant protein modelers as they engage molecular matter affectively and kinesthetically. As modelers *move with* 3D models on display consoles and workbenches, there is much more than automation that moves the image: gesture, intuition, and imagination come into play. The image experience enacts a “throwing of the senses,” to recall David Abram in *The Spell of the Sensuous*, toward human and nonhuman particle worlds. In their imaging/sculpting of living systems, the (art)n collective establishes viable collaborative zones between scientific and artistic experimentations. Pushing the frontiers of what images can do and what image experiences can be, these heterogeneous molecular visualizations conjugate -morphic images perpetually under construction.

Morphic as Flux: Virus Models at the Olson Lab

Arthur Olson and David Goodsell's impact on molecular visualization has few parallels. Trained in X-ray crystallography in the 1970s, Olson began writing on the first atomic resolution of an intact virus particle in 1976–77 and experimented with visualizing the molecular structure of the virus in 1979.[89] At the time, he made a physical model of a virus macromolecule from brass parts and began to experiment with animating protein assemblies on film. Olson had joined the Scripps Research Institute in 1981; when David Goodsell arrived there in 1987, their decades-long collaboration would commence. The collaboration produced some of the most important physical models, software programs, and simulation tool kits for imaging structural and dynamic data in the biosciences. Goodsell's scientific illustrations in *The Machinery of Life* (1993) and *Atomic Evidence* (2016) set standards for magnified images of cellular structures at atomic resolution complete with molecules in their proper place, size, and concentrations.[90] If Goodsell's *The Machinery of Life* adopted an artistic approach to the challenge of integrative biology, Olson saw 3D animations and dynamic simulations as the intuitive way to manipulate and learn from molecular models.[91] Two-dimensional images lacked "representation flexibility," Olson argued, while the "tangible, haptic surfaces" of 3D physical models and the "immersive perspective" in 3D visualizations imparted a "sense of reality" to the biomolecular structures under scrutiny.[92] (When I visited the Olson Lab, physical models of viruses were strewn everywhere, some on display, some for visitors to touch/play with.) In the pitch for immersive media, Olson remains eminently reflexive about practices of molecular visualization as they have evolved since the late 1970s. His interest in the cognitive processes of research spurred many of the Olson Lab's media-technological innovations. The lab's notable successes are many, among them the production of Autodock, a program for biomolecular structure analysis that has been adopted by four thousand laboratories all over the world.

Central to media-technological innovation was the Olson Lab's research on the HIV-1 macromolecule. Autodock enabled researchers to understand how molecules act in motion and how HIV docks in host cells, so that those processes could be modified and sometimes disabled. As part of the National Institutes of Allergy and Infectious Diseases (NIAID) AIDS-Related Structural Biology program (currently, the Centers for HIV Structural Biology), the Olson Lab developed at least a thousand structures of protease, one of three important HIV enzymes in the viral replication cycle. Research on the HIV-1 enzyme's biomolecular structures had everything to do with the lifesaving protease inhibitors, placing the Olson Lab squarely within ongoing efforts to develop better pharmacological solutions for "managed HIV." As such, the lab has produced profoundly significant epidemic media. It sits as one node in a huge network, the HIV Interactions in Viral Evolution (HIVE). With ten participating institutions, HIVE coordinates a number of projects that study protein assemblies and interactions for HIV (the network is labeled the "HIVE Interactome").[93] Collaborations are stable articulations between institution-based research centers and laboratories. For the Olson Lab, the collaborative nexus includes structural biologists, biochemists, computer programmers, and graphics experts. In keeping with trends in molecular graphics, the Olson Lab has adopted a more quantitative approach to modeling biomolecular structures, with Goodsell's watercolor illustrations as the methodological and aesthetic basis for new models. Goodsell's watercolor of the HIV macromolecule in blood plasma made in 1999 (plate 12) was later *transcribed into* a molecular visualization (plate 13) with cellPACK, a tool kit developed at the Olson Lab. By now, the lab has made as many as six models of the HIV-1 (HIV-1 1.2, 1.3 . . .), each manually curated from widely sourced data. This ongoing endeavor is a prime example of the -morphic image as malleable and constantly editable when new data emerge, and speculative where data are inadequate.

Interactive media platforms for research collaborators enable the study of molecular structures and the editing of existing models as new data come in. One software tool kit is the suite cellPACK, a biology-specific extension of AutoPACK. The suite was developed by Ludovic Autin and Graham Johnson, when the medical illustrator–turned–software designer Johnson—who now directs the Mesoscope Lab at the University of California, San Francisco—was a research fellow at the Olson Lab.[94] The impetus behind cellPACK is to combine data from all branches of biology into a comprehensive mesoscale model ranging from 0.1 micron to 10 nanometers. "Artistic depictions of cellular environments" built on the cellPACK suite can integrate data from ultrastructural (light and electron microscopy), infrastructural atomic (X-ray crystallography and nuclear magnetic resonance [NMR] spectroscopy), and biochemical (for concentrations and interactions) sources.[95] "Ingredients" from these data sources produce "recipes" (as the Olson Lab's extended cooking metaphor goes) for various parts of the model. Plate 13 is made up of seven different recipes (each with a different color coding) that are unified into a single hybrid model. On cellPACK, the lab's HIV-1 ultrastructure (the HIV envelope) functions as the polyhedral "mesh" or the "state space" for packing ingredients.[96] Adding time to geometric coordinates, a dimensional state space is a mathematical model of a physical system that is better able to handle the multidimensional complexity of biological systems. It is possible to *simulate* unfolding molecular events there and therein to calculate probable outcomes. I return to simulations shortly. But to continue with cellPACK: its virtuoso "packing algorithms" determine how the mesh is filled out with ingredients to produce a scalable image (plate 14). Endless updates to the "editable model of HIV" become possible in these plastic, malleable images. Each -morphic image liquidates and reconfigures the previous trace. The point of the constant update is to integrate large data sets that increase in volume every day. The Olson Lab's release of HIV 1.6 demonstrated the possibility of integrating crowdsourced structural data at speeds commensurate with the fast pace of HIV research.[97] The -morphic image is always already incomplete in the *imperfect* alignment to incoming research inputs.

During my visit to the Olson Lab, Stefano Forli, the pharmacology/biotech interface at the lab, explained how animating 3D models on new media platforms provided the opportunity not only to circle, view, and analyze cellular structures but also to calculate the densities, forces, and propensities of molecules as they interacted with each other. Real-time video tracking allows for moving molecules around, watching for folds, accelerating or decelerating molecular motion. As the molecules vibrated in Brownian motion, Olson noted that scientists could better understand the electrostatic complementarity and hydrogen bonding underlying molecular structures; more importantly, they could zoom in and out of structurally indeterminate sites. In this latter capacity, -morphic images at this lab remain improvisational, productively speculative. Simulating lively fluctuations and interactions as molecular events, making and remaking biomolecular structures, the images represent a multitude of probable outcomes. These outcomes integrate inputs from *different* synthetic spaces to hypothesize emergent wholes.

These synthetic spaces are "possibility spaces," as Manuel DeLanda describes them in *Philosophy and Simulation*, that can render a range of probable outcomes mathematically calculable. Structural data constrain all probabilities, he argues, making simulations ontologically sound. In his articulation, *biological* "spaces of possibility"—the space of genes, the space of protein assembly, and the space of biochemical processes—are computationally rendered as *synthetic* "possibility spaces."[98] The fluid exchange of biological "spaces of possibility" and synthetic "possibility spaces" situates the -morphic 3D image on a synthetic-biological continuum in this enriched mechanist account. Life is not uncontainable: it is calculable because mathematical logic converts all possibilities into probabilities. Three-dimensional images integrate data inputs in visualizations of "emergent wholes," aligning overlapping possibility spaces. In their theoretical orientation, these simulations are provisional: the -morphic image is but one version of what *might happen* in synthetic-biological space. Simulations can materialize "individual singularities" arising from "populations of agents" interacting with each other.[99] To turn to HIV research, secondary mutations of HIV born of interactions with drug molecules are individual singularities that are "stable" in that their genomic data have been decoded and registered, and yet the protein assemblies that stem from these changed gene instructions are a different matter altogether. They depend on genetic instruction but also on biochemical conditions for conformational change at the particular interactive domain.[100] What, then, are the new tendencies and capacities of genes in their interaction with biochemical singularities? Since genetic and biochemical changes occur as nonlinear processes, what holds true at one plane does not hold true at the other. They occupy different "biological spaces," so to speak. Simulations of complex living systems articulate these spaces together, rendering nonlinear processes mathematically calculable so as to predict numerous probable outcomes. -Morphic images materialize specific outcomes as insights to be further tested, providing provisional coherence that can give way to other probabilities. As an imperfect image, the -morphic gestures toward the temporal excess of lively fluctuations that constitute the biological complexity of living systems.

One can see how tool kits like cellPACK facilitate *integration* across synthetic possibility spaces, scaling images as they move in molecular and cellular domains.[101] Biological complexity necessitates such scalar dynamics: this is a lesson well learned from the annals of the HIV/AIDS pandemic. As Olson argues, the clinical consequences of HIV drugs like azidothymidine or AZT proved that finding the perfect new drug molecule was not enough; its interactions across the living system had to be anticipated in order to scuttle toxic side effects like lymphoma or liver failure. Speculative and dynamic, malleable and creative, the -morphic 3D image in molecular visualizations enables prediction at the scale of molecular events; it has integrative force. As images composed at one scale liquidate to reassemble into larger wholes, or vice versa, -morphic images not only present variable trajectories of virus-host interactions but also predict what is not yet known. They are crucial sites for creative actualizations of competing hypotheses based on mathematical probabilities. At one level, then, the -morphic image materializes biological complexity; at another, despite calculable outcomes, it lags behind the lively flux that exceeds all synthetic transcription and is haunted by the partially known. The incompletion of the -morphic embodies the unknown as biological uncertainty.

The broader picture is a steady movement toward synthetic reason manifest in the change of the Olson Lab's official name from the Molecular Graphics Lab

(1981) to the Center for Computational Structural Biology (2018). The change marks a paradigm shift toward complex systems thinking in which the isolated living organism is no longer the sublime object of virology. The study of nonlinear multispecies relations constitutive of viral emergence is at center stage. This theoretical orientation toward living systems finds full realization in systems biology that processes high-throughput data from specialized arenas of research.[102] The disciplinary shift means that the virus is increasingly a fuzzy concept: at once a submicroscopic particle, a genetic substrate, and a protein-lipid combo without cell walls. Its appearance *as* image brings together not only different scientific expertise in crowdsourced models but also artistic histories, technological skills, and design chutzpah. In the medial entanglement of the -morphic image, scientists and artists coemerge in embodied relation to the living systems they visualize.

Implicit in these stories of -morphic images are conceptions of life that are at odds with each other. DeLanda espouses a mechanist account of life as calculable; simulations of living systems afford a mathematical realism.[103] In contrast, Myers insists on a neovitalist understanding of excitable matter as recalcitrant to epistemic cuts.[104] *The Virus Touch* is less invested in rehearsing the vitalist-mechanist debate than in thinking how media-technological practices perform encounters with process-relational ontologies. Liveliness materializes the "excess" as the proverbial unknown, presenting new challenges for any kind of realism. This motivates the push for more machinic innovation and fine-honed aesthetic expression: the constantly dispersing image struggles to bring coherence to viral emergences. The imperative to engage this excess, to apprehend if not comprehend it, fuels a drive for multisensory encounters with living systems that vibrate and fluctuate. They appear within grasp in 3D image experiences even if some structural details are not (theoretically) calculable or (empirically) verifiable. Emplacing users/viewers in visual-haptic image spaces, 3D images present the spatial illusion of "being with" living systems and turn study into embodied encounter. As user and image coemerge, multisensory formats enfold users in active multispecies entanglements. Life as life itself continues to unsettle.

Coda: Images Unfolding

The scenes of image making/doing/enacting in this chapter are classic instances of epidemic media. Materializing viruses on a synthetic-biological continuum, the -morphic image is form, relation, and process. Amid epidemic intensities, these images are necessarily instrumental: the scientific insights they envision aim to alter molecular relationalities and to deliver those alterations as biotechnological solutions. As such, -morphic images of the postgenomic present are one stop in turning data into flesh. When new multispecies relations emerge, as they do in epidemic situations, it becomes all the more urgent to speedily integrate multiple data streams and to speculate on what is as yet unknown. Despite their overt functionality as speculative media, malleable -morphic images engage radical biological uncertainty. Their provisional status galvanizes all kinds of aesthetic and technical experiments in creative partnerships and collaborations among scientists, artists, engineers, and computer programmers. The "morph" as technique turns to mediation as prehension armed with new tools, creative image production, and rich aesthetic grammars. Seeking visual coherence, if molecular visualizations draw on scientific-cultural histories of visible forms, the consequent transcoding situates -morphic scientific images in larger media cultures, including artistic and industrial media practices. As the modern practitioners seek answers to viral emergences, they range beyond their specialized fields of scientific expertise *and* beyond the epistemic settings of basic science laboratories. This chapter's itineraries from bioscience laboratories to animation outfits to art galleries to studios attempt to plot the restless quest to comprehend a new multispecies relation.

Always processual, the -morphic designates the drive toward "realistic" capture, toward more precision, more accuracy, and greater efficiency *as a desire*. At the limits of visual-machinic capture, other inklings vibrate, compelling intuition. Those inklings provoke a multisensory entanglement with living systems in and beyond us. As biotechnical images engage more than the visual and the numerical, they disclose the virus touch.

THREE

THE SENSIBLE MEDIUM

Clinical Translations of Blood

A primal scene from the HIV/AIDS epidemic: the blood paintings of artist Robert Sherer, from the US South, who archives HIV+ and HIV− blood as a collective record. Sherer began to paint with his own blood after accidentally slicing an artery one day. At the time he was attending the Atlanta College of Art after obtaining a degree in biology from the University of Alabama. It was the early days of the HIV/AIDS epidemic. In 1998 the antiretrovirals (ARVs) were just out. Sherer's fellow artists had been dropping like flies, and blood had attained symbolic status as *the* mode of transmission for HIV. Like no other, the HIV/AIDS epidemic underscored the role of blood as a life-sustaining resource for both humans and microbes: its regenerative capacities had to be protected from death, and its operations as a medium of transmission had to be controlled. Blood nourished the virus; blood passed easily from host to host. Exhortations to get tested had become commonplace in American public life, as had biomedical knowledge of spiraling viral copies and diminishing T-cell counts. Heightened perceptions of vital processes were part and parcel of the biomedicalization of American life that sparked massive social transformations in the mid-1980s. As part of this changing landscape in the United States, patient-centered HIV/AIDS movements made the technical modification of blood, in tests and therapy, a collective enterprise. Blood was not only symbolic but *sensible* as a milieu for the unfolding drama of multispecies relations. Scientific and artistic compositions of blood across settings—from laboratories, biorepositories, databases, and clinics to homes, galleries, theaters, and other performance spaces—made blood public as an interior milieu under attack that was equally a medium recalcitrant to containment at the epidermal limits of the molar body. Amid mounting contagion hysteria, varying compositions of blood became the epidemic's sanguineous imaginary. This chapter traces processes of mediation that materialize blood in biotechnical spatial forms composed as *interior milieus*. I characterize these intensive time-spaces "read" for their multispecies distributions as "biotechnical milieus," probing the ecological and social implications of such compositions.

I focus on the mediatic processes that clinically translate this vital medium into three forms: frozen blood samples (for refrigeration), blood data (for the database), and blood pictures (for points of care/clinics). Taking volumetric and numeric forms, these biotechnical milieus are temporally organized as serial snapshots in the blood files. Media, in this chapter, are the technical apparatuses and devices that attempt machinic capture of the vital medium, imposing epistemic cuts to compose individual (the patient) or populational (the demographic) biotechnical milieus. But media are also the medial substrates constitutive of a vital medium whose molecular intelligibility makes delimiting the open spatiality of life impossible. In this tensioned space, blood swirls, restless and changeful, pointing centrifugally beyond the individuated blood file to what lies between populations within a species and beyond. To analyze the *milieu as medium* is to consider how biotechnical forms attempt to control, indeed govern, infection's risk environment so as to prepare it for targeted interventions. One articulation of control renders the extensive time-space of infection as highly intensive and localizes it as an interior milieu epistemically cut for study and consequently targeted for biomedical intervention. In blood samples, blood data, and blood pictures, the interior milieu emerges serially as the demarcated surrounds for tracking the actions of agents (such as CD4 cells or viral particles). Blood is the quiet backdrop to a multispecies drama transcribed as mathematical ratio (*x* particles in *y* milliliters). The numerical ranges that make infection intelligible command the lion's share of attention, recessing blood's volumetric form as the interior milieu. My focus on the spatial form, the milieu, follows notations of the environment in biological epistemologies and in media histories, even as the concept remains irrelevant to clinical-scale analytics. The point is to illuminate the difficulty of containing clinical-scale intensive time-spaces of infection, of securing the interior milieu from emergent life as biogeomorphic activity. In this regard, the trace of biological individuality that haunts the "interior milieu" indexes the political desire to localize, target, and govern infection's risk environment. The conceptual displacement of milieu in this chapter not only situates biological thought in environmental studies but also opens up anthropocentric clinical translations of blood to the multispecies question. The interior milieu, it turns out, disperses into disease milieus, and the latter into global hotspots of infection. An epidemic emerges in nested media environments as I follow blood across differentiated material settings—the laboratory, the biorepository, the database, the clinic. Blood dominates the scene because chronic blood surveillance for "managed HIV" has made this vital medium a staple in that pandemic's public sensorium.

The contagion hysteria of early AIDS, in this regard, was a blood sensing that perceived the intrinsic transitivity of the vital medium. Reflexive artistic compositions highlighted the significance of collective participation in *living* at the threshold of the "undetectable."[1] Without the clinical translation of blood as medium across settings, neither cutting-edge research nor the mass manufacture of drug therapies could stem the epidemic. The interior milieu had to become perceptible as a public sensorium. In the period known as early AIDS, artists such as Ron Athey "pleaded in blood" in performances that offered their audiences natural (blood, semen, saliva) and synthetic (margarine and ointment for anal penetration) bodily fluids; in the post-ARV era, artists drew attention to the biomedicalization of blood that involved detection and storage.[2] For all intents and purposes, the HIV/AIDS pandemic ushered in a *medicalized* epoch sanguinis, as Michel Foucault characterized it, in which this highly politicized, excorporated substance once more came to define social kinship.[3] After post- and pre-exposure prophylaxis (PEP and PrEP), there has been a deliberate de-escalation of the dramatic blood politics of the early AIDS era. But blood in the HIV/AIDS pandemic remains significant as a material substance because its components, the CD4 cells, are under threat, and therefore they have to be chronically monitored to control vital degeneration. Blood emerges *as a medium* at the point of radical alteration. As David Ho and his team made modifications of HIV RNA in vivo possible in the mid-1990s, all eyes turned to T-cells, foregrounding life at the molecular scale.[4] With ARVs, blood emerged as a biomedically malleable medium. Blood tests tracked mutations of HIV particles as HIV/AIDS became a chronic illness; blood repositories stored blood samples for new ARV designs. Against this backdrop, for Sherer, the bright spatter from his artery took on social salience. Emptying the ink from his quill pens, he began to paint in blood.[5] Trained in botanical illustration, he painted nature in its bucolic innocence, its delicacies. Alert to lively materialities, he thinned his blood with anticoagulants and mixed it with inks to increase its brightness. Soon an HIV+ friend donated her blood for a painting; shortly thereafter, Sherer's refrigerator was stacked with donations. As he framed each blood portrait in Victorian oval frames, the feared medium became collectible art.

Sherer's blood catalog opened as part of a thematic exhibition called *The Body as Commodity* at the Atlanta Contemporary Art Center (then known as Nexus) in 1999. The drawings were installed on a vivid red velvet-covered wall that immersed viewers in the vital substrates of the paintings and of infection. When I first interviewed him in April 2017, he picked *Sweet William*, the vital record of a fellow artist who had since passed, as the centerpiece (plate 15). This portrait in flowers harkened back to Sherer's grandmother's sense that the prettiest blooms were those cut down early. The opening in Atlanta became mourning work as those who recognized references broke down. In this sense Sherer's blood catalog represents HIV/AIDS artworks of the early period; the paintings mourn rather than engage with (post-ARV) chronic infection. But I was captivated by something else: by Sherer's excorporation of the vital medium that gave his "blood paintings" (as he calls them now) indexical value and by his relocation of the individual vital media into deceptively bucolic natural settings. Sherer's botanical milieus invoked the ecological dimensions of blood. The early paintings are replete with natural life: flowers in bloom, flowers in bouquets, bunnies nestling, insects abuzz, vegetables ripe and bursting. In my interviews with him conducted over a few years, he noted his interests came from living on a farm. One among these early pieces—a portrait of two nestling bunnies, one painted in HIV+ blood, the other in HIV− blood—stands out as a reflection on managed HIV (plate 16). An invitation to multispecies entanglements, the piece, titled *Love Nest*, drew attention to the opacity of blood in its surface appearances. Blood was incomprehensible as an infected milieu without molecular intelligibility; it had to be extracted, classified, and translated into data. Sherer's bunnies were a response to blood as sensible media. He challenged viewers of *Love Nest* to slip into *social* profiling without the technical notation of blood tests. Ironically, despite his challenge, several viewers insisted they could differentiate the HIV+ from the HIV− bunny. This portrait of sero-discordant bliss, a "living with" HIV and each other, further underscored the possibility of *living on* as multispecies—of staying undetectable. This sense of distributed subjectivity is stronger still in Sherer's insect paintings, where swarms saturate the visual landscape, recalling disease vectors and multiplying microbial life. In *Hookups*, insect saturation indexes southern climates as well as natural fecundities across species (figure 3.1). We are reminded of Dorion Sagan's crowded planet of commingling organisms that ingest, digest, procreate, and excrete each other.[6]

Figure 3.1. Robert Sherer, *Hookups*, 2012. HIV+ and HIV- blood on paper, 32×19 in. Credit: Robert Sherer.

In his later paintings, Sherer explored the biomedical imperatives under which one lives on: the periodic testing, the microactions of HIV, and the intensive immunological strife. These blood paintings exemplify all the ways in which art-science has mediated the epidemic experience of living as multispecies. In *Fathoming*, the vital medium is expressed as the oceans we carry within us; there we find industrial entanglements—mines, bombs, chains (figure 3.2). Industrial ruins in the ocean feature a breached interior milieu; deep within lies a ticking time bomb, the virus, no doubt referring to those hidden HIV reservoirs that even the most sophisticated tests cannot detect. In such portraiture the biotechnical milieu translates vital processes of altered life so as to fathom their depths. Blood emerges as a painterly medium, a denatured vital substance, yet the wild viscous spatter indexes those other spaces of commingling bodies, emplacing viewers in the extensive environments of infection.

Such a sanguineous imaginary brought home the complexities of the biomedical surveillance that had become quotidian to the HIV/AIDS pandemic. Chronic blood tests made body fluids intelligible as vital media to be governed and managed at clinical scale. To regulate multispecies distributions in blood realized global ambitions of epidemic management at the scale of the individual "patient" or of "key populations," the targets of biomedical research outcomes. In his painting *Test Results*, Sherer foregrounded the proverbial viral load test as a key control mechanism and as a chronic fact of life. To live distributed required the in vivo labor of staying below fifty copies of HIV-1 per milliliter of plasma. The viral load test monitored this every six months, scanning for redistributions. A count of more than a thousand HIV copies per milliliter of blood indicated viremia or increased viral proliferation, a sign that HIV had developed resistance to the present line of antiretroviral therapies (ARTs); then a second blood test was in the offing to confirm diagnoses before the inception of a new line of treatments.[7] Sherer's blood paintings are as much meditations on multispecies entanglements as they are on the public sensorium of managed HIV. As such, he engages biomedical blood surveillance from the perspective of the socially and ecologically distributed subject.

Epidemic Media

Blood makes an appearance in this chapter as tangible, print, and electronic media. If epidemic exigencies had made governing body-fluid exchanges a major preoccupation in the HIV/AIDS pandemic, blood as one risk environment for HIV infection had a dual valence: it was both a medium of transmission and vital media under threat of exhaustion. Hence, blood came to occupy a historical

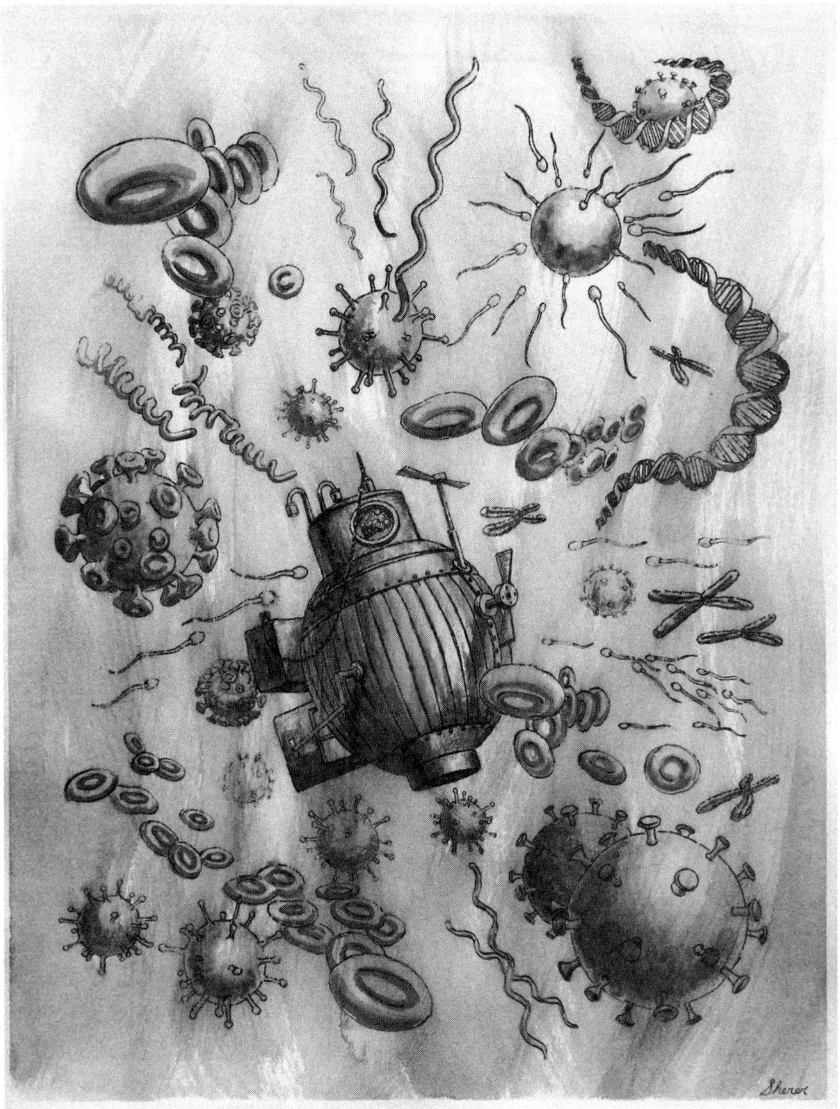

Figure 3.2. Robert Sherer, *Fathoming*, 2013. HIV+ and HIV- blood on paper, 33×25 in. Credit: Robert Sherer.

place like no other body fluid. Epidemic media as the machinic inscription of blood made this vital medium readable and manageable at the molecular scale. Mediatic processes that processed and stored blood mobilized media technologies and cultural techniques that are not conventionally within the remit of media studies: besides traditional apparatuses like microscopes and computers, for example, these include inscription devices such as detection platforms and centrifuges, fluorescent probes and chemical reagents. Importantly, blood's lively materiality—its unstable, fragile, and transitive qualities—continues to define what can be done at the machinic interface. The intrinsic qualities of blood compel fervent efforts to contain blood within well-demarcated milieus and to store it as such in temporally sequenced individuated records. Analyzing the making of biotechnical milieus, then, affords a closer look at efforts to *contain* multispecies entanglements by reimposing biological individuality. What might this mean for a *multispecies politics* in the domain of public health? The multispecies question is rarely a concern for public health even though epidemiological accounts of "natural" disease vectors and disease milieus are crucial to managing extensive (human) community transmission. In this chapter, my reframing of clinical translations of infection as multispecies distributions reveals the environmental politics of the book. Further, as a scholar of environmental media, I am interested in media-technological compositions of infection's environments that underlie the conduct of global public health materializing in individuated blood samples, data, and pictures. Understanding processes of mediation that transform risky epidemic media into biotechnical milieus provides a pathway into the inquiry.

A similar lacuna arises in environmental media studies, where the pursuit of *vital media* as media environments mostly relegates them to clinical scales. This is because bodily fluids (blood, semen, saliva, vaginal/rectal secretions, respiratory mucous) have restricted circulation. They are ontologically fragile, unable to survive for long outside their site of generation. But as I have noted earlier, almost always, these fluid media exceed their molar boundaries, whether by human habits or ecosystems. To think milieu as medium is to recognize biological-social (community transmissions) and biological-ecological (cross-species transmissions) time-spaces in which dynamic multispecies relations materialize. Interior milieus are fractal environments, mirroring unfolding processes in disease milieus—in the neighborhood, the town, the city, the province, the region, and outward. Epidemiologists characterize the geological, atmospheric, and biological (soil, humidity, and insect life, for instance) as well as geographic, industrial, and demographic (territories, transportation routes, and mobile populations, for instance) conditions of pathogenic emergence in these nested milieus. Such materialities fold the "disease milieu" into global hotspots for planetary-scale emerging infectious disease events; the latter are the subject of the next chapter. Following blood beyond its original site of production, in this chapter, illuminates multispecies entanglements as social and ecological relationalities. Technical mediation places us in communication with vital media bristling with multispecies signals, gesturing toward disease milieus. What one breathes and ingests, where one lives and travels, one's intergenerational vitality, all determine how infection unfolds in the intensive interior milieu. As the chapter progresses, the blood files composed at clinical scale ultimately reveal the difficulty of controlling planetary circulations of these vital epidemic media.

In the post-ARV era, the biomedical gaze appears as objective, medicalized, neutral in the machinic detection and calculation of viral matter in chronic viral load tests. The test extracts HIV genetic material from peripheral blood mononuclear cells (PBMC), probes and magnifies HIV RNA, identifies viral genome sequences, and then calculates the number of viral copies as a mathematical range. The virus-human ensemble becomes readable as a numerical threshold within a specified volume of blood. *The biotechnical milieu materializes in volumetric spatial form.*[8] If one medium reveals another, if the "ship alters the sea, or rather makes the sea navigable at all," as John Durham Peters puts it, then sophisticated inscriptive devices (detection platforms) navigate the vital medium, drilling down to the smaller and smaller numbers of viral copies.[9] Tests like the Roche Diagnostics viral load test can detect as few as twenty copies per milliliter of blood. Such precision is crucial because undetectable HIV reservoirs can lie latent for a while before exploding into viremia at a later stage.[10] Viral bioassays are the gold standard for tracking HIV infection: their capture of viral-particle distribution prepares interior milieus as biological targets for therapeutic intervention.

The chapter examines what it takes to materialize a life-sustaining medium as the controlled time-space of infection at clinical scales. These compositions occur across clinical points of care, clinical medicine laboratories, international research networks (such as the HIV Vaccine Trials Network [HVTN] or the AIDS Clinical Trials Group [ACTG]), and public health databases. Each site relies on the others in this biomedical network. Research in biomedical interventions relies on blood supply from HIV cohorts in specific disease milieus (a neighborhood or city), on longitudinal data (stored in databases), and on clinical trial protocols (for study designs). In each setting viral particles become readable as a ratio in the sensible milieu of host blood: fluids and solids, images and movements, translate into a number. In popular parlance, this number is a constant aspiration, as the mantra "staying undetectable" suggests. Beyond detecting the ratio, serial blood pictures are the chronological record of infection necessary for living with ARTs: they present the conduct of altered lives. To direct and regulate temporal fluctuations in host blood and in viral replication entails tracking *changes* in the interior milieu; this means *chronic* biomedical surveillance. As an epidemic medium, blood emerges in snapshots that stabilize changing multispecies distributions (as mathematical ratios) to prepare them for therapeutic modification. In this regard, blood surveillance regulates and controls the unfolding of life.

The blood files are storage technologies that maintain and transcribe the temporal record of chronic infection. On the one hand, clinical medicine laboratories with biorepositories bank blood as samples for biomedical research. On the other hand, following cross-network protocols, these laboratories generate confidential medical information that is then housed in databases and articulated with demographic and geospatial aggregative data. Drawing on media theorist Cornelia Vismann's critically acclaimed *Files*, I argue that files marshal blood as an alienable resource, render it readable, and archive it for future research. The blood files still the dynamism of multispecies distributions and fragment the time-space of infection. The accumulative capacity of the file makes it possible to sequence viral temporalities to some degree in asking: When will the virus mutate? When might a dormant reservoir become active? When will drug efficacies fail? What coinfections and comorbidities, habits and behaviors, will change the ratio of multispecies distributions?

This chapter unfolds the story of managed HIV through the itineraries of blood files as they move through clinical medicine laboratories, biorepositories, databases, and clinical patient records. I analyze blood processing and storage at the University of Washington's Clinical Retrovirus Laboratory (henceforth the Retrovirus Lab), which hosts one of the biorepositories for the Centers for AIDS Research (CFAR) system. This laboratory medicine facility serves as a nodal point for the preparation and distribution of blood samples and for uploading blood data into electronic storage systems. My turn to points of care includes three clinics: Seattle's Madison HIV Clinic, the largest federally funded clinic in the Pacific Northwest and one of the sources for the blood specimens housed at the Retrovirus Lab; Mumbai's Sanjeevani support outfit for MSM (men who have sex with men) and TG (transgender) communities, administered by the Humsafar Trust; and Cape Town's "HIV adherence clubs," funded by Médecins Sans Frontières (MSF), as three exemplary instances of community-based points of care embedded within global biomedical infrastructures. As blood materializes across this field of operations, captured, composed, and stored, it brings with it the messiness of biological, social, and ecological relations.

The Milieu

Following expansions in environmental media studies, I situate vital media as extensive media environments of infection. Body fluids such as respiratory mucous, saliva, semen, blood, and rectal and vaginal fluids are rendered calculable as *risk* environments for emergent multispecies relations that must be constantly managed to contain infection. The epidemic episteme of public health localizes these environments clinically to individuated bodies (e.g., body fluids) and demographically to population aggregates (e.g., community transmission). Interior milieus and disease milieus emerge as nested fractal forms. But containment is less and less tenable in the past four decades after the emerging infectious disease scares of the 1980s. To put it bluntly, infection as fluctuating multispecies relationalities unfolds extensively; when it does so at exponentially high speeds, scaling up across host populations, one form of recognition is a "global public health crisis." This recognition is a political fiat that privileges the biosecurity of human life. But if we locate infection in its nested milieus, we find interior milieus distending from cellular coordinates centrifugally outward into ecosystem vectors. How processes of mediation make vital media intelligible elaborates this centrifugal orientation to composing milieus.

BIOLOGICAL MILIEUS

The milieu has a significant history in the biological episteme. One of the most notable explanations that approaches the clinical scale is physiologist and physician Claude Bernard's notation of the *milieu intérieur* (interior milieu), a term that accentuates the internal autonomy of molar forms. While bodies are eminently permeable, living beings, Bernard explains, strive for an internal constancy of extracellular fluids, keeping blood sugar levels or platelet counts constant to ward off vital degeneration. Attempting to distinguish the chemistries of different species, Bernard famously saw the interior milieu as a struggle to keep the planet at bay: our ancestor organisms left the oceans to "carry the oceans with them," he argued, and henceforth struggled to maintain the internal constancy of their internal environments. For Bernard, that internal constancy (or homeostasis, as we know it now) "is the condition of a free and independent existence."[11] But this desired condition, a "free and independent existence," is an impossibility, as we know from contemporary environmental perspectives. Lungs are permeable, body fluids are exchangeable, chemicals direct molecular change, our genes register environmental dynamics . . . the list is endless.[12] Transitive epidemic media only underscore the point. One historical epistemologist who recognized infection's *extensive* risk environments but saw demarcating milieus as a pragmatic response to illness is Georges Canguilhem, a physician who was invested in the medical, social, and ecological dimensions of health. Importantly, for Canguilhem, the milieu is media—lively and bristling, the milieu is always a relative concept that refers centrifugally outward.

Canguilhem sees the milieu as a composition organized around the organism as epistemic object (much like Jakob Uexküll's *Umwelt*). The "milieu proper to man is the world of his perceptions," writes Canguilhem, "the field of his pragmatic experience, the field in which his actions, oriented and regulated by the values immanent to his tendencies, pick out quality-bearing objects and situate them in relation to each other and to him. Thus, the environment to which he is supposed to react is originally centered on him and by him."[13] But unlike Bernard, Canguilhem emplaces this centripetal composition *in* "nature" and plugs the individual body back *into* its living milieu. What organisms perceive as their milieu at any given point is an epistemic cut: it is *a* field of "pragmatic experience" that orients "our" actions. We not only compose a pragmatic time-space but populate it with relationally constituted "quality-bearing objects." In HIV infection, blood materializes as the individuated interior milieu whose solid components, the CD4 cells, are under attack from HIV particles. These cells and particles are the quality-bearing objects appearing in the drama of "life itself" unfolding in plasma as the medial extracellular fluid. The ARVs block the HIV proteins that hijack CD4 cell machineries by stalling the production of HIV enzymes (protease, reverse transcriptase, and integrase) that allow HIV to integrate its protein-making instructions into the host DNA. In this way, the therapeutic intervention of the ARVs alters and modifies the distributions of viral matter in blood so as to maintain the internal constancy of the hematic system. Taking ART, in Canguilhem's terms, makes new vital norms once one *falls into health*.[14] Health is always emergent, a horizon negotiated between doctor and patient. The epitome of health, Canguilhem maintains, is "lived in the silence of the organs"; only when the liver, stomach, or heart malfunction do we perceive something is amiss.[15] Then we *fall into health*. In this case, staying at the threshold of the undetectable, maintaining a stable ratio of multispecies distributions, becomes the new normal.

Positioning the milieu in terms of health as a moving target, Canguilhem elaborates Bernard's interior milieu as a historical construction and insists that the securing of organismic autonomy is a pragmatic solution for living in the greater milieu "out there." In histories of science, the "technical shaping" of the body, as the paleontologist André Leroi-Gourhan argued, imparted a sense of freedom from the milieu: the evolution of hands and feet were essential to this perception of freedom.[16] The milieu came to be projected as the environment *outside* the body. But Canguilhem's ecological perspective situates the interior milieu as always already interpenetrated with other living systems even as maintaining health delimits the time-space of infection. Diseases are radical disturbances in the articulation of living being with the milieu, compelling the making of new vital norms. If one has masked or practiced social distancing during COVID-19, the discomfort of these adjustments, the making of new vital norms, needs little explanation. Moving beyond the pragmatic standpoint, Canguilhem underscores a relative conception of the milieu. "The notion of milieu is an essentially relative one," argues Canguilhem, but we tend to forget its role as planetary connective tissue when we separate the body from its external environment.[17] We test vital media for HIV or SARS-CoV-2 distributions in the individuated interior milieu; we assess damage by a mathematical ratio, x *viral particles in* y *milliliters of blood*. Numerically inscribed in milliliters, the medium as epistemic object asserts an active volumetric presence. Meanwhile, the numerically recorded microbial presence that *comes from elsewhere* positions the interior milieu in the external environment—infection arrives from another body, a disease vector, an elemental medium. What, then, are the time-spaces for HIV or SARS-CoV-2 actions? How has the virus traveled to this intensive space? How transitive is the vital medium exchanged between host populations? Did it act as transport in cross-species transmissions? How far does the interior milieu *extend*? In this regard, the interior milieu is always a relative conception materializing in epistemic cuts that centrifugally gesture to other milieus beyond the molar limits of the individual body. The milieu as epidemic medium is rife with different agencies, in Canguilhem's account, bringing home the distributed *Homo microbis*, despite efforts to individuate, despite the medical isolation of "an" interior milieu.

CLINICAL MILIEUS

Media-technological processes inscribe, parse, and record specific signals in blood, rendering the medium intelligible for clinical research and care. A single blood specimen is separated into multiple samples, then probed, magnified, and calculated for its multispecies distributions; when frozen, excorporated blood components outlive their original interior milieu. Unlike other bodily archives such as "the ancient clocklike subsystems in our brains, extinct viruses in our DNA, bacteria in our guts," however, blood cannot survive outside the body for long without technical fabrication.[18] In frozen states, red blood cells last outside the body for thirty days, and platelets for even less, while plasma can be archived only when mixed with freezing reagents. This materiality mandates global logistics of blood storage. For example, conveying blood samples in vials requires cold-chain transport—something we have learned more about from logistics of transporting mRNA COVID-19 vaccines. Global logistics further indicate blood's excorporated existence as global commodity. Yet the vital medium's fragility ties it surely to its local site of production: blood is eminently a body fluid whose study must take into account individuated sites legible at the clinical scale.

When pursued beyond the individuated clinical scale, the social character of blood as a material-symbolic medium has dominated blood studies. Anthropological scholarship on blood dates back to Richard Titmuss's (1970) study of voluntary blood donation.[19] Recent books such as Janet Carsten's *Blood Work* and Jacob Copeman and Dwaipayan Banerjee's *Hematologies* track blood in the emergent relations between new biotechnologies and blood-collection practices. One of the few works that contextualizes blood in ecological perspective is Jairus Victor Grove's *Savage Ecology*; yet the book's main focus is on the global logistics of managing blood. Carsten's ethnography of laboratories is closest to my observation of blood processing in clinical medicine laboratories. But mine is not an ethnography of laboratories; it is a media analysis of the mediatic processes that detect signals in blood and compose them as frozen sample, data, and picture. There is also a range of scholarship on extractive markets and the legal impacts for alienable biological products (oocytes, blood, organs). Catherine Waldby and Robert Mitchell's *Tissue Economies* and Melinda Cooper and Catherine Waldby's *Clinical Labor* are exemplary instances of the genre. This literature on the markets, the law, and the politics of blood is important in establishing blood's controlled existence as excorporated substance. Social medicine scholarship such as Marsha Rosengarten's *HIV Interventions*, gauging the social impacts of HIV management (including blood tests), further informs my reading of blood processing as the clinical basis for therapeutic interventions.

In the context of these blood studies, blood's capture as a global commodity relies on the legibility of its multispecies distributions, as we know from the historical blood-donation bans. Global blood banks harvest plasma as an alienable resource, imposing stringent regulations controlling potential transmissions of pathogenic particles. The formidable apparatus for "securing" clean blood specimens, and surveilling them for infection, is a clear indicator of the vital medium's feared transitivity. Blood is always already under threat because the global commodity is inevitably a planetary multispecies milieu. The blood-donation panics of the HIV/AIDS pandemics exposed the impossibility of freedom from the extensive time-space of infection. If blood appeared as a *threatened* collective resource in the furor over contaminated blood banks, we live with that legacy even today. Blood-donation policies still constrain MSM from donating blood. In the early epidemic exigencies of COVID-19 panics, convalescent plasma became a valuable commodity as an antibody infusion for critically ill patients.[20] As television personality Andy Cohen noted on CNN, he was surprised to find the HIV/AIDS-era blood-donation ban was still on the books when he showed up to donate his plasma as a COVID-19 survivor; he was asked about his last date of sexual contact with another man.[21] No one intimated heterosexual contact conveyed HIV infection, even though decades of statistics have proved otherwise. Blood-donation bans intended to control blood exchanges between individual bodies arbitrate between interior milieus, sorting and segregating them into demographic groups. Canguilhem's mentee, Michel Foucault, would name such technological regulation of vital circulations *biosecurity*.[22] This well-charted history of blood-donation bans reveals the social governance of blood once multispecies distributions were molecularly intelligible. The patient-centered movements of the HIV/AIDS epidemics were critical to analyzing this social governance, exposing the desire for "clean blood" as not as objective as it might seem. Insisting on "parallel trials" for patients already on medication for AIDS-related conditions, AIDS activists made legible the costs of their exclusion from experimental treatments as a eugenic project.

The desire for clean and secure blood that haunts the global commodity points unerringly to the open spatiality of life. The body might emerge as enclosure, as the interior milieu epistemically cut for study, but environmental media studies attentive to molecular relationalities articulates this topological construct within overlapping ecosystems. What we understand as a specific milieu is an aesthetic composition that delimits the infinite open spatiality of life. The epistemic cut that locates blood as an interior milieu relies on human perceptions of *organismic difference* from the living milieu. But technical mediations complicate that boundary in divulging territories that we cannot touch or see—territories that extend well beyond the interior milieu.[23] Evidence of multispecies entanglements "in" our blood is but one slice of the greater recognition of the biological openness of living systems.

MILIEU AS MEDIA

Media studies provides conceptual frameworks for understanding how biotechnical milieus render blood intelligible. Processing blood for storage inevitably illuminates a human-animal-machinic perceptual complex engaged in these tasks. Basic immunology points to embodied perceptions unavailable to consciousness: the cognitive processes of macrophages enveloping, digesting, and then *presenting* fragments of the virus to the immune system as antigens, so that the immune system can *recognize* them and release a coordinated response. Media practices such as the viral load and hematic panel (including CD4 counts) tests compose accounts of these signal exchanges, disruptions, and failures. Media, as John Durham Peters observes, inscribe and transcribe some signals in the visual, auditory, verbal, numerical, and mechanical registers, but others remain imperceptible as noise.[24] Blood data and blood pictures are products of seeing, touching, and reading signals before their composition in the spatial forms of the interior milieu. As in the case of the -morphic image, the medial entanglements illuminate an infection environment that is *more than* comprehensible. In this chapter's stories, this medial entanglement is suggested by my characterization of blood as a *sensible* medium, one which embeds us in multispecies relationalities.

Contemporary media theorists provide rich accounts of machinic perceptions and their limits. In a refreshing reading of Uexküll's *Umwelt*, Inga Pollmann in *Cinematic Vitalism* emphasizes the productive machinic capture of vital media in considering Uexküll's romance with chronophotography. She argues that this media-technological practice provided a technical solution for a problem that haunted him: the inevitable anthropomorphizing of animal perception. As we know, Uexküll's milieu is a kind of soap bubble that carries a sensorily accessible perceptual world. He overcomes the problem of human understandings of animal perceptual processes, embedded in human psychology, only when he turns to a "third eye," argues Pollmann, that records the surface of the animal's behavior. The media practice of chronophotography affords a machinic eye stripped of human intention.[25] Like James Cahill, Pollmann pursues cinematic efforts to unthink anthropocentrism, forging continuities between analog and digital preoccupations with machinic capture. A tradition of cinematic vitalism is the upshot, one that builds on the entanglements of media apparatuses with lively materialities. A similar move is at work in my study of blood processing at clinical labs that render the vital medium sensible.[26] As blood becomes comprehensible as *x* particles in *y* milliliters of body fluid, strict procedures on the handling of blood indicate a sense of haptic

Plate 1. Viruses in Mexico's Cave of Crystals, screenshot from "Alien Worlds beneath Our Feet: Dr. Penelope Boston on Caves," 2014. Source: Boston, Lecture to Perimeter Institute of Theoretical Physics.

Plate 2 (*below*). Daniel Goldstein and John Kapellas, *Medicine Man* (detail), 2006. Life-size mixed-media sculpture. Credit: Daniel Goldstein and John Kapellas.

Plate 3 (*opposite*). Daniel Goldstein, *Medicine Man for South Africa*, 2009. Life-size mixed-media sculpture. Credit: Daniel Goldstein.

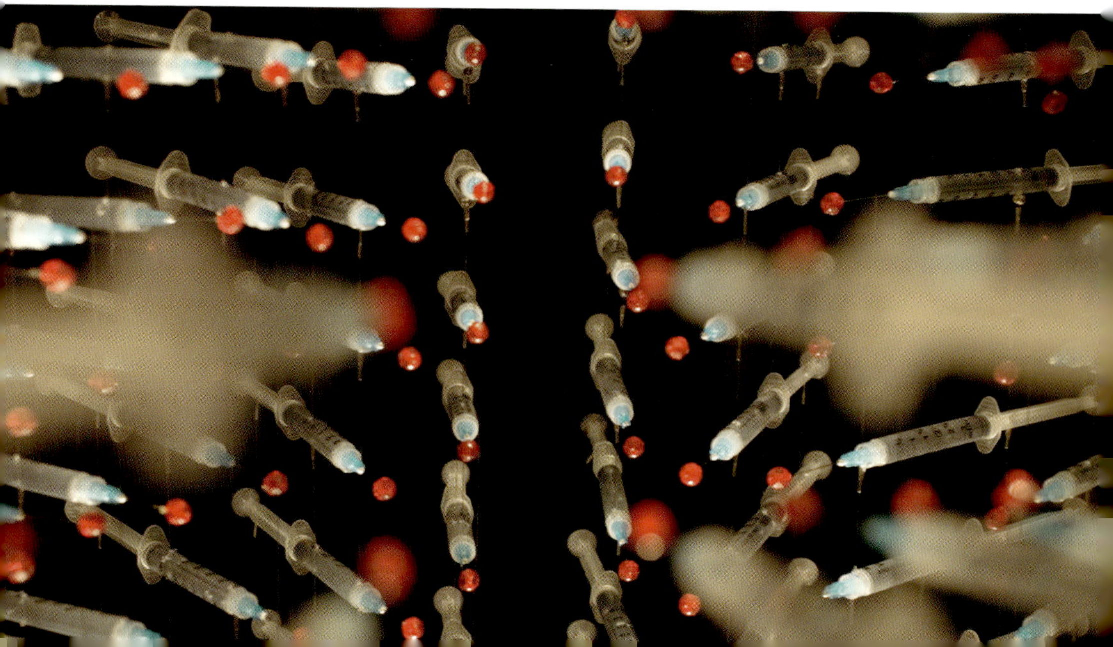

Lipoatrophy
Skin Rash
Fatigue
Neuropathy
Diarrhoea

Plates 4 (*above, top*), 5 (*above, bottom*), and 6 (*opposite*). Pato Hebert, all untitled, from the series *Lingering*, 2020–21. Archival pigment prints, 10 × 7.5 in. Credit: Pato Hebert.

Drug Facts
Peel
Active ingredient Purpose
Ethyl alcohol 62%..........Antiseptic
Uses ■ to decrease bacteria on the skin that could cause disease ■ recommended for repeated use
Warnings
For external use only-hands
Flammable, keep away from fire or flame
When using this product ■ keep out of eyes. In case of contact with eyes, flush thoroughly with water.
L0019096BA
*Effective at eliminating 99.99% of many common harmful germs and bacteria in as little as 15 seconds.
Distributed By: Vi-Jon • 8515 Page Ave • St. Louis, MO 63114
0 72785 13871 1

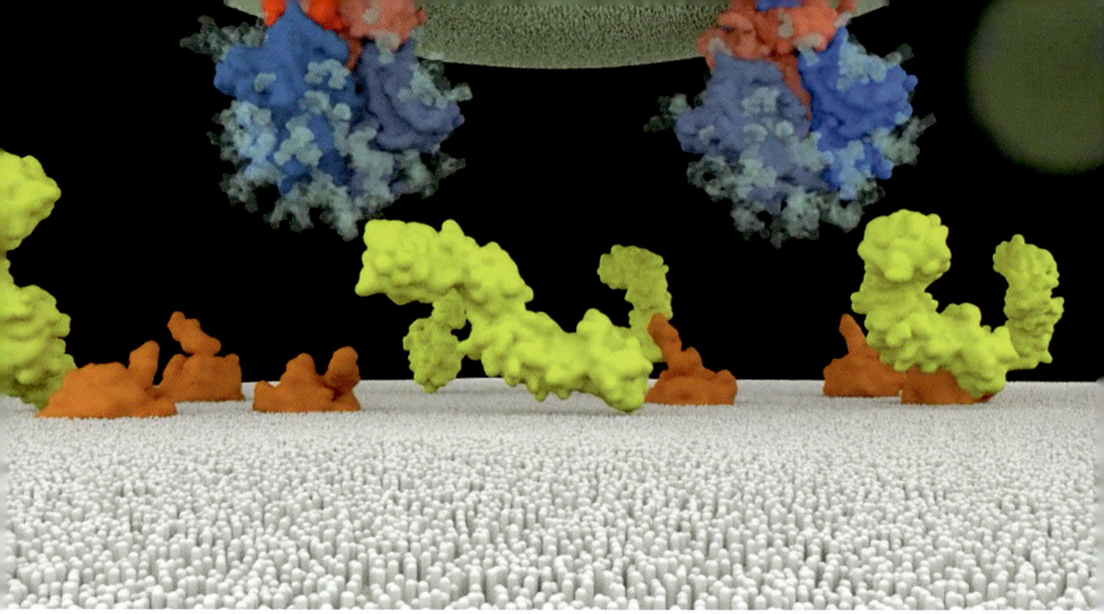

Plate 7 (*above*). Still from Janet Iwasa's protein-folding animation, 2018. Source: Iwasa, HIV *Life Cycle*.

Plate 8 (*opposite, top*). Still from Janet Iwasa's protein-folding animation, 2018. Source: Iwasa, HIV *Life Cycle*.

Plate 9 (*opposite, bottom*). *Messiah*, 1987/1990. Vintage PHSCologram, darkroom and computer interleaved Crosfield Cibachrome and Kodalith films, mounted on plexiglass, 96 × 60 in. Credit: Ellen Sandor and (art)n.

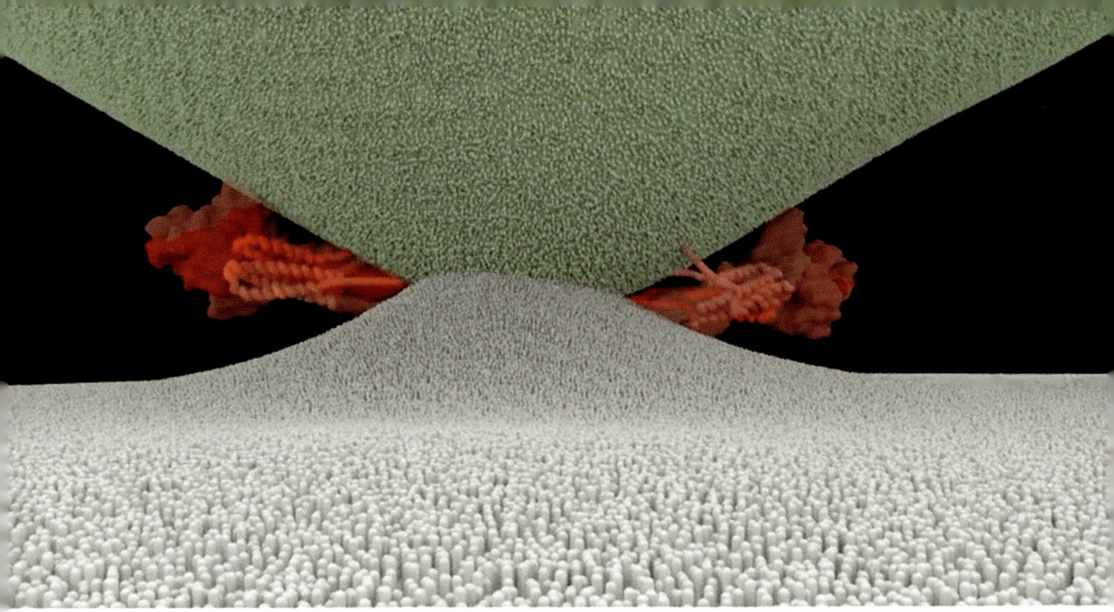

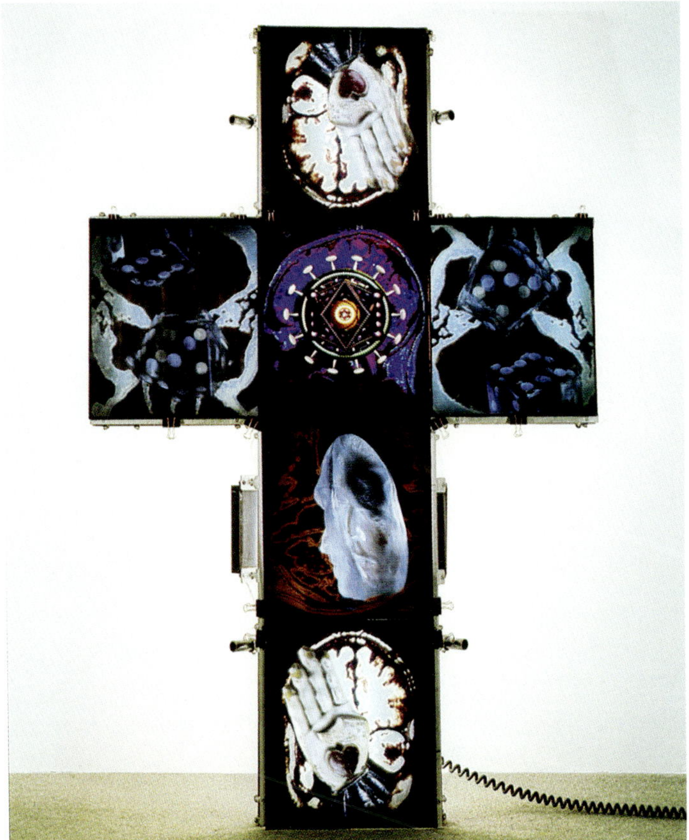

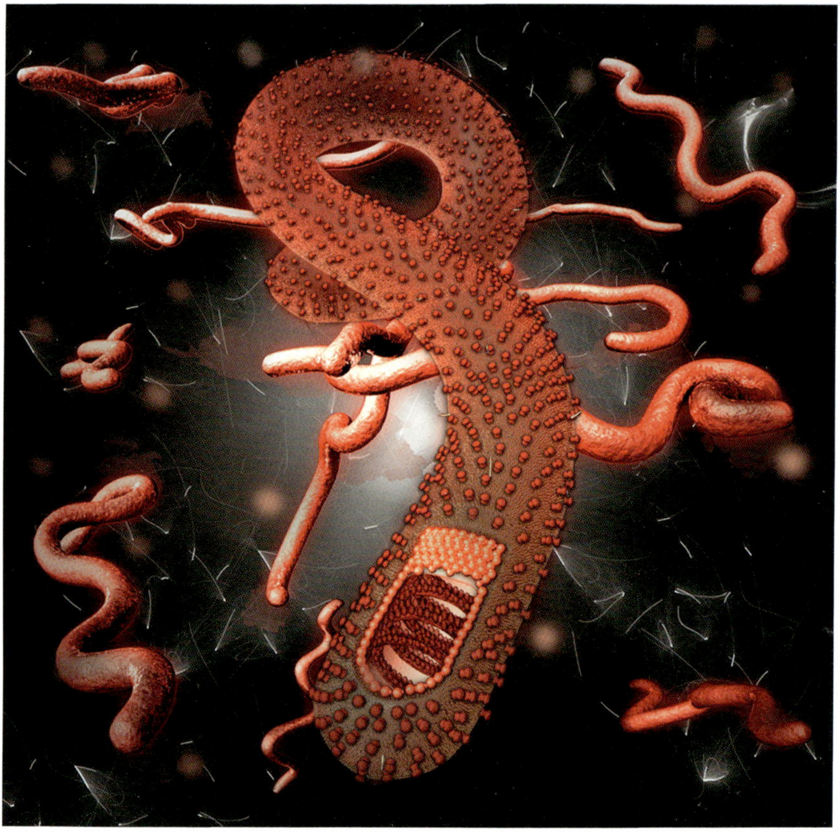

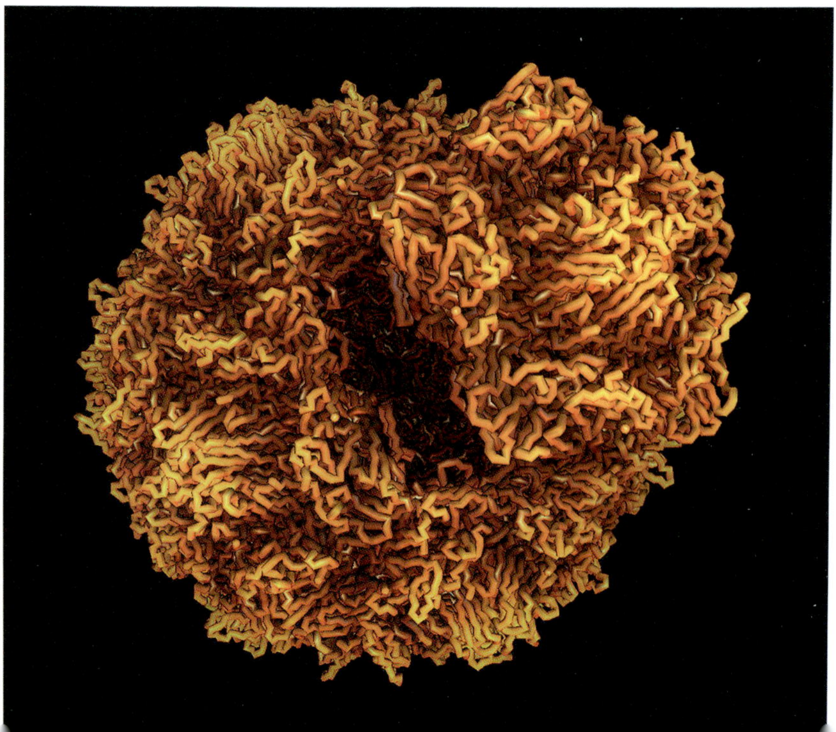

Plate 10 (*opposite, top*). *The Ebola Virus*, 2014. Virtual photo/PHSCologram. Duatrans, Kodalith, plexiglass, 30 × 30 in. Credit: Ellen Sandor and (art)n.

Plate 11 (*opposite, bottom*). *Nanoscape II, Viral Assembly*, 1999. Virtual photo/PHSCologram. Duatrans, Kodalith, plexiglass, 30 × 30 in. Credit: Ellen Sandor and (art)n.

Plate 12 (*above*). David Goodsell, *HIV in Blood Plasma*, 1999. Watercolor, 1,000,000× magnification. Source: Goodsell, https://ccsb.scripps.edu /goodsell/cellspace/.

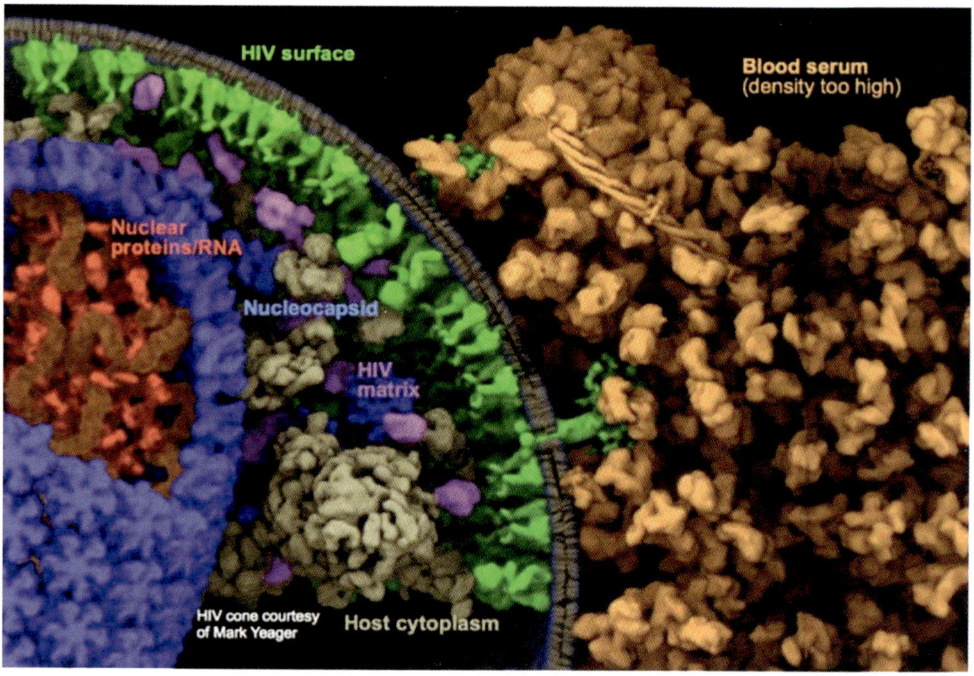
HIV surface
Blood serum
(density too high)
Nuclear
proteins/RNA
Nucleocapsid
HIV
matrix
HIV cone courtesy
of Mark Yeager
Host cytoplasm

Plate 13 (*opposite*). An HIV-in-blood-plasma model, 2015. Source: Johnson et al., “CellPACK,” figure 6a.

Plate 14 (*below*). CellPACK recipe illustrations, packing the HIV-1 mesh, 2014. Source: Johnson et al., “3D Molecular Models,” figure 2.

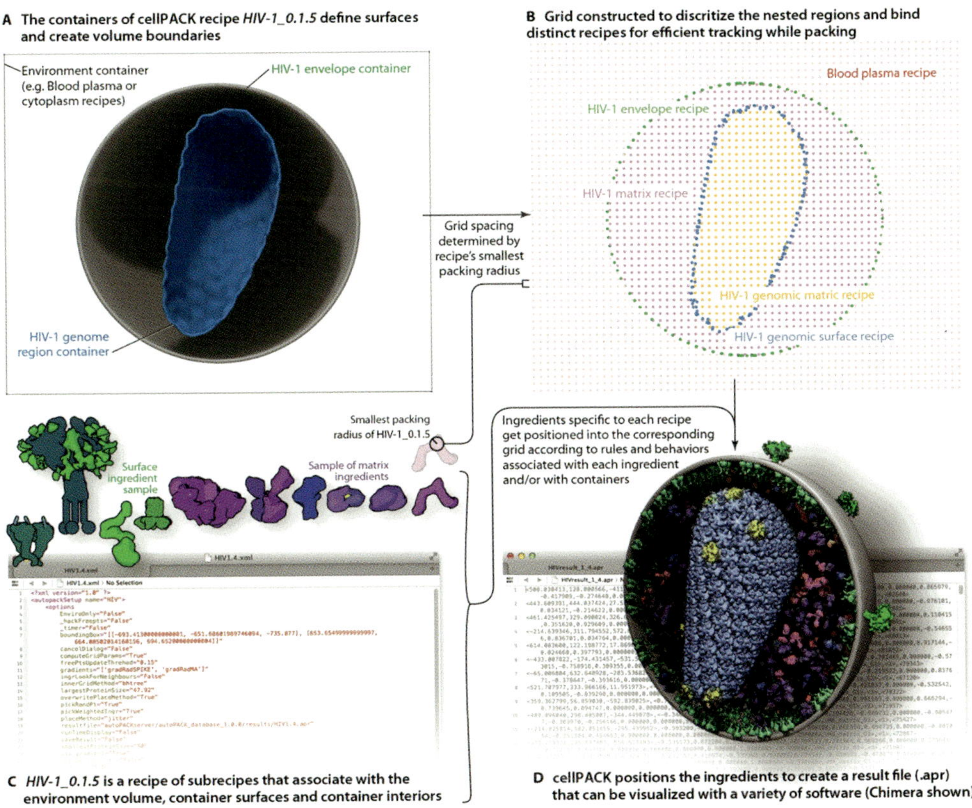

Plate 15 (*above*). Robert Sherer, *Sweet William*, 2004. HIV+ and HIV− blood on paper, 24 × 18 in. framed. Credit: Robert Sherer.

Plate 16 (*opposite, top*). Robert Sherer, *Love Nest*, 2005. HIV+ and HIV− blood on paper, 13 × 16 in. Credit: Robert Sherer.

Plate 17 (*opposite, bottom*). Blood resting after the first spin in a high-speed centrifuge. Source: Author photograph, 2017.

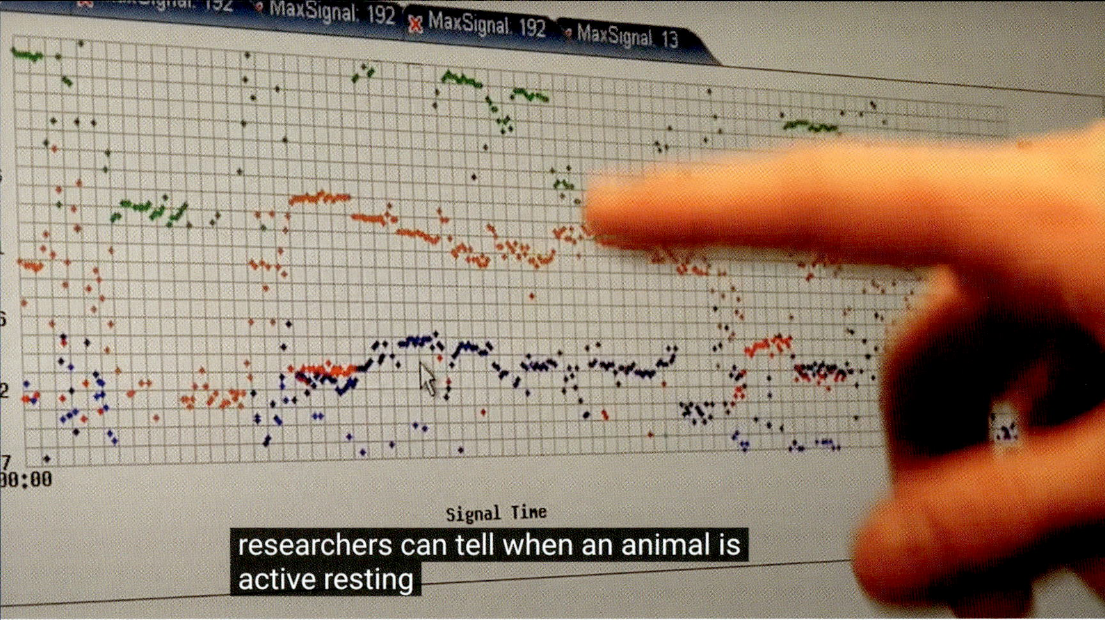
MaxSignal: 192
MaxSignal: 192
MaxSignal: 13
00:00
Signal Time
researchers can tell when an animal is
active resting

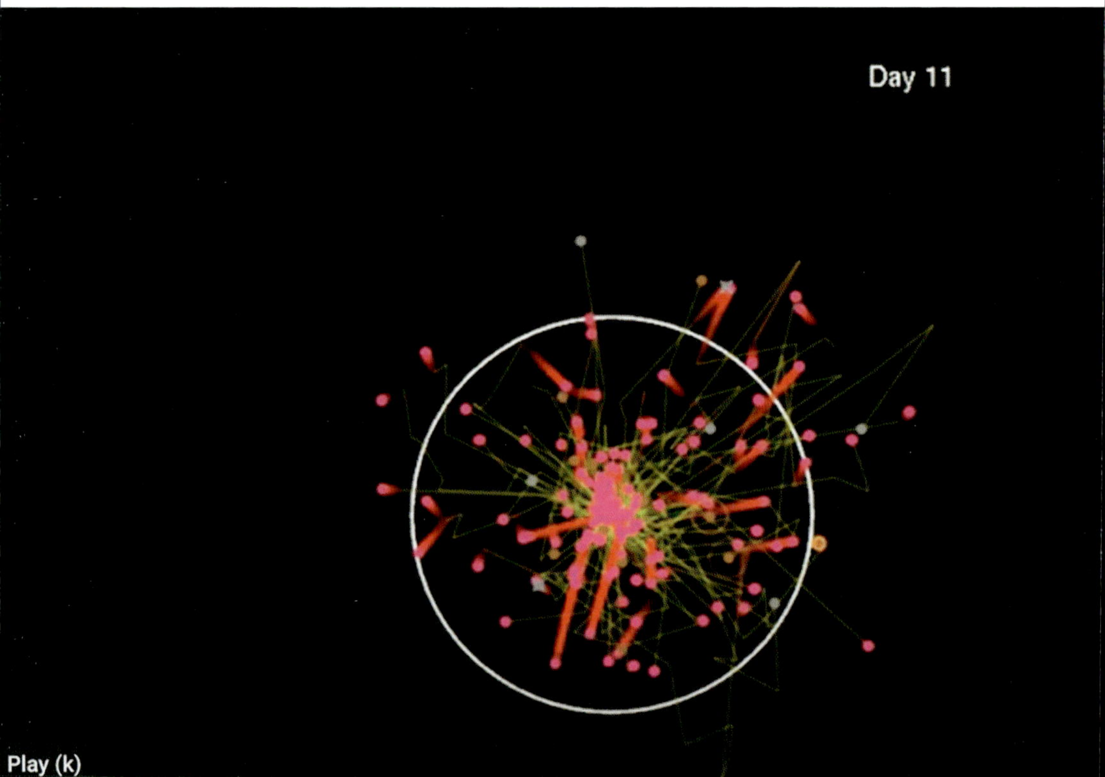
Day 11
Play (k)

Plate 18 (*opposite, top*). Radio-telemetry map, Barro Colorado Island, Panama, video still, 2010. Source: Smithsonian Tropical Research Institute, *Barro Colorado Island: BCI-Official Video*.

Plate 19 (*opposite, bottom*). *Seed Movement Fireworks* video still, 2012 (discussed by Jansen et al. in "Thieving Rodents as Substitute Dispersers of Megafaunal Seeds"). Source: *Seed Movement Fireworks*, https://www.youtube.com/watch?v=JebSa7d1e1M.

Plate 20 (*below*). Aerial canopy on Barro Colorado Island, Panama, video still, 2018. Source: North Carolina Museum of Natural Sciences, *Can Drones Help Count Rainforest Animals?*

Plate 21 (*bottom*). Filtering moving animals, screenshot, 2019. Source: Yousif et al., "Animal Scanner," figure 6.

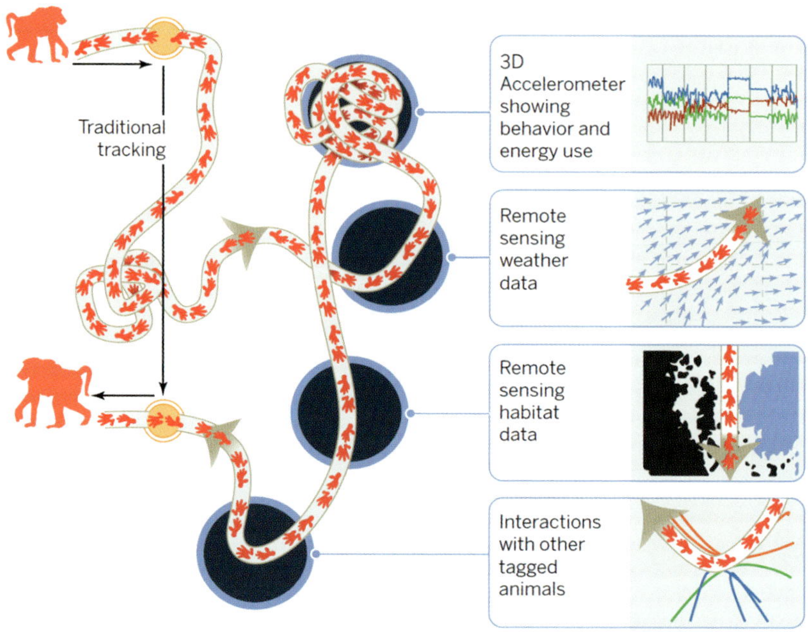

Plate 22. Big-data animal tracking, 2015. Source: Kays et al., "Terrestrial Animal Tracking," 1222.

danger. Even in the cool confines of the laboratory, blood engages the sensorium, exceeding its molecular intelligibility.

This sensible dimension is, for Jacques Rancière, intrinsic to all media. Reflecting on what a medium can mean, he argues that the medial substance (electronic, print, biological, or chemical) and the medium as neutral technical apparatus (the polymerase chain reaction [PCR] machine or the camera) often exist in tension.[27] To be sure, the machinic capture of imperceptible signals is automatic, nonhuman; as that capture objectifies blood as biological substance, it imposes an epistemic cut separating the vital medium from the disease milieu. The disease milieu persists as those undetectable multispecies relationalities that short-circuit any human-machinic mastery over lively materialities. Machinic apparatuses such as the centrifuge and the PCR platform that spin and probe biological substances work with known biological specificities, but they are also open to uncertainties. The major imperative is to craft an interior milieu on pragmatic grounds, and this composition is implicit in the protocols or study designs that accompany each blood specimen. But the vital medium continually signals what is partitioned away. Not all sensations—the glow of a probe, the cold of the freezer, the brightness of the sample—find record in the final composition of the blood sample, data, or picture. Those sensations make blood palpable beyond numerical or visual notation. Further, errors, redundancies, and noise index the material conditions of existence for blood: the condition of the infected body (marked as the specimen) and the implicit exchange of body fluids within the disease milieu. Noise, as Greg Siegel argues, remains an intrinsic part of decoding signals.[28] Amid epidemic intensities, *infected* blood gestures to the extensive time-space of infection, throwing the senses toward the radical openness of all living systems. Hence, despite winnowing blood down to clinical scale, the *sensible medium* alerts us to the inescapability of multispecies entanglements.

At the Lab: Blood Specimen to Blood Samples

The focus on the molecular basis of life that generally accompanied large-scale biomedicalization had a profound effect on the clinical management of HIV. Distributions of HIV particles in host blood had to be tracked over time to understand the efficacies of drug therapies and potential vaccines—the latter remains the holy grail in HIV/AIDS research. Laboratory medicine facilities nested within global biomedical infrastructures were key sites for processing and storing blood specimens for longitudinal studies. I understand infrastructures as technical systems that facilitate flows of signals, as Brian Larkin reminds us; their study involves looking at physical and cultural systems.[29] The laboratory medicine lab that I studied is one stop in a biomedical infrastructure that enables blood to circulate among laboratories, biorepositories, databases, and clinics. As parts of the global *biomedical* infrastructure, these locations take clinical health as a deliverable outcome.

I observed the translation of blood from its arrival as sample from HIV/AIDS clinics to its storage as frozen sample and blood datum at the University of Washington's Retrovirus Lab in 2017. One of the research cores of the CFAR that coordinates HIV/AIDS research, this lab composes blood samples into data in its articulation with the CFAR Network of Integrated Clinical Systems (CNICS); the latter aggregates blood data from eight HIV clinics and coordinates blood files for clinical research networks such as the AIDS Clinical Trials Group and the HVTN. The University of Washington's Madison and Roosevelt HIV/AIDS clinics supply blood samples for longitudinal studies, with patients enlisting to have thirty milliliters of blood drawn three times a year. Dr. Robert Coombs, who has been engaged in HIV/AIDS clinical medicine since 1985, heads the Retrovirus Lab, while his counterpart, Dr. Nina Kim, manages the University of Washington's HIV Info System (a CNICS core). The Retrovirus Lab is housed on an entire floor of the Harborview Research and Training Building, and its corridors are lined with massive refrigerators that store frozen blood specimens for future research. They comprise the refrigeration infrastructure for one of the CFAR biorepositories that archives frozen blood samples. This particular facility stores "plasma, serum, and PMBCs" from "clinically well-characterized HIV-infected patients," as the posters on the walls tell me.[30] The samples can be shipped to basic science laboratories upon request. The main aim of this biorepository is to assist researchers in translational medicine, a field focused on the connection between clinical study (tools, theories, methods) and its practical applications. As such, the Retrovirus Lab regulates knowledge transfers among laboratories, points of care, and clinical trials.

One of the main aims of the lab, embedded in a complex biomedical infrastructure, is to transform the vital medium into quality-controlled "biotechnical milieus," a descriptor not commonplace to this laboratory setting. The lab processes blood specimens arriving from clinics into data and freezes them as multiple samples. On a visit to the laboratory, a technician had drawn their blood so I could observe the daily cycle of blood processing; even as they were not entirely sure about the direction of my inquiry, they translated the scientific procedures and protocol with vigor. Throughout the day one benchmark came up repeatedly: the importance of quality control as the first order of business. Quality control of blood involves the proper preparation, detection, and composition of the blood samples, minimizing errors, redundancies, even indeterminacies, so that other laboratories can trust the data, and clinics can administer the best therapeutic options. The lab invests in state-of-the-art technologies and strictly adheres to standardized cross-network protocols and sample-processing techniques. Gradually, I came to realize that implicit in this mantra was a recognition of blood's lively materiality. The fact that a range of viral particles remained undetectable exposed the limits of machinic capture, while rigorous biosafety protocols for handling tangible media indexed haptic danger. But these preliminary observations—or, rather, my translations of the lab's craftwork—will become clearer with a closer look at the material construction of blood into biotechnical milieus. To this end, I focus on two mediatic processes, fractionation and quantification, that render blood readable: specifically, the centrifuge's physical and chemical differentiation of blood components, and RT-PCR (reverse transcription polymerase chain reaction) assays inscribing HIV RNA distributions and quantifying viral particles as a ratio per milliliter of blood.

Before I turn to these activities, however, let me situate quantification and fractionation within the story of what happens to blood specimens when they arrive at the lab. Even as the biosafety protocols recognize blood's characteristic transitivity, the blood specimens arrive in (what seemed to me rather ordinary-looking) iceboxes with a requisition form designating how the sample should be processed. Among other tags, the CFAR database provides blinded patient identifiers and specific protocol numbers for each sample. These details are locally retrieved from the Laboratory Data Management System (LDMS), which directs the division of individual specimens into multiple aliquots (small test tubes) and generates barcodes for them. Even at this stage we can see the gradual abstraction of the excorporated vital medium: the patient identifier anonymizes the multiple samples culled from one specimen even as the tie to one patient (including the location, place, and time of the draw) localizes the medium as an individuated interior milieu.

Anonymizing the patient's social history distills blood for clinical research so that the natural history of infection becomes the primary focus. Social history is reintroduced at a later point via the CNICS database for translational medicine applications to real-world settings. But at this first stage, classified under a "global ID," the samples fragment the original specimen and prepare it for different kinds of bioassays (PCR for viral fingerprints, Western blot for antibodies and antigens).[31] Each entry in the LDMS database comes with an enumerated protocol or a study design that defines the procedures for detection and composition: What information is sought from the sample? What are the precise settings for the media apparatuses? The design defines the form the blood sample will take. During my visit I watched the processing of blood samples based on the HVTN's protocol 704, which sought to study whether antibodies to HIV infection were induced by the vaccine for those who had signed up for the trial or whether they were induced by HIV infection. If the antibodies were "natural," detected as antigens (fragments of the virus), then the antibodies were infection induced. But if not, in the uninfected (previously identified in screening tests), the antibodies were vaccine induced—so the vaccine would have worked. This was just one protocol for the many shipments that the Retrovirus Lab receives from the HVTN per day: five shipments per day with fifty to four hundred specimens per shipment. Each specimen, as I have indicated, is then divided into multiple aliquots according to the protocol.

Fractionation divides and separates blood's components for later quantitative assessment. Typically, fractioned blood appears as a layered fluid, its components well demarcated by color and viscosity. Erythrocytes, or red blood cells laden with iron, are the heaviest components, so they sink to the bottom; the clear plasma floats to the top; in the middle lies a layer of leukocytes (white blood cells) and platelets known as the buffy coat. The process of fractionation commences with insertion into a centrifuge, a laboratory device that separates fluids, gases, or liquids based on density (figure 3.3). As the centrifuge spins the aliquots, the centrifugal force makes the denser particles migrate away from the axis while the lighter ones migrate toward the axis. All liquid is drained from the peripheral blood mononuclear cells (PBMCs), which form pellets for study; the PBMCs contain the valuable white blood cells (T-cells, B-cells, NK cells), some of which are under attack by HIV RNA particles. The protocol defines the speeds and number of spins necessary to prepare the sample; often, several spins are necessary to fractionate blood.

The Retrovirus Lab deploys a high-speed centrifuge that can handle larger volumes. After the first spin, I watched the aliquots at rest, settling and separating into varied hues—beige, off-white, deep red—glinting against the glass (plate 17). Washed and buffered with chemical reagents, the swirling blooms are eye-popping against the antiseptic confines of the biosafety cabinet. For me, the mediatic process was vividly aesthetic, replete with color bursts and gradients, with dense and light liquids, with seeping and separating globules. The technical procedures governing this area of the lab were rigorous: not only the donning of gowns and goggles but also the strict cleaning of surfaces. As it was repeatedly mixed with chemical agents, blood at the biosafety bench (figure 3.4) was always handled at arm's length with pipettes (droppers) and gloves. For it is not only the transitivity of blood but the toxicity of chemical agents that

Figure 3.3. High-speed centrifuge. Source: Author photograph, 2017.

Figure 3.4. The biosafety bench. Source: Author photograph, 2017.

can be harmful; they cannot be allowed to move beyond plastic and glass confines. One such chemical is a blue dye (trypan blue) that is added to the white blood cells that HIV infiltrates to check their viability. When the dye moves to the middle of dead cells, staining and demarcating them, it means HIV has exited these cells, leaving cellular havoc in its wake. My guide mixed chemical agents and reagents, diluting the sample, infusing a density gradient to further chemically separate blood components, and treating the blood with blue dye—all with the delicate care that painters adopt in mixing colors and pigments. I asked inquisitive questions about these treatments, about bovine serum or Ficoll-Paque (a sterile medium for separating lymphocytes), which are quite ordinary in this setting. Watching the dropper gently probe fractionated blood samples, I was intensely aware of blood as a tangible substance. Here blood was visual-haptic, activating the sensorium while we struggled for molecular intelligibility.

Spun, rested, washed with chemical reagents and dyes, blood appeared in biotechnical forms spatially composed as individuated frozen samples. Before freezing, we embarked on a manual count of each specimen (from which a sample was taken) to ensure its viability. Were there enough live PMBCs for storage? A small portion of the buffy coat layer was placed on a cytometer, or a slide with demarcated quadrants. Under the microscope viable cells were optically rendered and manually counted by toggling a lever on an accompanying meter (figure 3.5). The manual process felt something like the peripheral vision test at the optometrist. Looking into the microscope, I was deeply aware of my lack of technique as I struggled to make sense of what I was seeing while my guide patiently provided slow instruction. The manual count of live and dead cells established the degree of infection, and we entered the information on the requisition form. Here was a snapshot of infection as the biological substance transformed into its numerical form.

If color, depth, and viscosity accompanied the composition of blood in fractionation processes, such sensuous qualities were not readily available to the *human* sensorium in viral bioassays. Testing platforms apply light and heat; some are equipped with color cartridges to demarcate viral genomic bands in host DNA. But it is the machine that detects these signals and translates them algorithmically into numerical ranges of viral particles per milliliter of blood. The final composition is numerical data with the volumetric notation of blood implicit in the ratio. At the lab I watched several viral assays conducted on different platforms. The lab reverberated with the quiet hum of these machines; no one but a curious media researcher appeared preoccupied with the actual processes, when visible, within the machine. Once the settings were

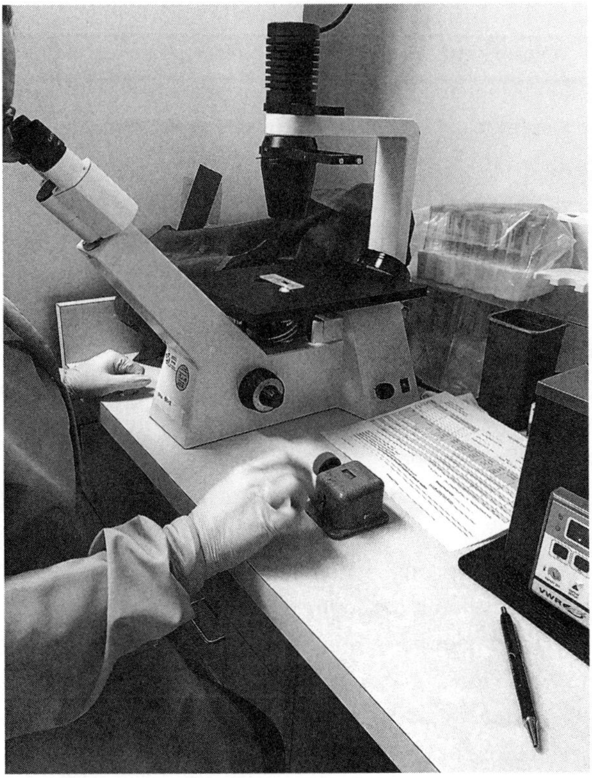

Figure 3.5. Microscope and cytometer. Source: Author photograph, 2017.

checked, typically machinic detection proceeded uninterrupted. Most captivating among the detection platforms was the Abbott M2000 machine, reputed for fine-grained and dependable detection of HIV RNA. As figure 3.6 shows, the aliquots are slotted into the trays in the foreground, while the screens in the background register the numerical transcriptions. The Abbott M2000 at the Retrovirus Lab machine runs a real-time RT-PCR assay to account for HIV-1 RNA. The PCR is a common laboratory technique that copies and amplifies a small segment of genetic material for clinical study. One of its applications is to detect viral genomic fingerprints by selectively amplifying viral genetic sequences and preparing them as epistemic objects; the point is to make larger samples for study. Viral RNA are first converted into double-stranded DNA (reverse transcription) when necessary (as in the case of SARS-CoV-2), and then "primers" or genetic sequences specific to the viral DNA are attached to the DNA strands slated for duplication; these strands are further marked by fluorescent dyes. With iterative COVID-19 testing, we often hear about the number of PCR cycles. These cycles (often twenty to thirty at least) create hundreds of

"DNA targets" for detection and further research. Once these targets are ready, the enumeration of viral copies per mL blood proceeds, yielding the viral load as a ratio. In these processes, blood emerges in the biotechnical forms, both as tangible media and as numeric representation, composed at individuated clinical scales.

In the quantification of viral RNA, the study design determines not only machine settings and cycles but also tangible media (quenchers, primers, and reagents). Wet processes including light emissions, and heat-induced DNA treatments accompany algorithmic transcription. For instance, the fluorescent probes that dye specific DNA targets emit light, while the linear exponential phase involves repeated thermal cycles for DNA amplification. These physical and chemical reactions folding into biological processes transmute blood into a *form of life*: a multispecies distribution emerges in the volumetric milieu of blood. Yet as we know from "limit of detection" (LoD) measures that not all viral particles are detectable.[32] The laboratory technique certified as Abbott Real-Time HIV-1 assay can detect 40 copies/mL within a 1.0 mL sample volume and the confidence interval for detecting HIV-1 concentration is 95 percent.[33] The Retrovirus Lab hopes to develop more sophisticated techniques that can count as few as seven to eight copies per milliliter of blood, drilling down to those HIV reservoirs from which infection can spike again. As we know, the successful elimination of the HIV reservoirs is touted as the cure, so this fine-grained detection is crucial to HIV eradication.[34] In this push for fuller inscription, the lively materiality of the vital medium exceeds its machinic capture.

These processes of mediation pick apart blood for its "value-bearing" agents that constitute the media environment of infection as an interior milieu. But this biotechnical form is always in rack focus: something from the edges, blood's leakiness, troubles the borders, exciting the clinical sensorium. Beyond the sensorium, the effort to drill down to the last viral particle further gestures toward an imperceptible agent hidden deep in the interior milieu. This species perspective is rare in these laboratory confines devoted to molecular intelligibility. And yet, at a few junctures, species difference crept into the clinical setting of the lab. My guide told me they had to process one blood specimen multiple times because of the astronomical viral load—they repeatedly thought it was an error. There was so much HIV-1 RNA, they noted, "It could have walked on its own!" In this offhand, humorous reference to "it" as uncontrollable and nonhuman, the species differences made a sudden appearance, the open spatiality of living systems haunting the individuated blood specimen. If the species scale returned somewhat inadvertently for the lab technician, for a media scholar it was semantically already present at the very start of the process: in the blood "specimen" (the example of a species) arriving via cold-chain transport.[35]

Figure 3.6. Abbott M2000 RT-PCR machine. Source: Author photograph, 2017.

In the shipping manifests accompanying the vials, the blood specimen was just a generic annotation, a discursively embedded reference preceding the making of molecular-scale epistemic objects. But, as Jacques Derrida once taught us, such traces expose what sets a epistemic orders in motion—in this case, a new multispecies relation that galvanizes the will to biosecurity.

Biorepositories and Databases: Blood Samples and Blood Data

Beyond clinical research, this floor of the Harborview building houses a CFAR biorepository. Here blood specimens are cryopreserved as blood samples and archived as blood data. Unlike depositories that preserve material accumulations, repositories are resting places: denatured blood is filed away until requisitioned for research. As the "selective [written] deposit of communicative acts," Vismann argues, the file remains open to *more* data accumulations in the future.[36] Unlike documents, which follow the logic of restricted circulation (the original must be distinguished from its copies), files proliferate and decay as their context changes. Their contents can be added to or discarded, trimmed or rearranged. This accurately describes what happens to blood at the biorepository. When retrieved for research, blood samples are used up; moreover, blood is divided into specific components (such as PBMCs) for preservation, much like materials are sorted, classified, and collated in print or digital files. The vital fragility of blood defines the parameters of sorting since blood components have different shelf lives: red blood cells, for instance, are viable in refrigerated form for only thirty-five days, so they must be cryopreserved and frozen between -80 and -140 degrees Celsius. The CFAR biorepository at the University of Washington preserves serum, plasma, and PBMCs at the requisite temperatures.[37] More generally, the technological infrastructure of refrigeration determines what can be stored and where: some famous repositories like the Centers for Disease Control and Prevention (Atlanta) and the State Research Center for Virology and Biotechnology (Novosibirsk), for example, intentionally archive (historical) viruses like *Variola* in various media, leading to conspiracy theories and conflicts over sovereignty over these biological substances.[38] As blood survives the patient, the CFAR biorepositories function as living archives dating back to the pre-ARV period. One can find early versions of HIV housed in blood samples from the late 1980s. There is a shadowy similarity to Robert Sherer's modest blood archive, even though the CFAR system *removes* personal indicators of in vivo labor from the biorepository's physical storage. Each frozen sample is a stilled anonymous biotechnical milieu stored in assemblages of aliquot and blood.

The physical infrastructure materializes in the large refrigerators lining the corridors, seven of which are liquid nitrogen freezers (at –140 degrees Celsius); thirteen others operate at –80 degrees Celsius (figure 3.7). Each refrigerator is nicknamed after a country; most workers at the lab simply shrugged when I asked them about this informal classification, indicating it was simply a matter of convenience. I surmised the national designations arose from an awareness of the core facility's nodal location in a global health infrastructure. That nodal character was repeatedly evident in the requisitions arriving from international networks (e.g., the HVTN). When blood samples are ready for cryopreservation, the HIV Algorithm Workflow System, linked to the LDMS database, designates where the sample should be filed. Each refrigerator carries a map with the box numbers, much like an old-fashioned card filing cabinet (figures 3.8 and 3.9). As the aliquots are placed in their compartments, the fluid medium freezes into a solid state. Removed from its site of origination, from the interior milieu of the blood specimen, the frozen blood samples appear as fragmented contents—raw materials for clinical research on therapeutic efficacies.[39]

In the CNICS database, the composition of the digital blood file returns geospatial, demographic, and diagnostic information to the anonymized blood

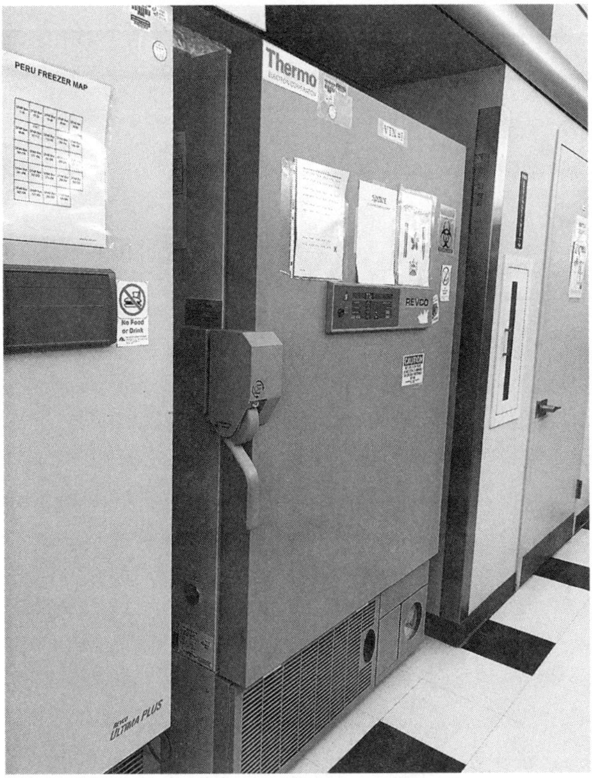

Figure 3.7. Biorepository refrigerators. Source: Author photograph, 2017.

specimen. A vast biomedical infrastructure connects the molecular compositions of blood specimens to longitudinal patient data, both individual and aggregative: the digital blood files collate, tag, and annotate the blood compositions. Studies focus on HIV cohorts whose blood profiles are read for indications of changing multispecies distributions.[40] Researchers can access data on patient-reported outcomes, ARV resistance, and vital status, among other elements, reinserting lab-based blood compositions back into specific disease milieus and biological pasts. Unlike open-access online services for basic science (such as the Protein Data Bank), CNICS data are protected because they articulate with electronic medical records.[41] There are rigorous access protocols, software firewalls, secured file transfers, and daily backups. All proposals for the use of the database and specimen biorepository holdings are closely vetted to assess how the data will be used and shared. Since I was a media scholar, I did not have direct access to the databases, but I culled my reading of their operations through a series of interviews.

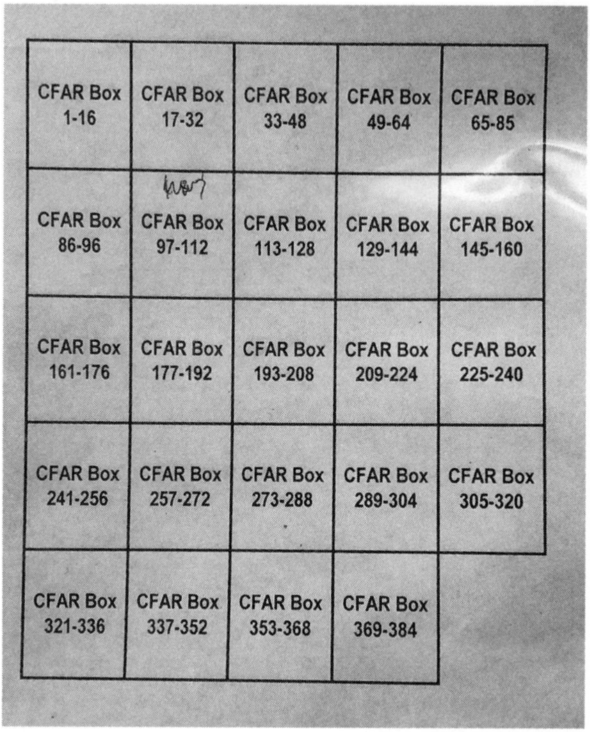

Figure 3.8. Sample file map. Source: Author photograph, 2017.

Figure 3.9. Freezer boxes. Source: Author photograph, 2017.

One of my interviewees was Dr. Nina Kim, who is based at the Madison HIV Clinic, the largest HIV/AIDS clinic in the Pacific Northwest. "Dr. Coombs and I," she told me, "tie researchers to patients and samples," confirming the nodal operations of the CFAR-CNICS pairing at the University of Washington.[42] The University of Washington's HIV Information System administers the database, as the researchers take "data custodianship" of patient records, "cleaning" and "protecting" data. Real-world information is codified and unlinked from personal situations. For example, the ICD-10 codes (from the International Statistical Classification of Diseases and Related Health Problems, approved by the World Health Organization [WHO]) standardize and code diagnoses—everything from clinical symptoms to social habits. A researcher studying drug efficacies for patients with heroin dependence, for instance, comes to CNICS to identify cohorts and access longitudinal studies. The researcher can access frozen samples from the biorepository and pull the various "time points" for each record. These operations provide a dual sense of the medium: blood is a localized interior milieu (specific to the "patient") *and* an aggregate (part of a cohort) in a particular demographic setting. The social disease milieu shadows the interior milieu as blood is reincorporated into real-world situations. Dr. Kim researches liver disease progression in people living with HIV (PLHIV) as a comorbidity for HIV infection. Such comorbidities and coinfections are specific to well-demarcated disease milieus: for instance, in Cape Town, clinical research on HIV is inevitably tied to tuberculosis coinfection, so each blood draw records HIV RNA distributions alongside that of the tuberculosis bacterium. In vivo complexities return in individual patient bodies, social aggregates, and localized disease milieus. Clinical notes accompany blood compositions (notes on the results of the Mantoux test for tuberculosis, for example) and become a part of the digital health record. Molecules, as Andrew Barry once noted, come to "embody their environments."[43] No longer isolated in molecular compositions, they are reembedded in social and ecological relations.

At the CNICS database interface, lively flux is managed in "cleaning" data. When I asked Dr. Kim about informal data such as patient logs and diaries, she noted that there was new research in natural language processing that would allow free-form texts (including data from questionnaires) to enter the record. The point of clean data is not to undermine patient perceptions of illness or health. Rather, it incisively tags, annotates, and classifies information for efficient retrieval in current clinical research. One of the advantages of CNICS databases is that they enable research in close to real-time analyses. In this regard, these databases retain the inherently dynamic capacities of files. As Wolfgang Ernst notes in *Digital Memory and the Archive*, digital archives that compress storage and transmission manifest dynamic material agencies.[44] Researchers can access, and sometimes annotate or tag, signals as they appear on-screen; access and update happen almost simultaneously. CNICS facilitates real-time research in mounting relational database management systems with efficacious, domain-specific languages (such as SQL, or Structured Query Language) for writing and interpreting, flexible text formats for reading and accessing (using XML, or Extensible Markup Language), and Java technologies for developing dynamic web content.

The database is regulated not just for scientific research but for community impacts. Blood compositions collected in the blood files, aggregated as populations, and controlled for multiple variables are the baseline for practical applications in real-world settings: How will heroin users adapt to new PrEP medications? What parameters of tuberculosis coinfection impact HIV vaccine dosages? Such research and development relies on public participation in clinical trials, and that participation is ideally protected by rigorous protocols. While at the Retrovirus Lab, I inquired about failed protocols and their social impacts. The HVTN protocol 505, I was told, met with early termination because the vaccine actually increased rather than decreased HIV infection in patient cohorts. In this story the social interface of community advisory boards that regulate drug and vaccine trials made a brief appearance amid the hum of machines and the data deluge. Both the AIDS Clinical Trials Group and the HVTN (clinical trial networks) impose fairly rigorous regulations on the reincorporation of blood data back into specific patient bodies. Community advisory boards are control points; in part, they function as watchdog groups. But they also assess the impact of social factors such as housing, food security, and sanitation on health. The fragility of blood becomes perceptible in the in vivo labor of living with HIV, with coinfections, and sometimes with precarious means that impact health. These real-world settings are the extensive media environments of infection: they are the disease milieus of altered lives that topologically stretch the interior milieu into an open spatiality.

The CNICS database interfaces with specific disease milieus and aggregated patient cohorts, opening into points of care where blood becomes individuated blood pictures. Before I turn to the clinics, however, it is important to note that the transit of blood from laboratories to real-world settings had a checkered history in the period known as early AIDS. Patient activism placed demands on the regulation of clinical trials by the US federal Food and Drug Administration (FDA); that activism galvanized funding for HIV/AIDS research. Within this well-documented history, blood's vital fragility—T-cells threatened, blasted, and destroyed—became sensible, entering the public sensorium. The FDA's

1988 move to allow patients already experimenting with drugs to participate in clinical trials (the Phase 0 trials of 1989) made blood pictures accessible during clinical trials. One could check results *before the completion* of the designed trials (the traditional Phase 1); research designs could be changed midway; experimental techniques were allowable; and decisions could be made on microdoses of the drug molecule under investigation before undergoing intensive screening for all possible results.[45] In other words, the Phase 0 trials tuned into a viral emergence that could not be entirely anticipated. Importantly, the Phase 0 trials made way for "dirty data" (as Jim Eigo notes in his ACT UP Oral History Project interviews) informally compiled in logs, diaries, and medical charts, all of which suddenly acquired technical value.[46] This history left an indelible impact on communal interfaces within the biomedical infrastructure. By now we are accustomed to alliances among scientists and clinicians, policy makers and representatives of governments, social scientists and health-industry workers, patient groups and journalists. But what remains historically significant is "the construction of lay expertise," as Steven Epstein named it, that won treatment activists a place at the table. Histories of AIDS health movements show how activists mastered biomedical knowledge practices so as to gain credibility with the scientific community: blood data translated as blood pictures underwrote an emergent "mesoscale" technical literacy.[47] Health became a deliverable public good to be exchanged in negotiations between medical institutions and HIV-affected communities. Once activists were on the committees of the National Institutes of Health and on FDA regulatory boards, treatment-activist revisions to biomedical knowledge and practice filtered upstream. Such a history points toward the clinic and beyond—to the street and neighborhood, home and hospice—where controlled blood data morph into blood pictures open to the radical uncertainties of managed HIV.

With COVID-19, it seems as if the entire world is preoccupied once more with the targeted management of infection's environments—with respiratory mucous, with breath, with particulates in air. Against this backdrop, the story of how blood became a *public sensorium* in the HIV/AIDS epidemics is instructive. On the one hand, in resource-rich settings, as HIV infection became a privately lived chronic infection, blood became accessible in biotechnical forms because of self-testing viral load kits streaming blood data or patients receiving viral counts within a day on their mobile devices. For self-quantifying, self-regulating consumer-patients, viral particles blooming in blood are an ordinary affair. This has much to do with biomedicine as a commercial enterprise, which includes brisk markets for personalized biosensors, connectivity infrastructures, and data-storage facilities.[48] In self-quant communities, the ideal patient is an ideal consumer.[49] On the other hand, a very different history unfolded beyond Europe, North America, and Australia before the South African struggle for HIV treatment access in the 2000s made the provision of therapeutics a global affair. Vinh Nguyen's *Republic of Therapy* provides an overview of the period immediately following the mass manufacture of ARVs after their FDA approval in 1995. The therapeutic citizenship born of the fight over clinical trials in North America and Europe became a worldwide phenomenon as drug trials moved elsewhere. With Merck's controversial 1997 "028" study in Brazil and fierce debates over nevirapine in Uganda, the colonial sphere would reconfigure globalized HIV treatment and care, with wide-ranging implications.

In South Africa, ART participation was tempered both as democratic entitlement and as a form of coercive discipline, no doubt because of the role that biometric registration played in colonial and, later, apartheid administrations. In their multidisciplinary ethnographic studies of blood surveillance among youth in the Eastern Cape, researchers at the AIDS and Society Research Unit at the University of Cape Town noted how patients approached state welfare provisions through bureaucratic instruments such as "passports"—a small exercise book with handwritten medical data that they brought to clinical visits.[50] In constantly updating these passports, patients became their own health-care archivists who could shape what nurses would "see" in their blood. In such logs and entries, blood inhabits the disease milieu even as it emerges as individual blood pictures. At informal points of care, the sensible medium discloses an interior milieu; at the same time, disturbances, periodic or unexpected, in the larger disease milieu determine these compositions. Nutrition and hygiene, employment and housing, coinfections and vital statistics, all complicate an exclusive focus on viral particle enumeration. The precarities of everyday life surfacing in a fragile vital medium become central to the biomedical enterprise of managed HIV.

At the Clinic I: Blood Pictures

On a sultry August afternoon in 2016, I entered the Humsafar Trust (HST) offices in Mumbai to meet representatives of Sanjeevani (meaning "Life Saver"). As India's largest nongovernmental organization promoting LGBTQ+ rights, HST has had counseling and health-care advocacy as part of its portfolio since 1994.[51] Sanjeevani is a community-based support unit for PLHIV that articulates with HST, the Mumbai District AIDS Control Society, and the federal NACO (National AIDS Control Organization). Sanjeevani was formed in March 2003 to serve MSM and TG communities, linking PLHIV to ten ART

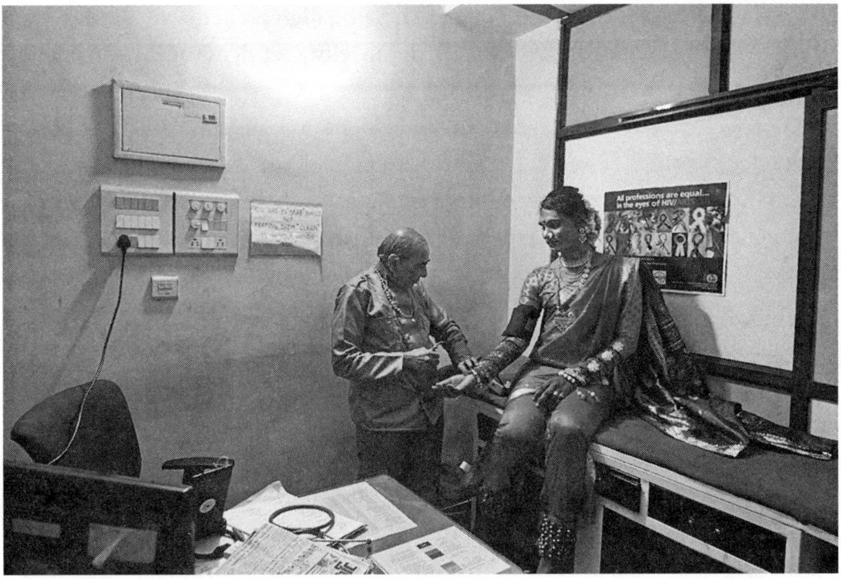

Figure 3.10. HIV clinic at Humsafar Trust, Mumbai, India, 2019. Credit: Photograph by Satyabrata Tripathi. Courtesy Getty Images.

centers. With access to the HST office facilities, Sanjeevani maintains records, keeps track of registered PLHIV, and follows up with referrals and health visits.[52] I met the Sanjeevani "team," which included a HIV/AIDS counselor and the self-disclosed HIV/AIDS activist Urmi Jadhav; the latter had just returned from the Durban AIDS conference of 2016.[53] I was keenly aware of my position as a researcher from the Global North in their interactions with me. A third interviewee whose medical records were stored at the offices displayed their file so I could better understand the particularities of the storage system. This interviewee identified as a member of the "key population," a standardized category in global epidemic risk surveillance, and indicated they were there as a personal advocate for the efficacies of Sanjeevani's community-based epidemic interventions. They drew my attention to the fact that it was HST's social credit in the wider MSM and TG communities that made them one of the success stories for HIV management. Despite the rhetoric of global biomedical development—the "team," the "partnership," and the "key population"—the range of Sanjeevani's burden in this resource-limited setting became increasingly clear as the interview proceeded. At present, HST has ramped up its integrated HIV health-care services: there are smart cards (blue for those with monthly incomes above Rs. 15,000/$67 and green for those below), a new ART Center (established in 2019), digital client-tracking systems (Avegen), and expanded mental health counseling services (figure 3.10 is at the new ART Center).

When I visited the HST offices in the Lower Parel neighborhood of Mumbai back in 2017, one accessed the facility through a large shopping complex with a thriving bazaar on the ground floor. A walk up the narrow stairway put me at the entrance of a few large rooms that constituted the HST work and social space. Past the foyer, several people were hanging out in a large lounge with couches and posters, chairs and tables; one passed through this social space to reach air-conditioned offices packed with computers, storage cabinets, and cubicles, and winged by a small conference room. As I entered the conference room, I eyed the file cabinets for what they might store. Where do those files originate? What kinds of data find their way into them? How do those blood data become legible to PLHIV registered with Sanjeevani?

In 2016 Sanjeevani supported over 300–350 PLHIV in Mumbai; in this regard, it served a local demographic in India's HIV/AIDS epidemic.[54] Sanjeevani facilitators handled the registration and temporal records of individuals under their care, and streamlined testing and treatments for HIV coinfections at several hospitals.[55] Interfacing with global nongovernmental organizations such as MSF for second- and third-line ARV and multidrug resistance (MDR) treatments, Sanjeevani focused on ARV adherence and therein the maintenance of viral thresholds. As such, it participated (and continues to do so) in India's Veehan, a "loss to follow" program that followed up with patients who have fallen off their meds, and in national health-care surveys of new and chronic infection. "Loss to follow" is a worldwide biomedical agenda mobilized in partnerships with the WHO, MSF, UNAIDS, and other global public health institutions working in the global AIDS field.[56] As those agencies infused sudden concentrations of resources into conditions of scarcity, mobilizations around HIV/AIDS social stigma mushroomed into energetic organizing around nonnormative sexualities, notes Gowri Vijayakumar, including the insistent social demand for better medical and legal dispensations.[57]

In all these ways, small-scale as it was, and eminently localized, Sanjeevani exemplified community-based points of care that locally implement global biomedical enterprises. Within those enterprises, such outfits are typically considered nodes of implementation that follow policies made elsewhere. Sanjeevani activists attend the world AIDS meetings and deploy nomenclature such as "key populations" or "loss to follow," indexing streamlined global biomedical knowledge practices. In line with other worldwide creative experiments in ensuring adherence, Sanjeevani hosts a litany of social programs for those who seek counsel there: it provides unhindered access to treatment and care, especially for those who cannot afford long waits to fill monthly prescriptions; nutritional advice based on dietary needs, medical histories, and economic constraints; yoga classes; and counseling on sexual practices and mental health.

As such, this multipronged organization exemplifies all the ways in which community-based organizations address the social materiality of a specific disease milieu along with their global (MSF, in this instance) and national (NACO, for India) interfaces within biomedical infrastructures. In conducting research on blood files, I visited several points of care in India, but I selected Sanjeevani because of its location in a bustling global urban center, a classic topography for infection concentrations; its localized constituency; and its trade in social trust. Most of these particulars sharply contrast with points of care such as the Madison HIV Clinic that have direct relationships with biomedical research networks; despite the differences, the efficacious management of blood is possible at the Madison Clinic in Seattle because it, too, has significant social credit with HIV-infected communities in the local area.

Sanjeevani facilitated the collection of blood specimens for laboratory processing, while the HST premises offered physical facilities for storing medical files. At the time of my visit, each PLHIV had a file in the form of a ruled exercise book that was populated with blood data from tests every six months. Standardized numerical data, date of draw, time, and place ensured clinical chronology; these were complemented by informal notes on missed visits, new coinfections, and other vital statistics. The informal notes embedded the numerical blood composition within the patient's disease milieu and life circumstances. In such notations a *blood picture* emerges, translating technical notations of infection fluctuations into a local grammar inclusive of everything from urban conditions (neighborhood changes, transportation routes, medical facilities) to historical experiences (weather events, political disruptions). The classificatory system for these blood files registers the somewhat precarious circumstances of the Sanjeevani "friends," as they are called. Since strong social stigma prevents the friends from keeping records at home, their medical files are stored at the HST offices and filed under the friend's mother's name. The nomenclature protects against disclosure: only the Sanjeevani friends can request the files once they give counselors the name as password. Many friends are socially vulnerable because they are LGBTQ+ or because they cannot divulge their serostatus at home: 83 percent of those on ART at Sanjeevani were MSM, and 17 percent were TG in 2016. Sanjeevani counselors enable the friends to navigate anger, frustration, grief, and sometimes suicidal ideation.

The moniker "friends" indicates Sanjeevani's physical and virtual spaces as safe spaces that engender the social trust necessary for successful chronic blood surveillance. The blood pictures in the medical record reflect the biological-social character of blood, as the Sanjeevani counselors translate the technicities of blood data for individual friends. The fact that TG and MSM patients *return* for periodic blood tests already indicates the depth of Sanjeevani's social credit; a recent assessment in 2020 put ART retention rates at 85 percent.[58] As with other such community-based points of care, Sanjeevani hosts a monthly social hour to coordinate testing and drug distributions; around twenty to thirty friends show up for each session. During the interview Urmi Jadhav made the point clear in their experience of a hospital visit *with* the HIV/AIDS counselor. In their joint recollection, it was clear not only that the counselor took slights to Jhadav personally but that Jhadav also found strength in the counselor's witness to the hospital's phobic response to their needs. Of course, such affection is possible because of the small scale of operations, but it is also the case that Sanjeevani's community investments are strengthened by their embedding in HST. In other words, the blood pictures trade on established social credit that imparts therapeutic value to this biomedical enterprise. In this case, as in others, we see why global institutions such as MSF necessarily partner with local grassroots organizations for the implementation of HIV treatment and care.

The blood files in Urmi Jadhav's story make evident a "particular entity that is taking shape while recording its own actions," as Vismann notes of files.[59] Tracing files from Roman times (when the file was an administrative dispatch) to Prussian state archives (when it was domiciled as "evidence" of governance) to modern state bureaucracies (when it governed the modern individual's relations with particular state or corporate entity), Vismann's media history underscores the role these storage technologies play in mediating relationships between individuals and states, corporations and bureaucracies. The constantly updated blood files at Sanjeevani mediate MSM and TG patients' relations with national and global biomedical infrastructures. The major communications infrastructure is mobile telephony (individual calls, texts, WhatsApp groups), as is the case in many parts of India.[60] The Sanjeevani counselors not only monitor and schedule periodic blood tests but also accompany the friends to test sites and bring along the medical file. When doctors access the file, the friends often encounter the administrative power of state-run medical institutions and their deep-seated homophobia. In the interview Urmi Jadhav repeatedly expressed deep anger at phobic state hospitals that, in a moral and punitive mode, delay treating the HIV+ socially vulnerable; their anger indicated the growing *social demand* for state medical care. In this sense, the file that initially structures one's encounter with an indifferent state bureaucracy motivates participation in the form of a push for more effective state dispensations.

The more precarious the circumstances, the higher the therapeutic value of lay experts like the Sanjeevani HIV/AIDS counselors. Uncertainties arising from changing residences, shifting work schedules, and overbooked outpatient clinics are major impediments to maintaining the kind of chronological medical file necessary for the sequential tracking of infection intervals. It is up to the Sanjeevani health counselors to store blood in legible compositions, to mark the periods and reasons for discontinuities, and to find appropriate solutions or workarounds. Under resource constraints, the Sanjeevani blood archive is haunted by impermanence: when friends disappear for long periods, the counselor can make the call to discard the file. Such disappearances are not surprising as the socially vulnerable migrate, fall off from ART regimes (despite free drugs financed by NACO), or fall into acute infection and coinfection. The materiality of the disease milieu continually determines the vitality of blood: the interior milieu is always already structured by the constraints of its disease milieu.

Around thirty-two to forty-five PLHIV become nonadherent, falling off their meds for one to three months at a time, so monitoring adherence is a key agenda.[61] The reasons for nonadherence can range from losing a job to "feeling healthy" again. It falls on the counselors to underscore the importance of monitoring blood. They must routinely make blood readable in blood pictures so that *staying undetectable* does not signify *regaining health*. Health remains a horizon: a changing molecular distribution of viral matter in blood that must be monitored. For these numerical data to become common knowledge necessitates clinical translations reliant on local expertise, including linguistic translations (between English and Hindi and Marathi, minimally) and creative narrations of biomedical data. Lay experts ameliorate what Akhil Gupta has called the burden of "restricted literacies"—in this case, of the local PLHIV constituency.[62] In evolving mesoscale literacies, patients become lay experts and counselors, and some begin to act as ambassadors for the local organization. In their pitch for medical self-governance, Urmi Jadhav is an exemplary modern practitioner moving between their roles as an activist-expert and a leader of a community-based organization. They attend AIDS conferences to listen in for new therapies, models of clinical care, and coinfection treatments. Within Mumbai they are recognizable as a representative of TG rights (presiding over the Kinnari Kastoori organization for the transgender community) and as an artiste in a local dance troupe (the Dancing Queens). It is not the city's blood exchanges but the management of blood that is the subject of their lectures; not containment but adherence as gritty altered life is the mantra. They see their public presence as intrinsic to "staying undetectable" as a collective enterprise. In all these ways, mesoscale experts inhabit life otherwise.

The blood files at the Sanjeevani clinic are baggy and heterogeneous because they contain all the information relevant to maintaining chronic surveillance. The files crosshatch personal reports with marginal notes and tables of blood data. The counselors struggle to reconcile singular patient needs with the macroimperatives of viral load tests. They note down weather conditions, nutritional changes, and water scarcities. Unlike CNICS data mining that aggregates social and economic data, here, there is a singularity to each medical profile: there is a pragmatic reassertion of the interior milieu that incorporates the disease milieu. The therapeutic value of these baggy blood pictures can hardly be underestimated as patients, doctors, and counselors negotiate ongoing changes in blood. The blood files come to be capacious technologies that accumulate and organize change while remaining open to dynamic lively materialities. Such capaciousness is not new in the annals of medical history.[63] As Annemarie Mol notes, illness/disease is a series of "material events" in which fragments of the body—the one the doctor sees, the one in the blood picture, the one popping pills, the one that loves—hang together as the "body multiple."[64] This body multiple surfaces and resurfaces in the blood file even as routine blood surveillance plots and streamlines life as chronological unfolding. Such a body emergent *in blood* and *with therapies* performs the altered life of ARV adherence.[65]

At the Clinic II: Blood Files

Following excorporated blood lights up a two-way street. In one direction, there is translational biomedical research necessary for clinical trials on new ARVs or HIV vaccines; in the other, there are clinics as points of care where blood is collected and processed, adherence monitored, and coinfections managed through chronic blood tests. Since the emphasis often falls on technologies and expert techniques, the creative labor of the lab, its exemplary blood processing, acquires greater value than the clinical labor of the donor. This accretion of surplus value around scientific research is a predictable story. For the HIV/AIDS pandemic, a biomedical triumphalism attributes "managed HIV" primarily to the pharmacological solution of ARVs and sidelines the clinical in vivo labor of staying undetectable. But when one tracks the circulation of blood within the well-oiled biomedical infrastructure, dynamic multispecies relations begin to surface, as does the distributed collective experiment that is managed HIV.

The last story of this chapter, from South Africa, illuminates this distributed experiment. Both the Sanjeevani clinic in India and the HIV adherence clubs in South Africa function as "string figures," to recall Donna Haraway's phrase, in the global public health story.[66] They tell stories *about* the global stories of HIV/AIDS. To vivify these places is to unravel a knowledge economy that reinforces managed HIV as a biomedical milestone and not a protracted collective endeavor. Yet the success of managed HIV in South Africa, as elsewhere, lies in the effective partnering of PLHIV and global health organizations that distribute health care at the grassroots. The following story concerns the HIV adherence clubs that first emerged in the sprawling partially informal township of Khayelitsha, bordering Cape Town. These "HIV ART Clubs," as they came to be known, have become scalable as global models under MSF to prevent virological rebound from noncompliance with ART regimes (the "loss to follow" problem). The local clubs exemplify other informal community-based models of health care—the many food pantries and clean-needle exchanges, the home-based care and hospices of the HIV/AIDS pandemic. I close with one woman's story to trace the success of managed HIV from the tiniest variable in the global public health infrastructure.

In 2017, I visited Khayelitsha's MSF Site B Community Health Clinic in search of Fanelwa Gwashu, the health activist/educator who started the first HIV ART Club in 2007. Diagnosed with HIV in 2004, she had been a client at Khayelitsha's Ubuntu Clinic, started by MSF in 2001.[67] At the time, she was out of work and living at Site B. Gwashu's lively participation in the HIV support groups made her a natural choice as a community educator for self-directed therapeutic ART compliance, which both the Treatment Action Campaign and MSF saw as a crucial frontier. The pilot HIV ART Club was launched in 2007 as an effort to stop "loss to follow" in drug regimens, considered the root of virological rebound. The point was to distribute ARVs after the 2004 rollout across demographic variables, keeping abreast of comorbidities and a migratory labor force that returned to the resource-poor Eastern Cape during the summer months. Gwashu recalled the excitement of the first venture: the response of ninety patients who signed up for the first club made the pilot both stimulating and overwhelming. With support from the Western Cape Department of Health and the Treatment Action Campaign, MSF organized thirteen clubs by 2009–10. It would take years to reach the ideal capacity of fifteen to thirty patients per club, meeting at community venues or at homes (when transportation or housework made travel difficult) at regulated intervals.[68] When the HIV ART Clubs were on a sure footing, Gwashu began to work in one of MSF's mobile clinics to widen the reach of clinical care (figure 3.11).

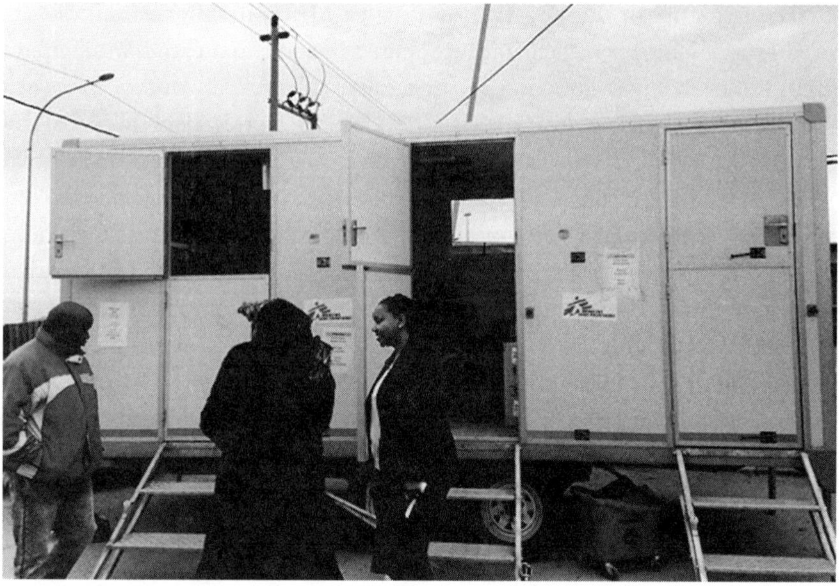

Figure 3.11. Mobile clinic, Site B, Khayelitsha, Cape Town, South Africa. Source: Author photograph, 2017.

Each registered HIV ART Club had a manager, a facilitator/educator, a data gatherer, a nurse, and a pharmacist (see registry entry in figure 3.12). The attendees were clinically screened for admission: patients with tuberculosis, for instance, could not attend a large social gathering. This meant that the blood tests for everyone included a sputum check. Those who had lower-than-detectable viral load distributions for a year and had been on the same ART for six months were the "stable" patients targeted in this model of long-term retention. Each patient was annually scripted for two visits—routine check-ins, clinical checkups, or blood tests (see figure 3.13, second column)—and brought a "Patient Treatment Card" with them as a chronological record (figure 3.14). At the social hour, patients found buddies, picked up their prepackaged ART, and did their "bloods" at periodic intervals.

In the print epidemic media of Khayelitsha's HIV ART Clubs, life emerges in its temporal distribution, an interior milieu sequenced in serial snapshots. The HIV ART Club registries mark the social temporalities of labor, travel time, and age. Anna Grimsrud of the MSF noted that the clubs are differentiated along demographic aggregates, some targeting young adults (ages fifteen to twenty-five), and others migrant laborers, addressing the known variables.[69] Life appears composed as biological events in these epidemic media that aim

Club:.......................... Club manager:..........................

Sticker	Phone Number Private (PVT) or Shared (S)	Drug Regimen		Standard Session (Month 0)	Standard Session (Month 2)
Club date				10/02/2010	11/04/2010
Place Patient sticker here, Or write Folder number First Name, Last Name Gender, Date of Birth	Write patient's cell phone number	ART drugs	Weight (W)	Weight or outcome	Weight or outcome
	Write "PVT" or "S"	Date of ART Start	Symptoms (S)	N or RTC	N or RTC
200005436 Bizikaia Tolominta Female, 02/05/1977	078145628	D4T, 3TC, EFV	W	75	67
	PVT	24/10/2005	S	N	RTC

Figure 3.12. Antiretroviral therapy club register sample entry. Source: MSF, Khayelitsha, Cape Town, South Africa, 2017. Author photograph.

Visit no.	Type of club visit	Activities	Script
Month -1		Recruitment + clinician scripting for 3 months	1 month supplied by pharmacy
Month 0	Enrolment visit	Scripting for 6 months	1 x 2m pre-packed
Month 2	Routine visit		1 x 2m pre-packed
Month 4	Blood visit	Bloods taken	2 x 2m pre-packed
Month 6	Clinical visit	Clinical consultation + Re-scripting for 6 months	3 x 2m pre-packed
Month 8	Routine visit		1 x 2m pre-packed
Month 10	Routine visit		2 x 2m pre-packed
Month 12	Re-scripting visit	Re-scripting for 6 months	3 x 2m pre-packed

Figure 3.13. Antiretroviral therapy scripts for individual patients. Source: MSF, Khayelitsha, Cape Town, South Africa, 2017. Author photograph.

to regulate its fluctuations by sequencing periodic tests. Life simultaneously appears in its multivalent socialities, since the HIV ART Clubs attempt to modulate "HIV lifeways" for individual persons and social groups.[70] Their success depends on scaling down to the particularities of each disease milieu. By 2014, MSF reported a success of 62 percent retention rate on ART for 2.4 million in South Africa, just four years after the rollout of the HIV ART Clubs. The heterogeneous venues for the HIV ART Clubs—allowing members to save time and money on transport and to share milieu-specific know-how—and the buddy system contributed to the success rate, so much so that the HIV ART Clubs were recognized as one pillar of decentralized ART delivery models in the WHO/UNAIDS Treatment 2.0 initiative.[71] This model of differentiated care of the Treatment 2.0 initiative—one size does not fit all—attends to the

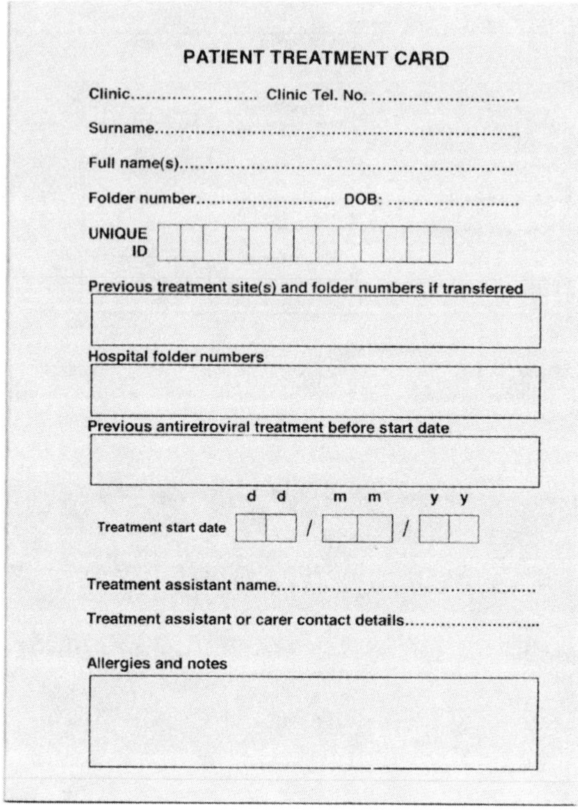

PATIENT TREATMENT CARD

Clinic........................ Clinic Tel. No. ....

Surname..

Full name(s)..

Folder number........................... DOB: ....

UNIQUE ID

Previous treatment site(s) and folder numbers if transferred

Hospital folder numbers

Previous antiretroviral treatment before start date

Treatment start date d d / m m / y y

Treatment assistant name..

Treatment assistant or carer contact details..........................

Allergies and notes

Figure 3.14. Antiretroviral therapy patient card. Source: MSF, Khayelitsha, Cape Town, South Africa, 2017. Author photograph.

"problem of multiplicities" (to recall Foucault) that persists in demographic aggregates.[72] Singular differentials are reconstituted as variables, which include everything from comorbidities (such as tuberculosis, hypertension, and diabetes) to housing, labor patterns, sanitation, and calorie intakes. At the adherence clubs, the variables scale down to address thirty individual cases documented in treatment cards, registries, and clinical files. The MSF literature recounts an in-clinic innovation that reduced going in for clinical care to specific days and limited hours, and which subsequently evolved into a scalable community-based program.[73] As the model scales up, Gwashu disappears from view as one of the designers of the scalable model, becoming a historical trace. If my attempt to trace the blood specimen in its unfolding as blood sample, blood datum, and blood picture *re-members* points of transfer and exchange in the global success story of managed HIV, Gwashu flashes up at the interstices.

Tracking blood articulates laboratories, biorepositories, databases, and clinics with each other, as I have done in this chapter, illuminating the different biotechnical forms of this vital medium. At each material site, biological and technological processes of mediation compose the interior milieu and its "value-bearing" contents as epistemic objects. The institutional sites within the biomedical chain of operations are discrete and invested in quality-controlled compositions of biological targets: I have tracked the privileging of some biological products (the denatured blood sample, the clean blood data) over others (the heterogeneous blood picture, the baggy blood file) in massive global biomedical infrastructures. Tuning in to blood's global circulation, however, relativizes this value production, exposing the seams of an underlying bioeconomy that attempts to govern living with HIV.

Coda: Media Leaking

Blood as a media environment has appeared in this chapter in three biotechnical spatial forms: as blood sample, blood datum, and blood picture. Mediatic processes ensure blood's excorporation as well as its technical-aesthetic composition as an interior milieu. During epidemics the three biotechnical forms of the interior milieu acquire immanent value for controlling and regulating infection. Looking closely at making/enacting/doing these epidemic media at discrete sites of clinical translation yields only a strong sense of how vital media extend beyond the molar boundaries of individuated bodies, transmuting and carrying viral particles in their transit within host populations. Nested fractal milieus centrifugally gesture to multispecies relations; they emplace us not only in disease milieus as extensive time-spaces of infection but also in the planetary hot spots of cross-species transmission. Thus, biotechnical milieus that make the vital media molecularly intelligible as interior milieus *also* open into sense perceptions of that *other space* of multispecies entanglements. This extension of a vital medium underscores the open spatiality of "the body" that is the epistemic ground of clinical intervention. It turns out blood is not simply a body fluid but a planetary-scale living system.

In the HIV story, blood occupies center stage in "falling into health," as Canguilhem once put it.[74] But more generally, one cannot think of surviving epidemics without genomic fingerprints or serological tests; in this regard, the story of blood extends to other vital media such as fecal matter (as we see in the next chapter) or saliva (at our current juncture). The only difference is that none of these other media have blood's stature as a global commodity. My discussion of mediatic processes in four locations—the laboratory, the biorepository, the database, and the clinic—demonstrates how vital media tagged as individuated specimens become biological targets of detection, of therapy, of future research.

The processes of mediation that seek blood's machinic capture constantly encounter lively materialities, leading, once again, to a push for everything from media technological innovation to better health-care dispensations. Amid these struggles, blood as an epidemic medium continues to trouble human-machinic efforts to make it entirely legible or entirely clean. Errors, redundancies, and excesses vibrate as noise, sometimes throwing a spanner in the works: samples become unusable; botched protocols raise alarms. The noise discloses mediation as prehension, as a grasping, a sensing, an intuiting of process-relational ontologies. As Sherer's portraits intimate, the sensible medium activates a sensuous multispecies entanglement.

We move inexorably toward cross-species transmission in the next chapter. But in this chapter the story of public health recounts socioeconomic challenges in composing infection's risk environments during global health emergencies. The colonial sphere of long-term harms is in full view, while the biosphere exerts spectral force in recessed multispecies talk. As blood processing renders vital states intelligible, health appears in its uneven distributions across the world. To stay with troubling differences names the desire for life otherwise as the remaking of a global health commons for pandemics now and those to come.

FOUR

THE MULTISPECIES KINESTHETIC

Tracking Animal Host Movement

A 1949 photograph of two Australian farmers surveying dead rabbits neatly strung between sturdy posts (figure 4.1) narrates one of the most famous episodes in the settler colonial anthropogenic engineering of the wilds. The story begins in 1859, when a settler, Thomas Austin, introduced twenty-four rabbits into his estates in Australia. The climate proved so favorable that within a year Austin counted more than thirty thousand. By the 1880s a billion rabbits were destroying crops and stripping farmers of stock feed. The unprecedented rabbit invasion led Louis Pasteur to dispatch his nephew, Adrien Loir, to carry out an experiment in ecological engineering: injecting a few rabbits with chicken cholera bacteria (*Pasteurella multocida*). The 1887 experiment was a failure as the bacterial plague killing not only the rabbits that ate the tainted food but also

Figure 4.1. Two men standing beside rabbit carcasses, Australia, 1949. Source: State Library of Victoria Pictures Collection.

the Australian birds.[1] By the close of the nineteenth century, a deadlier bioweapon against rabbits appeared on the horizon. Scientists in Uruguay discovered the myxoma virus, a new pathogen that killed laboratory rabbits. In 1950, myxomatosis, carried by mosquitoes, was introduced to rabbits in Australia. A huge "success," as one reading goes, the virus killed 99 percent of the rabbit population.[2] But within seven years, the rabbits developed immune resistance to the virus. As rabbit and virus coevolved into a biological partnership of opportunistic tolerance, the death rates fell below 70 percent. This struggle to artificially control rabbit populations "in nature" exemplified the difficulty of translating laboratory experiments in pathogenesis into wild ecosystems and of anticipating coevolving relations between animals and once pathogenic microbes. The Australian rabbit plagues would captivate those microbiologists who eschewed delimiting the study of disease emergence to the biological sciences alone.[3] Disease emergence came to be understood as novel multispecies relationalities whose nonlinear causalities ranged from genetic mutation to climate change to global transportation infrastructures.

The rabbit plagues inspired French-born American microbiologist, experimental pathologist, and philanthropist René Dubos to argue for a greater comprehension of nature not as an idyllic utopia but as an unseen world of permanent struggle. Animals and parasitic microbes were not engaged in deadly struggle but sought instead to reach "opportunistic tolerance."[4] The idea was not new. One could date thinking about human and animal health together to physician, pathologist, and anthropologist Rudolf Virchow, who coined the term *zoonoses* in 1855 to identify diseases that jump from animals to humans (e.g., distemper in dogs can cause measles in humans). In *Mirage of Health* (1959), Dubos elaborated a notion of emergence that would come to stay. While the confines of the laboratory lent certainty to disease etiologies, this experimental approach, Dubos argued, failed to account for the "conditions prevailing in the natural world" that play a part in the causation of disease.[5] Those conditions could be external or internal to organisms: from weather conditions to food scarcities, from working habits to emotional stress. Emergence as a "constellation of circumstances," as Dubos put it, scuttled the linear causality between a specific pathogen and a specific disease.[6] Pasteur's failed experiment with chicken cholera was a case in point. Among the many histories of disease emergence, Dubos recounts the disastrous 1845 potato blight in Ireland. Meteorological conditions—a chilling rain—led to the putrefaction of plants so that *Phytophthora infestans*, a fungus present in the potato plant since its introduction from Central America, could multiply.[7] The potato as a new source of food had led to an increase in the Irish population; with the introduction of the crop, the population doubled from 3.5 million in 1700 to 8 million in 1840. Famously, the "potato famine" arising from the blight galvanized susceptibility to tuberculosis; the rest is history, as they say, as the tuberculosis epidemic proved to be one of the motors of mass Irish emigration to America. The tuberculosis outbreak in mid-nineteenth-century Ireland, then, cannot be understood only in terms of a new mutation of *Mycobacterium tuberculosis*, as a biological change in the interaction between microbe and human, but rather as a multitemporal event whose causes were many, not the least of which was, in Dubos's story, an unprecedented change in the relation between fungus and potato. Microbial mutations arose not *only* as genetic changes but also as upheavals in entire coevolving ecologies. Written in the mid-twentieth century, *Mirage of Health* launched scathing criticism of the post–World War II strategic vision of a war on germs that could be won by mass biomedical intervention. Instead, Dubos offered a counterphilosophy of permanent struggle, calling for *preemptive resistance* to disease as a science. As the century wore on, disease emergence as multispecies relationalities continued to inspire calls to war against a singular enemy; we still hear the war cry pitching SARS-CoV-2 as "our" deadly foe. Central to Dubos's ecological reorientation was the anticipatory imperative of locating *potential* emerging infectious disease (EID) events before they exploded into extensive community transmissions.

Tracking zoonotic spillovers at organism-environment interfaces, the epidemic exigency explored in this chapter follows the anticipatory logic of preemption. The literature on the biosecurity measures of vital-systems preparedness has established this connection substantially.[8] But rethinking ecological health to understand EID events in the current epidemic episteme has moved well beyond the doctrines of warlike preparedness. Ecological health takes aim at the anthropogenic drivers of emergent multispecies relations such as deforestation, pasture expansion, extractive mining, wildlife trading, and industrial farming that can activate zoonotic spillovers. These are anthropogenic transformations wrought in the colonial sphere fueled by industrial capitalism. This chapter pursues epidemic media that detect and compose animal movement patterns in the wild, the "living laboratories" of the earth, to locate and identify the time-spaces of potential spillovers. As we shall see, the literature on zoonotic spillovers attributes them to novel interfaces between wild animal hosts and human populations, sometimes through intermediate hosts. Deforestation may fragment animal habitats, for example, changing patterns of feeding, birthing, and migrating; prospecting for natural resources might generate new animal-mineral-human assemblies; or wild animals in captivity with waning immune systems might carry novel viruses into new species populations. A group of curators of the interactive online *Feral Atlas* configure these time-spaces as the "patchy ecologies" of the more-than-human Anthropocene.[9] As anthropogenic change *drives* cascading effects, often ecologically threatening or deleterious, novel multispecies relations emerge as the "non-designed consequences of imperial and industrial infrastructure."[10] I return to the *Feral Atlas* toward the close of the chapter, but my point here is that locating potential zoonotic spillovers *materializes* "zones of virulence" where new multispecies associations "shape how viruses evolve, infect, recombine, and sometimes go pandemic."[11] Focusing on "zones of virulence" obviates the singling out of evolutionary phylogenetic data as the key to zoonotic spillovers, therein undercutting the depoliticization of agencies in the global hotspots for EID events.

The story in this chapter concerns virus-host coemergence as *viral transmissions* between animal hosts or "individuals," as they are called in species taxa. The implicit centering of species taxa immediately raises thorny questions, for crafting species difference conceived along a classificatory logic similar to racial taxonomies imposes an impossible organismic purity.[12] Stefan Helmreich notes organismic difference is especially difficult for microbial integrities, as we know from histories of their coevolution and rhizomatic assemblies.[13] This implosion of organismic difference is implicit in the very constitution of *animal hosts as multispecies*; as lively media for the transport of microbes, they are always already *not* one species. But they are configured as such—as isolable "animal hosts" moving in "their environments." This immanent figuration materializes in tracking and sensing biotechnical kinesthesia. Since viruses do not have locomotion, since they ride *in* their animal hosts, the ecological story of viral transmission is sensible in changing relations between individuals and populations in feral ecologies. One point of entry into this complex story is to track animal movement: as animal forms traverse space, they materialize their environments. These environments are subsequently composed as biogeographic regions, some of which are identified as global hotspots of EID events. This chapter analyzes processes of technical mediation that differentiate specific animal hosts from their environments (swaying grasses, leafy vibrations, diverse animal forms) and aesthetically recompose them as organism-environment assemblages in spatial forms of planetary habitation (maps and atlases). These mediatic processes ultimately produce the "multispecies kinesthetic" as the basis of controlling EID events. As in the two previous chapters, my inquiry conjugates two distinct but overlapping fields: multispecies ethnography and environmental media studies.

Movement can be understood as viral emergence in media such as air and water, blood and feces. Vital transmissions are legible only in their media-technological inscriptions, as we have seen with the PCR (polymerase chain reaction) assays for identifying genomic fingerprints in the previous chapter. In this chapter transmission indexes two movements: vital transmissions of viral particles (detected in genetic sequences) *and* animal host movements (detected as machinic signals, from electrical to electromagnetic). As motion sense, kinesthesia attunes us to this double valence of transmission. The *multispecies kinesthetic* gestures toward transmission as viral infection within and between species, accessed through animal movement patterns. Disease transmission becomes intelligible as the spatial distribution of life on earth: that is, how and where animals move, interact, and form new assemblies in the patchy ecologies of the more-than-human Anthropocene. The multispecies kinesthetic deploys geospatial technologies (radio collars, camera traps, and thermal sensors) and cultural techniques (walking the transect to object segmentation) in order to track changing animal movement patterns. These machinic signals find articulation in "organism-machine-environment" assemblages, as Jennifer Gabrys notes, even as machinic intervention, in the name of mechanical objectivity, erases itself in the organism-environment form as epistemic object.[14] In animal movement patterns, then tracking biotechnical kinesthesia as media-technological practice yields organism-environment assemblages as objects of study; subsequently located in specific biogeographies, these assemblages are encoded with phylogenetic, ecological, and geographic data from geographic information systems (GIS). The upshot is the multispecies kinesthetic.

The bulk of the chapter explores two efforts to track animal movements that illuminate the ecological orientation toward disease emergence. The projects under scrutiny are not directly organized around viral emergence, but this is exactly the point about emergence as a nonlinear multitemporal event irreducible to specific factors; rather, viral appearances, mutations, and jumps are provisionally projected into the past (as we shall see with the HIV story) or into the future (the coming pandemic). The tracking experiments that I explore are biodiversity research: they plot animal movement patterns as the story of changing habitats whose drivers are anthropogenic. Both tracking projects are inextricable from extant histories of cross-species transmission; the animal hosts they track are some of the prime reservoirs of pathogenic viruses. These are nonhuman primates (NHPs) in central Africa and in western Amazonia, the biogeographic centers of primate diversity. (Since the NHPs in these projects range in tropical rain forests, I mostly use the colloquial moniker *wild primates* rather than this technical term.) In these areas 49 percent of wild primates are threatened by either direct exploitation or habitat fragmentation; 25 percent of zoonotic spillovers are ascribed to these animal hosts. Old World (African) wild primates—specifically, our closest relatives, chimpanzees—are widely recognized as host reservoirs for HIV-1 (group M). We shall see what the HIV "origin story" reveals about the significance of multispecies traffic to disease emergence. In contrast, New World wild primates—specifically, howler monkeys—are sentinel populations for the yellow fever virus (of the genus *Flavivirus*).[15] Drawing attention to mosquitoes as disease vectors, as I have argued elsewhere, the early twentieth-century yellow fever outbreaks in the Americas are significant in the annals of disease emergence because they played a definitive role in public health emergency protocols. Even today, the Yellow Jack flag from these epidemic episodes warns of acute infection in designated spaces (a camp or hospital, for instance). Hence, these New World primates are included in the viral emergence story of this chapter. Following zoologists and wildlife biologists, I ask: How are wild primate animal hosts tracked as moving forms in changing environments? What media-technological processes detect and compose their movement trajectories? How do their movement patterns materialize extensive infection environments? The chapter closes with two modes of spatial composition—maps and atlases—that transcribe animal movements and habitat disturbances: one is normative, drawing on extant scientific and cultural forms, and the other is experimental, reflexive, and improvisational, constellating diverse knowledge in field reports. Both are dynamic, open-ended locative media that emplace changing multispecies relations in threatening ecologies. In both, the multispecies kinesthetic orients us toward threats to structural one health.

Structural One Health

The complex notion of disease emergence as novel multispecies relationalities found greater elaboration in the 1980s, coalescing at the 1989 Emerging Viruses: The Evolution of Viruses and Viral Diseases conference of the National Institute of Allergy and Infectious Diseases and the National Institutes of Health. Most scientists agreed *novel* had many meanings: it often meant particular viruses had *newly appeared* in populations and were rapidly expanding their range. Although there was some effort to track viruses as stemming from gene mutation or a new variant de novo ("from the beginning"), at this juncture, molecular epidemiologists tracking nucleotide substitutions (calculated at a uniform rate over five to forty years) could not account for decisive evolutionary changes. Phylogenetic schemata could track a group of viruses to a common ancestor, as was the case of the simian viruses that became HIV. But there was no evolutionary big bang for a virus's emergence as a pathogenic actor in human populations. Stephen Morse maintained that *viral emergence* in "EID events" could be attributed to two processes: first, cross-species transmission, or the introduction of the virus into a new species, often through a vertebrate or arthropod vector; and, second, the concurrent dissemination of the virus from a small to a larger population (host-to-host transmission). The first part of this "two-step" process, as Morse described it, identified a "zoonotic pool" of viruses that skipped the species barrier from original reservoirs to new host populations, sometimes via intermediate hosts (such as the pig, civet, or pangolin).[16] This recognition drew attention to the pivotal role of animal hosts as reservoirs and intermediate hosts in the ecological story. As molecular biologists joined hands with veterinarians and biodiversity advocates, rigorous collaborations emerged between these coteries and citizen-scientists, wildlife enthusiasts, Indigenous experts, local farmers, educational institutions, and policy makers in multisectoral alliances that have become the convention in the twenty-first century.

The current preoccupation with animal hosts in novel multispecies relations draws on decades of research on spillover zones. Reputable EID models suggest that 60.3 percent of EIDs are zoonotic; among these, 71.3 percent originate from wildlife.[17] These days we have bats on our mind, much like our obsession with wild primates in recent decades or with rodents as plague agents in centuries past. All these animal populations are reservoirs, intermediate hosts, sentinels. Reservoirs are understood as hosts in which viruses create little trouble, for there is little incentive toward a "dead-end host."[18] The biodiversity of animal hosts compels curiosity; their sickness alarms us. We are hyperaware of their multispecies constitution, their migrations, their sickness and health, the density of their populations, and of how anthropogenic disturbances impact their movement patterns. As the authors of "Global Hotspots and Correlates of Emerging Zoonotic Diseases" argue, EIDs more often than not involve "dynamic interactions among populations of wildlife, livestock, and people in rapidly changing environments."[19] The stories are as profound as they are disturbing: deforestation that destroys habitats (e.g., disrupted fruit bats carrying the Nipah and Hendra viruses), industrial farming techniques (e.g., bovine spongiform encephalopathy resulting from sheep intestines in cow meals), or large-scale industrial change (e.g., the disturbance of mosquito habitats during the Panama Canal hydroelectric project) . . . the vast list of anthropogenic activities that have had transformative effects on ecosystems grows.[20] These stories of anthropogenic ruin illuminate the colonial sphere of ongoing catastrophes. Now we are alert to changing animal movements and new contact zones. Bats forage beyond their home range; rodents come in contact with farmers. The bacteria and viruses that they bear enter new hosts. It is clear that the best investment in epidemics is to develop a transdisciplinary multisectoral approach that crosshatches human health (public health), animal health (veterinary expertise), and ecosystem health (biodiversity agendas). Such an approach was enshrined in the "one health" principles drafted a year after the 2003 Ebola outbreak.[21]

Importantly, structural one health does not privilege animal or ecosystem health *over* human health. Not only is the impact of environmental degradation unevenly distributed across the globe, affecting historically vulnerable communities with the greatest severity, but conservation efforts are often criticized as colonial hangovers that put the well-being of animals before that of humans; bans and prohibitions as well as new enclosures change human social patterns, mobility networks, and food sources, with deleterious consequences.[22] Ursula Heise's *Imagining Extinction* plots a cultural history of such conflicts to underscore the socioeconomic context underlying biodiversity agendas and policies. Her discussion of the Stanford Graphic Novel Project's *Virunga*, a story featuring mountain gorillas in the Virunga National Park, unpacks wild primate conservationist agendas. Following Heise's notations, one of the animal movement tracking projects in this chapter, the wildlife biologist Anne Laudisoit's search for a relict population of thirty-six chimpanzees through the Ituri highlands (on the border between the Democratic Republic of Congo [DRC] and Uganda), might be misconstrued as primarily conservationist. But a closer look yields a complex picture. Trained as an epidemiologist, Laudisoit espouses structural one health in her affiliation with EcoHealth Alliance. As such, her starting point is to consider health distributed across living systems, including animals and forests; there is no fetishization of one species over another, as is the case in the lasting colonial legacies of conservation. Beyond the critique of conservation, the multispecies politics of the epidemic episteme complicates what must be protected and at what cost: as extinction/loss hangs in the balance with abundance/flourishing, we are forced to acknowledge that not all life as unfolding activity mandates conservation in the Anthropocene. Deflecting from animal conservation, structural one health focuses on the biodiversity of all living systems and targets the material conditions that underlie pathogenicity. The point is to root out the anthropogenic drivers of ever-emergent threatening ecologies that harm animal, plant, and human assemblies as well as soils, air, and water. Following animals such as relict chimpanzees, then, is not driven by conservation alone but by complex negotiations of biodiversity among multiple stakeholders. This is clear in Laudisoit's goals, which are thickly configured by her long-standing local and regional affiliations and are not dictated by top-down imperatives to conserve.

Structural one health guides EcoHealth Alliance's many collaborations on human-animal health initiatives. A New York–based nonprofit, EcoHealth Alliance is a multinational enterprise that coordinates research in the biosciences, animal health, and biodiversity agendas. One of the participants in PREDICT 1 (2009–14) and PREDICT 2 (2014–19), the US government's pandemic preparedness initiatives (funded by the US Agency for International Development), EcoHealth Alliance has identified as many as 981 new viruses, including adenoviruses in rodents (in the DRC), herpes viruses in macaques (in Malaysia), and Ebola viruses in bats (in Sierra Leone).[23] A key figure in the Global Virome project, Peter Dasazk, who is one of EcoHealth Alliance's celebrity scientists, made headlines during the COVID-19 pandemic for his collaborations with the Wuhan Institute of Virology. EcoHealth Alliance joins hands not only with global research institutions but also with local laboratories, farmers, animal experts, and universities. The aim is to track disease emergence as well as to build capacity in communities vulnerable to spillovers. I focus on scientist and wildlife biologist Anne Laudisoit's "walk with" chimpanzees in the Ituri highlands as one EcoHealth Alliance initiative relevant for the HIV spillover story. Laudisoit has taught at the University of Kisangani in the DRC for a decade and works in close collaboration with academic researchers and students there as well as with local guides and Lendu villagers. Laudisoit's embedded tracking practice deploys techniques of on-the-ground observation, camera traps, and specimen collection, representing noninvasive immersive methods of tracking multispecies traffic.

A second vector in understanding the impact of anthropogenic change on animal biodiversity is movement ecology–based enterprises that remotely sense and quantify animal movements, define trajectories and patterns, and then classify and curate big data on animal movement. Movement ecology is a deeper dive into structural one health as simulations built on animal movement records predict what habitat loss implies for the survival of animal populations. Movebank, hosted by the Max Planck Institute for Animal Behavior, and the eMammal database, hosted by the Smithsonian, are notable repositories that rely on geospatial (GPS/GIS) and sensor technologies to detect multispecies kinesthesia. I consider zoologist Roland Kays's projects tracking wild primates at the famous Smithsonian Tropical Research Institute's Biological Station on Barro Colorado Island, Panama, as an exemplary instance of new initiatives around animal-machinic coemergence. Collaborating with ornithologist Martin Wikelski, director of the Max Planck Institute of Ornithology, Kays had for years been exploring media-technological affordances (optical, acoustic, and thermal) for and methodological questions on tracking animals, well before the wide availability of low-cost geospatial technologies. Together, Laudisoit and Kays provide a glimpse of technical mediations that track multispecies traffic, which is ground zero for zoonotic spillovers.

The ecological outcome of structural one health is to relearn how to inhabit a planet that we do not own. Whether through extractive mining or deforestation or land use for crop and pasture, 50 to 70 percent of the earth's surface is currently modified for human activities.[24] Parasitic relations highlight the logic of planetary resource distribution since they are obvious relations of dependency. Environmental thought positions humans as parasites as well as an ecosystems-dependent species and a species that converts life-sustaining substances into resources, then hoards them, changing the distributions of life on earth. Life unfolds as a distribution of resources in the epidemic episteme. The epidemic media of the wild orient us toward life otherwise, in which we develop long-term planetary relationships with species within us and beyond—even those that retreat from us into the intractable habitats we call "the wilds." For any threat to *their* health is *our* loss. Unless we can make such recognition the basis of a multispecies politics, resource extraction and colonial dispossession will, in the final account, demand our cellular submission to pathogens. Sensing animal hosts as they move for food, water, nesting, and birth is epidemic media that emplace us in inescapable multispecies and ecosystem entanglements.

The Rules of Traffic

In 1989 Stephen Morse proposed new research into disease transmission as multispecies kinesthesia. He named the new agenda an inquiry into the rules of "viral traffic."[25] I take my cue from this turn toward detecting movement as crucial to regulating and controlling disease emergence. *Traffic* points to the multitemporal movements constitutive of epidemics. First, *traffic* suggests microbial kinesthesia in cross-species transmissions: viruses hitch a ride on media into new hosts because they spot an opportunity for more resources. Second, *traffic* indexes population densities within the demarcated surrounds we name an *environment*. The density of host populations, including those with a common ancestor (various primate species, for example), has much to do with the ease of cross-species transmission. Third, *traffic* names economic activities, from wildlife trading to food practices, that have been identified as the major drivers of pathogenic emergence. And, finally, *traffic* suggests machinic signal transmissions of animal movements. In all these ways, traffic foregrounds the distribution of "life on earth" in biological and ecological, social and economic terms, as well as its transcription in spatial forms. All these dimensions are at play in making the multispecies kinesthetic.

The HIV story is illuminating, once again, because there is wide agreement on the multistage process of HIV transmission.[26] Natural histories of cross-species transmission based on molecular phylogenetics locate HIV's emergence in the southeastern corner of Cameroon in the early twentieth century (possibly between 1921 and 1933, although some date it earlier).[27] Molecular phylogenies hypothesize evolutionary histories from serological samples probed for genomic fingerprints; the effort is to locate a common source for the spillover event (the most recent common ancestor).[28] Phylogenetic trees trace the evolution of viruses, assessing probable outcomes for zoonotic spillovers based on viral traits such as DNA or RNA composition, enveloped or nonenveloped structures, and genome length. Beyond phylogenetic trees, the natural histories of viral emergence direct us to changing multispecies relations. These natural histories evaluate the viral richness in animal reservoirs such as bats or wild primates. Some animal reservoirs teem with viruses that share similar traits; they exhibit great viral biodiversity. This viral richness implies that these animal hosts provide adequate provision for similar viruses: for instance, several coronaviruses live in opportunistic tolerance with bats. In the case of spillovers into human populations, the same logic prevails: viruses will try to find hosts that are phylogenetically proximate to the animal reservoirs they already occupy. As we know, African wild primates carry SIVs (simian immunodeficiency viruses), which are the simian strains of multiple HIVs. Simian immune systems tolerate the virus, so the SIVs are not highly pathogenic. Bats, too, can tolerate a diversity of viruses because their high metabolism provides them immunity from viral takeovers; they not only have high viral biodiversity but also, as the only mammals powered with flight, can transmit viruses over large distances. Studying bat colonies for over fifteen years, Chinese virologist Shi Zhengli observed a natural genetic library for viruses in the bat populations of the Yunnan province; her studies included the coronaviruses.[29] The viral biodiversity of bats along with their phylogenetic proximity to mammals increases the possibility of cross-species viral transmission from these reservoir hosts.[30] But not all zoonotic shifts into new hosts constitute an EID event. Molecular analytics record HIV shifts several times before two strains in chimpanzees (who have genomic sequences 98 percent similar to that of humans) became established in human populations. Epidemics must also take root in host populations through host-to-host transmissions; in public health, this is the community transmission phase. The HIV-1 (group M) caused the global pandemic, but HIV-1 (groups N, O, P) had far narrower reach; for example, HIV-1N community transmission was localized as endemic to Cameroon. First genetically detectable in 1990, SIV was found in thirty-six wild primates in sub-Saharan Africa.[31] One history of evolutionary biology highlights two strains of SIVcpz (a variant) as "sources" that became HIV-1 in crossing into human hosts. Research on the strains' phylogenetic histories is ongoing, with some scientists tracing them back to red-capped, spot-nosed mustached, and mona monkeys. Paul Sharp, George Shaw, and Beatrice Hahn suggest that SIVcpz is the combination of two strains from these monkeys that mingled in a chimpanzee coinfected with both; here, once more, horizontal gene transfers stemming from coinfection enable viral evolution, displacing the logic of descent.[32] The jury is still out on tracking *the* original reservoir for SIV strains, leading many to describe reliance on phylogenetic analysis alone as a fool's errand. What is clear is that "mammalian sympatry" or the overlap of phylogenetically proximate mammals in a biogeographic area is an important factor in zoonotic shifts. Viruses search for similar hosts that can tolerate their parasitic needs. In other words, genetically similar mammals present already familiar internal environments for parasitic survival.[33] Since the Kinshasa strain of SIVcpz is associated with the global HIV/AIDS pandemic, the "eastern chimpanzees" of the DRC have attracted a large degree of scientific attention in the search for HIV origins. Among them, isolated populations are particularly captivating for the clues they offer to the historical movements of SIV strains.

With mammalian sympatry, biogeographies enter the picture. Where do phylogenetically similar populations range? Multispecies histories convert into geospatial coordinates, spatializing disease emergence. It is now possible to spatiotemporally "map" possible zones of virulence in which zoonotic shifts can potentially become EID events. Composing global hotspots constellates phylogenetic, ecological, and geographic data to segment the earth's surface into distinct biozoogeographic zones. One widely used model from the University of Copenhagen's Center for Macroecology, Evolution and Climate, for instance, programs the earth into thirty-four biozoogeographic zones; I return to their use in EID event maps later in the chapter. In geospatially mediated hotspots, animal reservoirs and intermediate hosts come into view: wild species dislodged from their habitats, animals in captivity, farmed livestock rubbing shoulders with their wild counterparts. These are "feral ecologies" in the blasted ruins of the Anthropocene. Now there is greater awareness of EID events traced to captive animals such as pigs (H1N1) and dromedary camels (MERS-CoV) as well as to traded exotic wildlife such as civets (classic SARS) and (possibly) pangolins (SARS-CoV-2). Their sickness in captivity, signaling waning immunity and proliferating viral copies, serves as a warning of potential spillovers into human populations.[34] As hosts wane, viruses seek new ones: hence the motivation to skip into a new species and, consequently, the emergence of *novel* multispecies relations. Frédéric Keck's ethnography of the SARS outbreak in Hong Kong in 2003 situates farm-raised chickens as sentinel animals whose illness should have served as a warning.[35] Such studies underscore the urgency of tracking animal movement patterns, of reservoirs and intermediate hosts, and of the regulation of livestock farming and wildlife trade. For primates, there are innumerable scientific papers on high-risk host shifts resulting from the consumption of meat from wildlife, illegal trading (holding animals in captivity), and large-scale deforestation that fragments habitats.[36] The HIV-1M emergence story places these shifts from wild primates to humans within seven hundred miles of Kinshasa, DRC. As the city grew into a transportation hub, the virus surely spread among human host populations across the globe. In other episodes, such as the yellow fever epidemics in the Americas, the virus affected human and animal populations with equal ferocity. These stories illuminate emergent ecosystems as always "diverse and invaded, neglected but resilient, anthropogenic but wild," as Eben

Kirksey notes, returning us to entangled natural and social disturbances on a damaged planet.[37]

Some historians and anthropologists recast "natural histories" of HIV emergence, drawing on oral interviews, archival sources, and social histories. They argue that central African communities had millennia-long histories of NHP-human contact, so the conditions for cross-species transmission plotted by virologists, epidemiologists, primate scientists, and evolutionary biologists were already present. Yet colonial transformations of the early twentieth century and accelerated industrial production in the mid-twentieth century wrought substantial anthropogenic changes that enabled HIV-IM to establish itself in human populations. Based on sixty-two oral history interviews conducted in southeastern Cameroon, Stephanie Rupp and colleagues argue that critical changes in hunting access, agricultural expansion, commercial rubber collection, and medical interventions, for instance, played a key role in this establishment.[38] Tamara Giles-Vernick and colleagues track a range of factors from the commercial production of coffee, cocoa, and timber, to expanding transportation systems, to changing sexual practices, to reoriented mobility networks, to blood transfusion practices as constitutive of this multitemporal event.[39] All these scholars debunk the myth of the "cut hunter" as the progenitor of HIV-IM, typically projected as a lone male figure carrying the strain from the Sangha Basin to Kinshasa on a steamer.[40] Such social, economic, and ecological histories firmly situate HIV emergence in the colonial sphere.

Structural one health involves tracking anthropogenic encroachments into geographically classified wildlife "species home ranges" as contact zones for potential disease outbreaks. Some of these are easier to plot than others. Studying human-wildlife and human-livestock-wildlife interfaces in African, South Asian, and Southeast Asian contexts, Melinda Rostal of EcoHealth Alliance, for instance, followed the mosquito-borne Rift Valley fever in South Africa to settings where wild buffalo, kudu, springbuck, and blesbok, among other wild animals, commingle with sheep, goats, and cattle (figure 4.2).[41] When the livestock become infected, they transmit a zoonotic virus (of the phlebovirus genus) to humans, as we know from the 1955–56, 1973–76, and 2010–11 outbreaks in South Africa.[42] These EID events arrive with weather, soil, and vegetation changes that emplace livestock within the home ranges of their wild species counterparts. Tracking disease emergence this way, the hope is to draw attention to the "unintended consequences" (as Dubos notes) of changing land use and thereby to influence industrial-agricultural plans and policies. Rostal has also tracked rotavirus exchanges between humans and rhesus macaques

Figure 4.2. Sheep among bucks in Free State near Northern Cape, South Africa. Source: Rostal et al., "Understanding Rift Valley Fever," 157.

(monkeys) in Bangladesh, populations that live in close proximity to one another in urban settings—these are exemplary feral ecologies. The molecular phylogenies of the rotavirus reveal a complex reassortment of mutual infection as the virus mutates across and between host populations.[43] In urban contact or farmland cases, organic samples from both populations are readily accessible, as are direct observations of their movements. Far more difficult to trace are cross-species transmissions in the wild that can account for zoonotic spillovers, hence the need for media-technological animal motion–sensing to track multispecies traffic.

The mediatic processes involved in tracking multispecies traffic have many histories, some of which do not find elaboration in animal media studies. Much has been said about animals' "material semiotic" trace (to recall Donna Haraway) in analyzing *animal-tracking* as an ancient media practice.[44] But inquiries into these media are rarely linked to media-technological studies of disease-surveillance networks. The digital surveillance of changing multispecies relations in EIDS surfaced in the late 1980s after the 1989 conference. One might trace syndromic surveillance infrastructures back to Stephen Morse's 1994 low-cost, nonprofit disease-surveillance network (DSN) ProMED-mail, one of the first *digital* disease-detection tools of the twentieth century.[45] The World

Health Organization's Global Outbreak Alert and Response Network (GOARN) and the CDC's (Centers for Disease Control and Prevention) FluNet are the digital successors to Alexander Langmuir's much-discussed mid-twentieth-century Disease Detective programs.[46] Toward the close of the twentieth century, these DSNs tracked viral chatter not only in human social communication (emails, mobile phone uploads, web crawling) but also in molecular phylogenetics—in the biological chatter of genetic mutation.[47] In their landmark book *The Exploit*, Alexander Galloway and Eugene Thacker characterize these contemporary DSNs as "networks fighting networks" in an informatic war between machines and microbes.[48] Among the DSNs, molecular virologist Nathan Wolfe's nonprofit Global Viral founded in the San Francisco Bay area in 2007, attends to the geospatial coordinates of potential zoonotic shifts. Global Viral's virus-hunting activities took place in Southeast Asia, China, and sub-Saharan Africa.[49] Their forecasts conjugated predictors such as industrialization, deforestation, and urban expansion with densely populated environments in which secondary transmission might ensue.[50] Close to the Pearl River Delta, Hong Kong, for instance, is one such geospatial interface between the wild terrain of human-animal contact and a dense, globally connected, urban geography; as such, this is an exemplary global hotspot. Such syndromic surveillance with interactive smart grids meant building technological infrastructure, from mobile labs equipped with lab-on-a-chip viral diagnostic technologies to web-crawling technologies to mine "rumor registries" (from mobile phone and email uploads). Biological samples of vital media were translated into digital files in the field, while SMS feeds were crunched at Global Viral's centers in San Francisco and Washington, DC. In 2019, the nonprofit morphed into the for-profit risk-modeling firm Metabiota and joined the PREDICT coalition. With partners such as EcoHealth Alliance, it was clear that disease surveillance should look beyond mining viral chatter to the bigger picture: *the complex problematic of EIDs as biological, social, and ecological crisis events*. For EID modelers engaged in structural one health, there is hope of influencing social and economic policies on large-scale land-use change (including logging and mining concessions, dam building, and road development) and of building the capacity for preempting EID outbreaks *in* global hot spots. The most likely hot spots targeted by the EcoHealth Alliance are in Côte d'Ivoire, Liberia, the DRC, Egypt, Jordan, Bangladesh, India, Indonesia, Malaysia, Thailand, and China. On the other end are biodiversity imperatives to protect fast-disappearing habitats whose loss can generate novel human-animal interfaces. Animal movements at the frayed edges of habitats, diminished communities, and vanishing food sources and breeding grounds all index the changing rules of traffic that can usher in an EID event.

The Multispecies Kinesthetic

Animal movement records shared on open-access databases acquire immanent value in the epidemic episteme as indicators of potential EID events. The multispecies kinesthetic presents one way of thinking about the processes of mediation constitutive of those records. This entails converting vital signals of entangled species movements within individuals, populations, and ecosystems into machinic transmissions to be decoded, filtered, sorted, and classified so as to render them as "animal movement records." Several media-technological processes work in tandem: first, the inscription of vital media (heartbeat, temperature, bodily fluids) into machinic signals (electromagnetic and electrical) and the decoding, filtering, sampling, and encoding of those signals into information (animal forms and movement patterns); and, second, the composition of information into animal movement records with predictive efficacy. The two stories of detecting animal host movements in tropical rain forests in this chapter elaborate different modalities of these processes; both rely on a priori compositions of the habitat (the island, the highlands) where tracking practices ensue, and both engage forest kinesthetics to compose organism-environment assemblages. My interviews with Anne Laudisoit and Roland Kays flesh out specific operations of the multispecies kinesthetic.[51] The chapter closes with two modes of technical-aesthetic composition that situate biotechnical kinesthesia geographically: one is EcoHealth Alliance's multitemporal EID world maps, and the other is the improvisational *Feral Atlas*.

But why a kinesthetic? While the Greek root verb *kineîn* simply means "to move," *kinesthesis* refers to an embodied "feeling of motion" that detects bodily position, weight, or movement of muscles, tendons, and joints. A sense of something else beyond proprioception or self-movement, kinesthesis picks up signals from a moving force field. The *kinesthetic* refers to perceptions of movement within a demarcated surround that we constitute as an environment. The organism-environment relation emerges as information from a surfeit of signal and noise. *Multispecies* in this chapter underscores the animal (individual or population) as always distributed and networked with other species and ecosystems. Viruses emerge in animal hosts' extracellular and cellular environments; animal hosts emerge with other species, plants, and ecosystem agents. The multispecies kinesthetic disentangles process-relational ontologies, isolating them as organism-environment assemblages—as epistemic objects of study. As viral traffic materializes in biotechnical forms, as kinesthesia finds composition in EID maps and atlases, animal motion stills in spatially composed movement patterns.

This reading of the multispecies kinesthetic draws on current research on animal movement patterns at the frontiers of environmental science. In part, this research is made possible by exponential advances in sophisticated geospatial technologies. Jennifer Gabrys's *Program Earth* is devoted to examining the implications of these technologies: specifically, how "distributed and networked environmental sensors within more earthly realms" transcribe animal movements.[52] A range of embedded technologies—from miniaturized radio transmitters to light-leveled geolocators and RFID (radio frequency identification) tags—transmit signals through GPS satellites recording atmospheric (ambient temperature, humidity, wind or air flow), geological (altitude, soil, vegetation), and biological (heart rate, pressure, oxygen levels) data in real time.[53] As Etienne Benson argues in *Wired Wilderness*, this monitoring and surveillance of the environment dates to the post–World War II era, a history that Gabrys elaborates in her analyses of computationally enabled sensors. Most compelling is Gabrys formulation of the organism-machine-environment emerging together. Biological organization, she argues, is anterior to machines; animal perceptions, their kinesthesis, inform how they interact in the environment. Following Isabelle Stengers, she goes on to argue that "the construction of the experimental device" in no way "ensures that the being we wish to mobilize will agree to show up."[54] Here, the animal's agency transforming what machines can do hints at the mutually transformative processes of medial entanglement—Barad's intra-active agencies and Chow's ricocheting active and reactive relations.[55] Of course, there is considerable anthropological, historical, and philosophical literature on humans as animals "writing" or inscribing other animals in acts of technical mediation. But Gabrys's elaboration is a crucial reference for the biotechnical in this chapter because she focuses on animal-movement tracking, specifically; I follow her lead in thinking the different agencies operative in organism-machine-environment assemblages. Since animal "individuals" are explicitly multispecies in my analysis, the organism in the organism-environment assemblages of this chapter does double duty. Organisms isolated for study in biotechnical forms are microbes living in animal media *and* animal hosts moving in their habitats.

Such a relational biotechnical form relies on sensing heartbeats and body temperatures, humidity and ambient light; on inscribing detected signals into data; and on transcribing them into information. Media technologies convert ecological and biological signals into data: for instance, motion sensors respond to radiant heat energy and convert that energy into infrared signals (part of the electromagnetic spectrum invisible to the eye). Relayed through GPS, these transmissions are further transcribed via GIS into data layers. In turn, GIS interfaces with existing programs mapping bio- or zoogeographies to compose cultural forms such as EID atlases. Animals roam in these spatial configurations, their changing movement patterns catching our attention. The programmed earth surfaces in global databases and remote-sensing platforms that allow scientists to follow animals and to understand their spatial distributions. State-of-the-art projects such as the International Cooperation for Animal Research Using Space (ICARUS) tracks animals as they move for food, breeding grounds, and rest by embedding miniaturized transmitters in animal bodies that will not impede animal movement.[56] In this way, sophisticated sensor and geospatial technologies establish the biogeographic ranges of animals as they move through space.

Before turning to animal movement patterns, however, I pause on one researcher, the director of the Movement Data Science Lab (MOVE) at the University of California, Santa Barbara, Somayeh Dodge, who was my guide into this increasingly complex field of study. Dodge also introduced me to Roland Kays, a cutting-edge builder of animal movement tracking software. Her own published research provides insight into quantitative experiments in measuring the temporal and spatial scales at which individual animals move. Dodge not only tracks animal movements in her collaborations with the Environmental-Data Automated Track Annotation (Env-DATA) system but also models *probable* movement patterns from GPS observations.[57] One of her projects studies movements of tigers in Thailand, accounting for their daily patterns of hunting and regular patterns of patrolling home-range boundaries for an average of seven days to three weeks. Her writings propose modes of "object segmentation" to differentiate between low- and high-frequency movements, and different "time series simulations" to model probable movement patterns.[58] Mapping predator movements makes visible changing ecosystems: the shortage of prey, the drying up of streams, and the clearing of grasses where tigers crouch, all indicative of habitat fragmentation and loss. That fragmentation drives these predators toward new interactions in search of new prey; new interfaces emerge in the spatial distributions of changing predator-prey relations. Dodge's research first introduced me to configurations of habitat loss in movement ecology. In its constellation of media-technological practices, movement ecology's discrete agendas—tracking animal movements, assessing habitat loss, locating animal hosts—are crucial for my conjugation of biodiversity, disease surveillance, and media studies.

Throughout the book epidemic media are media and apparatuses, infrastructures and systems governed by the epidemic episteme. My focus on processes of mediation highlights the interlocking biological and technological processes constitutive of biotechnical forms. In this chapter that form materializes animal movement as *biotechnical kinesthesia,* which becomes the basis of composing the *multispecies kinesthetic.* I begin with tracking media, drawing on media studies scholarship on remote-sensing technologies and geospatial infrastructures.[59] Then I move to signal processing that transcribes animal motion through space as movement patterns through sampling, layering, and classifying images. Both processes act together to constitute animal movement pattern records. Since the technical notations of contemporary tracking media may not be commonplace as yet, a few brief definitions are in order before a more sustained engagement with the two tracking projects.

One key process for embedded tracking practices is *segmentation,* evidenced in the "transect method." Like the laboratory protocol in the previous chapter, a transect is a study design that draws on scientific-cultural methods: it segments a classified biogeographic environment (forests, grasslands, rocky mountainous areas) and prepares the segment as representative sample for information extraction. As such, transects are scientific-cultural enactments of an epistemic cut. The transect is a priori to the embedded media-technological practices of tracking animal movements. Traditionally, the transect is a straight line that traverses a part of an area and transcribes the area as measurable square footage. A portion of a forest is selected as a sample whose information can be statistically projected to understand the whole forest. Walking a transect includes direct observation and sample collection (blood, urine, saliva, feces) in tandem with setting up automated sensor technologies such as camera traps. Typically deployed in ecological surveys, the transect yields information about environmental gradients: for example, the increased salinity in soil or decreases in animal population densities. Anne Laudisoit's transect in the Ituri highlands exemplifies this method of segmenting a forest to compose animal movement patterns. Then there is the *sensor-technology design*: this includes everything from the miniaturization of transmitters to camera trap designs and the programming of controls for ambient temperature, light, humidity, or air flow. Roland Kays's experiments on Barro Colorado Island reveal sensor design as ever a media-technological frontier, always to be rebuilt and developed, discarded or archived, refined and modified. Both Laudisoit and Kays experiment with the spatial placement of embedded and remote, noninvasive and invasive, media technologies to better capture animal motions and to minimize background noise. But as we shall see, the noise is not necessarily machinic failure; rather, it often records animal and vegetal agencies registering as biotechnical kinesthesia. Finally, *object formation* transcribes signals into biotechnical forms. *Formation* is not a technical term in animal movement pattern detection, but I deploy it to indicate the aesthetic "form-making" processes of signal transcription. In the Latin etymology, *form* is the external appearance of a thing cut out from a background; in its understanding as figure, the (back)ground accompanies form. Put differently, the background as noise *accompanies* the biotechnical cutout in processes of mediation. *Formation* references both figure and ground, cutout and surplus. Unprocessed lively materialities fold into biotechnical kinesthesia as the form's sensuous qualities, activating an awareness of deep entanglements. All these notations underscore the subtraction expressive in the epistemic cut, a necessary cut-out for making multispecies relations intelligible as animal movements: for one, weeding out excessive kinesthesia, animal and vegetal, is necessary for a coherent configuration. Animals emerge as epistemic objects in biotechnical forms, moving within the biogeographically constituted environments that sustain them.

Tales of Forest Kinesthetics

Both Anne Laudisoit and Roland Kays bring their backgrounds in wildlife biology to their methods and techniques of tracking animal movements. Laudisoit trained as an epidemiologist, and her research on the bubonic plague took her to the DRC, where she spent a number of years trapping rodents. But she soon turned to the study of endemic monkeypox, which led her to other pastures: forests disappearing at the rate of 12 percent per year, at whose edges rodents and squirrels encountered farmers. Increasingly drawn to forests as "living laboratories," Laudisoit began to track a newly discovered community of chimpanzees with colleagues at the University of Kisangani, the Biodiversity Monitoring Center, and local Lendu villagers with expert knowledge of chimpanzee migrations in search of water. Using direct observation, automated camera traps, and collection of fecal matter, Laudisoit combined biological, cultural, and technical methods for her study of biodiversity in chimpanzee populations that range in the high-altitude fragmented Ituri highlands. She exemplifies the field specialist with institutional links—straddling both the University of Kisangani and international centers for the study of primatology—and long-term community ties in the region.[60]

Roland Kays, in contrast, has been building animal-sensing technologies for a number of years. Trained as a zoologist, Kays holds a double appointment at North Carolina State University and the North Carolina Museum of Natural Sciences (where he runs a biodiversity lab). Before widely accessible GIS technologies, Kays built an automated radio-telemetry system that tracked animals fitted with radio collars on Barro Colorado Island, Panama, but once movement ecology found realization in GIS/GPS technologies that capture animal movements at high resolution and with far more precision, Kays teamed up with Martin Wikelski to theorize and build new technologies. His writings and field experiments exemplify the theory and practice of animal sensing based in movement ecology. His book on camera traps, *Candid Creatures*, for instance, assesses the efficacies of camera technologies, while his writings with Wikelski explore the promise of "born digital" transcriptions of animal movements.[61] As animal movement becomes increasingly quantified, researchers like Kays reflect on *how* media technologies render living forms folded into an environment intelligible and on the challenges that accompany such transcription. Machine, organism, and environment coemerge in the search for the lightest sensor or the most noninvasive satellite imaging that does not impede animal movement. Importantly, both Laudisoit and Kays are keenly aware of tracking media as provisional, exploratory knowledge-practice, despite the ongoing refinements of tracking media technologies.[62] Thinking of these modern practitioners together affords a closer look at biotechnical kinesthesia that is always emergent, always attuned to viral rules of traffic.

WALKING WITH CHIMPANZEES IN THE ITURI HIGHLANDS

I interviewed Anne Laudisoit online in June 2020, while she was in Uganda. Looking for ecologists studying primates in central and western Africa, I had stumbled on her project through my conversations with scientists and media specialists at EcoHealth Alliance. Laudisoit had joined the nonprofit in 2017. When I interviewed her, she had reached the border between the DRC and Uganda after a trek through the relict forests in the Ituri highlands along the Albertine rift escarpment, an isolated region. As steep as they are dangerous, the highlands range over the "red zone" of Hema-Lendu internecine conflicts, she told me, as a lush, verdant landscape yawned behind her at the video interface. She had completed a documentary on the trek to follow a chimpanzee community that her team had tracked for a full year. Their habitat was increasingly fragmented, with human settlements disrupting the continuity of forested areas; as the forests became islands, the wild primates crossed close to villages and other settlements in their journey toward water sources.[63] *MBudha: In the Chimpanzees' Footsteps*, a film that Laudisoit codirected with Caroline Thirion, follows the chimpanzees' journey, drawing on Laudisoit's immersive animal-tracking footage. Although made to solicit public resources for biodiversity agendas, the film functions as an audiovisual field report on the trek. The film unfolds as a straightforward quest narrative that closes with a glimpse of the elusive chimps. Local villagers living one kilometer from the forest in northeastern DRC reported occasional glimpses of the chimps. Laudisoit had heard their screams while on another project but had never sighted them. You'll find them at their water source, said the villagers, who had a long-term relationship with the animals. Highlighting animal cultures, they sketched mourning rituals, birthing habits, and food and water sources for Laudisoit and her team. I wondered why an eco-epidemiologist became interested in a relict population. She had been tracking monkeypox outbreaks in the DRC, Laudisoit told me, mostly small-scale endemics that had occasionally broken into epidemics. When monkeypox showed up in the United States in 2003, the CDC invested in tracking this disease emergence. Transmitted through lesions, body fluids, and respiratory droplets, as an *orthopox* (the same family as smallpox), the virus spread easily among a generation no longer vaccinated for the famous eradicated disease. Working with local nurses, Laudisoit traced viral movements in human populations, but as an ecologist, her expertise lay in the animal hosts, whose genetic characteristics would show whether or not the virus was indigenous to the region or imported. The monkeypox virus had multiple animal hosts, including wild primates, all displaced from their home ranges because of habitat fragmentation. Curious about wild primate biodiversity in a region that houses half the chimpanzee population in the world, populations that make the IUCN's (International Union for the Conservation of Nature) Red List of Threatened Species, Laudisoit grew invested in the story of habitat fragmentation.[64] The genetic characteristics of a relict population of eastern chimpanzees, remnants of a once diverse and widespread population, could illuminate the impact of anthropogenic change. Moreover, their relative isolation could prove insightful for the study of viral strains. The search for the sudden abundance of flourishing parasites had led to an inquiry into a relict population fleeing anthropogenic change. Tracking disease emergence had become a will to structural one health, motivating the trek to the Relict and Refuge Altitude Forest of the Albert Lake Escarpment in search of the eastern chimpanzees.

The University of Kisangani had previously funded a project on the chimps, and this gave Laudisoit's National Geographic–funded effort the base team and expertise necessary for the arduous quest.[65] Accompanied by Pasteur Jérôme Dz'na (interpreter and agronomist) and her longtime guide Otis Kpanyoyo, Laudisoit embarked on a trek along the high-altitude escarpment bordering Lake Albert. The goal was to document animal movement with noninvasive motion-sensing methods such as direct observation (physical signs like handprints, smells, sounds), digital-optical capture (in automated camera traps), and the collection of vital traces (like fecal matter). As the team tracked the movement of the chimpanzees, they recorded the plants, soils, and animals of the habitat's ecosystems.[66]

This required a study design that demarcated forested areas of the Ituri highlands as the environment. A meticulously designed "transect" segmented the forest for close analysis drawing on extant scientific and cultural knowledge. The transect establishes a straight line around which a sample area is surveyed and documented. Figure 4.3 shows two of the three transects undertaken by Laudisoit's team (the two diagonal lines peppered with dark dots). For every kilometer of the transect, the team recorded everything five meters to the left and five meters to the right of the straight line (for a total width of ten meters at any given point). Such records could assess gradual changes in the habitat over time. Changes in portions of the transect—in an area of ten meters by ten meters square, for instance—could be statistically modeled based on processed sample data; subsequently the models could be deployed to assess biodiversity transformations in the area. As Laudisoit shared her transect designs with me, the forest emerged medially as a segmented space metonymically extending to encompass the larger region. A minimal black line demarcated the whole area for cartographic classification, while the color-coded satellite images (figure 4.3, right corner) rendered the vegetal density of the environment.

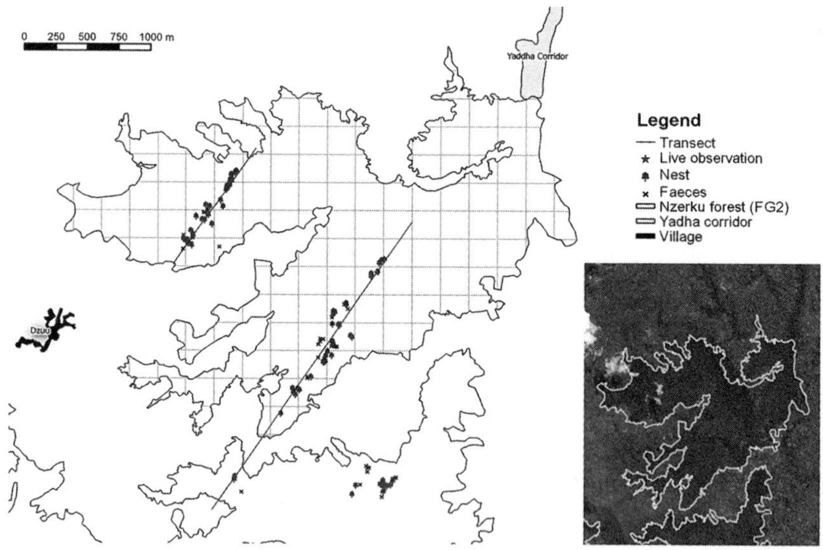

Figure 4.3. Transect diagram for Ituri Highlands, Democratic Republic of the Congo, 2017. Credit: Anne Laudisoit.

The designs for the team's three transects established the Ituri highlands as a *concrete biogeography* with named forests (such as Nzerku or Tsili-Bai), ecological corridors (Yadha), and villages (such as Dzuu and Kpagboma) and an *abstract diagrammed space*. In such combination, the earth appears segmented, sampled, and quantitatively assessed for environmental gradients. An environment emerges in the biotechnical form of a natural habitat for animal hosts.

In this environment wild primates appear as image, sound, and touch, in their habits and behaviors, movement trajectories and resting places. Tracking media institute a rack-focus effect pulling from the organism-environment assemblage as biologists and ecologists try to differentiate moving animals from the noise of undecidable signals, degraded data, and habitual derailments. Animals appear foregrounded in admixtures of vital and digital signals. These include sensuous signals with long histories in tracking practices: histories of interpreting bird song, the howl of the wolf, the monkey's scream, a physical and sensual language that institutes the human as animal.[67] In tracking as a modern practice, the differentiation of animal forms moving in the environment requires media-technological expertise: spatial designs (transect), technical know-how (camera traps), biological training (preparing samples for PCR bioassays), and mechanical knowledge (hand or footprint tracking). In contrast to new remote animal-sensing technologies that accumulate data faster and more efficiently, walking a transect is physically laborious, especially at these forbiddingly high altitudes; more generally, the embedded tracking practice is "multivariate, historically produced, often fleeting, dauntingly complex and uncontrollable," as most fieldwork tends to be.[68] Toward the close of *MBudha*, the team glimpses the chimpanzees resting in their journey through the forests; by that time the team has crossed the border into Uganda. Laudisoit noted that the moment documented in the film took a year to arrive. For the most part, the chimpanzees remained cryptic and shy, eluding their trackers. The chimpanzees' participation, sometimes scuttling, at other times playfully engaging machinic capture, indexes the animal agency constitutive of *bio*technical kinesthesia.[69]

On the trek, the team painstakingly followed vital signs such as hand and footprints (figure 4.4), nests in the arboreal canopies, and fecal matter (figure 4.5). The legend in figure 4.3 documents the team's mechanical methods, which included a combination of making live observations, counting nests, and amassing feces. Such documentation and organic sample collection require a deep immersion in the wilds and are reliant on Indigenous knowledge earned over time. Laudisoit's transect exemplifies the rigorous local relationships necessary for ecosystems to appear as such. Without this partnering, without diverse knowledge communities, one ends up with skewed and insufficient data

Figure 4.4. Tracking imprints, film still from *MBudha*, 2018. Credit: Anne Laudisoit and Caroline Thirion.

Figure 4.5. Washing fecal matter, film still from *MBudha*, 2018. Credit: Anne Laudisoit and Caroline Thirion.

on biogeographic regions, weakening the prognosis of disease emergence. With each vital sign, the team was better able to comprehend the role the primates play within the ecosystem.

Fecal matter, for instance, yielded seeds dispersed by the chimps as they moved through the environment; we know seed dispersal is invaluable in maintaining plant biodiversity. Fecal matter is, of course, also critical for its genetic information. Unlike the taking of serological samples, gathering fecal matter is a noninvasive technique: after all, animals excrete and leave the substance behind as a vital trace. Laudisoit explained the methods of washing and drying fecal matter to preserve it in pellet form. One part is observed for animal diet, which includes seeds and insects. The other part is saved for genetic analysis; PCR machines are expensive and not easily available on the trek, so the samples must be buffered to maintain the quality of the nucleotide sequences. Denatured with buffers, animal vital traces are temporarily preserved as records of their multispecies distributions. Then the search is on for microbial genomic fingerprints. The DNA viruses are hardy; they can be buffered in ethanol and preserved in dry silicate gel. But RNA virus nucleotides are difficult to preserve without cold-chain transport (they must be frozen at –80 degrees Celsius). Without cold storage, the team's findings, surmised Laudisoit, would mostly capture the genetic fingerprints of DNA viruses. The explanation of the process indicates the fragility of vital media that degrade without technical fabrication (buffers and temperatures). Laudisoit's explanation points to the technological limits of processing vital media. Addressing those constraints, efforts are underway to create DNA barcoding techniques that can inscribe vital matter in the field and therefore quicken the process of genomic identification.[70] For fecal pellets, buccal swabs, and blood samples remain crucial for the study of disease emergence: they are required for the detection of viral genomic fingerprints. Once the prepared samples are processed in PCR assays, as described in chapter 3, the nucleotide sequences are compared to identified genomic sequences stored in open databases. Simian and viral genomic data provide evidence of ecosystem relations: of the primate genes, of their interaction with other animals, and of the microbes they host. The story of vital trace collection exemplifies one difference between embedded tracking practices and remote-sensing methods, yet both aim to materialize the biotechnical kinesthesia of moving animals in changing environments. As we shall see, there are also differences in the articulation of knowledge communities in the two kinds of tracking media: one relies on long-term local alliances, and the other on harvesting citizen-science data.

Given the agential *non*participation of the chimpanzees in their machinic capture, as documented as their absence for most of the film, Laudisoit's team relied on automated camera traps to detect chimpanzee movement patterns. Camera traps, or motion-sensitive wildlife cameras, have been a staple in tracking animal movement from a static point in space for at least fifty years. Cameras brands such as Reconyx and Bushnell HD are widely accessible and affordable for scientists and wildlife enthusiasts alike. Most take three trigger images at a time, and these are most useful for recording medium or large animals; smaller animals (66 percent of animals, 81 percent of birds on earth) are another matter. Camera traps are now conventional "photo-vouchers" of the animal specimens, replacing museum specimens of yore.[71] Twenty-seven Bushnell Trophy HD Cams placed along the three transects were key to Laudisoit's investigation. They were fitted with passive infrared (PIR) sensors, which are commonly used in motion detectors, so the camera shutter was triggered by any movement within one hundred feet of the sensor. The PIR sensors detect and measure heat energy in infrared wavelengths along the electromagnetic spectrum. All objects emanate heat energy in the form of radiation not visible to the naked eye; the sensor measures this incoming energy, which, at certain infrared wavelengths, triggers the shutter. One can program the camera to recognize ambient temperatures in the forest and to differentiate them from the higher heat energy of moving forms: that is, animals that cross the sensor field. This prevents temperature noise from triggering the shutter since the cameras remain in the forests for a number of months.[72] Here the forest as environment is the background noise to be technologically subtracted in order to sense animal motion and to track that motion serially across the transect. The cameras can operate in temperatures from –4 to 140 degrees Fahrenheit and have a locking mechanism that guards against disruptions in settings. Lithium batteries power automated visual capture; the images are stored for months on SD cards (one set of batteries can run as long as twelve months). For Laudisoit's initial venture into the region, the team placed cameras that gathered footage between March and June and again in June through August 2016 (batteries and SD cards were replenished midway, in June of that year). When she received the National Geographic grant in 2017, the team placed cameras along the transects for a whole year. The latter footage shows up in *MBudha*.

The hybrid-mode camera allowed both still photographs and video capture: each camera was set to capture one still and a one-minute video of animals within five to six meters of the focal lens. In figure 4.6 we see Laudisoit and D'zna programming the Bushnell Trophy HD Cam to those settings. Crucially, the night-illumination mode captured a number of animals that typically camouflage themselves as protection against predators during the day. In *MBudha* we see a curious monkey approach the camera in night vision (figure 4.7); the team sorting through their raw footage (as recorded by Thirion in *MBudha*) delights in such glimpses, especially when they are of rare animals in this biogeography. The chimpanzees' direct approach along with other antics—blocking the lenses with fur, tilting the lenses—conveys their awareness of the machines as new actors in the forest. Yet their intentions, motives, desires, or what Chow characterizes as the "reactive relation" of being "captured" on camera, remains opaque. Are the chimps just curious? Are they playing with the cameras? Do their motions signal aggression? Do they even care about the machinic eyes? The film's narration of the moment of capture as wonder, as captivation, as sensorial and affective overload, exemplifies an "overburdening" that, for Chow, is an apprehension of those "mysterious connections" between human, machine, animal, and environment. In short, these scenes record the sensuous entanglements of machinic capture. Despite the most noninvasive of interventions, machine and organism are deeply embroiled in each other's affairs.

Rather counterintuitively, the still-camera mode is capable of capturing a greater number of animal specimens than the video setting since trigger speeds for photographing are faster than those for video capture. A small animal such as a bat could escape the latter, but a photograph would catch the movement. Such nuances illuminate interlocking vital and machinic properties in the making of biotechnical kinesthesia: animal motion speeds and bodily gestures, alongside shutter speed, camera lenses, and placement equipment are all rolled into the organism-environment relation. Camera traps, argued Laudisoit, are the "eyes of the forest," and they are her preferred technique because of their noninvasive character (they do not involve embedding chips or collars). The Bushnell's "no glow" model sports an antireflection mesh, so that the LCD viewer screen does not glint and attract undue attention. Beyond media-technological affordance, Laudisoit spoke expansively about her camera trap spatial design, a cultural technique key to tracking animal movements with new sensor technologies.[73] Camera traps follow the Eulerian method of tracking movement, which essentially captures all animal movements at a given spatial point. This is typically opposed to the Lagrangian method, which follows one population in its movement trajectories. Laudisoit's trek fits the latter in tracking relict chimpanzees, but her camera trap design with the twenty-seven fixed cameras in the sensor-mediated forest space adapts the Eulerian method for her purposes.[74] Most of her cameras were placed forty to sixty centimeters from the ground, so as not to miss smaller animals; five were placed in the arboreal canopy through which the monkeys swing. The camera trap placement segmented the forest vertically into cells of two hundred meters by two hundred meters, rendering vertical space intelligible. The forest appears as much in its vegetative undergrowth as in its soaring arboreal canopies.

The tracking media in Laudisoit's laborious transect illuminate machinic modes of detection that materialize moving animals and forest ecosystems. At the same time, camera traps are activated by the lively materialities of the forest and the participation of the animals. Epidemic media, once again, operate

Figure 4.6. Setting camera traps, film still from *MBudha*, 2018. Credit: Anne Laudisoit and Caroline Thirion.

Figure 4.7. Night visitor, film still from *MBudha*, 2018. Credit: Anne Laudisoit and Caroline Thirion.

on a biological-technological continuum, mingling machinic signals with vital signs—the animal's excreta, body temperature, rapid heartbeat, and muscular speed articulated with collection equipment, chemical agents, cameras, computers, and routers. All the while, the machinic eye sits quietly in the forest in hopes of recording multispecies kinesthesia. As biologists and ecologists walk behind their primate ancestors, a technically mediated kinesthesis brings awareness of shared ecosystems. Segmented and parsed, the tropical rain forest becomes medially comprehensible. The resultant organism-environment assemblage makes the case for what it takes to live with viruses in green dwellings.

EXPERIMENTS IN SENSING TECHNOLOGIES: BARRO COLORADO ISLAND

Zoologist Roland Kays has been following animals in the Americas for decades. A theorist and practitioner of animal-tracking technologies, he has been involved in designing animal-sensing infrastructures and camera traps and writing software for more precise signal detection in the age of big data. In "Born-Digital Biodiversity Data," Kays, William McShea, and Martin Wikelski argue that data management systems such as eMammal and Movebank are fast replacing traditional natural history museums as specimen collections, which traditionally indexed "the spatial distribution of life on earth."[75] Since collecting physical specimens is on the wane, photo-vouchering specimens with camera traps has become crucial to the endeavor. Movebank currently sports 1.5 billion photo-vouchered specimens as spatial ecology avails itself of new technologies and infrastructures. This is all the more reason for experiments with media-technological affordances and all the more incentive to test their capacities and limitations. Associated with the Smithsonian Tropical Research Institute, Kays has carried out some of his experiments in the controlled setting of Barro Colorado Island (BCI) in Panama, a "scientific jewel" in the Smithsonian's crown from the beginning of the twentieth century. In this regard, Kays's projects occupy the opposite end of the spectrum from Laudisoit's ventures. The biogeographic region he traverses is one of the most studied living laboratories in the world. Hence, it is an excellent setting for launching new experiments on machinic transmissions in tropical rain forests.

Barro Colorado Island became an island when the Chagres River was dammed in 1913 as part of the Panama Canal's construction. The island is only six square miles but houses 1,400 plant and 100 mammalian species. The Biological Research Station was established in 1923, and the island was declared a nature reserve; as a colonial space of conservation, it is the locus of hundreds of scientific experiments every year. The histories of industrial construction, disease emergence, and conservation efforts are inextricable from each other in this biogeography. We know that yellow fever threatened canal construction, fueling research into the mosquito as the arthropod vector for the (yellow fever) *Flavivirus*. Research into canopy-dwelling mosquitoes, in part, drove the establishment of the Biological Research Station on BCI.[76] Against this backdrop, wild primates make a historical appearance as sentinel populations. Two yellow fever outbreaks in 1948 and 1956 among howler monkeys that skipped into human populations drew attention to wild primates. On BCI, the American primatologist C. Ray Carpenter, who was one of the first scientists to film and videotape primates in their natural habitats, started his studies in the 1930s, setting early standards for primatology. Investigations in wild primate population density and immune systems joined the virological enterprise to biodiversity research. For all these reasons, the howler monkeys of BCI are part of the global story of cross-species virus transmissions. The island's history frames Kays's experiments with animal movements there. In all his endeavors, he poses medial concerns: How can we distinguish animal forms as foreground and the environment as background? What are the mechanisms that translate signals into measures of distance? What are the challenges for camera traps and radio waves in tracking movement? In what follows, three experiments illustrate Kays's long reflection on the technical mediation of animal movements.

Launched in 2003, the automated radio-telemetry system on BCI mounted several radio-telemetry receivers for signals from radio collars attached to small animals. The very high-frequency transmitters were attached to 374 individuals for six years. As part of this experiment, Kays focused on the methodological problem of "location estimation."[77] The point was to analyze "range-free" localization techniques: Could the signal strength of the radio wave capture distance accurately? Radio waves generally lose intensity as they travel over space; the greater the distance covered, the weaker the signal. Signal strength, then, could be the measure of distance and therefore enable plotting the animal's movement trajectory (see signal strength plotting in plate 18). In a discussion of the collaborative project, Kays analyzed the many challenges facing this technique. On the one hand, radio collars fitted with the smallest batteries delivered weak, hard to detect, signals. On the other hand, there was tremendous noise interference in the buzzing tropical rain forest. One might say the milieu was a discernibly active agent in formulating the organism-environment assemblage. As Brian Larkin has argued, "the unstable consequences" of media (as noise) interrupt and alter media (signals) that seek to govern: in this case, the tropical forest continues to emerge as the sensuous quality of biotechnical kinesthesia.[78] The forest is media for multispecies distributions; the biotechnical form, it turns out, is much more than decoded machinic signals. Biotechnical forms embody human, machinic, and plant materialities that emplace embedded or remote trackers "in" their environment. Errors and redundancies, even failures, are significant for this reason: throwing the senses toward the nonhuman world, they emerge as the sensuous quality of biotechnical form.

Kays's automated radio-telemetry experiment prompted a reassessment of ecological constraints on signals alongside the more conventional problem of invasive GPS localization technologies. One of the greatest challenges for the latter is to fit small animals with the smallest transmitters—amounting to something like less than 5 percent of the animal's body weight—and still retain transmitter efficacy. Kays experimented with small transmitters in a related project, the Agouti Enterprise, on BCI, which equipped agoutis or giant rodents with radio collars and radio-tagged the seeds they carry. Agoutis live in conditional mutualism with plants, carrying seeds through space. These rodents are partly beneficial in seed dispersal because they carry and cache seeds. But they are partly harmful as well (therefore, their mutualism is conditional) because of the competitive relationships within the agouti population. In the visualizations of seed dispersals, the researchers struggled to make sense of seed scattering: one seed moved 99 meters, and then back and forth, until it ended up 280 meters from the original point (plate 19). Over time, the Reconyx camera footage caught "robber agoutis" stealing 84 percent of the seeds cached by others; some of the rodents were not collared but appeared on camera. Also caught on the camera were ocelots, or wildcats, that hunted agoutis, a predator-prey relation that affected the mutualism between agoutis and plants. As researchers transcribed the camera-footage data into data visualizations to gain insight into agouti movement complexities, they found a proverbially complex story of evolving ecosystem relations among seeds and hiding places on the forest floor, agouti competitors and predators, radio collars and camera traps (plate 19).

A second experiment tracked howler monkeys among other wild primates on BCI. Unlike Laudisoit, Kays did not train in epidemiology but zoology; hence, his concerns are about the biodiversity of animal populations and not disease emergence per se. As a protected reserve, BCI is a laboratory for studies with far-reaching implications for the South American tropical rain forests. One of the difficulties in tracking wild primates living in these environments is the verdant and dense arboreal canopy. Needless to say, with deforestation comes severe habitat loss of these arboreal homes. In "Hot Monkey, Cold Reality," Kays and colleagues write about an experiment with flying drones fitted with radiometric sensors and cameras to track four species of wild primates on BCI: mantled howler monkeys, black-handed spider monkeys, kinkajous, and white-faced capuchins.[79] As in the Laudisoit-Thirion film *MBudha*, Kays made a video accompanying the research as an audiovisual field report of sorts on this remote-tracking venture.[80] The drones (DJI Matrice 600 Pro Drone) were fitted with radiometric thermal sensors for measuring the temperature of surfaces and with a fixed Canon EOS 5DS RGB camera

Figure 4.8. Fixing the drone camera, video still, 2018. Credit: North Carolina Museum of Natural Sciences, *Can Drones Help Count Rainforest Animals?*

for snapping footage (figure 4.8). Both were angled straight down at the ground in nadir view.

Isotherms located the thermal signatures of animal bodies, ranging from 27 to 53 degrees Celsius; tree-canopy temperatures were much cooler (23 to 25 degrees Celsius). The highest temperature, 53 degrees Celsius, identified spider monkeys, whose black fur absorbed heat from the sun during the day. The differences in temperatures—warm animal bodies, cool arboreal canopies—made it possible to discern moving forms against the environment as background. Plate 20 shows a thermal video capture of moving howler monkeys taken at the same time and place as the inset photograph. The red codes for daytime temperatures, while the white spots are the "hot" monkeys. Cooler nocturnal temperatures heighten the contrast between form and background in this thermal kinesthetic. The cameras and sensors were programmed with meteorological data, ambient-light specifications, and morphological identifiers to distinguish the biotechnical kinesthesia of the moving animals. The inset photograph from drone footage illustrates the difficulty of visually tracking wild primate movement in arboreal canopies without thermal sensors. As ever, Kays documents the challenges posed in the experiments, including the distracting noise of the drones and the problem of flying drones in this thickly forested region. But the drones had the advantage of mobility, keeping up with animals faster than biologists walking a transect in the forest could.[81] When I interviewed him in July 2020, Kays was unenthusiastic about the results of this experiment, for it did not yield precise data. But what the experiment revealed were the machinic parameters of signal detection (inscribing radiant heat energy emanating from animal bodies) before their transcription as RGB visual data. For the signals to cohere as data, and for data to become information, required filtering out the vibrant milieu as background noise. This was object formation in all its complexity.

Kays took up the challenge of subtracting the background from the animal form in his experiments using software tools. In "Animal Scanner," Kays and his coauthors explored ten images from two hundred camera traps to create data sets for testing newly developed software.[82] Of course, as mentioned earlier, Kays has deep expertise in camera trap designs for motion-sensitive game cameras.[83] But the capacity to record animals "automatically, continuously, and simultaneously," as he put it, presents its own problem: with voluminous data arriving faster and faster from citizen-scientists armed with low-cost cameras, developing software for processing organism-environment understandings has become urgent.[84] As an educator, Kays has been heavily involved in citizen-science efforts and is therefore aware of the need to develop computer vision tools that can filter, sort, and classify big data streams. In one experimental tool, he focused on filtering out "empty pictures" such as images showing humans (hikers, for instance) and other false triggers (like vegetal movement) so as to identify *animals* and *their* movements. The basis of the filter was methodical "object segmentation" that first identified the animal, then subtracted the background, and finally assembled animal motion over space to calculate the movement pattern. This meant neural-machinic processing of differences across colocated frames based on the "deep learning classifications" of image processing.[85] Each frame in the three images per trigger was segmented into 736 blocks. The software identified and extracted specific features from these blocks to assess if these features had changed in colocated blocks. The *calculation of change* rested on detecting a minimum feature distance between the same features in colocated blocks; a change or difference in the feature is understood in spatial terms as distance. If the minimum feature distance was large, indicating an increased difference between colocated blocks, then something had *moved*. Human-neural systems processed this spatial change as movement. But beyond detection, it was further necessary to figure out what the change signified—whether it was activated by animal, vegetal, or human presence. This transcription entailed subtracting the background from foreground regions: the bounded boxes in plate 21 capture the objects that are foregrounded for further analysis by assigning them mathematically calculable values. In this example, humans are classified in white-bounded boxes, animals in black-bounded boxes. The software aims at weeding out errors: the last row in plate 21, for example, shows a misclassification, a common problem attributed to object deformation, occlusion, and low contrast. As in the case of cameras embedded in the forest, digital transcriptions pose their own challenges. Once the images are cropped and the background subtracted, the forms in bounded boxes specify what exactly moved and how much. Comparing a training set (with three classes of movement) against a testing set (of randomly chosen movements) from thirty thousand images enabled Kays's team to fine-tune the filtering algorithms for proper detection. Aside from filtering algorithms, "deep object graphs" selected and sorted specific inputs from cluttered RGB maps to model the background. The selection of specific features and deep object graphs draws on scientific and cultural information about the biogeographic region to differentiate the environment from the animals and therein track their movement across space. Organism and environment emerge together, once more, as biotechnical kinesthesia. This third experiment offers a deeper look into digital image-processing techniques that transcribe *moving animal forms* layered against a *moving ecosystem*. Rendered calculable, the sampled images encode traffic in animal hosts.

These experiments in embedded and remote-tracking media present two very different constellations of knowledge communities (see plate 22). Laudisoit harvests long-term relationships with local and regional experts, institutional (at the University of Kisangani) or not (Lendu villagers), some living at human-wildlife interfaces of potential zoonotic spillovers. Kays, by contrast, engages massive citizen-science projects mounted on platforms such as eMammal or Zooniverse. eMammal, for one, hosts Snapshot USA every year, a monthlong challenge for wildlife enthusiasts and local experts to document "mammal richness" within habitats of their choosing, thereby generating voluminous data streams.[86] These networks oriented toward biodiversity research forge diverse knowledge communities. In this regard, both Laudisoit and Kays are exemplary modern practitioners consistently accommodating other worlds in their own scientific practices. Tracking animal movements, they are part of collective creative experiments that take account of the multispecies distributions on the planet.

As animals appear in biotechnical kinesthesia against their programmed environment, they are multispecies, carrying microbes. In the New World ecologies, white capuchin and howler monkeys are often studied for the pathogens they carry.[87] Since New World monkeys such as marmosets and squirrel monkeys block SIV-1 infection at the stage of viral entry into cells, they are of interest as animal models for biomedical research.[88] Furthering research in

HIV-1 pathogenesis, serological samples from these primates present potential therapeutic and prophylactic solutions to HIV infection in other primates. In all these ways, wild primates occupy a curious place in HIV research, at once animal reservoirs and animal models for biomedical study. The multispecies kinesthetic documents the ecological threat under which they live as their habitats become increasingly fragmented. As wild primates swing through vast arboreal canopies, pausing for food, birthing, and rest, the struggle to understand molecular phylogenies and biological functions continues in the quest to live with viruses. Perhaps the multispecies kinesthetic can serve as our best warning system against falling into ecological ill health.

Composing the Multispecies Kinesthetic

Animal movement tracking is one piece of the puzzle in rendering biodiversity loss as ecological threat. The spatial forms of maps and atlases based on the information extracted from signal detection are compositions that plot present and potential zones of virulence. Since maps and atlases are inextricable from extant cultural histories, these are indisputably aesthetic forms. I close with two modes of aesthetic composition salient to the study of spillovers: the first is a standard model, a normative conjugation of biodiversity research and potential EID hot spots, and the second is an experimental, curated yet improvisatory compendium of "field reports" on threatening ecologies. Considered together, the two media practices direct us to the processes of mediation constitutive of living between loss and abundance in the epidemic episteme.

Geospatial epidemic media capture novel multispecies associations as species distributions in biogeographic regions. Program earth appears as the normative world map (figure 4.9, right) layered with data from various sources that articulate published research with live satellite data inputs. These articulations compose the (dis)joints of globe and planet. EcoHealth Alliance produces zoonotic surveillance models that track viral sharing networks so as to map phylogeographic regions with high likelihood of zoonotic spillovers. Predictions of viral interconnectedness within and between mammalian orders, they maintain, are a public health research priority.[89] The heat maps visualize phylogenetic data from published research ("all data" from the 1940s onward) and "stringent data" (from viral bioassays and direct evidence) to analyze high viral diversity within a species and viral sharing across species.[90]

Published in a paper coauthored by Noam Ross, one of the data scientists at EcoHealth Alliance, the table accompanying the world map aggregates viral richness in different mammalian orders (which includes 4,196 mammals) (see

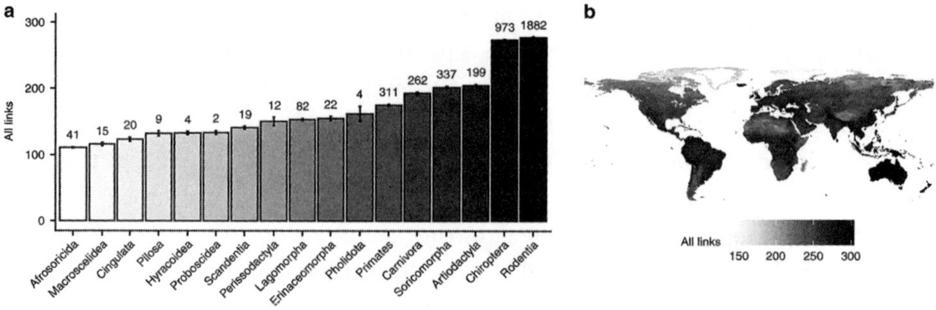

Figure 4.9. Heat map detail of taxonomic and geographic distributions. Source: Albery et al., "Predicting the Global Mammalian Viral Sharing Network," 2020

figure 4.9, tabulation on the left). Wild mammals are of particular importance as high-risk sources of pathogenic viral transmission. Existing data from 591 recorded viral associations show that rodents (Rodentia) and bats (Chiroptera) have "high viral interconnectedness," which means a host of viruses are exchanged within and between bat and rodent populations.[91] The research shows that this phylogenetic aggregation is one of the conditions for zoonotic spillovers. These data are articulated as biogeographic distributions since viral sharing networks are stronger in areas where there is an overlap of different species as well as high diversity within each species. Such notations draw on IUCN data on species ranges in biogeographic regions. In the presentation of results, scientific papers visualizing phylogeographic data account for geographic bias, adjusting the model to accommodate the lack of data (or scant data) from some relatively inaccessible biogeographic regions.[92] The point of the model is to project probabilities based on available data even as the scientists and modelers remain reflexively tuned to data still to be gathered. In an interview Noam Ross, who was trained as a forest/plant ecologist specializing in plant epidemiology, explained the efficacies of generalized additive models in evaluating these data over the black box option. In my limited understanding, black box models are productive in big-data analysis: the model is viewed for its inputs and outputs rather than for the internal workings of the system.[93] General additive models, however, attend to the known functions of a system. In this case, "all data" from phylogenetic trees and IUCN "species ranges" yield considerable information on the processes of viral sharing, but there is the understanding that new data streams might warrant modifications of those functions. Hence, such maps may appear to be totalizing forms, but they are *provisional* snapshots. Once data are information, aesthetic compositions of the results crosshatch available tools, noted Ross, such as a Mixed Gam Computation Vehicle (MGCV) package for R (an open-source programming language) and the University of Copenhagen's QGIS geoprocessing tool for designating thirty-four zoogeographic zones. The consequent mathematical transcriptions find expression in cultural forms (the world map) coded with commonplace referents—red for hot, blue for cool. The maps mobilize open-access programs, tool kits, and models, alongside geospatial technologies that enable the composition of live data into prediction. Increasingly, such open-ended maps hosted on publicly accessible sites situate EID events as ecological threats in the epistemic episteme.

A rather different effort unfolds in the curated *Feral Atlas* as an interactive online model for inhabiting the more-than-human Anthropocene. As Jennifer Deger and colleagues argue, "field-based and historically grounded observations" attentive to the uneven cascading effects of the Anthropocene "are more necessary than ever before" as a complement to the planetary-scale modeling of program earth.[94] Based on anthropological imperatives, the atlas as a compendium constellates "reports, essays, artworks, code, and design" from more than a hundred contributors to investigate relationships that stimulate "ferality"—the tangle of nonhuman entities with human-built infrastructures.[95] The evolving assemblies produce threatening ecologies of present and future harms. Such an approach convenes diverse knowledge communities and includes field reports from communities most vulnerable to ecological degradation. The "uneven geographies" of the *Feral Atlas* highlight harms to nonhuman entities and human communities, closing the divide between biodiversity research and environmental justice agendas; the aim is to think both together. In all these ways, the *Feral Atlas* facilitates a thoroughfare between transdisciplinary collaborations and in situ observations necessary for engaging imperial and industrial ruin.

As one enters the site, the seventy-nine field reports appear as mobile icons—a rabbit, microbial DNA, water bodies, plants, a rat, cows, fungi, an ant, a mosquito, nuclei in cells, fires, smokestacks, the parched earth. . . . Figure 4.10 is one snapshot of this moving feast. No world map appears to locate us in these dynamic assemblies. The dynamism of evolving ecologies is performed by the floating icons that move in and out of the frame; they function as portals into heterogeneous field reports. To take a snapshot of this processual form, as I have done, is rather counterintuitive since the point of the atlas is to destabilize the "capture" of ecological relationalities in static world pictures. Users are invited to find their own way in singular trajectories through the atlas. If there is a visible conceptual architecture, users can view it in the four nodes

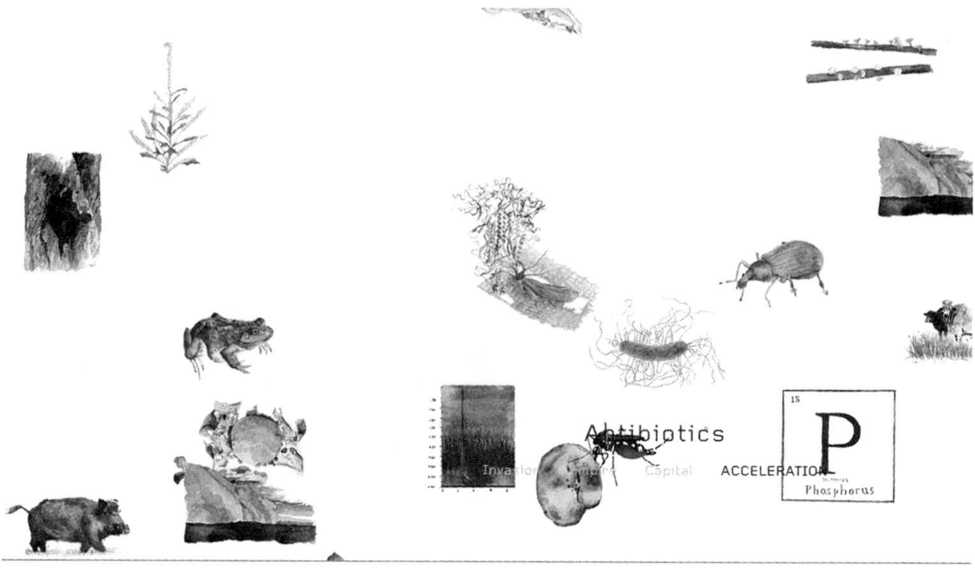

Figure 4.10. Online *Feral Atlas* navigation portals (screenshot). Source: Tsing, Deger, Saxena, and Zhou (curators), *Feral Atlas*, Stanford University Press, 2021. https://feralatlas.supdigital.org/

that organize the index: invasion, empire, capital, and acceleration, a listing accessible by clicking the floating key at the top left-hand corner. These rubrics present recognized anthropogenic regimes in whose historical shadow pathogenicity emerges. When visual arrangements or stable configurations appear, they are heterogeneous—a grid, a diagram, a flow map, mobile drawings, rather than cartographies. Figure 4.11 is the illustration for the "empire" node of the atlas: tagged as an "Anthropocene Detonator Landscape," it signals Indigenous codifications of changing ecologies.

I followed specific icons such as rabbits, rats, coronavirus, potato blight, and radioactive insects, among others, that make more-than-human social worlds. Exploring the interactive atlas generates unexpected pathways connecting patchy ecologies: for example, clicking on a mosquito or rabbit does not yield scientific information or epidemic histories of these creatures. Rather, one journeys into theories and reports, histories and visual illustrations, to apprehend the story of planetary damage. Disease emergence is but one ecological threat we stumble on in this vast compendium of threatening ecologies. The multiple sites of knowledge production in the *Feral Atlas* demonstrate the possibilities of thinking life otherwise. Dislodging us from normative habit, epidemics emerge as multitemporal crisis events—as Dubos's constellation of

Figure 4.11. "Anthropocene Detonator Landscape: Empire," screenshot of *Feral Atlas* website, 2020. Source: Tsing, Deger, Saxena, and Zhou (curators), *Feral Atlas*, Stanford University Press, 2021. https://feralatlas.supdigital.org/world/empire

circumstances. The atlas compels users to engage the past and present harms of anthropogenic change apprehended every day but perhaps not entirely intelligible. The multispecies kinesthetic materializes in interactive and relational affordances of digital forms and platforms, building large, heterogeneous knowledge communities committed to figuring out how to live on a damaged planet.

Coda: Living Otherwise

All evidence shows that EID events driven by anthropogenic change are ecological threats that will keep coming unless we apprehend them as more-than-human processes and relations. The provocation is to expand the epidemic episteme beyond the exterminating and wrecking games of the post–World War II period. To encounter these processes and relations poses the question of mediation: What mediatic situations push us to live otherwise in the more-than-human Anthropocene? How can media dislodge old harmful habits whose uneven effects on nonhuman entities and vulnerable human communities continue to proliferate? How do media implicate us in threatening ecologies?

Apprehension immediately conjures mediation as prehension, our perceptual grasp of ontic relationalities. Acting responsibly in the patchy Anthropocene requires an expansive understanding of media as/in the environment that scholars across the field of environmental media studies explore together. The search is on for new research paradigms in media studies that analyze how media operate *and* what they can do in apprehending ecological threats. Following EIDs as ecological threats (narrowed to zoonotic spillovers in this chapter) affords a closer look at animal, machinic, and human prehension as a perceptual complex, pressing beyond mandates of ever more precise machinic capture. To study mediation orients media scholars toward in situ mediatic processes—interpreting vital traces, navigating drones, placing camera traps—that are the bases of planetary-scale models. If the latter compel institutional action, research agendas, and environmental policy, they build on diverse knowledge communities, from citizen-scientists to local and regional experts. To focus on mediation is to zoom in to such participatory world building at concrete sites and to zoom out to transdisciplinary collaborations around widely shared imperatives. Thus, the chapter commences with tracking as media practice, always a situated one, whether embedded or remote, and closes with compositions that render information comprehensive in globally legible forms (the world map and the atlas). In both detection and composition, knowledge is provisional, open-ended, conjectural; more importantly, perhaps, the sensuousness of biotechnical kinesthesia apprehends multispecies entanglements.

Understanding the media situation, then, is crucial to the epidemic episteme. While the short-sightedness of emergency might propel immediate capture and control, placing extermination on the table, lessons from Anthropocene histories should direct us toward the long game. I write this amid widespread impatience with not catching up with wily variants, with changing health recommendations, with increasingly uneven resource distributions. Perhaps the HIV story should remind us how to apprehend abundance and loss. For these axes of multispecies politics remain constitutive of the more-than-human Anthropocene. Perhaps refracting our gaze to mediation might alter the course of history returning as farce. What media—as medium, apparatus, and infrastructure—apprehend the threatening ecologies of the epidemic episteme? Opening to new possibilities of living otherwise, we might ask: What are media becoming?

CONCLUSION

Media Theory (in a Pandemic)

As a witness to the period known as early AIDS, Paula Treichler wondered how to have theory in an epidemic of grievous losses when abstractions hurt.[1] Looking back to Albert Camus's 1947 *The Plague*, she mused on his melancholic observation on theory's abstractions amid the modern plagues. "Still," writes Camus, "when abstraction sets to killing you, you've got to get by with it."[2] Treichler's aim was to situate scientific facts and findings in the social and cultural structures that underwrite them—in other words, to concretize their historical materiality. *How to Have Theory in an Epidemic* undertook that task with cultural theory as its theoretical object and critical practice. Amid the linguistic turn, Treichler, among others, unraveled the cultural dimensions of science that had turned a health emergency into a moral cesspool. The AIDS epidemic, Treichler argued, "does not exist to demonstrate the value of contemporary theory. If anything, it puts theory stringently to the test, serving as a useful and often dramatic correction for inadequate theoretical formulations."[3] My retrospective look frames the present juncture of daily confrontations with scientific theories, clinical instructions, and public health policies; abstractions hurt as losses turn into statistics, and health policy seems to arrive all too late. For media scholars attuned to the first fully digital pandemic, mediatic processes that materialize the pandemic require closer scrutiny. Questions concerning the mediation of life arise, pushing the disciplinary boundaries of what media once were. One might rephrase Treichler's animating query for the current situation: How to have *media theory* in a pandemic? How does the epidemic paradigm put media studies to the test?

This book's reflections on the scientific-technological mediation of "life" in the epidemic episteme place media studies and the biosciences at the center. With life an increasingly elastic concept in the multiform biosciences, those who study mediatic processes in science laboratories often focus on lively matter and medial processes rather than on representations alone. For inquiries into making/doing/enacting epidemic media habitually disclose the entangled materiality of living processes and relations. The material settings for my inquiries have ranged from the cool confines of laboratories to vibrating tropical forests to modest clinics—all in the messiness of raging pandemics. The structuring event-horizon of emerging infectious diseases orients epidemic media in health emergencies toward instrumental goals. Delivering biotechnological and biomedical solutions may be epidemic media's telos, but is that all epidemic media do? Pursuing this line of inquiry, a second question inspires, this time from the closing chapter of Natasha Myers's account of making proteins. Myers closes her ethnography musing, *What is life becoming?*[4] To focus on the virus, a boundary object, already keeps faith with this open question. But in tracking epidemic media, another rephrasing is in order: *What are media becoming?* I conclude this book with Treichler and Myers to mark the historicity of *The Virus Touch*, a book that spans two global epidemics. "Finished" in the midst of a global pandemic, it eschews mastery of its theoretical object, epidemic media, because pandemic pasts and presents unsettle. Abstraction, it turns out, continues to hurt.

My study has theorized epidemic media as critical media practices that materialize an immanent multispecies relation to control infection. As image making, record keeping, and motion sensing make that relation intelligible, they *still* life's becomings in stable configurations. These biotechnical forms are intra-active performances, as we have seen, that are constrained by their material settings. Such a reading attends to their historical materiality, taking a page from science studies scholars who underscore scientific facts as constructions. When we are faced with a *new* emergence, this general feature is more accentuated: we see this routinely in the many performances of scientific findings and (sometimes publicized) debates over the novel coronavirus during the COVID-19 pandemic. Epidemic media materialize these facts and findings, some empirically verifiable, others theoretically calculable. Amid impatience and suspicion, the histories of making HIV epidemic media illustrate the significance of such conjectural forms in the steady progress toward viable solutions. In the furious acceleration of pandemic time, epidemic media's speculative bent is simply historical necessity in the face of radical uncertainty. We might remember that propositions and hunches, intuitions and theoretical insights, are what made possible the hyperendemicity of HIV infection. Situating the research on SARS-CoV-2 in this historical frame recasts the present conjuncture as one stop in the slow craftwork of modifying pathogenic multispecies relations.

The present seems all too slow and simultaneously vanishing under the weight of epidemic pasts and pandemic futures. We can scarcely hold on to the now in the untimeliness of pandemic urgencies. This *thick temporality* structures epidemic media. Nothing is ever enough, or complete; something out there beckons. Pattern recognition from pasts—everything we have learned about spiked orbs, about vital media, about reservoir hosts—acquires value, opening myriad trajectories into the future. All pathways are relevant even as there are efforts to monetize just one: Remember the hydroxychloroquine game in the early months of COVID-19? The pathways we go down can have long-term consequences, as we know from the deadly DDT strategy of the mid-twentieth century. This thick temporality informs my approach to epidemic media as the animating research concept that informs media analyses and media histories in *The Virus Touch*.

The qualifier *epidemic* as a structuring event-horizon for thinking about what media are aligns this book with other explorations of media actions "during harmful events," as Lisa Parks and Janet Walker put it, in a special issue on "disaster media." "Thinking about these and related processes through the disaster media lens has led us to ask all over again what 'media' are and to contend with how, especially during harmful events, media in various modalities proliferate, transform, translate, and inevitably sculpt the environment," they write. Media in/as environment, they continue, "give shape and meaning to disasters themselves, and become integral to the ways disasters are imagined, experienced, and felt."[5] Complex temporalities of harm underwrite the world-making force of media in this analysis, directing what media *are* and what they *do*; how to *situate* media practices, temporally and spatially; and what critical methods are most salient to evaluating their role. What, indeed, are media becoming? Studying different modalities of disaster media has been immensely productive for media theory: for instance, writings on climate change or toxicity provide specific insights about deep timescales, about chemical relationalities, expanding the paradigms of media study. In the same vein, one could ask where this inquiry into epidemic media leads.

Epidemic media is a research concept adjacent to disaster media since epidemics are crisis events organized around harm, ongoing and anticipated. There are *historical* lessons from pandemics past that have installed a "new memory" since the early 1980s, one that articulates (emerging infectious disease) epidemics as nonlinear multitemporal biological, social, and ecological catastrophes. One might say this nonlinearity pertains to other disasters such as climate change or ozone layer depletion. For all disasters, "new memories" are not universal but marked by differential vulnerabilities, depending on where the disasters unfolded, who was affected, what was made intelligible, and what remained obscure. We know these historical differences from criticisms of the Anthropocene as a catchall term for all anthropogenic disasters. Yet epidemics are distinct *as* environmental crises. First, they privilege *making life* as the central problematic at a time when large-scale disasters make it urgent to think living and nonliving process-relations together, and at a time when the distinction of "life" is under pressure even in the biosciences. The immanent value of life in epidemic intensities sits uneasily in ongoing efforts to unthink anthropocentricism and to reflect on the coemergence of human and nonhuman relations. But as I have argued, life in the current epidemic episteme is fundamentally about unfolding ecological processes and relations with multispecies entanglements occupying pride of place. In this strain of environmental thought, the biosciences that take life as their theoretical object are in the lead. Second, there is no wide agreement on the narrative of incremental harm for infectious disease epidemics. There is no "5°C temperature rise" equivalent for these "sudden" emergences that generate questions about qualitative shifts, about how to model or predict them. It is possible to stabilize conditions of possibility for pathogenicity in emergent multispecies relations when infection is zoonotic in origin. But neither phylogenetic evolutionary histories nor well-demarcated hotspots offer a stable timeline of harm. In all these ways, as a research concept for thinking media as/in the environment, epidemic media are not recognizably disaster media like floods, fires, and earthquakes; the relation is one of adjacency.

To track epidemic media, then, requires attending to the very historicity of the concept. Epidemics harken back to ancient times, but those epidemics are not the same as epidemics in the modern episteme. After the viral emergences of the early 1980s, the epidemic materialized as a specific kind of event organized around a rereading of what is harmful. In the current knowledge configuration, killing pathogenic germs is a shaky option at best; controlling and regulating infection across time-spaces is more viable. This historicity shapes what we understand to be epidemic media of the more-than-human Anthropocene. But what can this current epidemic paradigm illuminate for media theory?

#Intensity

After affect studies, *intensity* is a buzzword in media theory. As a quality of epidemic media, it acquires particular definition. Think of what the delta variant has done. We are, once again, in the midst of a qualitative shift, confronted with racing viral temporalities (see Note 1).[6] The animating question for epidemic media is: What precisely makes this variant of SARS-CoV-2 more efficient? How to render that efficiency intelligible in unfolding molecular events?

> *Note 1*
>
> The delta variant has changed the game, we hear. The variant first emerged in India in December 2020 and soon proved 40 percent more transmissible than the first variant, the alpha strain that emerged in the United Kingdom. To understand its biological mechanisms, we plunge back into molecular investigations. For some of us, we are back to following the discussions over enzymes: those proteases that had to be inhibited to block HIV entry into human cells. We learn that a human enzyme, a protease called furin, helps the SARS-CoV-2 spike fuse into human cellular membranes. As the virus nears the cell, a spike protein (the S protein) bends toward specific receptors in our respiratory cells. Human enzymes "cut" or prime the spike for entry, usually twice for SARS-CoV-2. But the delta variant needs but one cut; it has become more efficient in its fusion capacity. This change in the virus is miniscule to nonexperts—just one change in the amino acids (P681R) that make up the S protein. All eyes are on the furin cleavage site: epidemic media render it visible even as much remains uncharted. There are debates, conjectures, in the slow work of catching up with this mutation. The gaze is intensely micro, but the implications are extensive, frighteningly so. Amid epidemic intensities, making epidemic media is urgent in this trajectory of harm. Meanwhile, the delta variant speeds ahead, changing the world as we know it.

How to plot theoretical possibilities for altering this relation? The questions are *intense* because they materialize elements of the intensive environment that enable efficient infection. The time-space of infection stretches tight between embodied molecules (of vital media) and excorporated molecules (of vital media transforming into elemental media). Epidemics are intense experiences that collapse distance from the epistemic object; one is hyperaware of being viscerally entangled "in" the very media environment one studies. At the same time, the time-space of infection spirals out extensively in accelerating infection trajectories. This sensuous entanglement is difficult to set aside under epidemic conditions: one cannot escape a "throwing of the senses" toward multispecies relations even when they feel most difficult. As processes of mediation place media makers in the flux of participation, knowing multispecies entanglement becomes unavoidable in making/doing/enacting epidemic media. Caught in a vortex of lively agencies, the knowing subject struggles for objective mastery: to bring clarity, precision, and accuracy to the problematic multispecies relation.

Intensity further informs my preoccupations with the tangibility of epidemic media. "Tangible media" (Natasha Myers) or "wet" media (Eugene Thacker) surface in predictable ways accompanying processes of optical capture or digital transcription.[7] Vital traces such as handprints or feces are just as important to tracking media practices as chemically denatured vital samples are to probes that quantify viral particles. Tangible media are intermediaries of the sensuous experience that complement machine vision. The material settings for tangible media are diverse as I plot the gathering of feces in forests, the positioning of camera traps, the drawing of vital fluids at clinics . . . these concrete sites proliferate in the book. Machines are equally sensuous in the physicality of hardware: the spin of the centrifuge, the clasp of headgear for 3D images, the lightness of the hemocytometer lever, and the gleam of glass pipettes activate embodied participation. Some tangible media and machines are not conventional to media studies, so their inclusion in this book lays trails for new media histories.

Beyond these additions, the insistence on tangible media intervenes in media studies of life as mathematical abstraction. The genomic revolution set in motion understandings of life as code: tampering with code was *the* god trick. A mathematical realism that rendered life as calculable has energized media theory ever since as theorists ponder biological and technological processes. It is not that attending to life as code shunts the embodied experience; quite the contrary. This is especially the case in media studies of artificial intelligence and of synthetic life. But the orientation toward code too often institutes an intellectual *rupture* between analog and digital mediatic processes. In part, the separation has to do with the kind of deep expertise media historical work demands. But theorizing epidemic media mandates making "partial connections" (as in Isabelle Stengers) between *media practices*—between the digital and the analog, the tangible and the intangible—that target controlling infection.[8] The separation between digital and analog obtains not just in biomedia studies but in controlled experiments elsewhere. Remote-sensing animal motion as a media practice is separated from the embedded transect, for example, with the latter positioned as the analog anterior. This occludes scrutiny of tangible processes: the position of camera traps, the weight of geolocative devices, the vegetal situation. The two stories of animal motion sensing in this book deliberately constellate embedded and remote practices as tracking media. The study of tangible media, then, poses different questions of media practices: What does it take to prepare a sample for PCR (polymerase chain reaction) assays? How does one place a camera in the forest? What hardware materializes machine visions of living systems? A focus on tangibility repeatedly closes the analog-digital gap and broadens understandings of contemporary media practices. Remote sensing and embedded transects are *tracking media*, mathematical models and immersive image experiences constitute *molecular visualization*, and freezing blood samples and uploading blood data together produce the *blood files*. These juxtapositions return readers to concrete situations, to material specificities, where "scientific study" fails without making partial connections.

The stories of people and things, animals and plants, soils and air, machines and the senses, aim to emplace readers in epidemic intensities. The senses partitioned away return to dislodge abstraction, and medial actions are embodied as material performances. Sensuous "knowing" as a mode of being places media makers in the intimate entanglement of infection. My emphasis on tangibility underscores this other kind of knowing when epistemic cuts tend toward abstraction.

 # New Memory

The scattering of media practices in *The Virus Touch* sets it apart from media inquiries that focus on one media practice (e.g., molecular animation, microcinematography, video games), one historical period/genre (e.g., early scientific film, HIV/AIDS video, cell culture technologies), or one media theoretical trajectory (e.g., classical film theory or biomedia studies). This scattering is a critical method dictated by the pandemic event-horizon. As emergences, pandemics are frustratingly nonlinear. Just when vaccines are out, a black fungus emerges (see Note 2); just when all eyes turn to bats, a lab leak theory arises (see

Note 2

Suddenly COVID-19 erupts in color. Even as the visualized spiked orb made the submicroscopic particle SARS-CoV2 aesthetically ubiquitous, COVID-19 infection remained symptomatically indiscernible until saliva tests proved otherwise. But something different emerged amid India's second wave: a new life-form, mucormycosis, or black fungus, accompanying SARS-CoV-2. Ill-health from COVID -19 hit the visual register in blackening, necrotizing skin, among other disfiguring symptoms. This was not a previously identified comorbidity; it arose from immunosuppression (especially, aggressive steroid treatments). More importantly, the fungal spores made landfall in those who had long stays at hospitals with mechanical ventilators and oxygen pipes/cylinders. As is the case with ontologies of harm, the coemergence of virus and fungus activated many theories; some were pointed accusations about crumbling hospital infrastructures, not the least of which were unhygienic pipes. This was an illustration of industrial mediation in threatening ecologies of infection. For this was indisputably a human-made disaster. In the year after the initial lockdown of March 2020, the Narendra Modi–Amit Shah government had done very little to amplify health-delivery systems. In May 2021 government representatives cowered away from the public as black cremation smoke choked the skies and bloated bodies wafted down the Ganges. Spectacular and chromatic, the black fungus left its calling card, installing a new memory of anthropogenic harm.

Note 3).[9] This nonlinearity informs how media theories/histories and bioscience research are conjugated in this book.

Media histories spark this conjugation; without them, this nonlinear constellation working toward a "new memory" of pandemics would not be possible. In this regard, *The Virus Touch* builds on well-worn ground. One history is particularly salient to this book: the alliance between microbiology and optical media technologies in the mid-nineteenth century. Microbiology was born in the crucible of germ theory, but its theoretical propositions were not verifiable without optical technologies, notably the microscope. Bacteria and viruses do not "appear" in morphological distinctions before the mid-nineteenth century; they are not among Ernst Haeckel's illustrations, not among Antonie van Leeuwenhoek's wiggling creatures. It is germ theory that orients the study of infection toward the technical mediation of imperceptible microbial agents and their life processes. The mid-nineteenth-century conjugation of media and biology directs the book's historical forays, but mine is not a continuous media history. Rather, it constellates discontinuous media histories around a *historical turn*: the current epidemic episteme, in which the specter of viral emergence comes to overwrite the epidemic as crisis event. That emergence commands conjugations of discrete media histories. The epistemology of sudden infection generates a rupture and galvanizes the temporality of shocks and jolts. We live with uncertainty, with pandemics as perpetual futurity. Epidemic media make/enact new memories as partial, motivated, and dynamic, always arriving with every shock. Surely we knew this was coming; we should have read the stars.

Amid uncertainty, prior global pandemics are historical lifelines. Global pandemics materialize sudden synchronicities orienting different agendas, different experiences of harm, different needs toward a shared telos. While that telos can manifest as particular solutions—tried and tested antiretroviral therapies, effective vaccines—global pandemics can activate much broader negotiations among multiple stakeholders. One threshold for these negotiations is "health" as a collective enterprise. As an iconic global pandemic, HIV/AIDS has shown how the world could indeed come together around illness, dying, and surviving in negotiations that recast health as a moving target. Whether it was the insistence on health as care practices and infrastructures, or health as global commons, or health as structural one health inclusive of nonhuman others, the target put a symbiotic agreement on the table. As another jolt, COVID-19 opens a pathway into this new memory with vast archives, including the well-crafted histories of the AIDS crisis. Following one strand of epidemic media, then, can provide a historical pathway through thick temporalities. That pathway installs new memories of how we came to live in ecological and social ruins.

#Discordance

The lab leak theory seeks clarity (Note 3).[10] It seems intolerable that we still do not know where the virus emerged; so it *must have been* engineered, or so human hubris suggests. Seeking coherence is survival during epidemics, whether that is in linear causalities or elegant directives. The messiness of viruses skipping species barriers—where? how? when?—is troubling, especially since preventing such jumps in the future is a herculean task. We can't get the world to agree there is climate change. Imagine international agreements on regulating illegal

Note 3

The lab leak theory casts doubt on the Hunan Seafood Wholesale Market as the possible source of a spillover event. China's cagey response to the World Health Organization's investigation of the site exacerbates claims that there is something to hide: the possibility that the Wuhan Institute of Virology, which had been working on coronaviruses, had engineered a more virulent pathogen in a "gain of function" experiment. And it had leaked, accidentally. Fingers point to three laboratory workers who had strange pneumonia-like symptoms in November 2019, before the first cases in Wuhan. Amateur sleuths uncover an "incident" of six workers at the Mojiang mine in southwestern China's province of Yunnan who fell ill with pneumonia-like symptoms while scrubbing bat feces off a copper seam way back in 2012. Ideological battles erupt on the global stage and nationally in the United States. After all, the Wuhan Institute of Virology had received funding from the National Institutes of Health. Meanwhile, Shi Zhengli, the head of the institute's Virology Lab, stringently protests the theory. Several notable virologists claim natural origins, possibly from an intermediate host, but the lab leak theory offers a clean resolution, clear blame. We find it difficult to confront the wildness of natural origins for it implies moving across discordant landscapes, placing us in industrial ruin and ecological disrepair.

wildlife trade or restricting deforestation in global hotspots. Better to blame human malevolence or carelessness. I may be eating these words in the near future, but the ecological diagnosis is quite clear from pandemics in the past: from HIV, from Ebola, from H1N1, from SARS, from MERS. A similar point may be made about the unfolding public health crises. A stay-at-home policy, for instance, must have clear guidelines translatable across contexts. And yet we know the variables: home is a shared bedroom or spacious mansion; home is a street and a shelter. Unanticipated disasters arise precisely around stay-at-home orders as infections fester in multigenerational family spaces or a million migrants trek home to their villages. Home turns out to be a deadly trap, a place of exile and not of refuge. These pandemic memories afford a distributed sense of home, and not all of them map as geopolitical differences between richer and poorer nations. These discordances are inevitable for global emergencies in general, but acute infection highlights unmanageable time-space extensions, global and planetary. We experience discordance—not only in what is to be done but in where we should intervene.

Epidemic media materialize in discordant landscapes, facing the challenge of making objects and relations, sites and scales, cohere. The chapters offer a range of epidemic media as practices of willed coherence. We have seen how media technologies such as PCR machines and centrifuges detect and compose numerical distributions of "viral particles" in "host blood" at the clinical scale. The "interior milieu" makes molecular drift cohere, cutting off blood's vicissitudes in databases or clinics. Or we have seen how incoming data of different sorts, from genomic to biochemical, cohere in images of virus macromolecules. Scientific images faithful to accurate data constrain aesthetic vivification that renders them lively; the image experience is secondary to precise capture. These instances illustrate the purposeful organization of diffuse information in media practices. Dissipation coheres, notes Stengers, privileging specific epistemic objects and occluding others.[11] It would be annoying for a molecular biologist to be bothered with species-level analyses, or indeed for a clinician to be involved in policy on habitat fragmentation. But in the stories of collaborations and negotiations, the modern practitioners make such partial connections across material settings. Such negotiations over ontologies of infection—dealing with failing lungs, with communal losses—is but historical necessity. If the experience of COVID-19 teaches us anything, it is to keep abreast of pandemic scatter: to think vaccine development alongside legislation on illegal wildlife trade, to think social anomie alongside clinical comorbidities in vulnerable populations. Or else we are faced with the surety that crisis events such as COVID-19 will arrive every so often, demanding expensive solutions that take decades to distribute. Hence the intentional politics of this book, oriented toward making new memories for living with pandemics.

The HIV/AIDS activist Emily Bass first drew my attention to "scattering" as an analytic when we both contributed to the volume *AIDS and the Distribution of Crisis* (2020).[12] The collection appeared as the COVID-19 pandemic broke, motivating the conveners, Jih-Fei Cheng, Alexandra Juhasz, and Nishant Shahani, to orchestrate a series of online events on what the HIV/AIDS crisis teaches us about the present moment. I came to understand better the project of new memory. *The Virus Touch* deliberately proliferates skills and talents, institutions and industries, agents and actors. We find molecular biologists, structural biologists, evolutionary biologists, epidemiologists, data scientists, programmers, engineers, animators, health-care workers, nurses, health educators, painters, sculptors, computer graphics technicians, academics, caregivers, and AIDS activists, alongside viruses, bacteria, plants, animal hosts, molecules, genes, optical devices, tool kits, software programs, and motion sensors, among other nonhuman agents, in the story of HIV emergence. As epidemic media emerge, they invite us to probe the edges of specialized fields and to inhabit the discordant landscapes of media studies.

I mark my debt to fellow scholars, artists, scientists, and activists, among so many others, who taught me the difficult arts of negotiation: to occupy an unsettled critical space between disciplines. These modern practitioners made collaborative knowledge making the cornerstone of surviving pandemics. Some of them are no longer with us. How indeed to have theory in an epidemic?

Notes

INTRODUCTION

1 I am echoing Michael Balter's iteration in his coverage of the HMP, launched in 2008. Balter, "International Human Microbe Program." The HMP was *the* new "big science" initiative, generating the same degree of excitement within scientific communities as the international Human Genome Project did a decade ago. A collaboration between the National Institutes of Health in the United States and the European Commission, the HMP plans to sequence approximately nine hundred microbial genomes of bacteria, viruses, and fungi from samples collected from specific sites of the human body (the digestive tract, the mouth, the skin, the nose, and the vagina), first from healthy volunteers and, later, from humans with specific illnesses. The European Commission's Metagenomics of the Human Intestinal Tract Project (MetaHIT) specializes exclusively in the microbiome for the human gut; other partners include major science and health agencies in France, Japan, Canada, and several other countries. See Yong, "Microbiome Sequencing."

2 Sagan's "The Human Is More Than Human" (in *The Cosmic Apprentice*) calls for a defamiliarization of the human based on a symbiotic perspective on planetary evolution. I return to the basis of his claims—to symbiogenesis—in chapter 1. Here I invoke Sagan as a key figure who constellates scientific and cultural histories of multispecies emergence. Helmreich discusses Sagan's essay in writing about the implications of the HMP in "*Homo microbis*."

3 Dietert, *Human Superorganism*, 2.

4 Yong, *I Contain Multitudes*, 1857.

5 Carl Zimmer, "How Microbes Defend and Define Us," *New York Times*, July 13, 2010, https://www.nytimes.com/2010/07/13/science/13micro.html; and Helmreich and Paxson, "Perils and Promises of Microbial Abundance."

6 Sagan, *Cosmic Apprentice*.

7 Rheinberger, *Epistemology of the Concrete*.

8 Murphy, "Afterlife and Decolonial Chemical Relations."

9 A long-wave epidemic is one that emerges over the years with different modalities of impact. The first stage is usually when infected people are not visible to medical science; stage 4 commences when the number of cases threatens to overwhelm health resources. See Whiteside, *HIV/AIDS*.

10 Writing on the chemosphere, medical anthropologists such as Nicholas Shapiro and Alex Nading, among others, have tracked the epidemics—such as chemical poisoning and kidney diseases—that do not register as political emergencies primarily because they unfold as long-term harm among vulnerable (often racialized) communities with little recourse to mechanisms of political redress. See Shapiro and Kirksey, "Chemo-Ethnography"; and Nading, *Mosquito Trails*. On metabolic disorders, see, for instance, Nobert, Birkenfeld, and Schulze, "Global Pandemics Interconnected."

11 Povinelli, *Between Gaia and the Ground*.

12 Cheng, Juhasz, and Shahani, *AIDS and the Distribution of Crisis*.

13 See Online Etymology Dictionary, s.v. "emergence," accessed July 26, 2022, https://www.etymonline.com/word/emergence.

14 Clark and Hird track the politics of microbes encountering each other and humans encountering microbes. Clark's oeuvre represents a swathe of critical geography that grapples with the spatialization of entanglements, interconnectivities, and enfoldings in human and non-human agencies. See Clark and Hird, "Microontologies."

15 In her oft-cited notion of "reciprocal capture," Stengers elaborates the point as the "dual process of identity construction" that unfolds in species relations: "one values the other," giving rise to "immanent modes of existence." Stengers, *Cosmopolitics I*, 35.

16 In recent years, there has been a return to Alfred North Whitehead's critique of Newtonian physics as an account of the universe in discrete fragments. Whitehead, following the radical empiricism of Henri Bergson and William James, argues for the "togetherness of things," which nature exemplifies. This relatedness of nature is available to us in two modes of perception: pure perception (colors, sounds, smells) and a perception of causal relatedness (an intuitive knowledge) based on experience. In the midst of ecological catastrophe, Whitehead's insistence on our deepening awareness of processes and relations between the living and the nonliving makes sound sense for scholars of environmental media and of philosophies of science. See Stengers, *Thinking with Whitehead;* and the essays in Gaskill and Nocek, *Lure of Whitehead*.

17 Van Dooren, *World in a Shell*.

18 The Rockefeller Foundation–*Lancet* Commission on Planetary Health situates human health within human systems: "The threats that our species faces are not abstract physical risks," they argue, "such as disease, climate change, ocean acidification, or chemical pollution. The risks we face lie within ourselves and the societies we have created. When we consider climate change, the main metric of danger is greenhouse gas emissions. But that measure should also include the capacity of human systems to monitor the threat, understand its importance, and act on that

knowledge. Second, planetary health concerns the natural systems within which our species exists—for example, the health and diversity of the biosphere. Human beings live within a safe operating space of planetary existence. If the boundaries of that space are breached, the conditions for our survival will be diminished. Currently, natural systems are being degraded to an extent unprecedented in history, with known and as yet unknown and unquantified effects on human health." Horton and Lo, "Planetary Health," 1921.

19 Anna L. Tsing, Jennifer Deger, Alder Keleman Saxena, and Feifei Zhou curate the online *Feral Atlas* (https://feralatlas.org/), which includes contributions from over a hundred participants. I discuss the atlas at greater length in chapter 4.

20 See, for instance, Redvers et al., "Molecular Decolonization."

21 Chow, *Entanglements*, 12.

22 There is excellent scholarship on contagion fiction and nonfiction, movies and television shows, video games, and comic books; see Wald, *Contagious*. I discuss science journalism on EID outbreaks at greater length in chapter 1.

23 In *The Order of Things* (first published in 1966), Michel Foucault explains how all empirical observation materializes objects by placing them in a system of elements or a "grid" that differentiates them. Social power underwrites "grids of intelligibility" that encode what I describe as epistemic objects.

24 Wang et al., "Airborne Transmission of Respiratory Viruses."

25 A loaded term, *vital* carries with it universes of debate that echoed throughout the nineteenth and early twentieth centuries. Vitalism is a strain of thought that argues that the processes of life (organic life) are not explicable by physics or chemistry alone. Living organisms have a distinctive organization that cannot be compared to that of machines (as opposed to the mechanist argument of the human as differing only in degree of complexity from mechanical devices). Going back as far as the Stoics, vitalism (the old vitalism of the nineteenth century) saw itself in opposition to the "mechanist" theories of life; theorists struggled to explain how life emerged, its internal trigger, the essence revitalized by electricity. Unlike traditional vitalism, which located the inner principle of life in the soul, the modern vitalists were materialists concerned with the organization of matter and preoccupied with distinguishing biological transformations from physico-chemical ones. Writing the Gifford Lectures delivered at the University of Aberdeen, 1906–8 (published as *The Science and Philosophy of the Organism*), the German biologist and philosopher Hans Driesch (1867–1941) argued for that which escaped prediction and control. Driesch christened this "something" *entelechy*, while Henri Bergson named it *élan vital* in his early twentieth-century classic, *Creative Evolution* (1907). Both drew on Immanuel Kant's notion of *Bildungstrieb*, which is the self-organizing power of organisms that gives matter its coherence. For Kant, this agentic power, as Jane Bennett explains in *Vibrant Matter*, is an invisible presence that is not explicable through physico-chemical reactions. How the egg grows and changes, its *morphogenesis* or becoming manifold in space, is proof of this presence. But while Kant finally situates this agentic force in a divine power, Driesch and Bergson variously theorize it as a driving biological force active in nature. They largely eschew the mechanist

model of life, which tuned in to patterns of change and to variations in organismic complexity but saw the "aim" of the organism as predictable: it sought to replicate and readjust to a pattern it recognized as its own (autopoiesis). The neovitalists argued that the "pattern" made by small incessant changes (variations) could not be foreseen or predicted; living organisms "see" the pattern in retrospect. Human "intelligence" grasps and organizes this changefulness as duration in the organism's life: a now and then, a past, present, and future; but much of the flux remains unavailable to consciousness.

26 Joshua Neves, "Technology + Pharmacology: Notes on Current Research," *Heliotrope,* September 15, 2021, https://www.heliotropejournal.net/helio/technology-pharmacology.

27 See "Gas Clouds Demonstrate Their Ability to Travel Great Distances," a video embedded in Lydia Bourouiba's "Turbulent Gas Clouds and Respiratory Pathogen Emissions." This close-up view of a sneeze filmed at two thousand frames per second (duration 0.25 second) shows it's a hot, moist, turbulent gas cloud containing air and mucosalivary droplets that travel as far as twenty-six feet (seven to eight meters). See also, Anfinrud et al., "Visualizing Speech-Generated Oral Fluid."

28 Pato Hebert, "Trying to Catch Your Breath," 2008.

29 Stengers, "Challenge of Ontological Politics," 91.

30 Elaborating Félix Guattari's *The Three Ecologies,* Ivakhiv provides an architecture for thinking the threefold nature of ecology. First, there is ecology as the material relation between things (appearing as objects); second, there is ecology as the experience of processes (the subjective or social relation); and third, there is ecology as mediation (the basic relational act). Making possible the first two relations, the third, mediation, is the focus of environmental media studies. See Adrian Ivakhiv, "Why *Three* Ecologies?," *Immanence: Ecoculture, Geophilosophy, Mediapolitics* (blog), January 15, 2021, https://blog.uvm.edu/aivakhiv/2021/01/15/why-three-ecologies/; see elaborations in Ivakhiv, *Shadowing the Anthropocene.*

31 See Landecker, "Metabolic History of Manufacturing Waste"; and Neubauer and Landecker, "Planetary Health Perspective."

32 Landecker, "Metabolic History of Manufacturing Waste," 531–32.

33 The "furin cleavage," for instance, is under investigation for evaluating the infectiousness of the delta variant; furin is a protease made by the human body. See Xia et al., "Role of Furin Cleavage Site."

34 See the elaboration of speculation as a critical-creative practice that confronts uncertainty in Uncertain Commons, *Speculate This!*

35 Chow, *Entanglements,* 12.

36 Chow, *Entanglements,* 12.

37 Abram, *Spell of the Sensuous,* 57–58.

38 Peters, *Marvelous Clouds.*

39 Furuhata *Climatic Media*; Starosielski, *Undersea Network*; Mukherjee, *Radiant Infrastructures*; Helmreich, *Alien Ocean*; and Jue, *Wild Blue Media.*

40 By now there are several methods for quantifying the viral shedding in the stool of COVID-19 patients as fecal data that can yield localized epidemiological estimates.

See, for example, Natarajan, "Standardized Preservation, Extraction, and Quantification Techniques."

41 Helmreich, "*Homo microbis*," 54.

42 Helmreich, "*Homo microbis*," 55.

43 Some of the most famous cases of art practitioners performatively probing the limits of "making life" are Eduardo Kac's GFP Bunny, which generated controversy, and the Critical Art Ensemble's *E. coli* culture, which resulted in a raid on cofounder Steve Kurtz's home. See Eduardo Kac, "Rabbit Remix," accessed July 26, 2022, https://www.ekac.org/gfpbunny.html; and Critical Art Ensemble, *Digital Resistance*. Berrigan's experiments, featured in "Life Cycle of a Common Weed," are of significance to my work because of their emphasis on living with HIV. On theorizing multispecies distributions, see Helmreich and Paxson, "Perils and Promises"; Celia Lowe, "Infection"; and Nigel Clark and Myra Hird, "Microontologies."

44 See "Introduction to Feral Atlas," accessed July 26, 2022, https://feralatlas.supdigital.org/?cd=true&rr=true&cdex=true&text=introduction-to-feral-atlas&ttype=essay.

45 Latour and Woolgar, *Laboratory Life;* Rheinberger, *Epistemology of the Concrete*; and Knorr Cetina, *Epistemic Cultures.*

46 Latour and Woolgar, *Laboratory Life*, 64.

47 Latour and Woolgar, *Laboratory Life*, 106.

48 Stengers's contribution to the collaborative project of making worlds references her long engagement with the discordant landscapes of science. In "The Challenge of Ontological Politics," she addresses making partial connections (as proposed by Marilyn Stathern) with reference to a few successful environmental coalitions: the worldwide "GMO event," as she calls it, and a negotiation between multiple stakeholders on dunes in the Cape Flats, South Africa.

49 Latour, "Circulating Reference."

50 Latour and Woolgar, *Laboratory Life*, 62; see also, Karen Barad, *Meeting the Universe Halfway*. Despite the common usage of *craftwork* as a moniker for do-it-yourself practices, I deploy the phrase to describe medial actions in laboratories so as to highlight the provisional "making do" of epidemic media under pandemic/epidemic situations.

51 Following the morphing thyrotropin releasing factor hormone or TRF(H), Latour and Woolgar in *Laboratory Life* note the set of positions within which an object takes shape; it acquires meaning and significance depending on a particular network of individuals. See also Latour, "On Technical Mediation."

52 As de la Cadena and Blaser describe it in their scholarly elaboration of the Zapatista invitation to reworlding. See de la Cadena and Blaser, "Introduction."

53 Stengers, "Challenge of Ontological Politics."

54 Central to the biotech industry is the growth of the information industry. Tracing the historical conjunctions of molecular biology and the information sciences from the 1970s, Thacker argues for the turning of flesh (biological DNA) into information (digital file) and then again into flesh (e.g., new proteins in proteomics) as constitutive of processes of optimization. His books—*Biomedia* and *The Global*

Genome—take as their inspiration the genomic revolution that led to the mapping of the human genome in 1990.

55 Sarah Franklin's *Dolly Mixtures*, a cultural history of the first cloned animal in the United Kingdom, remains another staple in assessing the social impacts of the biotechnological enterprise. The Roslin Institute in Scotland successfully cloned "Dolly" in 1996, attempting to create "better" genetically modified livestock; the search was on to isolate and develop genetic substrates through digital modulations.

56 "Making life" involved writing code, as in the stellar example of the J. Craig Venter Institute's development of the first entirely synthetic cell in 2010. A digital code of an organism's entire genetic code was rendered into chemical DNA (made by Blue Heron Bio), stitched into longer fragments grown in yeast culture, and then transplanted into bacteria (*Mycoplasma capricolum*). The new synthetically programmed (and watermarked) DNA replaced the former code (*Mycoplasma mycoides*), giving birth to a new synthetic cell. Such innovations in potential autografts and allografts gave new impetus to organ-transplant and stem cell research. Aside from the gene, cells have further emerged as ground zero in the technological control of life. As they slice and dice, design and build life itself, biotechnologies are at the front and center of both social debates and legal controversies. See, for example, Burgess, Thurtle, and Mitchell, *Biofutures*.

57 Kember and Zylinska draw on the Bergsonian concept of vital fluctuations as tiny variations in life as unfolding activity. The notion is typically attributed to French philosopher Henri Bergson, especially in *Creative Evolution* (1907), a work considered a seismic shift in the world of letters. Where mechanistic notions intimated that the organism will always try to retain its original structure/pattern, and therefore there is no change per se, Bergson emphasizes living/surviving as creative progression: each state is different from the previous one, but the difference means the previous state also exists or continues into it.

58 DeLanda, *Philosophy and Simulation*; and Myers, *Rendering Life Molecular.*

59 Gabrys, *Program Earth.*

60 Myers's ethnography of protein modelers moving with the molecules that they excite for study describes the force of that affect. Myers, *Rendering Life Molecular*. Excited by material presences that are sensible, protein modelers perform embodied encounters even as institutional constraints determine what is ultimately composed.

61 Parikka, *Geology of Media*.

62 Sampson and Parikka, "Operational Loops of a Pandemic."

63 Kirsten Ostherr, interview with Pujita Guha, Surojit Kayal, and Maile Aihua Young, *The Digital Pandemic Interviews* (podcast), parts I and II, November 14, 2020, https://podcasts.apple.com/us/podcast/the-digital-pandemic-interviews/id1531208911.

64 See Myers, *Rendering Life Molecular*, 75.

65 The study of living matter is far older in the ancient, medieval, and early modern sciences: one could venture as much into Aristotelian theories of spontaneous generation as one could into Islamic golden age physiology. But biology would emerge

as a modern discipline post-Enlightenment: for example, the botanist, physician, and zoologist Carolus Linnaeus refers to the Latin *biologi* in his *Bibliotheca Botanica* ([1736] 1968), a book that proposed a massive classification of plant genera and species in the known world. A century later, by 1838, biologists had established the cell as the basic unit of life and theorized principles governing life from this perspective. Over the course of the nineteenth century, biology evolved into different branches, from physiology to microbiology; by the early twentieth century, not only was biology gradually differentiated from physics, but the life sciences also underwent internal differentiations (physiology, genetics, zoology, botany, and so forth).

66 Stengers, "Challenge of Ontological Politics."

67 The partition of the senses as central to aesthetics refers us to Jacques Rancière's much-discussed *The Politics of Aesthetics* (2004), in which Rancière elaborates the governance of the human sensorium in artworks that meet the mandates of propriety.

68 The grid is elaborated in Foucault's *The Order of Things*; see note 23.

69 Uexküll, "Stroll through the Worlds of Animals and Men."

70 Abram, *Spell of the Sensuous*, 44.

71 Abram, *Spell of the Sensuous*, 59.

72 Siegel, *Forensic Media*. In the chapter "Black Boxes," Siegel develops a theory of noise with reference to the "black box" on flights, whose recorded signals are forensically deciphered as an account of "what really happened." Following Michel Serres's notions of the parasite, Siegel makes a case for what the noise accomplishes, including situating listeners in the affective chaos of death.

73 In one of the best articulations of the turn, the editors of *New Materialisms* argue for "thinking anew the structure of matter has far-reaching normative and existential implications." Coole and Frost, "Introducing the New Materialisms," 15. For my purposes, their emphasis on the new promises and threats of the new models of living matter arriving from molecular biology and its cognates in biomedicine and biotechnology is particularly relevant.

74 Myers, *Rendering Life Molecular*.

75 Barad, "Invertebrate Visions," 227.

76 See Thurtle, *Biology in the Grid*, on making epistemic objects in the grid.

77 Siegel, *Forensic Media*, 136; and Larkin, *Signal and Noise*, 239.

78 I owe the point to Hannah Landecker's discussion of her paper, "Coming Home to Roost," presented at a workshop ("Altered Lives") organized by Vincanne Adams, Lochlann Jain, and Kelly Knight, February 2022.

79 Stengers, "Ontological Politics."

80 Foucault, *Order of Things*, 303.

CHAPTER ONE. THE EPIDEMIC EPISTEME

1 Exactly what proportion of the population died of smallpox is the locus of debate among historians: some argue for one-third to one-fifth, while others believe the it was as high as half in some provinces and only a little less in others. Whichever

the case, there is consensus on a demographic collapse in central Mexico in the sixteenth century that contributed to the fall of the Aztec and Nahua kingdoms. See McCaa, "Spanish and Nahuatl Views." Robert McCaa offers a strong critique of historians who minimize the impact that the unknown pathogen had on the area, as he meticulously tracks the many references to the disease in Spanish and Nahautl texts.

2 The emergence of terms seeking to describe the disease, with its hemorrhagic fevers with ulcers or pustules (that was perceived as leprosy at first sight)—*cocoliztli, huey zahauatl totmonaliztli*—historians argue, is etymological evidence that smallpox was not known in the region before this historical juncture. The evidence is garnered from Spanish-Nahuatl dictionaries and glossaries of the period. There is consensus that smallpox was an Old World disease that the Spaniards brought with them, with some disagreement from those who argue that the virus skipped into Nahua and Aztec populations from rodents during a period of extreme drought in the region.

3 The smallpox epidemic of 1519 to 1520 killed 5 million to 8 million people, while the more catastrophic epidemics that began in 1545 and 1576 subsequently killed an additional 7 million to 17 million people in the highlands of Mexico.

4 Manuel Orozco y Berra, *Historia Antigua y de la Conquista*, 4:445–46.

5 McCaa, "Spanish and Nahuatl Views," 407.

6 The competing accounts circle the question of agency: To what extent did the smallpox epidemic contribute to the fall of Mexico's central valley in the sixteenth century? Were there two protagonists, Spanish and Amerindian, or three, adding *Variola*, in this global history? Historians interpret these data along two timescales, the human and the natural. Most traditional historical accounts present multiple social, political, and economic determinants of the weakened condition of the great Aztec warriors: forced migration and enslavement, as well as the new pestilence, a disease already known in the Old World. The newness of the pestilence meant there were few social, political, or technological solutions to address radically deteriorating vital states. Research on the Hopi and Pueblo smallpox epidemics of the late nineteenth century shows that the emerging modes of care reduced fatalities by twelve times. McCaa, "Spanish and Nahuatl Views," 423. By then, civic interventions into epidemics had been institutionalized to some degree. But in sixteenth-century central Mexico, there were few defenses against virulent strains of *Variola*.

7 The outbreaks in Spain were more akin to measles and understood as a disease of childhood. See Crawford, *Viruses*.

8 In the 1830s the attempted governance of vital forces within a demographic became institutionalized as a public health enterprise. Historians remind us that such governance hails back to at least the Middle Ages with politico-theological regulations against leprosy (usually involving banishment); the politico-economic regulation of the plague, both the Black Death in Europe (1347–51) and the later Great Plague of London (1665), catalyzing the first quarantines and mortality records of disease fatalities; and the politico-medical control of smallpox epidemics through inoculation campaigns in the eighteenth century. The mortality tables of the Great Plague (John Graunt's record of weekly burials and acute and chronic diseases in 1662

was one of the first scientific assessments of disease distributions) present one of the most abiding of epidemic media forms; mortality and morbidity rates would remain the unshakable index of deadly microbial circulations within a given population. By the mid-nineteenth century, statistical interpretations gave new significance to morbidity statistics, opening the door for inferential prognosis of disease outbreaks. In years to come, demographers began to not only collect, tabulate, and synthesize data on population vital statistics but also establish methods and procedures for epidemiological forecasts.

9 In thinking about what constitutes an event, Povinelli points out that while scholars of the biosphere privilege the "coming catastrophe," those living with long-term anthropogenic damage from colonial dispossession live out "ancestral catastrophes." Povinelli, *Between Gaia and Ground*. Arnold, in *Colonizing the Body*, argues that the vaccination campaigns in the British colonies, fiercely fought by local communities, had as much to do with the disruption of local hegemonies as with extant understandings of therapies ritualized in the worship of the goddess Sitala.

10 Reinhart Koselleck's monumental *Futures Past* rethinks historical temporalities and, specifically, the making of pasts. The "future anterior" corresponds to the future perfect tense, designating an action that will have happened in the future. The phrase is deployed to address what might have happened in the past that would have opened a vein into futures that are not present in dominant historiographies.

11 Scientists now understand *Variola* to be a rodent virus that crossed the species barrier from rodents to camels and humans in farming communities almost ten thousand years ago. The "Antonine plague" that hit the Roman Empire in AD 166 is the first recorded instance of a smallpox epidemic. Historians understand the Athenian plague of 430 BCE also as smallpox. Smallpox would ravage human populations through the centuries; in the twentieth century, smallpox killed 300 million. See Crawford, *Viruses;* and Oldstone, *Viruses, Plagues, and History.*

12 Extracting pus containing the vaccinia virus, Jenner reserved the serum in quills for cutaneous insertion in uninfected human subjects. The dairymaid is the central protagonist in this apocryphal tale of an artisanal brew, an intrepid physician-scientist, and science at its experimental best. In his account of smallpox cases in the farms of Berkeley, Gloucestershire, Jenner observed the curious phenomenon that dairymaids who had previously contracted the common (and not deadly) cowpox infection, caught from bovine teats and udders, suffered a far milder form of smallpox than others on the same farm. Members of the household who solicited Jenner's services died while the dairymaids lived on, somehow able to fight the ravages of the *Variola major* or *Variola minor* virus. Hence, Jenner decided to first infect James Phipps, the son of Jenner's gardener, with the *vaccinia* virus in May 1796. Once the boy had suffered the typically mild episode of cowpox, Jenner infected him with infectious matter from smallpox pustules later that year. And, indeed, Phipps failed to contract smallpox altogether. Elated, Jenner cultivated reserves of cowpox matter; he sent the serum to fellow physicians for their research; he

published pamphlets on his discovery; he received parliamentary grants of £30,000 for his efforts and honorary degrees from Oxford and Harvard universities. And there lie the near-mythic origins of modern immunology, enshrining an aggressive, preemptive biomedicine. At its center is the physician-scientist: the responsible reader of "vital signs" (the pox), the researcher willing to risk a patient for the greater public good, the prophylactic thinker invested in biomedical prevention, and the public health campaigner (writing on preventive medicine).

13 The West African strain of the monkeypox spread globally in 2003 (including to six US states) led the CDC to invest in its research; the first case of monkeypox ever reported was in 1957. See Shah, "Could Monkeypox Take Over."

14 Preston, *Demon in the Freezer*. In the closing chapters of the smallpox story, the last episode of infection in the world, in 1978 (two years before the WHO declared the disease eradicated), resulted from an accidental leak from a University of Birmingham Medical School reservoir of the pathogen. When smallpox was officially certified as eradicated in December 1979, an agreement was reached under which all remaining stocks of the virus would be either destroyed or passed to one of two secure laboratories—one in the United States and one in the Russian Federation. That process was completed in the early 1980s, and since then no other laboratory has officially had access to the virus that causes smallpox. See World Health Organization, "Smallpox," accessed July 7, 2022, https://www.who.int/teams/health-product-and-policy-standards/standards-and-specifications/vaccine-standardization/smallpox.

15 Osterholm and Olshaker, *Deadliest Enemy*, 20.

16 Murphy, "Alterlife," 497.

17 There are many accounts of "first sightings," some as far back as 1959 (cases now disproven by AIDS researcher, physician, and virologist David Ho); the first case in the United States was that of Robert R., who died in 1969. Usually, early cases are the pre-1981 cases (1981 is when AIDS became known to the medical profession). See *Wikipedia*, "Timeline of Early HIV/AIDS Cases," last modified April 12, 2022, 1:35 (UTC), https://en.wikipedia.org/wiki/Timeline_of_early_HIV/AIDS_cases. See also Mann, "AIDS."

18 At the level of international organizing, AIDS was seen to be an epidemic erupting in multiple contexts as early as 1986. In only the second IAC (Paris, 1986), Bila Kapita, the chief of internal medicine in Kinshasa, Democratic Republic of the Congo, already spoke openly about the pandemic in Africa. When he was jailed for his speech, the international community mobilized to free him. But AIDS would be constituted as a pandemic requiring global modular forms of prevention and care a few years later. In 1992, the IAC in Amsterdam was the first to announce a global agenda: the theme that year was "A World United against AIDS" with eight thousand attendees. The emergence of HIV as a global phenomenon therefore had two phases: the epidemic (perceived in localized infection topographies) and the pandemic (an accelerated movement between infection localities).

19 As Priscilla Wald has noted, the outbreak narrative forecloses efforts toward ameliorating the global conditions for diseases (nutrition, health-care access, housing).

In *Contagious* (2008) and a recent discussion of the COVID-19 outbreak, she points to the lost possibilities of the 1978 Alma-Ata Declaration, which committed signatories to work for universal access to primary health care. "At a 1978 conference called the Conference of Alma-Ata, a place formerly in the Soviet Union, 134 nations and 67 NGOs [got] together and said they were affirming the UN definition of health as a fundamental human right. The idea was that all of these signatories would commit to this definition of health not as the absence of disease, but as proper nutrition, access to primary healthcare, proper shelter and clothing and basic needs for human wellbeing." Wald and Weed, "COVID-19 and the Outbreak Narrative."

20 The contributors to the volume *Against Health,* edited by Johnathan Metzl and Anna Kirkland, present a range of arguments for focusing on the conditions that constitute ill health, signaling "health" as a multisite, differential horizon of possibility.

21 Speaking at the World Economic Forum, Bill Gates noted that HIV/AIDS research prepared the way for the COVID-19 vaccines. At least twenty vaccines for HIV/AIDS were in clinical trials before the emergence of COVID-19. See Bill Gates, "How HIV/AIDS Prepared Us to Tackle COVID-19," World Economic Forum, July 27, 2020, https://www.weforum.org/agenda/2020/07/bill-gates-hiv-aids-covid19/.

22 *We Are Having This Conversation Now* mounts a dialogic presentation of what it means to talk about AIDS at the current juncture. Once there was a silence about a little-known disease; then, a second silence after the normalization of AIDS in the post-antiretroviral period as a chronic condition to be privately lived in the doctor's office. Such silences obscure the continuing struggle for access in under-resourced settings and the corollary vibrant organization of care. Centering their conversation around the "Beshabi video tape" that documented African-American women's experiences in early 1980s Philadelphia, Alex Juhasz and Theodore Kerr draw readers into an intensely moving, deeply experiential, and sharply analytic discussion on the cultural production of AIDS. In *Viral Cultures,* Marika Cifor attempts to "reckon with the AIDS past in the pandemic present" with her archival ethnography on queer, intergenerational HIV/AIDS activism in the United States (displacing the centrality of AIDS as a predominantly gay white, middle-class crisis) and on the curatorial care work of HIV/AIDS activists who lovingly circulated bottom-up knowledge practices (4).

23 National Institutes of Health, "Experimental mRNA HIV Vaccine Shows Promise in Animals," NIH Research Matters, January 11, 2022, https://www.nih.gov/news-events/nih-research-matters/experimental-mrna-hiv-vaccine-shows-promise-animals.

24 In 2020, 37.7 million were living with AIDS (including 1.5 million new infections), and 680,000 died of AIDS-related causes. See updates at "HIV/AIDS," Global Health Observatory, WHO, accessed July 8, 2022, https://www.who.int/data/gho/data/themes/hiv-aids.

25 Postexposure prophylaxis (PEP) is a triple combination drug therapy for four weeks, while pre-exposure prophylaxis (PrEP) is ongoing prevention at one or two ARV doses per day. Both contain HIV replication through either blocking entry into T-cells or disabling reverse transcription.

26 Wald, *Contagious.*

27 Lederberg outlined his observations in a book, *Emerging Infections,* coedited with Robert Shope and Stanley Oaks.

28 See WHO, HIV Fact Sheet, June 27, 2022, https://www.who.int/news-room/fact-sheets/detail/hiv-aids.

29 See Patton, *Inventing AIDS*; Treichler, *How to Have Theory*; and Epstein, *Impure Science.*

30 Garrett won the Pulitzer Prize for Explanatory Journalism in 1996.

31 Scientific institutions have had varied responses to these publications: notably, former scientists at the CDC criticized Preston's *The Hot Zone* for its exaggerations and speculation on the transit of HIV along the Kinshasa highway. See McCormick and Fisher-Hoch, *Level 4.* Some argued that the route across the Democratic Republic of the Congo and Uganda was not a highway but a series of roads; others maintained that some of these roads in the eastern Congo had been built long before HIV's emergence. On the movie front: Fox Studios had earmarked *The Hot Zone* for a film, but Warner Bros. stole the show with *Outbreak* (1995).

32 Anderson Cooper, "Scientists Believe Covid-19 May Have Roots in These Bats," CNN, June 12, 2020, https://www.cnn.com/videos/health/2020/06/12/bats-covid-coronavirus-cnn-special-report.cnn. Post–lab leak theory, Peter Daszak, the president of EcoHealth Alliance, who appeared on Cooper's CNN segment, has been caught in the political crosshairs because of his long-term collaborations with the Wuhan Institute of Virology. See Subbaraman, "'Heinous!'"

33 Brilliant is an illustrious figure who during his travels to the subcontinent in 1973–76 had been exhorted by a Hindu sage (Neem Karoli Baba) to wipe out a ten-thousand-year-old disease that killed 300 million people in the twentieth century alone. Thus began his long hunt to eradicate *Variola.* He is known to have met the last survivor of the disease in Bangladesh. He went on to become a public advocate for stopping the next pandemic for decades after. See Brilliant, *Sometimes Brilliant.*

34 In the film *Contagion*'s heavy-handed closing sequence, audiences get the final picture: the causal chain of events behind the emergent associations, linking reservoir mammals with intermediate hosts (farmed or captured animals) with humans. A bulldozer razes palm trees in a rain forest, dislodging a bat eating a banana, which shelters in a barn; a pig that eats the dropped fruit is later slaughtered; it is handled by a chef, who doesn't wash his hands. A handshake at a restaurant initiates the community transmission in humans.

35 There are innumerable histories of the global pandemic and of regional epidemics, so many, in fact, that one would have to categorize them according to genre. Some genres relevant to this project are investigative journalism pieces, such as Craig Timberg and Daniel Halperin's recent *Tinderbox*; popular synthetic histories, such as Jonathan Engel's *The Epidemic*; and online archives of testimonies, movements, and public documents (such as the ACT UP Oral History Project, accessed June 20, 2021, http://www.actuporalhistory.org).

36 Kevin Esvelt proposed editing the virus in the wild but with necessary caution. See Ledford, "Caution Urged over Editing DNA"; and Specter, "Rewriting the Code of

Life." The very recent cure involves wiping out the last reservoirs by using anti-Nef antibodies. See Kelly Malcom, "Antibiotic Molecule Enables Immune System to Kill HIV Infected Cells," *M Health Lab* (blog), September 7, 2020, https://labblog.uofmhealth.org/lab-report/antibiotic-molecule-enables-immune-system-to-kill-hiv-infected-cells.

37 With reference to the first name for the HIV/AIDS epidemic, GRID (gay-related immunodeficiency), Patton recounts scientific occlusions in the early years of the epidemic that trained disease-surveillance systems on *a* target population with devastating consequences. Patton, *Inventing AIDS*.

38 Much activist and critical work on the HIV/AIDS crises in the late 1980s and early 1990s, grounded in Foucault's work on disciplinary societies, treated AIDS as a singular disease with a singular etiology. Activists, writers, and art practitioners privileged informal networks of information and care against institutions ready to "let die" disposable populations (Simon Watney, Douglas Crimp, Catherine Waldby); the major push for social change, as we know from ACT UP histories, targeted public policy, funding for HIV/AIDS research, prevention (clean needles, condoms, advertising), and care (counseling, hospice, alternative medicine).

39 See T. Jones, Wear, and Friedman, *Health Humanities Reader*, especially Allison Kavey's "A Brief History of Love."

40 When patients hyperattuned to their vital states actively seek, collate, and organize data into biomedical information, they become active participants in emergent "bioscapes," as Regula Valérie Burri and Joseph Dumit describe them, or the shared knowledge practices of living a medical condition. Burri and Dumit, "Indeterminate Lives, Demands, Relations." As uncertainties—about genetic testing, about high-tech knowledge, about corporate medical and scientific infrastructures, to name just a few—accumulate even as numerous, often consecutive, decisions must be made, the medical situation is increasingly stratified. The ensuing uneven terrain, an ethical plateau, means that what health is, could be, or should be is no longer a unilateral decision made by one medical authority.

41 In the early years of the HIV/AIDS epidemic in the United States, patients and caregivers, doctors and nurses, struggled to stabilize a diagnostic snapshot of the new disease. Their testimonies now proliferate in institutional and communal archives: activist enclaves assemble patient and caregiver testimonies in multiple media platforms, such as ACT UP's Oral History Project or HIV/AIDS videos (distributed through indie media channels such as VideoDataBank, an international video art distribution organization), while medical institutions such as the National Institutes of Health embark on digitizing accounts from doctors, nurses, clinicians, and public health officials (for instance, the In Their Own Words database, accessed June 15, 2022, https://history.nih.gov/display/history/In+Their+Own+Words. Such databases provide a glimpse into the transformation of biomedical information economies in the past thirty years, a change that made emergent scientific hypotheses a matter of public debate and made the medical progression toward health a collaborative venture.

42 Osterholm and Olshaker, *Deadliest Enemy*, 16.

43 Three graduate students—Surojit Kayal, Maile Young, and Pujita Guha—embarked on a podcast project in fall 2020, after an independent study on the place of the biological in environmental studies. *The Digital Pandemic* (podcast), accessed July 27, 2022, https://podcasts.apple.com/us/podcast/the-digital-pandemic-interviews/id1531208911.

44 The archiving of the HIV/AIDS pandemic is now a generational endeavor in widely discussed documentaries such as David France's *How to Survive a Plague* (2012), Jim Hubbard's *United in Anger* (2012), and Dylan Mohan Gray's *Fire in the Blood* (2012); scholarship on AIDS art and activism, as in Deborah Gould's *Moving Politics* (2009) or Christopher Castiglia and Christopher Reed's *If Memory Serves* (2011); and commemorative gestures, such as Kris Nuzzi and Sur Rodney's curated history of visual aids, *Not Over: 25 Years of Visual AIDS* (La MaMa Gallery, New York, June–September 2013) or the traveling *Art AIDS America* exhibits (2016–17, originally shown at the Bronx Museum of Arts, New York).

45 Roitman, *Anti-crisis*, 93.

46 Povinelli, *Between Gaia and the Ground*.

47 There are many reasons, from epidemiological perspectives, that pandemics wane, including herd immunity, and a variety of models forecast this rise and fall; meanwhile, virologists base their analyses on the genetic trajectories of the virus that enable or disable it from evolving into biological partnerships with hosts.

48 The Greek *krisis*, or "decision" (from the root *krinein*, meaning "to decide") made its way into late Middle English from medical Latin (where it signified the turning point of a disease). The general sense "decisive point" dates from the early seventeenth century. See *Online Etymology Dictionary*, "crisis," accessed July 27, 2022, https://www.etymonline.com/word/crisis.

49 See Martin and Martin-Granel, "2,500-Year Evolution of the Term Epidemic."

50 During the 2009 H1N1 pandemic, amid debates over the phenomenon, the National Institute of Allergy and Infectious Diseases defined pandemics by eight distinct criteria. See Morens, Folkers, and Fauci, "What Is a Pandemic?"

51 Wald writes about Typhoid Mary and Gaetan Dugas as two classic instances, tracking the phobic circumstances under which the two figures carried the cultural burden of the epidemic origin story. See Wald, *Contagious*. For a debunking of the Gaetan Dugas myth, see Worobey et al., "1970s and the 'Patient 0' HIV-1 Genomes."

52 On Shi Zhengli, see Qiu, "Chasing Plagues."

53 See, for instance, Jason Moore's discussion in *Anthropocene or Capitalocene?*

54 See Slater, *War and Disease*.

55 In "After the Age of Wreckers and Exterminators," Eva Giraud mines scholarly conversations on chemical and biochemical interventions after DDT toxicity and the emergence of antimicrobial resistance. See also Kinkela, *DDT and the American Century*.

56 See, for instance, infectious disease epidemiologist, Anne Rimoin's interview on NPR: Michaeleen Doucleff, "Scientists Warned Us about Monkeypox in 1988: Here's Why They Were Right," May 27, 2022, https://www.npr.org/sections

/goatsandsoda/2022/05/27/1101751627/scientists-warned-us-about-monkeypox-in-1988-heres-why-they-were-right.

57 Smallpox was eradicated because we took the human body, its vital medium, out of *Variola*'s reach. In this regard, the "cure" meant containing *Variola*'s ability to "come alive" by removing the conditions for host-to-host exchanges.

58 One of the sustained readings of this crossing appears in Cooper's *Life as Surplus*. "Viral storms" is celebrity scientist Nathan Wolfe's evocative term for episodic viral emergences. Wolfe, *Viral Storm*.

59 Shah, *Pandemic*.

60 "One Health" was first mentioned in a story about Ebola hemorrhagic fever on April 7, 2003, when Rick Weiss of the *Washington Post* quoted William Karesh (at EcoHealth Alliance) as saying, "Human or livestock or wildlife health can't be discussed in isolation anymore. There is just one health." See Rick Weiss, "Africa's Apes are Imperiled, Researchers Warn," *Washington Post*, April 7, 2003, https://www.washingtonpost.com/archive/politics/2003/04/07/africas-apes-are-imperiled-researchers-warn/fc37f619-d7fe-407f-8f6e-b0d202eeb04a/. In 2004, the Wildlife Conservation Society held a conference at Rockefeller University in New York called One World, One Health, out of which the twelve Manhattan Principles were created. See the Wildlife Conservation Society and The Rockefeller University hosted meetings, "One World, One Health: Building Interdisciplinary Bridges to Health in a Globalized World" September 29, 2004. Posted on the One Health Commission website on November 29, 2004 (https://www.onehealthcommission.org/index.cfm/37526/93958/one_world_one_health_building_interdisciplinary_bridges_to_health_in_a_globalized_world).

61 See note 18 of this volume's introduction.

62 Lowe, "Infection," 302; see also Wallace et al., "Dawn of Structural One Health."

63 The time lag is in part attributed to the rise of Nazi Germany: Fleck's research was disrupted when he was imprisoned in Auschwitz and Buchenwald; he survived the war and returned to the question of historical epistemology in the postwar years.

64 As early as 1872, German physiologist Emil du Bois-Reymand, delivering one of the first lectures on the history of science at the Academy of Sciences in Berlin, would insist, "We teach science and its history at the same time." In tracing the work of historical epistemology—in Gaston Bachelard (*Essai sur la conaissance approchée*, 1927), Edmund Husserl (*The Crisis of the European Sciences and Transcendental Phenomenology*, 1934–37), Ludwik Fleck (*Genesis and Development of a Scientific Fact*, 1935), and Georges Canguilhem (*Knowledge of Life*, 1952)—Hans-Jörg Rheinberger highlights Fleck's observation that "every epistemology must be brought in relation to the social, and further, with the history of culture, if it is not . . . to come into sharp contradiction with the history of knowledge and everyday experience." Quoted in Rheinberger, *Epistemology of the Concrete*, 18.

65 In *The Epistemology of the Concrete*, Rheinberger explores the material and institutional histories that constructed scientific objects of inquiry (such as the cell or the gene), model organisms (the fruit fly or the tobacco mosaic virus), laboratory techniques (such as the sample preparation), and protocols (instructions for setting

experiments in motion). As these change over time, what appears self-evident is unsettled: thus, the "gene," for instance, is a remarkably "fuzzy object" in its migrations from structural biology (focused on gene instructions for assembly) to molecular biology (focused on code) to evolutionary biology (focused on mutations over time).

66 What became known as the Koch postulates were the four criteria for establishing disease causality formulated by Friedrich Loeffler and Robert Koch in 1884 and subsequently polished and published by Koch in 1890. The postulates were: (i) finding the causative microorganism in abundance in the diseased organism (and not a healthy one); (ii) extracting and growing the causative agent in a pure culture; (iii) when reintroduced into a healthy host, it should cause disease; and (iv) finally, it should be reisolated and compared to the original.

67 Notably, the first virological discovery was of immediate *economic* interest since the tobacco mosaic virus had wreaked havoc on lucrative tobacco harvests. Crop damage in the Ukraine, Bessarabia, and (later) Crimea was the primary motivation for Ivanovsky's pursuit of the pathogenic microbial agent, in Ivanovsky, "On Two Diseases of Tobacco."

68 For an account of these early beginnings, see Lustig and Levine, "One Hundred Years of Virology."

69 Beijerinck, in an address to the Koninklijke Akademie van Wetenschappen in Amsterdam, quoted and translated by Gerrit Iterson, *Martinus Willem Beijerinck: His Life and Work*, 120.

70 In 1926, when Rivers was invited to speak at a meeting organized by the Society of American Bacteriology, he first pronounced, "Viruses appear to be obligate parasites in the sense that their reproduction is dependent on living cells." Quoted in "The Birth of Modern Virology," Hospital Centennial, Rockefeller University, accessed June 20, 2020, http://centennial.rucares.org/index.php?page=Modern_Virology. An obligate parasite is an organism that cannot live without a host (that is, it cannot process all the cellular components it needs to regenerate itself), as opposed to a facultative parasite, which can live independently but becomes parasitic under certain conditions.

71 Boycott, "Transition from Live to Dead," 94. The debate continued in the publication with Geoffrey Samuel writing in response to J. J. Davis's proposition that this group of microorganisms be classified as "vitamol." See Samuel, "Nature of Disease-Producing Viruses," *Nature*, January 11, 1930, 51; see Davis, "Viruses and Life."

72 Boycott, "Transition from Live to Dead."

73 Schrödinger's landmark book *What Is Life?* was culled from a series of lectures delivered in Dublin in 1943. He underscored a *qualitative* difference between physics and the life sciences: it was not enough to trace life back to its physical and chemical reactions; instead, one needed to elucidate specific laws governing complex living bodies or organisms.

74 Landecker, "Metabolism, Reproduction."

75 There are a host of questions about the usefulness of distinguishing life and nonlife, which I cannot pursue at length. One line of inquiry pursues the politics

of valuation. In *Geontologies*, Elizabeth Povinelli, for example, sees the distinction as crucial to processes of extraction, accumulation, and monetization in late liberal societies. What life (humans, plants, animals) generates is up for capture, but nonlife (rocks, minerals, soil) is even more so because of its abject status as passive inert matter. Nonlife does not appear to produce anything; it can be used up, moving toward the negative entropy that life-forms resist. Yet this is equally true of biological substrates (from oocytes and tissues to cells and genes) at present: they can be extracted, harvested, modified, and altered as alienable products. The thorough interpenetration of biological and technological processes toward the close of the twentieth century has made possible a brisk market for "biologicals" and new forms of biovalue. The virus has not escaped capture. When troublesome, viral genes can be snipped with zinc scissors to disable specific actions; more benign genres (such as lentiviruses) can be used to insert, modify, or delete genes. In all these ways, life in alienable forms is not so different from nonlife. Another line of thought points to synthetic life as evidence of plastic machinic life-forms in new conjunctions of the biosciences, computational sciences, engineering, and burgeoning industries. See, for instance, Roosth, *Synthetic*. What has life become, if its biological substrates can be so radically altered and modified? What is life when we can build it from synthetic compounds? For the latter inquiry, the biological organization of matter—the set of procedures defining life—serves as a model for what life can become.

76 Dietert, *Human Superorganism*, 235.

77 Lederberg et al, *Emerging Infections*.

78 Helmreich, *Sounding the Limits of Life*, xiii.

79 Helmreich, *Sounding the Limits of Life*, xii.

80 Jonas and Seifman, "Do We Need a Global Virome Project?," e1314.

81 See Margulis and Sagan, *What Is Life?* Russian scientist Vladimir Vernadsky coined the term *homeostasis* in the early twentieth century, but it took on new life after James Lovelock popularized it in *Gaia* (1979). The term was associated with living forms: a steady state of internal condition that living things maintain. The term had entered biological discourse in the 1930s with the publication of Walter Cannon's *The Wisdom of the Body* (1932); see Rodolfo, "What Is Homeostasis?"

82 Named after the Greek goddess who personified earth, Gaia was largely dismissed as neo-pagan mythology between 1969 and 1977, even as, in the early twenty-first century, ecologists took it seriously but found its implications to be dangerous (the competing Medea thesis launched in 2009 by paleontologist Peter Ward at the University of Washington, saw life as biocidal). As a chemist, Lovelock was invested in planetary chemical compositions; he saw the earth's potent mix of oxygen and carbon-hydrogen tending toward combustion as *different* from that of Mars and Venus. Lovelock had joined NASA's space program in the 1960s; his inquiries into the possibility of life on other planets motivated NASA's two Viking explorer missions in 1976. These missions were foundational to NASA's space biology program: 150 scientists would put together a twenty-year Astrobiology Roadmap in 1999 to speculate on the future of evolution. If life could emerge from

nonorganic matter, it was possible to create entire biospheres or life-worlds on earth and elsewhere (terraforming). In this view, life was emergent: as microorganisms processed energy (metabolism) amid ongoing geological, atmospheric, and chemical disturbances, they were active agents in making the biosphere. In *What Is Life?* (cowritten with the popular science writer Dorion Sagan, 1995), Lynn Margulis presses forward her theory of *endosymbiosis*—mutualistic existence of formerly free-living prokaryotic cells (bacteria) in eukaryotic cells (human). Instead of the Darwinian emphasis on competition, Margulis maintained two species could emerge together—a vision of planetary cooperation. Ironically, even as Gaia spells ecological danger, Margulis's theories of biological mutualism gained new momentum in the early twenty-first-century Human Microbiome Project (HMP). See also Melinda Cooper's excellent discussion of Gaia in *Life as Surplus*, ch. 1.

83 Margulis and Sagan, *What Is Life?*; and Helmreich, *Sounding the Limits of Life*.

84 The notion of organic systems as comprising individuals in cooperative and competitive relationships first arose in the second half of the nineteenth century to complement individual-based conceptions in the life sciences. But a century later an epistemological shift would occur across the biosciences, galvanized by irrefutable metagenomic evidence. See Gilbert, Sapp, and Tauber, "Symbiotic View of Life."

85 Lowe, "Infection," 302; and Sagan, *Cosmic Apprentice*.

86 Kirksey, Shapiro, and Brodine, "Hope in Blasted Landscapes."

87 The "Multispecies Salon" met in New Orleans after Hurricane Katrina in 2010 at a warehouse that was turned into a gallery space for art-science practitioners. The meetings were later published in a volume. See Kirksey, *Multispecies Salon*.

88 Jean-Philippe Chognot (reporting for AFP) signals the release of viruses from the permafrost melt in Russia in 2016. Chognot, "As Permafrost Melts It's Unleashing Ancient Viruses, Carbon—and Now Fuel Spills," *Science Alert*, June 7, 2020, https://www.sciencealert.com/as-permafrost-melts-ancient-viruses-and-now-fuel-spills-are-being-unleashed. In tracking microontologies, Nigel Clark and Myra Hird provide numerous instances of global warming liberating unknown numbers of microbes cyrogenized in the deep ice reservoirs of the Arctic and the Antarctic, some dating to the mid-Pleistocene era (Clark and Hird, "Microontologies").

89 Haraway, *Staying with the Trouble.*

90 As Anna Lowenhaupt Tsing, Andrew Mathews, and Nils Bubandt ("Patchy Anthropocene") characterize the uneven effects of planetary damage.

91 M. Cooper, *Life as Surplus*, ch. 3.

92 The rubric conventionally refers to the periodizing article: Paul Crutzen and Eugene Stoermer's "The Anthropocene."

93 Tsing, "Blasted Landscapes," 87.

94 In its first notations in the seventeenth century, the environment signified geophysical enclosures, vigorously contested, before the nineteenth century's suture of the environment with the natural world. Even then, nineteenth-century global histories of environmentalism record worldwide struggles over particular surrounds—a river, a wilderness area, an urban neighborhood. But it is in the twentieth century that intellectual framings consolidated and reformatted these

struggles against modern industrial metabolism as a global environmental movement with universal ambitions for planetary repair. See Alston, "Environment."

95 Tsing, *Mushroom at the End*, 85.

96 As the late health activist Jonathan Mann, the founding director of the Global Program on AIDS at the WHO, maintained that the dominant feature of this first period was silence, during which the spread of HIV was unchecked by awareness or any preventive action and approximately 100,000 to 300,000 persons may have been infected. Mann, "AIDS, Health, and Human Rights," 41. The moral panics of the 1980s—what Simon Watney (*Policing Desire*, 1997) memorably named the punitive palisade of images—in the postindustrial world (North America, Europe, Australia) are now regarded as tales from a hoary past. President Reagan memorably broke that silence only when Ryan White, a nine-year-old, died of AIDS, together with Reagan's Hollywood colleague, Rock Hudson (who died in 1984). Equally memorable were those who spoke from the far right, perhaps exemplified by the unforgettable call for an AIDS tattoo by conservative intellectual William F. Buckley (editor of the *National Review*), writing an op-ed for the *New York Times* on March 18, 1986: "Everyone detected with AIDS should be tattooed in the upper forearm, to protect common-needle users, and on the buttocks, to prevent the victimization of other homosexuals." Buckley, "Crucial Steps in Combating the Aids Epidemic; Identify All the Carriers," *New York Times*, March 18, 1986, https://archive.nytimes.com/www.nytimes.com/books/00/07/16/specials/buckley-aids.html.

97 There are many models for a critical method appropriate to thinking biological, social, and ecological crises together. Tsing, for one, follows an epistemic object, the matsutake, as an opening into natural milieus and social worlds; neither the mushrooms nor the mushroom pickers appear as unitary subjects. The story in *The Mushroom at the End of the World* discloses divisions and negotiations, creative solutions and setbacks, singular achievements and collective triumphs.

98 Farmer, *Infections and Inequalities*, 14. Farmer argues that in outbreaks "fundamental social forces and processes come to be embodied as biological events." A dynamic, critical, and systematic approach tracks rapidly changing molecular and clinical changes to biomedical and connectivity-infrastructure changes, instead of treating them separately as biological processes.

99 The social status of elites and expatriates, for one, ensured that they received high-quality service, while the poor at the Mission Hospital were at the mercy of unsterile syringes.

100 Farmer (1999, 22) cites this phrase in his account of the first cases emerging in Haiti, in 1979, reported by dermatologist Bernard Liautaud. In time, once Caribbean-wide data became available, a more complex view emerged about the role of North American sex tourism and commerce and Haiti's role in the West Atlantic system. This framing retold the story of Haiti's Port-au-Prince Carrefour district and its sex trade, which had been at the basis of the claim that AIDS originated in Haiti.

101 See Farmer's discussion in his preface to *Infections and Inequalities*, 21–34.

102 Farmer, *Infections and Inequalities*, 608.

103 M. Cooper, *Life as Surplus*; and Sunder Rajan, *Pharmocracy*. The Global North and Global South are the historical shorthand for geopolitical differences between industrialized and industrializing contexts; these are amoeboid geographies rather than cartographic projections since innumerable scholars note that the Global South exists in historically resource-rich Europe, North America, and Japan.

104 Richardson, *Epidemic Illusions*, 1.

105 See Montagnier, "25 Years after HIV Discovery."

106 Several global health theorists have pointed to the imbalances in research that is inattentive to chronic health conditions such as lower respiratory infections, diarrheal diseases, and malaria that shape therapeutic solutions to HIV's attack on the immune system (conditions endemic to the Global South).

107 Emily Bass, an AIDS activist, notes that PEPFAR as a response to HIV/AIDS spans four American presidents and ten Congresses, offering a blueprint for resource allocation. The program was responsible for putting 17.2 million people into ART; currently, the US has invested $85 billion in the program. See Bass, *To End a Plague*; and "PEPFAR 2021 Annual Report to Congress," 5 (https://www.state.gov/wp-content/uploads/2021/02/PEPFAR2021AnnualReporttoCongress.pdf).

108 Vijayakumar, *At Risk*. Vijayakumar argues that India's AIDS crisis was positioned against "African AIDS" in racist terms, in which the latter was the catastrophe that was already here, as opposed to the coming Indian crisis.

109 As early as 1986, the WHO's third director-general, Hafdan T. Mahler was authorized by the executive board to create programs that could address the coming health emergency; the result was the Control Programme on AIDS. The program was rechristened and recalibrated, gaining prominence under Jonathan Mann. In 1996 UNAIDS began its formal operations; still later, the Global Fund to Fight AIDS, Tuberculosis and Malaria was formed solely as a funding agency. Several nongovernmental organizations (NGOs), like the Bill and Melinda Gates Foundation, stepped into to scale up ART delivery.

110 Private donors entered the fray, even as the World Bank (with its famous report *1993 World Development Report: Invest in Health*) became an increasingly central actor in estimating the efficacy of global public health interventions. See Youde's discussion, *Global Health Governance*, 46.

111 Foucault's phrase has now become commonplace; see chapter 11 of *"Society Must Be Defended."*

112 The first cases of AIDS appeared in southern Africa, initially categorized as the wasting disease "Slim," in Uganda in the early 1980s. In South Africa the first recorded cases were among mobile travelers, white gay men in 1983, leading to the consolidation of sweeping government powers to examine any South African citizen who tested positive and to detain and deport noncitizens (migrant miners, in particular, were forcibly tested). Within a decade, the National AIDS Plan, launched in 1994, became one of the largest public health initiatives in global history.

113 As Jeremy Youde recounts, South African exercises in involuntary quarantine and vaccination date back to the colonial era Public Health Act of 1883 (Youde, *AIDS, South Africa, and the Politics of Knowledge*). Equally well known are last-ditch

apartheid-era efforts to configure the HIV/AIDS epidemic as a "Black African" problem, efforts that included a secret bioweapons program that would transform the virus into a biological agent for inducing sterility in Black South African women. M. Cooper, *Life as Surplus*, 68. In 1992, the African National Congress convened health experts and activists to develop a National AIDS Plan and doubled the budget for HIV/AIDS treatment and prevention after taking the reins in 1994. And yet the institutionalized racism around the HIV/AIDS infection of the apartheid era would continue to haunt the new government.

114 South Africa presents a clear instance of how national policies remain central to epidemic mediation, even when international actors, organizations, and institutions provide supplies, staff, and expertise. While, in the United States, white men who have sex with men still remain a major demographic for HIV infection, in South Africa 18.9 percent of adults of all sexual orientations between the ages of fifteen and twenty-five are infected; thus, young adults are often the target of epidemic interventions. Volumes have been written on President Mbeki's denialism that delayed the rollout of authorized cheap drugs for three years after the South African government legally won their case against forty-one pharmaceutical companies suing to stop generic ARTs (costing $350 a year as opposed to $10,000–$15,000 for brand drugs) from hitting the market. As Melinda Cooper explains, the reasons for Mbeki's refusal of ART's efficacies are complex, a neonationalist pushback against both expanding global markets (accused of "making money" off the African poor) and the racism of the "African AIDS" media blitz in the Global North. M. Cooper, *Life as Surplus*, ch. 2.

115 Rebecca Hodes notes that many African leaders responded to that media blitz with anger: in the Congo, the French acronym for HIV, SIDA, was quickly turned into "Syndrome Imaginaire Décourager les Amoureux," a foreign myth discouraging African sexual enjoyment and biological reproduction. Hodes is the deputy director of the AIDS and Society Research Unit at the University of Cape Town; see Hodes, "HIV on Documentary Television."

116 The generics produced by the Indian drug companies CIPLA and Ranbaxi demonstrated that AIDS therapies for the chronically ill could be inexpensive, but big pharma could not pass up the golden opportunity to make money from those who could afford expensive drugs in resource-rich contexts. Hence, the long-wave epidemic of AIDS was held hostage to the cost-benefit calculus, and AIDS activism turned to the great pharma wars of the 1990s. In the midst of heightening biocapitalism, the WHO returned surreptitiously to the 1970s agenda of institution building: this time, for smoother articulations among international organizations, civil society groups, and private philanthropic organizations. Youde, *AIDS, South Africa, and the Politics of Knowledge*.

117 Usher, "South Africa and India Push."

118 See Lakoff, *Unprepared*; and Collier and Lakoff, *Biosecurity Interventions*.

119 Lakoff, *Unprepared*, ch. 2; and Fishel, *Microbial States*.

120 The essay was later republished in Chakrabarty's *The Climate of History in a Planetary Age*.

121 Chakrabarty, *Climate of History*, 3. See also Chakrabarty's discussion of Andrew Goudie and Heather Viles's *Geomorphology in the Anthropocene* (2016).

122 Earth systems scientists are its historians: they gather astronomical and geological perspectives that place the planet in "communicative relationship to humans." "To encounter the planet," maintains Chakrabarty, "is to encounter something that is the condition of human existence and yet profoundly indifferent to that existence." Chakrabarty, *Climate of History*, 4–5.

123 Latour, *Facing Gaia*; and Connolly, *Facing the Planetary*.

124 The demographic and geographic localization of the cholera epidemic in London in 1854 is legendary, a collaboration between John Snow (an anesthesiologist) and William Farr (head of the Office of Public Records), despite the differences in their interpretation of cholera etiologies. Snow's map of London famously tracked the cholera outbreak to a polluted public water pump, establishing epidemiology's geographic calculus. Cholera hit England hard in 1831–32, fueling public concern over bad air, polluted water, and the specific disease milieus. Prevailing miasma theories attributing disease to rotting organic matter directed experts to the locations and disease milieus. While Snow did not espouse miasma theory, he was well versed in sanitary endeavors that sought to improve public hygiene: personal, social, and environmental. See Shah, *Pandemic*, ch. 7.

125 Shah recounts a similar story about the clearing of forests in Guinea, as one of the drivers of the 2014 Ebola outbreak. Shah, *Pandemic*, 16.

126 Thomas, "Pandemics of the Future."

127 Rose, "Multispecies Knots of Ethical Time," 128. Rose's article represents one strain of multispecies thinking among decolonial scholars. There are many others; for example, scholars like Kim TallBear work on metagenomic findings. A snapshot of different approaches can be found in the special issue coedited by Angela Willey and Kim TallBear, "Critical Relationality."

128 Rose, *Wild Dog Dreaming*, 51.

129 See Mukharji, "Cat and Mouse."

130 Paxson, "Microbiopolitics," 116; see also Paxson, "Post-Pasteurian Cultures."

131 Ginn, Beisel, and Barua, "Flourishing with Awkward Creatures," 114.

132 Giraud et al., "Abundance in the Anthropocene"; see also Giraud, *What Comes after Entanglement?*

133 Lorimer, "Parasites, Ghosts, and Mutualists."

134 Nigel Clark and Myra Hird, in "Microontologies," call for the flexible "subtending" of relations with emergent microbial life that constantly arrives in threatening microontologies; what these subtended multispecies relations imply is a new politics of space, global and planetary.

135 Haraway, *Staying with the Trouble*.

136 Haraway, *Staying with the Trouble*, 62.

137 Autopoiesis was developed by the Chilean neurobiologists Humberto Maturana and Francisco Varela in their landmark *Autopoiesis and Cognition* (1973). Autopoiesis relies on the capacity to reaffirm the structural integrity of the interlocking living systems that we call an organism. Faced with new perturbations in its

relations, the organism maintains a snapshot of how things were—a kind of self-referential memory. New perturbations may be the streaming inorganic chemicals that change circuits, reset channels, or redirect flows, and yet the feedback-response modification references the organismic state before perturbation.

138 Combining the etymons *sym* (meaning "together") and *biosis* (meaning "live"), *symbiosis* was a general term for human social mutualism hailing back to ancient Greece before its recent domestication in biology in 1879. Studying fungi, the German mycologist Heinrich Anton de Bary would adopt the cultural concept to describe the biological living together of unlike organisms; shortly thereafter, symbiosis became a generic biological moniker for long-term interactions between living organisms that include mutualism, commensualism, *and* parasitism. Contemporary theorists draw firmer boundaries around the evolutionary prospects of living (*biosis*) together (*sym*). See Douglas, *Symbiotic Habit*; Paracer and Ahmadjian, *Symbiosis*; and Margulis and Sagan, *Microcosmos*.

139 In her latest work on symbiosis (*The Symbiotic Habit*), Douglas returns to the persistence of this behavior among organisms in light of new thought on the microbiota crucial to immune function and the pragmatic promotion of symbiosis (reintroducing indigenous plant species in an effort to defragment habitats) as a bulwark against deleterious anthropogenic effects. Following *Symbiotic Interactions* (1994) and *The Biology of Symbiosis* (1987), *The Symbiotic Habit* ventures into the role of human ecological and medical interventions in the processes of symbioses and, for my purposes, includes a reevaluation of certain organisms originally considered pathogenic as potentially symbiotic in the evolutionary future. Douglas, *Symbiotic Habit*, 8. Symbiosis-at-risk is one step on a spectrum of relations between parasites and hosts, but some relationships never move past that point. Symbiotic relations are those that are mutually beneficial to the participants for the major duration of their lifetime. This does not mean that parasitism is not symbiotic but that pathogenic parasitism is not. Less virulent parasites are at a selective advantage in this regard, since they do not deplete the resources of the host. Douglas, *Symbiotic Habit*, 29.

140 Stengers, *Cosmopolitics I*.

141 Pato Hebert, "Lingering," 2020–21, https://patohebert.com/section/494902-Lingering.html.

142 Pato Hebert, interview by author, June 15, 2021.

143 Pato Hebert, "In, If Not Always Of," *Fraction*, no. 85 (2014), http://www.fractionmagazine.com/pato-hebert.

CHAPTER TWO. THE -MORPHIC IMAGE

1 Published in Ellermann and Bang, "Experimentelle Leukämie bei Hühnern" (1909).

2 Rous, "Transmissible Avian Neoplasm"; Rous, "Sarcoma of the Fowl." At the time of their publication, Rous's papers were not celebrated, since the relevance of cancer in birds to research on human cancers was not clear. Leukemia was not recognized as a neoplastic disease until after 1930. In fact, at the time of Rous's

discovery of Rous sarcoma virus (RSV), physicians strongly opposed the idea that cancer could be caused by infection. Patrick Moore and Yuan Chang's "Why Do Viruses Cause Cancer?" provides a historical account of virological research on cancer.

3 Landecker, *Culturing Life.*

4 See Kirsten Ostherr's discussion of this early film in "Animating Informatics."

5 Cahill, *Zoological Surrealism.*

6 The most salient treatises on machinic objectivity are Lorraine Daston and Peter Galison's *Objectivity* and Evelyn Fox Keller's *Making Sense of Life*.

7 In developing a theory of zoological surrealism, Cahill discusses "Notes on Drawing," where Eisenstein argues that, despite artifice, Mickey Mouse's plasmatic form and vitality contour our relation to milieu. See Cahill, *Zoological Surrealism*, 145.

8 Latour and Woolgar, *Laboratory Life*, 62.

9 Stengers, "Challenge of Ontological Politics."

10 As Georges Canguilhem explains, the cell is considered the sole constant in most living things and is always produced by an existing cell. See Canguilhem, *Knowledge of Life*, ch. 2.

11 Tufte, *Envisioning Information*, 81–97.

12 DeLanda, *Philosophy and Simulation*, 3, 185–86.

13 Flusser, *Into the Universe*, 31–40 (ch. "To Envision").

14 Thurtle, *Biology in the Grid*. Thurtle's history takes us all the way back to Ernst Haeckel's "art forms in nature" that inscribe life-forms and Haeckel's location of those forms *in relation* to others. Morphology, in this sense, is deeply relational in instituting visible differences between forms.

15 Manovich, *Language of New Media*, 63.

16 Lippit, *Atomic Light (Shadow Optics)*, outlines the "optical fantastic" in the first half of the twentieth century triangulating the development of X-ray technologies, the splitting of the atom, and psychoanalysis. See also my account of the cellular agon in "Animating Uncommon Life." In animated scientific edutainment, the orchestral music, for example, colors the molecular and cellular processes as a planetary adventure.

17 Molecular visualization began to cohere commercially in the late 1980s (although the precedents in molecular graphics go back much further). The first SciVis meeting (the Visualization in Scientific Computing Conference), in 1987, brought together industry, academics, and government officials. Thus began the industrial enterprise of new media platforms that allowed scientists and animators to produce images based on experimental data necessary for designing source materials (digital files for synthetic compounds) that could be actualized as marketable "biologicals" (biotechnological products). See Colonna, "Scientific Visualization."

18 Ghosh, "Toward Symbiosis."

19 Armitage, "On the World," 119.

20 See "HIV Drug Resistance Database," Stanford University, accessed June 30, 2021, https://hivdb.stanford.edu/.

21 DeLanda, *Philosophy and Simulation*, 19 and 164.

22 Thacker, *Biomedia*; Kember and Zylinska, *Life after New Media*; Myers, *Rendering Life Molecular*; and Thurtle, *Biology in the Grid*.

23 Rheinberger elaborates on one such organism, the fruit fly (*Drosophila*), which has the longest history as a model in genetics and developmental biology. Rheinberger, *Epistemology of the Concrete*, 224. See also Richard Twyman, "What Is a Model Organism?," *Encyclopedia of Life*, National Museum of Natural History, accessed January 19, 2021, https://education.eol.org/articles/model_organisms.pdf; and Kohler, *Lords of the Fly*.

24 Viruses can be named after the places in which they first emerge as objects of scientific research: for instance, Marburg virus, a virus that jumped into human populations from monkeys imported from Uganda for research at Behring Works, Germany, takes its name from the town in which the research unit is located.

25 See Montagnier's citation of the Barré-Sinoussi et al., "Isolation of a T-Lymphotropic Retrovirus."

26 Montagnier, "25 Years after HIV Discovery."

27 Latour, *Pandora's Hope*, ch. 5.

28 Latour, "Historicity of Things."

29 As early as the seventeenth century, the lens maker Antonie van Leeuwenhoek had observed spermatozoa, erythrocytes, and bacteria through a single biconvex lens, exclaiming at the "little living animacules, very prettily a-moving." Quoted in Dubos, *Unseen World*, 8.

30 See Rasmussen, *Picture Control*.

31 The former won the Nobel Prize for electron optics in 1986 even as he always insisted that it was his brother Helmut Ruska's methods of preparing biological samples that made electron microscopy possible. Ernst Ruska provided evidence in an article published in the inaugural volume of the *Archiv für die Gesamte Virusforschung* (now *Archives of Virology*), in 1939, where he insisted that it was Helmut's "ultramicroscopy" (of viruses) that made possible the development of electron microscopy. See Helmut Ruska et al., "Die Bedeutung der Übermikroskopie für die Virusforschung." The credit for crystallizing TMV (isolating the nucleoprotein that displays virus activity) in 1938 goes to biochemist and virologist Wendell Stanley, who won the Nobel Prize for his endeavors in 1946.

32 There are many histories of the discovery of the gene, starting from George Mendel, but the watershed point is James D. Watson and Francis Crick's definition of the molecular structure of DNA in 1953. The latter drew substantially on chemist and X-ray crystallographer Rosalind Franklin's research, which was not credited as such.

33 Thacker, *Biomedia*.

34 The recent "cleaning up" of DNA strands in the Chinese twins—research data that have not been externally verified by the scientific community—only underscores the ethical specter haunting biology. The use of zinc scissors to snip DNA segments (CRISPR technologies) enabled the first gene-edited babies in China: Lulu and Nana are reported to have a genetic mutation (of CCR5) that makes it harder for HIV to invade and infect their white blood cells. See Megan Molteni, "Scientist

Who Crispr'd Babies Bucked His Own Ethics Policy," *Wired*, November 27, 2018, https://www.wired.com/story/he-jiankui-crispr-babies-bucked-own-ethics-policy/.

35 Silkworm experimenters in the mid-1800s had shown that exposing silkworm eggs to sulfuric acid or rubbing them lightly with a brush could induce parthenogenesis. This set the stage for Loeb's early work with substituting physiochemical manipulation for spermatozoa. Loeb recorded his work in *Die chemische Entwicklungserregung des tierischen Eies* (1900).

36 Emerging in the 1970s, in vitro fertilization by the twenty-first century had become a global technological platform spanning clinical and laboratory practice, a thoroughfare exemplified in the material "hole in the wall." Franklin, *Biological Relatives*, 20–21. Thus, Franklin compares it to the "looking glass" that allows the prepubescent Alice access to the topsy-turvy universe of mutant exchange—a world in which women have not as yet become symbolic coin (as in exogamous kinship systems). Before normalization, such technology has the capacity to reset relations with strange kin. For Franklin, this disruption is the true promise: the capacity to rethink biology in its golden age.

37 Brenner, "In the Beginning," 137.

38 Stengers, *Challenge of Ontological Politics*, 86.

39 Myers, *Rendering Life Molecular*, 10.

40 Iwasa, "Crafting a Career in Molecular Animation."

41 I interviewed Janet Iwasa first on January 4, 2013, and I have subsequently followed up, corresponding with her on email on June 28, 2020, and March 3, 2021.

42 Showcase on the online platform Clarafi (produced by Digizyme) features Iwasa's works and offers tools and training for Molecular Maya (mMaya). See https://clarafi.com/animators/janet-iwasa/, accessed July 10, 2021. mMaya draws on biomolecular geometries from the Protein Data Bank; as a programming language, it combines modular elements of Python and MEL (Maya Embedded Language). See Nocek, *Molecular Capture*, 49–50.

43 "Dengue Invades a Cell," production by Irene Bosch, Michael Astrachan, and David Bolisnky; animation by Janet Iwasa, Gaël McGill, and Digizyme; composing, editing, and art direction by Michael Astrachan, XVIVO (Boston: WGBH Education Foundation, 2008).

44 See Harrison, "Whither Structural Biology?," 13.

45 Harrison, "Whither Structural Biology?," 14.

46 McGill, quoted in Ryan, "Molecular Movie Stars," 383.

47 Scholars argue that scientific intuition and hunches are epistemological cousins, but they differ substantially in terms of what they materialize. Intuition involves seeing/sensing the whole pattern of logical sequences underlying a single process *for an instant*, but a hunch focuses on a part that is *not yet empirically verifiable*. Lois Isenmen, in "Toward an Understanding of Intuition and Its Importance in the Scientific Endeavor," distinguishes between the hunch and the intuition, claiming a place for both in experimental research as the motor of scientific advance.

48 Stengers, *Cosmopolitics II*.

49 Iwasa, "Animating the Model Figure," 699.

50 Iwasa, "Animating the Model Figure," 699.

51 Tom Kirchhausen, "Clathrin Mediated Endocytosis by Janet Iwasa and Tom Kirchhausen 2012," YouTube, May 18, 2013, https://www.youtube.com/watch?v=o_EUHu4OJus.

52 Robert Lue's eight-and-a-half-minute animation, *The Inner Life of the Cell* (2006), won the coveted SIGGRAPH (Special Interest Group on Computer Graphics and Interactive Techniques) award for that year. See XVIVO Scientific Animation, "The Inner Life of the Cell," accessed June 12, 2022, http://www.xvivo.net/the-inner-life-of-the-cell. Other animations for public platforms include Iwasa's work in Jack Szotak's lab at Harvard University (for example, animations of single-strand RNA molecules surrounded by a fatty acid membrane).

53 For instance, Nikon hosts the "Small World" contest in microphotography every year to showcase new talents *and* sell their new instruments. Meanwhile, the National Science Foundation hosts a Visualization Challenge every year for animating data, creating apps, or illustrating engineering concepts.

54 Coren, "Fold It Gamers Solve Riddle of HIV."

55 Milburn, *Nanovision*; and Chang, *Playing Nature*. Milburn's works have consistently shown the closing distance between scientific research and popular science, first in *Nanovision* and then in *Mondo Nano*; Chang's new work in *Playing Nature* elaborates the point, pursuing the ecological vision of video games.

56 Cromley, "Digital Images Are Data."

57 Nocek, *Molecular Entertainment*, ch. 1.

58 Iwasa, *HIV Life Cycle*, Science of HIV, accessed July 1, 2022, https://scienceofhiv.org/wp/life-cycle/.

59 It would be tendentious to insist on too strong an opposition between the artifice of these moving images. As media scholars such as Kirsten Ostherr have shown, the "denaturing of life," has always persisted in moving images of vital processes despite the illusion of indexical realism in microcinematography. See Ostherr, "Animating Informatics."

60 Iwasa, *HIV Life Cycle*.

61 Tufte, *Envisioning Information*, 91.

62 Myers, *Rendering Life Molecular*.

63 See "HIV Life Cycle Illustrations by David S. Goodsell (2015)," Science of HIV, accessed July 24, 2022, https://scienceofhiv.org/wp/goodsell-gallery/.

64 Ferdinand Saussure, *Course in General Linguistics*.

65 Latour, "Visualization and Cognition," 27.

66 The (art)n collective patented the PHSColograms in 1989. See Ellen Sandor and (art)n, "What Is a Phscologram (Skol-o-Gram)?," accessed July 27, 2022, https://www.artn.com/phscolograms.

67 Ellen Sandor, interview by author, June 27, 2020.

68 (art)n confronts the viewer head-on with the presence of the computer and its ability to visualize the unseen. Such artists, drawing on the computer's inherent strengths, are creating works that are less self-conscious and apologetic than works of the past. The consequence of this boldness is a SIGGRAPH art show that

may be viewed as a watershed by future critics. See LeWinter and Baron, "Bold Statements."

69 Ellen Sandor, interview by the author, June 27, 2020.

70 Grau, *Virtual Art*.

71 Grau, *Virtual Art*, 15.

72 Ellen Sandor and (art)n, "Visualizing in a New Light," accessed July 27, 2022, https://www.visualizinginanewlight.com/. In the online gallery, one can see the displays of viral PHSColograms. See also Ellen Sandor and (art)n, "Invisible Visibility: Viral," accessed July 1, 2022, https://www.artn.com/viral.

73 Description of "The AIDS Virus, Third Edition," at Ellen Sandor and (art)n, "Invisible Visibility."

74 Myers, *Rendering Life Molecular*, ch. 1.

75 Cyrus Levinthal et al., "Proteins" (MIT, 1966), Early Interactive Molecular Graphics Movie Gallery, History of Visualization of Biological Macromolecules On-line Museum, https://www.umass.edu/molvis/francoeur/movgallery/moviegallery.html.

76 Levinthal, "Molecular Model Building by Computer," 52.

77 The Research Collaboratory for Structural Bioinformatics (RCSB) is the US data center that hosts the Protein Data Bank (PDB). The PDB started in 1971 and remains one of the oldest worldwide open-access databases for scientific study.

78 Cox wrote some of the earliest essays on art-science collaborations around scientific visualization. Particularly, influential were "Using the Super-Computer to Visualize Higher Dimensions" (published in *Leonardo*, 2008) and a public presentation, "Renaissance Teams, Visualizations, and Virtual Reality," delivered at the Hayden Planetarium, American Museum of Natural History, New York, June 28, 2001. Cox coined the phrase "Renaissance teams" for interdisciplinary clusters of actors engaged in visualization, with reference to artists who worked with scientists to make the most seminal images of botany and anatomy. Cox's lasting impact was recognized in her Distinguished Artist Lifetime Achievement Award from SIGGRAPH in 2019. See Cox, Sandor, and Fron, *New Media Futures*.

79 Sandin was trained by Tom DeFanti, one of the earliest pioneers in computer graphics. For their work on the CAVE, see Cruz-Neira, Sandin, and DeFanti, "Surround-Screen Projection-Based Virtual Reality."

80 The collaboration included Donna Cox, George Francis, and Ray Idaszak of the NCSA and Tom DeFanti and Dan Sandin of the EVL.

81 Cox, Sandor, and Fron, *New Media Futures*.

82 The *AIDS Virus* was made by Ellen Sandor and (art)n, with Stephan Meyers, Randy Johnson, and Jim Zanzi. In the virtual online exhibit, it is labeled as a "Vintage PHSCologram," indicating the collective's move from analog to digital technologies. See Sandor and (art)n, "Invisible Visibility." The piece is titled "AIDS Virus, Third Edition," 1989–1990. It was made with interleaved Cibachrome and Kodalith films.

83 In her seminal critique of early scientific discourse on HIV/AIDS, Cindy Patton dates the reinstitution of science as the premier war front to 1988, right after a widely discussed issue of the *Scientific American* (October 1, 1988) captioned "What Science Knows about AIDS" sported seminal images (micrograms and

diagrams) of the virus. The issue included Robert C. Gallo and Luc Montagnier's "AIDS in 1988." Patton argues that, in such articulations, science appears in opposition to nonscience or commonsense, and it "knows, rather than posits, imagines, or thinks" the virus separated as object from its human host. Patton, *Inventing AIDS*, 65.

84 See *Messiah* (1987), at Sandor and (art)n, "Invisible Visibility."

85 The Feature Gallery, directed by the late art-dealer who went by Hudson, first showed the *AIDS Virus* image in Chicago and then in Soho, New York. The Independent Curators Inc. included *Messiah* in a traveling show, "From Media to Metaphor: Art about AIDS, 1992–94," before the US Art in Embassies Program picked it up. When the program showed *AIDS Virus* in Harare, Zimbabwe (1998–2000), it gained international stature: "The AIDS Virus is clearly the most talked about piece in our collection," noted Anne Marie McDonald at the American Embassy in Harare. "The PHSCologram offers us a chance to discuss AIDS in an informal, less threatening way, but nonetheless important way. Zimbabweans are drawn to the technology that the piece evokes. Americans are stunned by the artistic feel, the vivid color and amazing shape of 'the disease.'" McDonald, quoted in Sandor and (art)n, "Invisible Visibility."

86 *Beautiful Strangers* was the name of the exhibit at the Feature Gallery, New York, March–April 1989.

87 Their many collaborations include the Scripps Research Institute, NASA, and other research hubs at major universities.

88 Michel Ségard, "Deconstruction in the Virtual World: Building Peace by Piece," an essay introducing an art(n) collective exhibition with the same title, November 3–14, 2015, https://static1.squarespace.com/static/5b75e7b9f93fd47ebf0d806f/t/5ca286410022910001485a57/1554155075238/SANDOR_NAC_NYC.pdf. See also K. Johnson, "(Art)n at Feature." Ken Johnson writes, "The things that (art)n chooses to represent PHSColographically are not of the normally visible world. Rather, the group works in collaboration with other scientists to produce images that usually exist only as speculative or theoretical entities. . . . Thus the idea animating the (art)n enterprise is that the heretofore invisible worlds being explored by various kinds of scientists may, for both functional and esthetic purposes, be rendered 'visible.'" Cited by Sandor and (art)n, "Invisible Visibility."

89 See Stephen Harrison, Arthur Olson, Clarence Schutt, Fritz Winkler, and Gérard Bricogne on the tomato stunt virus image produced at the Harrison Lab, Harvard University, 1978. Harrison et al., "Tomato Bushy Stunt Virus."

90 Goodsell is often compared to the pathbreaking Irving Geis, whose 1969 "ribbon diagrams" of the molecular structure of protein folds still hold sway in the aesthetic grammar of molecular visualizations. See Goodsell, Olson, and Forli, "Art and Science of the Cellular Mesoscale."

91 See Olson's full-length account of what 3D models offer in "Perspectives on Structural Molecular Biology Visualization."

92 See Olson's argument on perceptual cognitive processes in "Self-Assembly Gets Physical," 728.

93 "HIV Interaction and Viral Evolution Center," Scripps Research, accessed July 1, 2022, https://www.scripps.edu/fightaidsathome/_internal/templates/full%20width%20page.html.

94 cellPACK was developed at the Olson Lab (with Antin) while Johnson was finishing his postgraduate work. The open-source program integrates structural biology and systems biology data with packing algorithms to assemble comprehensive 3D models of cell-scale structures in molecular detail.

95 See G. Johnson et al., "cellPACK," 2.

96 In DeLanda's terms in *Philosophy and Simulation*.

97 See G. Johnson et al., "3D Molecular Models of Whole HIV-1 Virions."

98 DeLanda, *Philosophy and Simulation*, 5.

99 DeLanda, *Philosophy and Simulation*, 125.

100 Conformational changes can mean hundreds of thousands of "degrees of freedom" for proteins to fold; the point is to calculate the ones expending the least amount of energy for theorizing probable outcomes.

101 In her theory of scale, Alenda Chang in *Playing Nature* examines scale making by geographers, mapmakers, and computer scientists; she argues that scale is not just a graded system of measurement but has interobjective relativity in video games. Nonlinearity is the norm, which means that what holds at one scale will not hold at another.

102 As the late twentieth-century successor to genomics, systems biology materializes the disciplinary turn to data integration, repositioning genomic data as one part of the network constitutive of the living system in order to study multileveled perturbations in living systems. In the case of virological study, perturbation is not only what *viruses* do to human cells but also what scientists can do with viruses in their biotechnological interventions. Perturbations are simulations of biological events experimentally run together on multiple fronts for a prognosis of systemic adjustments, modifications, compensations, or reorientations. See Pulendran, Li, and Nakaya, "Systems Vaccinology."

103 DeLanda, *Philosophy and Simulation*.

104 Myers, *Rendering Life Molecular*.

CHAPTER THREE. THE SENSIBLE MEDIUM

1 Ghosh, "Becoming Undetectable."

2 Athey is an American performance artist associated with post-AIDS sexual artworks. Athey became the target of controversy in 1994 when he was falsely accused of exposing the audience to HIV-infected blood at a performance piece with Divine Fudge at the Walker Art Center, Minneapolis. While Athey had received only $150 from the National Endowment for the Arts (NEA), right-wing demagogues such as Jesse Helms targeted his performance pieces as too extreme, an affront to public taste, much like the work of the famous NEA four (Tim Mills, Holly Hughes, John Fleck, and Karen Finley), who fought a case for freedom of speech in the Supreme Court. Athey's embodied transformations onstage (bleeding,

cutting, swelling, twisting, penetrating) sought to "offer" the HIV+ body to audiences as an object of pain/pleasure. The politics of his work is extensively discussed in Jennifer Doyle's *Hold It against Me*.

3 See Foucault's discussion of the symbolics of blood in *History of Sexuality*, Vol. I, 148–50.

4 See "Time Names AIDS Scientist Man of the Year," *Los Angeles Times*, December 22, 1996, https://www.latimes.com/archives/la-xpm-1996-12-22-mn-11799-story.html.

5 The story of the blood paintings is as follows: In an effort to save several drawings from the bloody flow, Sherer emptied a nearby jar of pencils to cover the puncture and then watched with morbid fascination as the container filled. Soon, however, his curiosity was overcome by sheer exhaustion. He bandaged his wound with duct tape, sealed the jar and placed it in his minirefrigerator, and left the mess to get some sleep. Rested and refreshed, the artist returned in the morning to clean up the gruesome scene he had left in his studio. His drawings were ruined, and blood was everywhere. Yet despite the grisliness of the spectacle before him, the artist noted a compelling beauty in the dried spatters that covered his work. Then he recalled the jar of blood in the refrigerator, and his traumatic memory of the previous night vanished as a myriad of creative possibilities presented themselves. Sherer uncovered the jar, grabbed a brush, and began to experiment with his new liquid medium on scraps of paper. Very quickly he discovered that after only five to ten small brushstrokes, the exposure to air caused the blood to begin clotting, so he began to experiment. Subsequent research into the nature of his new medium led Sherer to explore a variety of other anticlotting additives and procedures. See Sherer, *The Blood Works*.

6 Sagan, *Cosmic Apprentice*.

7 See discussion of "WHO Guidelines" in Ghosh, "Becoming Undetectable." The guidelines are a publication of the Access Campaign, Médecins Sans Frontières.

8 *Undetectable* marks the suppression of viral generation. Contra the term, the condition is mediatically detectable: amplified viral particle signals are numerically transcribed, and the resultant quantification represents a volumetric blood picture. "Low" viral loads mark the ratio of viral particles to blood components before saturation. The majority of commercially available instruments (costing $10–$70) draw blood as the chosen body fluid; samples are prepared for plasma (55 percent of blood content) extraction and examination at laboratories. Many tests, such as those made by Abbott, Biocentric (Generic HIV Viral Load Test), and bioMérieux, use nucleic acid–based technologies that require a cold chain of transport for liquid plasma, which means laboratory storage and refrigeration are necessary. See Ghosh, "Becoming Undetectable."

9 Peters, *Marvelous Clouds*, 104.

10 Unlike the first test for HIV, the ELISA–Western blot test introduced in 1984 that checked for antibodies rather than for viral particles, the viral load test is currently the gold standard for tracking the progression of disease. This does not mean that each blood specimen (divided into several samples) is not run through other tests; indeed, antibody tests for volunteers in the HIV Vaccine Trials Network (HVTN) and T-cell tests for clinical care are also routine.

11 Canguilhem cites Bernard's notion of freedom in *Knowledge of Life*, 16.

12 Stacy Alaimo proposes "transcorporeality" as a mode of understanding the molar body's material distribution in its environment in *Bodily Natures*; Elizabeth Povinelli probes the life/nonlife boundary in *Geontologies*; and Mel Chen elaborates the queer affects of the distributed subject in *Animacies*.

13 Canguilhem, *Knowledge of Life*, 118.

14 See the discussion in chapter 3, "Health: Popular Concept and Philosophical Question," in Canguilhem, *Writings on Medicine*, 43–52. Canguilhem's *Writings on Medicine* is a collection that was posthumously published. The French edition was organized by Armand Zaloszyc, a psychiatrist and psychoanalyst who studied under Canguilhem. In their introduction to the collection's English translation, Stefanos Geroulanos and Todd Meyers (the translators) explain that Canguilhem himself had drawn up a similar ensemble of his own writings in the 1970s.

15 Canguilhem borrows the phrase from the surgeon René Leriche. See Canguilheim, *Normal and the Pathological*, 91. As a historian of science, Canguilhem was invested in developing a historical epistemology (spanning thinkers such as René Descartes, Auguste Comte, and Claude Bernard) that exposes the intellectual ground on which contemporary understandings of life take hold. Scholars describe the ensuing theory as a "negative vitalism" that presents the "living body" in constant negotiation with its dynamic milieu. See Geroulanos, "Beyond the Normal and the Pathological," 291. Canguilhem is less interested in defining the "powers" of living organisms than he is in the *process of living*. All organisms are irregular in that they must permanently remake their own norms to survive. In this sense, the normativity of life is a creative process that *individualizes* every living being. Health turns out to be a social process of *negotiating* one's vital norms in the doctor's office. Canguilhem's lean toward the singular search for a dynamic equilibrium places the patient-subject squarely at the center of the medical solution—neither the scientist nor the doctor is the prevailing authority. As he puts it, "The living body is thus the singular being whose health expresses the quality of forces that constitute it: it must live with the tasks imposed on it, and it must live exposed to an environment that it does not initially choose. The living body is the totality of the powers of a being that has the capacity to evaluate and represent to itself these powers, their exercise, and their limits." Canguilhem, *Writings on Medicine*, 48.

16 Leroi-Gourhan's *Gesture and Speech* (*Le geste et la parole*) establishes walking and chewing as the first intimations of the body's technological armature.

17 Canguilhem, *Knowledge of Life*, 113.

18 Peters, *Marvelous Clouds*, 266.

19 Titmuss, *Gift Relationship*.

20 While there is a great deal of controversy about whether or not convalescent plasma (with high amounts of antibodies) should be used to treat COVID-19, there is a brisk business for the medium. For-profit companies (like Takeda Pharmaceuticals) are buying convalescent plasma donations for as much as $800 a pop. See Jonel Aleccia, "Market for Blood Plasma from COVID-19 Survivors Heats Up," NPR,

May 11, 2020, https://www.npr.org/sections/health-shots/2020/05/11/852354920/market-for-blood-plasma-from-covid-19-survivors-heats-up.

21 See discussion of blood-donation bans directed at MSM donors in Sarkar and Ghosh, "Media and Risk."

22 In *Security, Territory, Population*, Foucault is directly concerned with the governance of epidemics and, therein, of vital circulations (blood, plasma, hormones, microbes, toxins, proteins, or lipids) during the earliest state-run inoculation campaigns. Distinguishing a third mode of power—distinct from sovereign juridical power that punishes or kills and disciplinary power that surveys, observes, and corrects—that *calculates* and *intervenes* in the vital circulations of human life, Foucault argues that the locus of this third kind of power is not *this* subject of law or *that* docile body but our very biological existence.

23 Stephanie Fishel's "microbial states" and Nigel Clark's "microontologies," discussed in chapter 1, conceptually signal this open spatiality.

24 Peters, *Marvelous Clouds.*

25 Pollmann, *Cinematic Vitalism,* 780.

26 Karin Knorr Cetina's analysis in *Epistemic Cultures* is particularly illuminating for my concerns with molecular-scale analytics, in challenging the sense of a unified science in the field of molecular biology.

27 Rancière, "What a Medium Can Mean."

28 Siegel, *Forensic Media.*

29 Larkin, *Signal and Noise.*

30 The peripheral blood (PMBC) of the circulating hematic system, as opposed to blood sequestered in the lymph, spleen, liver, or bone marrow, is one reservoir for integrated DNA (which embeds HIV protein-making directions within host DNA) and is therefore a key fluid for cure protocols.

31 Other tests include an initial rapid diagnostic test at the clinic, followed by a screening test for CD4 counts that accompanies the viral load test. The latter are processed at the Retrovirus Lab.

32 See Arnaout et al., "SARS-CoV2 Testing."

33 Pyne et al., "Evaluation of Abbott," 350.

34 The recent "HIV cure" refers to the São Paulo Patient: after receiving an especially aggressive combination of ARV drugs and nicotinamide (vitamin B_3), the São Paulo Patient went off all HIV treatment in March 2019 and has not had the virus return to his blood. This is regarded as an "intriguing—but far from proven—HIV cure." J. Cohen, "Intriguing—but Far from Proven—HIV Cure."

35 I owe Melody Jue for pointing this out to me in response to one of many talks on this part of my research.

36 Vismann, *Files,* 10.

37 From March 1987 to 2019, the CFAR/CNICS collected and stored 1,043,374 aliquots of biological specimens from 18,188 HIV-infected patients, which include viable frozen and snap-frozen PBMCs. See CFAR Network of Integrated Clinical Integrated Systems (CNICS), "Specimens," accessed July 1, 2022, https://sites.uab.edu/cnics/specimens/.

38 Some of the conspiracy theories are recounted in science journalism (for example, Richard Preston's *Demon in the Freezer*); more serious disagreements have broken out between nations, as we know from the struggle to preserve H7N9 (avian flu) strains at the Animal Health Research Institute of Taiwan and not transfer them to China, a struggle over "viral sovereignty" (see Frédéric Keck's discussion in *Avian Reservoirs*).

39 One paper with multiple authors, including Robert Coombs and Joan Dragavon from this lab, tracked the effects of PrEP on seroconversion (Partners PrEP Study) based on specimens from Kenya and Uganda. See Donnell et al., "Effect of Oral Preexposure Prophylaxis."

40 Tailored for scientific leadership in HIV research, CNICS makes possible interdisciplinary collaborations among scientists, clinicians, and social scientists. The advantage that CNICS has over traditional electronic medical records data held at specific centers is a large and diverse sample, in terms of both populations and biological specimens.

41 If the drive to unify health interventions through the medical record persisted throughout the twentieth century. The more complex electronic health record, argues Kirsten Ostherr, linking financial and medical information, risk assessments, and self-care protocols, embeds patients more firmly than ever in the biomedical knowledge economy. What makes it into the authorized medical file, now reconstituted as the electronic health record accessible to patients, is decided on a case-by-case basis. Against the backdrop of sprawling techno-services and biosensor markets, biological processes are palpable as microactions in private homes and public recreation facilities, schools and workplaces, shopping areas and parks. See Ostherr, "Risk Media in Medicine."

42 Dr. Nina Kim, virtual interview by author, April 24, 2017.

43 Barry, "Pharmaceutical Matters."

44 See Ernst, chapter 4, "Archives in Transition: Dynamic Media Memories," in *Digital Memory and the Archive*, 95–101.

45 M. Cooper and Waldby, *Clinical Labor*, 203.

46 Jim Eigo, interview with Sarah Schulman, March 5, 2004, MssCol 6148, ACT UP Oral History Project Videotapes, Manuscripts and Archives Division, the New York Public Library, https://archives.nypl.org/mss/6148.

47 Epstein, "Construction of Lay Expertise." Epidemic print media with local footprints, like the San Francisco–based *AIDS Treatment News* and the New York–based *Treatment Issues*, aiming to educate local disease constituencies, made that mastery possible.

48 The earliest self-quant community, the Quantified Self, started in 2008 and has meetups in 119 cities and 38 countries. The mantra is "*n* of 1" (the number of cases is oneself) as self-experimentation.

49 Still, the confrontation with regulatory institutions continues: biosensor technologies such as the NightScout, for instance, which includes a DIY smart screen for continuous tracking of blood sugar, await FDA approvals. Online self-quant communities have developed mesoscale literacies about testing protocols and result interpretations (#WeAreNotWaiting). Neff and Nafus, *Self-Tracking*.

50 Vale et al., "Bureaucracies of Blood and Belonging."

51 Among India's community-based organizations, HST was the first to take up LGBTQ+ rights and health. See "Integrated HIV Clinic," Humsafar Trust, March 13, 2020, https://humsafar.org/wp-content/uploads/2020/03/Session-1.1-Integrated-HIV-Clinic-HST-Presentation_13.03.2020.pdf; and Robertson, "Humsafar Trust."

52 Starting with 1,000 members of the MSM and TG communities in 1999, HST currently provides care to 8,500 members every year. See Humsafar Trust, "About Us," accessed July 1, 2022, https://humsafar.org/about-us/.

53 During the interview, when I asked about using their actual names in my writing, both expressed willingness since they already had public poresence as registered counselor (for Karamba) and community advocate/activist (for Jhadav).

54 Piña et al., "Antiretroviral Treatment Uptake."

55 The hospitals include Lokmanya Tilak Municipal, Sion, BYL Nair Charitable, J.J. Hospital, and KEM Hospital in Mumbai.

56 Gowri Vijayakumar notes that in 1996 there were 2.1 million HIV-infected people in India, the third-highest number in the world at the time, but the percentage was small in terms of India's population. The sheer numbers understood in the global public health frame prompted the sense of a crisis to come. Vijayakumar, *At Risk*, ch. 2.

57 Vijayakumar, *At Risk*. As sexual minorities and sex workers engaged the state, groups like the AIDS Bhadbhav Virodhi Andolan led the charge against AIDS-related discrimination.

58 The Humsafar Trust, *Knowledge and Program Sharing Meeting Report*, March 12–13, 2020, https://humsafar.org/wp-content/uploads/2020/04/Brief-report_HST_KSM_Final.pdf.

59 Vismann, *Files*, 78.

60 Rodrigues et al., "Supporting Adherence to Antiretroviral Therapy."

61 See Piña et al., "Antiretroviral Treatment Uptake."

62 Gupta, *Red Tape*.

63 Social science scholarship has long drawn attention to the value of informal therapeutic logs. Medical ethnographers habitually debate the value of informal logs: for instance, new mothers cataloging their newborns' vital signs present data for pivotal decisions in clinical care. Heimer, "Conceiving Children."

64 Mol's critically acclaimed *The Body Multiple*, a study of atherosclerosis through interviews with medical practitioners (radiologists and surgeons) and patients, reorients us toward diseases as enactments framed by different modes of expertise. For the pathologist, atherosclerosis comes into view as a cross section of an artery under a microscope; for the patient, the illness is the pain one feels climbing the stairs. Cataloging this series of material events, Mol alerts us to multiple fragments that "hang together" as the body multiple.

65 Cindy Patton, in her study of HIV metabolic disorders, shows how the overemphasis on the blood data of HIV infection alone loses sight of drug-therapy side effects that often trigger ARV noncompliance. See Patton, "Mobile Knowledge."

66 Haraway, chapter 1, "Playing String Figures with Companion Species," in *Staying with the Trouble*, 9–29.

67 In 2001, MSF began to provide ART at three dedicated HIV clinics in Khayelitsha, a township of 500,000 inhabitants located on the outskirts of Cape Town. Khayelitsha carries one of the highest burdens of both HIV and tuberculosis in the country. See the Médecins Sans Frontières account in Ghosh, "Becoming Undetectable."

68 Anna Grimsrud at the MSF elaborated the calibrated delivery model by forming clubs for family care, youth, and adults, some of which were client led, while others were clinic or hospital based or involved home outreach. Grimsrud, interview by the author, Cape Town, September 6, 2017.

69 Grimsrud, interview by the author, Cape Town, September 8, 2017.

70 As Brian King characterizes them in *States of Disease*. See King's chapter 2, "HIV Lifeways," in *States of Disease*, 51–80.

71 World Health Organization (Department of HIV/AIDS) and UNAIDS, "Treatment 2.0 Framework for Action."

72 See Foucault on the "problem of multiplicities" in *Security, Territory, Population*, 11.

73 By December 2011 there were ninety-eight clubs linked to six clinics in Khayelitsha. Since then, MSF has assisted with the broad replication of this model by city and provincial authorities; by 2014 there 40,000 patients enrolled in the clubs across Cape Town. Kathryn Stintson, "Cohort Profile." For the MSF timeline, see https://www.msf.org/hiv-depth, accessed June 30, 2021.

74 Canguilhem, "Health: Popular Concept and Philosophical Question," 43–52.

CHAPTER FOUR. THE MULTISPECIES KINESTHETIC

1 Dando-Collins, *Pasteur's Gambit*.

2 See Yong, "Next Chapter."

3 In *Spillover*, David Quammen argues that this coevolution was less a simple advancement toward mutual tolerance than a dynamic process of adjustment between rabbit and virus. He elaborates the work of Australian microbiologist Frank Fenner and his colleagues, who followed the rabbit plagues for years. Fenner identified five strains of myxoma virus in the wilds, from Grade 1 (the most lethal, which had a kill rate of 100 percent) to Grade 5 (which was very mild). Curiously, the middle strain, with a 67 percent fatality rate, survived. Fenner (reports Quammen) argued that that the virus needed open lesions for transmission to occur; if the aggressive strain killed the rabbit too quickly, the chances of host-to-host transmission diminished. Conversely, if the strain was too mild to cause lesions, then transmission also slowed. Hence, the middle strain of the virus survived. The moral of the story for Quammen: the balance for the virus is not "don't kill your host," but "don't burn your bridges until after you've crossed them" (65).

4 Dubos, *Mirage of Health*, 65.

5 Dubos, *Mirage of Health*, 86–90. Dubos did not contest the fact that a pathogen identified in laboratory research—say, *Variola* for smallpox—was the cause of a particular disease, but he drew attention to the multitemporal event of pathogenesis. When a population—of plants, animals, or humans—is exposed to a pathogen with which it had no past experience, exposure may bring about severe disease in many of

its individuals. The generalized epidemic, however, soon calls into play adaptive changes in both the host population and the infective agent that bring about an ecological equilibrium between them. The infective agent may remain widely distributed in a community, but its presence need not be associated with injurious effects. Disease, when it occurs, is due to changes in the conditions under which the ecological equilibrium evolved (79).

6 Dubos, *Mirage of Health*, 98.

7 Quammen notes that the fungus could arrive intact because the shortened travel time on steamships enabled its survival. Quammen, *Spillover*, 79.

8 See Melinda Cooper's *Life as Surplus* on the adoption of Dubos's doctrine of preemption in biosecurity regimes; see also Andrew Lakoff's *Unprepared* and the essays in Stephen Collier and Andrew Lakoff's *Biosecurity Interventions*.

9 Tsing et al., "Patchy Anthropocene."

10 Tsing et al., "Introduction to Feral Atlas," accessed July 26, 2022, https://feralatlas.supdigital.org/?cd=true&rr=true&cdex=true&text=introduction-to-feral-atlas&ttype=essay.

11 Fearnley, "Phylogenetic Trees." All the short essays in the curated cluster "Visualising COVID-19 as a Zoonotic Disease" on the Visualizing the Virus website are relevant to this chapter's preoccupations with cross-species transmission (accessed June 14, 2021, https://visualizingthevirus.com).

12 The definitive distinctions between species were first developed by evolutionary biologist Ernst Mayr's landmark *Systematics and the Origin of Species from the Viewpoint of a Zoologist* (1942), in which he drew on Mendelian and Darwinian theories.

13 Helmreich, *Alien Ocean*.

14 Gabrys, *Program Earth*.

15 See Ghosh, "Costs of Living."

16 Morse, *Emerging Viruses*.

17 One notable assessment that analyzes 335 EID events between 1940 and 2004 ascribes 54.3 percent of these to bacteria and rickettsia and the rest to viruses. K. Jones et al., "Global Trends."

18 Quammen, *Spillover*, 44.

19 Allen et al., "Global Hotspots," 2. The paper develops insights from K. Jones et al.'s "Global Trends in Emerging Infectious Diseases" and includes scientists engaged in EcoHealth Alliance, such as Peter Daszak and Kevin Olival as well as Stephen Morse.

20 On bats carrying viruses, see Robbins, "Ecology of Disease"; on mosquitoes and water lettuces, see Winegard, *Mosquito*. Bovine spongiform encephalopathy, or "mad cow disease," was tracked to a modified protein (a prion) that caused progressive neurological degeneration in the cow. Humans who ate beef had become infected with the disease beginning in 1986, but cases peaked in 1993 (at almost 1,000 per week). See CDC, "About BSE," October 18, 2021, https://www.cdc.gov/prions/bse/about.html.

21 See WHO, "One Health," September 21, 2017, https://www.who.int/news-room/questions-and-answers/item/one-health.

22 Addressing the shutting down of wet markets after the COVID-19 outbreak, Tamara Giles-Vernick draws a parallel to prohibitions against butchering bushmeat after HIV and Ebola in central Africa that drove these practices underground and made them difficult to track. The hardest hit were the economically vulnerable, who relied on wild meat for protein. Instead of lockdowns and bans, Giles-Vernick suggests other pragmatic solutions such as animal-surveillance systems and investments in safety-protocol pedagogy. See Giles-Vernick, "Should Wild Meat Markets Be Shut Down?"

23 After the completion of PREDICT in 2019, a new proposal is on its way, appropriately named not PREDICT but STOP (Strategies to Prevent) Spillover.

24 See Tucker et al., "Moving in the Anthropocene." The authors use measurements in the Human Footprint index of built environments, crop pasture, population density, nighttime lights, roads, and railways as one vector of assessing habitat fragmentation and loss. The index ranges from 0 for Brazil's Pantanal to 50 percent built density for New York City.

25 Morse, *Emerging Viruses*, 16.

26 In the case of HIV, the debate over the origins of HIV entry into the human population was fierce: while wild monkeys were the privileged vector, some argued that contaminated polio vaccines (live vaccines cultured in monkey tissue) and the transportation of African monkeys into the United States for laboratory research were the cause of the transfer, while others argued for the butchering of bushmeat.

27 See Tamara Giles-Vernick and colleagues' dating of HIV-1M emergence in "Social History, Biology, and the Emergence of HIV in Colonial Africa." There are volumes written in on the subject, including widely read books such as physician-anthropologist Jacques Pépin's *The Origin of AIDS*, historian John Illife's *The African AIDS Epidemic*, and journalist Craig Timberg and medical anthropologist-epidemiologist Daniel Halperin's *Tinderbox*.

28 Databases such as Duke's Global Health Institute's "Global Mammal Parasite Database" enable such genomic identification and consequent species classifications. See Global Health Institute, "Global Mammal Parasite Database," accessed July 26, 2022, https://globalhealth.duke.edu/projects/global-mammal-parasite-database#:~:text=The%20Global%20Mammal%20Parasite%20Database,transmission%2C%20prevalence%20and%20global%20location. Currently, there are 827,000 viruses in the animal world; as we know now, SARS-CoV-2 is a *Betacoronavirus*, one among the seven that infect human populations: see Wolfe, Dunavan, and Diamond, "Origins of Major Human Infectious Diseases."

29 Cohen, "Wuhan Coronavirus Hunter Shi Zhengli Speaks Out."

30 See the predictive paper by EcoHealth Alliance's Kevin Olival et al., "Host and Viral Traits Predict Zoonotic Spillover from Mammals."

31 Twenty-five percent of zoonotic spillovers into human populations can be traced to NHPs (chimpanzees, sooty mangabeys, and Asian macaques), including AIDS, malaria, and dengue and yellow fevers. Kevin Olival et al., "Host and Viral Traits." Humans have also infected NHPs with polio, influenza A, syphilis, and measles. Mosquitoes are well-known intermediate hosts that transmit viruses, hence the

massive worldwide efforts to control mosquito population densities, attacking the standing water where they breed.

32 Sharp, Shaw, and Hahn, "Simian Immunodeficiency Virus Infection." In a visualization of the "zoonotic diagram," Lyle Fearnley presents the Wuhan Institute of Virology's argument that the phylogenetic resemblance of SARS-CoV-2 to RaTG-13 (from bat feces) indicates probable bat origins for the virus. Fearnley, "Phylogenetic Trees." The reliance on the phylogenetic tree, however, tries to establish an evolutionary history that overlooks other factors in making viruses go pandemic, as Fearnley puts it, which are "contemporary assemblages of humans and animals, landscapes and microbes," that shape how viruses evolve, infect, recombine.

33 There is some debate over mechanistic hypotheses that establish causalities between biodiversity and disease risk, since the relationship is "complex, context-specific, and idiosyncratic." Allen et al., "Global Hotspots," 5. But predictive models that sample large-scale research data (including environmental, demographic, and host-diversity variables) and measure multiple sources of uncertainty attempt to close the gap between predictors and a priori hypotheses.

34 Strategic global public health measures have always included destruction of (e.g., the once popular spraying of DDT for mosquitoes) and protection against (e.g., mosquito nets for the US armed forces in World War II) vector species, as well as the elimination of their habitats (e.g., stagnant water).

35 Keck, *Avian Reservoirs*.

36 The Federation of Laboratory Animal Science Associations reports the illegal trade of seventy thousand individuals a year illegal (some for the biomedical industries). See Narat et al., "Using Physical Contact Heterogeneity and Frequency."

37 Kirksey, *Emergent Ecologies*, 3.

38 Rupp et al., "Beyond the Cut Hunter."

39 Giles-Vernick et al. "Social History, Biology."

40 Rupp et al., "Beyond the Cut Hunter."

41 Rostal et al., "Understanding Rift Valley Fever."

42 Rostal et al., "Understanding Rift Valley Fever."

43 Islam et al., "Molecular Characterization."

44 Haraway's *Primate Visions* is a key text in animal studies salient to the specific animal hosts in this chapter. See Etienne Benson's "Animal Writes" for a long history of animal tracking, beginning with hunters, who defined a certain trajectory of human-animal relations. Disease surveillance refracts this gaze to the animal as multispecies.

45 Morse was the progenitor of ProMED (the international nonprofit Program for Monitoring Emerging Diseases) and the originator of ProMED-mail, an international network inaugurated by ProMED in 1994 for outbreak reporting and disease monitoring using the internet. Still active, ProMED-mail's (accessed June 20, 2021, http://www.promedmail.org) moderated email list has over 37,000 subscribers from 150 countries.

46 The CDC's Disease Detectives program was the brainchild of Langmuir, an epidemiologist in the US Army in 1942–46, who was largely responsible for establishing

the Epidemic Intelligence Service at the CDC in 1951 (motivated by concerns over biological warfare during the Korean War). Langmuir argued that the potential weaponizing of pathogens during the Cold War required a trained cadre of epidemiologists; when Congress marshaled funds, the first twenty-two disease detectives were recruited in 1951. See Hamilton, "Epidemic Intelligence Service." The CDC Museum's Disease Detective Camp continues an outreach program for building such a cadre.

47 Nathan Wolfe and colleagues underscore the necessity of grasping viral intelligence for the epidemiological sciences: "By determining how humans become a part of the life cycle of pathogens rather than how pathogens enter human populations, we can understand the factors associated with emergence and improve the quality of public health responses." Wolfe et al., "Wild Primate Populations," 154.

48 Galloway and Thacker, *Exploit*, 15. The Rapid Syndrome Validation Project, the Real-Time Outbreak and Disease Surveillance System, and Early Notification of Community-Based Epidemics are just a few state-of-the-art infrastructures for this modality of surveillance.

49 The areas include Cameroon, Equatorial Guinea, the DRC, the Republic of the Congo (ROC), the Laos People's Democratic Republic, Gabon, the Central African Republic, Malaysia, Madagascar, and São Tomé. Originally founded as the GVFI, Global Viral is a 501(c)(3) not-for-profit that received seed funding from Google and the Skoll Foundation in 2008. Such imminent threats are precisely why Wolfe received funding from both the US government's Defense Advanced Research Projects Agency (DARPA) and the National Institute for Medicine to set up Global Viral.

50 In remote regions with lower population densities, host die-offs limit transmission; these hot spots are different from urban geographies in which secondary transmission across populations is made possible because of host traffic (transportation, trade, other forms of travel).

51 Roland Kays, interview by the author, July 7, 2020. Mine is a secondhand look, for I did not accompany either Laudisoit or Kays into their living laboratories (despite invitations); there is no participant observation in my accounts. Rather, I have talked with them and read field reports and published papers based on their direction.

52 Gabrys, *Program Earth*, 4.

53 Worldwide GPS satellite-based navigation systems have expanded to twenty-four satellites from 1978 to 1994. A GIS helps people use the information from GPS satellites.

54 Gabrys, *Program Earth*, 105.

55 Barad, *Meeting the Universe Halfway*; Chow, *Entanglements*.

56 ICARUS: Global Monitoring with Animals, "Animals on the Air," accessed July 1, 2022, https://www.icarus.mpg.de/28874/sensor-animals-tracking.

57 The Env-DATA system is a set of free tools on Movebank that links animal movement data with information from global environmental data sets, like weather models and satellite imagery. "The Env-DATA System," Movebank: For Animal Tracking Data, Max Planck Institute of Animal Behavior, the North Carolina Museum of Natural Sciences, and the University of Konstanz, accessed July 2,

2022, https://www.movebank.org/cms/movebank-content/env-data. The GPS data sets provide estimates for hundreds of environmental parameters—such as wind conditions, land use, vegetation, and snow cover—for the whole world, with many measurements available from the 1970s to the present.

58 Dodge, "Revealing the Physics of Movement."

59 Lisa Parks has a formidable oeuvre in media infrastructures, especially satellite technologies constitutive of a "vertical public sphere." For a sample of her work, see Parks and Starosielski, introduction; and the chapter "Satellite Archaeology: Remote Sensing Cleopatra in Egypt," in Parks, *Cultures in Orbit*.

60 Center for International Collaboration and Advanced Studies in Primatology, "The PrimateCast #58: Talking EcoHealth and Unexpected Chimpanzees with Dr. Anne Laudisoit," *The PrimateCast*, April 12, 2020, http://www.cicasp.pri.kyoto-u.ac.jp/news/podcasts/anne-laudisoit.

61 See, for example, Kays, McShea, and Wikelski, "Born Digital Biodiversity Data."

62 We might recall Carlo Ginzburg's unforgettable account of tracking as an ancient science, a form of conjectural knowledge on par with criminal forensics, psychoanalysis, and medical diagnostics. See Ginzburg, *Clues, Myth, and Historical Method*.

63 As Laudisoit's transect maps showed, the fragmented forest habitats are continuous with the Yadha corridor. Ecological corridors are critical for conservationists, for they allow animals to move between habitats and continue to play their roles as ecosystem actors.

64 The eastern chimpanzee is currently classified as endangered on the IUCN's Red List; it lives in the Central African Republic, the DRC, Sudan, Uganda, Rwanda, Burundi, Tanzania, and Zambia.

65 See Hicks et al., "Bili-Uéré."

66 Laudisoit et al., "Chimpanzees Surviving."

67 Abram, *Spell of the Sensuous*.

68 Henrika Kuklick and Robert Kohler temper the assumption that research is driven by theory (in histories of science) by noting that fieldwork is ever a multivariate combination of craftwork, material culture, and practical reasoning since "natural sites" are never exclusively scientific domains. Kuklick and Kohler, "Introduction," 3.

69 The question of animal agency has been extensively discussed in philosophical terms, following Jacques Derrida's *The Animal That Therefore I Am*, as the ethical problem of the animal writing the animal.

70 Walker et al., "Species from Feces."

71 Kays, McShea, and Wikelski, "Born-Digital Biodiversity Data."

72 The Fresnel lens in this genre of camera traps focalizes incoming electromagnetic radiation onto a pyroelectric sensor: this is an infrared receiver chip with pyroelectric crystals that converts temperature change into an electrical current. Subsequently, the electric current triggers the shutter. But setting the threshold for the infrared receiver to "see" the warm bodies presents a whole set of difficulties: there are false triggers and missing images (in light of other evidence of animal presence like footprints). Some argue that the problems lie with imprecise calculations of "ambient temperature" across the forest; the ground temperature,

for example, can vary greatly with changing soil composition, precipitation, and vegetal degrowth. At the same time, camera trappers disagree over what a warm body *is*, given the variance of surface and core temperatures of furry creatures. How then to mark the exact point of temperature difference? After all, setting the wrong threshold can lead to flawed hypotheses or misleading interpretations.

73 Laudisoit, interview by the author, June 20, 2020.

74 In her next venture, Laudisoit argued, she would experiment with the altitude gradient by placing camera traps in the midsection space of the forest.

75 Kays, McShea, and Wikelski, "Born-Digital Biodiversity Data," 644.

76 In fact, an entomologist specializing in termites, James Zetek, was the founding director of the Canal Zone Biological Area, located on BCI.

77 Kays, Tilak, et al., "Tracking Animal Location and Activity."

78 Larkin, *Signal and Noise*, 10.

79 The experiment captured the first three: see Kays, Sheppard, et al., "Hot Monkey, Cold Reality."

80 North Carolina Museum of Natural Sciences, "Can Drones Help Count Rainforest Animals?," in Kays, Sheppard, et al., "Hot Monkey, Cold Reality." This embedded video was sponsored by a number of institutions, including the Smithsonian Research Institute.

81 A biologist walked one and a half kilometers with binoculars as a test run of a twelve-hectare survey grid before the drone photography to get a sense of the size, morphology, and habits of the animal individuals, and set the parameters for machinic detection.

82 Yousif et al., "Animal Scanner."

83 Kays, *Candid Creatures*.

84 Kays, "Born-Digital Biodiversity Data."

85 These are classified as deep convolutional neural networks. See Yousif, "Deep Neural Networks."

86 The challenge defines specific parameters for the documentation: seven to forty camera traps, particular camera brands, and ten to forty locations for each spatial design. Participants who propose a project are invited to upload their records for review. If they pass muster, the records are archived at the Smithsonian. For primates, platforms such as Chimp&See (https://www.zooniverse.org/projects/sassydumbledore/chimp-and-see) invite participants to scan, interpret, and annotate seven thousand hours of footage collected from across Africa under the aegis of the "Pan-African Programme: The Cultured Chimpanzee." As Mimi Arandjelovic at the Max Planck Institute for Evolutionary Anthropology notes, this conservation initiative aims at tracking chimpanzee population densities, food competitors, and human pressure in chimpanzee habitats (see http://www.mimiarandjelovic.com/).

87 A novel primate hepadnavirus has been tracked to the white capuchin. See de Carvalho Dominguez Souza et al., "Novel Hepatitis B Virus Species."

88 See LaBonte et al., "Blockade of HIV-1 Infection."

89 See Albery et al., "Predicting the Global Mammalian Viral Sharing Network."

90 Noam Ross, virtual interview by author, May 30, 2020.

91 Albery et al., "Predicting the Global Mammalian Viral Sharing Network."

92 On extending observations from available phylogeographic data to places where there is no information—which involves plotting "missing zoonoses" and "missing viruses"—see Olival et al., "Host and Viral Traits."

93 For a sustained media analysis of black boxes, see Siegel, *Forensic Media*, 89–142.

94 Jennifer Deger, Alder Keleman, Anna Lowenhaupt Tsing, and Feifei Zhou, "Mapping Feral Flows," Anthropocene Curriculum, June 15, 2021, https://www.anthropocene-curriculum.org/contribution/mapping-feral-flows.

95 See Deger et al., "Mapping Feral Flows."

CONCLUSION

1 Treichler, *How to Have Theory*.

2 Camus, *Plague*, 130.

3 Treichler, *How to Have Theory*, 2.

4 Myers, *Rendering Life Molecular*, 230.

5 Parks and Walker, "Disaster Media."

6 Callaway, "Mutation That Helps Delta Spread."

7 Myers, *Rendering Life Molecular*; and Thacker, *Biomedia*.

8 Stengers, "Challenge of Ontological Politics," 91.

9 See Emily Schmall, "In the Wake of India's COVID Crisis, 'Black Fungus' Epidemic Follows," *New York Times*, June 20, 2021, https://www.nytimes.com/2021/06/20/world/asia/india-covid-black-fungus.html; and L. Cohen, "Colors of Rot."

10 Davidson, "Battle over the Coronavirus Lab Leak Theory."

11 Stengers, *Cosmopolitics I*.

12 Bass, "To End a Plague"; and Ghosh, "Costs of Living."

Bibliography

Abram, David. *The Spell of the Sensuous: Perception and Language in the More-Than-Human World*. New York: Penguin Random House, 1996.

Alaimo, Stacy. *Bodily Natures: Science, Environment, and the Material Self*. Bloomington: Indiana University Press, 2010.

Albery, Gregory F., Evan A. Eskew, Noam Ross, and Kevin J. Olival. "Predicting the Global Mammalian Viral Sharing Network Using Phylogeography." *Nature Communications* 11 (2020): 2260. https://doi.org/10.1038/s41467-020-16153-4.

Allen, Toph, Kris A. Murray, Carlos Zambrana-Torrelio, Stephen S. Morse, Carlo Rondinini, Moreno Di Marco, Nathan Breit, Kevin J. Olival, and Peter Daszak. "Global Hotspots and Correlates of Emerging Zoonotic Diseases." *Nature Communications* 8 (2017): 1124. https://doi.org/10.1038/s41467-017-00923-8.

Alston, Vermonja. "Environment." In *Keywords for Environmental Studies*, edited by Joni Adamson, William A. Gleason, and David N. Pellow, 93–96. New York: New York University Press, 2016.

Anfinrud, Philip, Valentyn Stadnytskyi, Christina E. Bax, and Adriaan Bax. "Visualizing Speech-Generated Oral Fluid Droplets with Laser Light Scattering." *New England Journal of Medicine* 382 (May 21, 2020): 2061–63. https://doi.org/10.1056/NEJMc2007800.

Armitage, John. "On the World of the Virus: Remaking Image Theory Anew." *Cultural Politics* 17, no. 1 (2021): 114–23.

Arnaout, Ramy, Rose A. Lee, Ghee Rye Lee, Cody Callahan, Christina F. Yen, Kenneth P. Smith, Rohit Arora, and James E. Kirby. "SARS-CoV2 Testing: The Limit of Detection Matters." *bioRxiv*, preprint, June 4, 2020, 131144. https://doi.org/10.1101/2020.06.02.131144.

Arnold, David. *Colonizing the Body: State Medicine and Disease in Nineteenth-Century India*. Berkeley: University of California Press, 1993.

Bachelard, Gaston. *Essai sur la connaissance approchée*. 1927. Paris: J. Vrin, 1968.

Balter, Michael. "International Human Microbe Program Looks Ahead." *Science*, March 22, 2012. https://www.science.org/content/article/international-human-microbe-program-looks-ahead.

Barad, Karen. "Invertebrate Visions: Diffraction of the Brittlestar." In Kirksey, *Multispecies Salon*, 221–43.

Barad, Karen. *Meeting the Universe Halfway: Quantum Physics and the Entanglement of Matter and Meaning*. Durham, NC: Duke University Press, 2007.

Barré-Sinoussi, F., J. C. Chermann, F. Rey, M. T. Nugeyre, S. Chamaret, J. Gruest, C. Dauguet, et al. "Isolation of a T-Lymphotropic Retrovirus from a Patient at Risk for Acquired Immune Deficiency Syndrome (AIDS)." *Science* 220, no. 4599 (May 20, 1983): 868–71. https://doi.org/10.1126/science.6189183.

Barry, Andrew. "Pharmaceutical Matters: The Invention of Informed Materials." *Theory, Culture, Society* 22, no. 1 (2005): 51–69. https://doi.org/10.1177/0263276405048433.

Bass, Emily. *To End a Plague: America's Fight to Defeat AIDS in Africa*. New York: Public Affairs, 2021.

Bennett, Jane. *Vibrant Matter: A Political Ecology of Things*. Durham, NC: Duke University Press, 2009.

Benson, Etienne. "Animal Writes: Historiography, Disciplinarity, and Trace." In *Making Animal Meaning*, edited by Linda Kaloff and Georgina M. Montgomery, 3–16. East Lansing: Michigan State University Press, 2011.

Benson, Etienne. *Wired Wilderness: Technologies of Tracking and the Making of Modern Wildlife*. Baltimore, MD: Johns Hopkins University Press, 2010.

Bergson, Henri. *Creative Evolution*. Translated by Arthur Mitchell. 1907. New York: Modern Library, 1944.

Bernard, Claude. *An Introduction to the Study of Experimental Medicine*. Translated by Henry Copley Greene. 1865. London: Macmillan, 1927.

Berra, Manuel Orozco y. *Historia Antigua y de la Conquista de Mexico*. Vol. 4. London: Forgotten Books, 2019.

Berrigan, Caitlin. "Life Cycle of a Common Weed." In Kirksey, *Multispecies Salon*, 164–81.

Boston, Penelope. "Alien Worlds beneath Our Feet: Dr. Penelope Boston on Caves." Public lecture delivered to Perimeter Institute of Theoretical Physics, Waterloo, Canada, December 4, 2014. Excerpts from lecture available at https://www.youtube.com/watch?v=gaD9iTOcoc4. Full lecture available at https://pirsa.org/13120045.

Bourouiba, Lydia. "Gas Clouds Demonstrate Their Ability to Travel Great Distances." JAMA Network video, March 26, 2020. https://jamanetwork.com/journals/jama/fullarticle/2763852.

Bourouiba, Lydia. "Turbulent Gas Clouds and Respiratory Pathogen Emissions: Potential Implications for Reducing Transmission of COVID-19." *Journal of the American Medical Association (JAMA)* 323, no. 18 (2020): 1837–38. https://doi.org/10.1001/jama.2020.4756.

Boycott, A. E. "The Transition from Live to Dead: The Nature of Filtrable Viruses." *Nature* 123 (1929): 91–98. https://doi.org/10.1038/123091a0.

Brenner, Sydney. "In the Beginning Was the Worm. . . ." *Genetics* 182 (2009): 413–15.

Brilliant, Larry. *Sometimes Brilliant: The Impossible Adventure of a Spiritual Seeker and Visionary Physician Who Helped Conquer the Worst Disease in History*. New York: HarperOne, 2016.

Burgess, Helen, Philip Thurtle, and Robert Mitchell. *Biofutures: Owning Body Parts and Information*. Philadelphia: University of Pennsylvania Press, 2008.

Burri, Regula Valérie, and Joseph Dumit. "Indeterminate Lives, Demands, Relations: Emergent Bioscapes." In *Biomedicine as Culture: Instrumental Practices, Technoscientific Knowledge, and New Modes of Life*, edited by Regula Valérie Burri and Joseph Dumit, 223–28. New York: Routledge, 2008.

Cahill, James. *Zoological Surrealism: The Nonhuman Cinema of Jean Painlevé*. Minneapolis: University of Minnesota Press, 2019.

Callaway, Ewen. "The Mutation That Helps Delta Spread Like Wildfire." *Nature* 596 (August 20, 2021): 472–73. https://www.nature.com/articles/d41586-021-02275-2.

Camus, Albert. *The Plague*. Translated by Laura Marris. 1947. New York: Knopf, 2021.

Canguilhem, Georges. *Knowledge of Life*. Translated by Stefanos Geroulanos and Daniela Ginsburg. 1952. New York: Fordham University Press, 2008.

Canguilhem, Georges. *The Normal and the Pathological*. Translated by Carolyn R. Fawcett. 1966. New York: Zone, 1991.

Canguilhem, Georges. *Writings on Medicine*. Translated by Stefanos Geroulanos and Todd Meyers. New York: Fordham University Press, 2012.

Cannon, Walter B. *The Wisdom of the Body*. London: Kegan Paul, 1932.

Carsten, Janet. *Blood Work: Life and Laboratories in Penang*. Durham, NC: Duke University Press, 2019.

Castiglia, Christopher, and Christopher Reed. *If Memory Serves: Gay Men, AIDS, and the Promise of the Queer Past*. Minneapolis: University of Minnesota Press, 2011.

Chakrabarty, Dipesh. *The Climate of History in a Planetary Age*. Chicago: University of Chicago Press, 2021.

Chang, Alenda Y. *Playing Nature: Ecology in Video Games*. Minneapolis: University of Minnesota Press, 2019.

Chen, Mel Y. *Animacies: Biopolitics, Racial Mattering, and Queer Affect*. Durham, NC: Duke University Press, 2012.

Cheng, Jih-Fei, Alexandra Juhasz, and Nishant Shahani, eds. *AIDS and the Distribution of Crisis*. Durham, NC: Duke University Press, 2020.

Chow, Rey. *Entanglements, or Transmedial Thinking about Capture*. Durham, NC: Duke University Press, 2012.

Cifor, Marika. *Viral Cultures: Activist Archiving in the Age of AIDS*. Minneapolis: University of Minnesota Press, 2022.

Clark, Nigel, and Myra Hird. "Microontologies and the Politics of Emergent Life." In *Handbook on the Geographies of Power*, edited by Mat Coleman and John Agnew, 245–58. Northampton, MA: Edward Elgar, 2018.

Cohen, Jon. "An Intriguing—but Far from Proven—HIV Cure in the 'São Paulo Patient.'" *Science*, July 7, 2020. https://www.sciencemag.org/news/2020/07/intriguing-far-proven-hiv-cure-s-o-paulo-patient.

Cohen, Jon. "Wuhan Coronavirus Hunter Shi Zhengli Speaks Out." *Science* 369, no. 6503 (July 31, 2020): 487–88.

Cohen, Lawrence. "Colors of Rot: The Pandemic's Fungal Turn." *Positions Politics*, September 1, 2021. https://positionspolitics.org/colors-of-rot-pandemics-fungal-turn/.

Collier, Stephen, and Andrew Lakoff. *Biosecurity Interventions: Global Health and Security in Question*. New York: Columbia University Press, 2008.

Colonna, Jean-François. "Scientific Visualization: A Means of Reconciling Artists and Scientists?" In *Frontiers of Scientific Visualization*, edited by Clifford A. Pickover and Stuart Tewksbury, 181–212. Hoboken, NJ: Wiley, 1994.

Connolly, William E. *Facing the Planetary: Entangled Humanism and the Politics of Swarming*. Durham, NC: Duke University Press, 2017.

Connolly, William E. *The Fragility of Things: Self-Organizing Processes, Neoliberal Fantasies, and Democratic Activism*. Durham, NC: Duke University Press, 2013.

Coole, Diana H., and Samantha Frost. "Introducing the New Materialisms." In *New Materialisms: Ontology, Agency, and Politics*, edited by Diana H. Coole and Samantha Frost, 1–47. Durham, NC: Duke University Press, 2010.

Cooper, Melinda. *Life as Surplus: Biotechnology and Capitalism in the Neoliberal Era*. Seattle: University of Washington Press, 2008.

Cooper, Melinda, and Catherine Waldby. *Clinical Labor: Tissue Donors and Research Subjects in the Global Bioeconomy*. Durham, NC: Duke University Press, 2014.

Copeman, Jacob, and Dwaipayan Banerjee. *Hematologies: The Political Life of Blood in India*. Ithaca, NY: Cornell University Press, 2019.

Coren, Michael J. "Fold It Gamers Solve Riddle of HIV." *Scientific American*, September 20, 2011. https://www.scientificamerican.com/article/foldit-gamers-solve-riddle/.

Cox, Donna. "Renaissance Teams, Visualizations, and Virtual Reality." Lecture at the Hayden Planetarium, American Museum of Natural History, New York, June 28, 2001.

Cox, Donna. "Using the Super-Computer to Visualize Higher Dimensions: An Artist's Contribution to Scientific Visualization." *Leonardo* 41, no. 4 (2008): 390–400. https://doi.org/10.1162/leon.2008.41.4.390.

Cox, Donna, Ellen Sandor, and Janine Fron, eds. *New Media Futures: The Rise of Women in the Digital Arts*. Champaign: University of Illinois Press, 2018.

Crawford, Dorothy H. *Viruses: A Very Short Introduction*. Oxford: Oxford University Press, 2018.

Critical Art Ensemble. *Digital Resistance: Explorations in Tactical Media*. Brooklyn, NY: Autonomedia, 2001.

Cromley, Douglas. "Digital Images Are Data: And Should Be Treated as Such." In *Cell Imaging Techniques*, edited by Douglas J. Taatjes and Jürgen Roth, 1–27. Totowa, NJ: Humana, 2012. https://doi.org/10.1007/978-1-62703-056-4_1.

Crutzen, Paul J., and Eugene F. Stoermer. "The Anthropocene." *Global Change Newsletter*, no. 41 (2000): 17–18. http://www.igbp.net/download/18.316f18321323470177580001401/1376383088452/NL41.pdf.

Cruz-Neira, Carolina, Daniel J. Sandin, and Thomas A. DeFanti. "Surround-Screen Projection-Based Virtual Reality: The Design and Implementation of the CAVE." In *SIGGRAPH '93: Proceedings of the 20th Annual Conference on Computer Graphics and Interactive Techniques*, 135–42. New York: Association for Computing Machinery.

Dando-Collins, Stephen. *Pasteur's Gambit: Louis Pasteur, the Australasian Rabbit Plague and a Ten Million Dollar Prize*. New York: Vintage, 2008.

Daston, Lorraine, and Peter Galison. *Objectivity*. Princeton, NJ: Zone, 2007.

Davidson, Amy. "The Battle over the Coronavirus Lab Leak Theory." *New Yorker*, June 13, 2021, 1–4. https://www.newyorker.com/magazine/2021/06/21/the-battle-over-the-coronavirus-lab-leak-theory.

Davis, J. J. "Nature of Disease-Producing Viruses." *Nature* 124 (1929): 267. https://doi.org/10.1038/124267c0.

Davis, J. J. "Viruses and Life." *Nature* 125 (1930): 351. https://doi.org/10.1038/125351c0.

de Carvalho Dominguez Souza, Breno Frederico, Alexander König, Andrea Rasche, Ianei de Oliveira Carneiro, Nora Stephan, Victor Max Corman, Pia Luise Roppert, et al. "A Novel Hepatitis B Virus Species Discovered in Capuchin Monkeys Sheds New Light on the Evolution of Primate Hepadnaviruses." *Journal of Hepatology* 68, no. 6 (2018): 1114–22. https://doi.org/10.1016/j.jhep.2018.01.029.

de la Cadena, Marisol, and Mario Blaser. "Introduction: Pluriverse." In *A World of Many Worlds*, edited by Marisol de la Cadena and Mario Blaser, 1–22. Durham, NC: Duke University Press, 2018.

DeLanda, Manuel. *Philosophy and Simulation: The Emergence of Synthetic Reason*. New York: Continuum, 2011.

Derrida, Jacques. *The Animal That Therefore I Am*. Translated by David Wills. New York: Fordham University Press, 2008.

Dietert, Rodney R. *The Human Superorganism: How the Microbiome Is Revolutionizing the Pursuit of a Healthy Life*. Boston: Dutton, 2016.

Dodge, Somayeh, Robert Weibel, and Eshan Forootan. "Revealing the Physics of Movement." *Computers, Environment, and Urban Systems* 33, no. 6 (2009): 419–34.

Donnell, Deborah, Eric Ramos, Connie Celum, Jared Baeten, Joan Dragavon, Jordan Tappero, Jairam R. Lingappa, Allan Ronald, Kenneth Fife, and Robert W. Coombs for the Partners PrEP Study Team. "The Effect of Oral Preexposure Prophylaxis on the Progression of HIV-1 Seroconversion." *AIDS* 31, no. 14 (2017): 2007–16. https://doi.org/10.1097/QAD.0000000000001577.

Douglas, Angela E. *The Symbiotic Habit*. Princeton, NJ: Princeton University Press, 2010.

Douglas, Angela E. *Symbiotic Interactions*. Oxford: Oxford University Press, 1994.

Doyle, Jennifer. *Hold It against Me: Difficulty and Emotion in Contemporary Art*. Durham, NC: Duke University Press, 2013.

Driesch, Hans. *The Science and Philosophy of the Organism, 1906–8*. London: Adam and Charles Black, 1908.

Dubos, René J. *Mirage of Health: Utopias, Progress, and Biological Change*. New York: Harper, 1959.

Durán, Fray Diego. *Historia de las Indias de Nueva-España y islas de Tierra Firme*. Mexico: Imp. de JM Andrade and F. Escalante, 1867.

Ellermann, Vilhelm, and Olaf Bang. "Experimentelle Leukämie bei Hühnern. II." *Zeitschrift für Hygiene und Infektionskrankheiten* 63 (1909): 231–72. https://doi.org/10.1007/BF02227892.

Engel, Jonathan. *The Epidemic: A Global History of AIDS*. New York: Smithsonian Books/Collins, 2006.

Epstein, Steven. "The Construction of Lay Expertise: AIDS Activism and the Forging of Credibility in the Reform of Clinical Trials." *Science, Technology, and Human Values* 20, no. 4 (Autumn 1995): 408–37. https://doi.org/10.1177/016224399502000402.

Ernst, Wolfgang. *Digital Memory and the Archive*. Edited by Jussi Parikka. Minneapolis: University of Minnesota Press, 2012.

Farmer, Paul. *Infections and Inequalities: The Modern Plagues*. Berkeley: University of California Press, 1999.

Fearnley, Lyle. "Phylogenetic Trees and the Genealogical Origins of Viruses." Visualizing the Virus, July 1, 2021. https://visualizingthevirus.com/entry/phylogenetic-trees-and-the-genealogical-origins-of-zoonotic-viruses/.

Fishel, Stephanie. *Microbial States: Global Thriving and the Body Politic*. Minneapolis: University of Minnesota Press, 2017.

Fleck, Ludwik. *Genesis and Development of a Scientific Fact*. Translated by Fred Bradley and Thaddeus J. Trenn. 1935. Chicago: University of Chicago Press, 1979.

Flusser, Vilém. *Into the Universe of Technical Images*. Translated by Nancy Ann Roth. 1985. Minneapolis: University of Minnesota Press, 2011.

Foucault, Michel. *The History of Sexuality*. Vol. 1, *An Introduction*. Translated by Robert Hurley. New York: Vintage, 1990.

Foucault, Michel. *The Order of Things: An Archaeology of the Human Sciences*. Translated by Alan Sheridan. New York: Vintage, 1973.

Foucault, Michel. *Security, Territory, Population: Lectures at the Collège de France, 1977–78*. Translated by Graham Burchell. New York: Picador, 2009.

Foucault, Michel. *"Society Must Be Defended": Lectures at the Collège de France, 1975–1976*. Translated by David Macey. New York: Picador, 2003.

France, David. *How to Survive a Plague: The Story of How Activists and Scientists Tamed AIDS*. New York: Public Square Films, Ninety Thousand Words, 2012.

Franklin, Sarah. *Biological Relatives: IVF, Stem Cells, and the Future of Kinship*. Durham, NC: Duke University Press, 2013.

Franklin, Sarah. *Dolly Mixtures: The Remaking of Genealogy*. Durham, NC: Duke University Press, 2007.

Furuhata, Yuriko. *Climatic Media: Transpacific Experiments in Atmospheric Control*. Durham, NC: Duke University Press, 2022.

Gabrys, Jennifer. *Program Earth: Environmental Sensing Technology and the Making of a Computational Planet*. Minneapolis: University of Minnesota Press, 2016.

Gallo, Robert C., and Luc Montagnier. "AIDS in 1988." *Scientific American* 259, no. 4 (1988): 40–51.

Galloway, Alexander R., and Eugene Thacker. *The Exploit: A Theory of Networks*. Minneapolis: University of Minnesota Press, 2007.

Garrett, Laurie. *The Coming Plague: Newly Emerging Diseases in a World out of Balance*. New York: Farrar, Straus and Giroux, 1994.

Gaskill, Nicholas, and A. J. Nocek, eds. *The Lure of Whitehead*. Minneapolis: University of Minnesota Press, 2014.

Geroulanos, Stefanos. "Beyond the Normal and the Pathological." *Gesnerus* 62, no. 2 (2009): 288–306.

Ghosh, Bishnupriya. "Animating Uncommon Life: U.S. Military Malaria Films (1942–1945) in the Pacific Theater." In *Animating Film Theory*, edited by Karen Redrobe, 264–86. Durham, NC: Duke University Press, 2014.

Ghosh, Bishnupriya. "Becoming Undetectable in the Chthulucene." In *Saturation: An Elemental Politics*, edited by Melody Jue and Rafico Ruiz, 161–84. Durham, NC: Duke University Press, 2020.

Ghosh, Bishnupriya. "The Costs of Living." In *AIDS and the Distribution of Crisis*, edited by Jih-Fei Cheng, Alexandra Juhasz, and Nishant Shahani, 60–75. Durham, NC: Duke University Press, 2020.

Ghosh, Bishnupriya. "Toward Symbiosis: Human-Viral Futures in the 'Molecular Movies.'" In *Sustainable Media: Critical Approaches to Media and Environment*, edited by Nicole Starosielski and Janet Walker, 232–47. Durham, NC: Duke University Press, 2016.

Gilbert, Scott L., Jan Sapp, and Alfred I. Tauber. "The Symbiotic View of Life: We Have Never Been Individuals." *Quarterly Review of Biology* 87, no. 4 (2012): 325–41. https://doi.org/10.1086/668166.

Giles-Vernick, Tamara. "Should Wild Meat Markets Be Shut Down?" *Somatosphere*, March 6, 2020. http://somatosphere.net/forumpost/wild-meat-markets/.

Giles-Vernick, Tamara, Ch. Didier Gondola, Guillaume Lachenal, and William H. Schneider. "Social History, Biology, and the Emergence of HIV in Colonial Africa." *Journal of African History* 54, no. 1 (2013): 11–30. https://doi.org/10.1017/S0021853713000029.

Ginn, Franklin, Uli Beisel, and Maan Barua. "Flourishing with Awkward Creatures: Togetherness, Vulnerability, and Killing." *Environmental Humanities* 4, no. 1 (2014): 113–23. https://doi.org/10.1215/22011919-3614953.

Ginzburg, Carlo. *Clues, Myths, and the Historical Method*. Translated by John and Anne C. Tedesci. Baltimore, MD: Johns Hopkins University Press, 1989.

Giraud, Eva. "After the Age of Wreckers and Exterminators: Confronting the Limits of Eradication and Entanglement Narratives." *Cultural Politics* 17, no. 1 (2021): 37–47. https://doi.org/10.1215/17432197-8797501.

Giraud, Eva. *What Comes after Entanglement? Activism, Anthropomorphism, and an Ethics of Exclusion*. Durham, NC: Duke University Press, 2019.

Giraud, Eva, Eleanor Hadley Kershaw, Richard Helliwell, and Gregory Hollin. "Abundance in the Anthropocene." *Sociological Review* 67, no. 2 (2019): 357–73. https://doi.org/10.1177/0038026119830907.

Goodsell, David S. *Atomic Evidence*. New York: Springer, 2016.

Goodsell, David S. "HIV in Blood Plasma." Educational Portal of the Protein Data Base, Molecular Landscapes by David S. Goodsell, 1999. https://pdb101.rcsb.org/sci-art/goodsell-gallery/hiv-in-blood-plasma.

Goodsell, David S. *The Machinery of Life*. New York: Springer-Verlag, 1993.

Goodsell, David S., Arthur Olson, and Stefano Forli. "Art and Science of the Cellular Mesoscale." *Trends in the Biochemical Sciences* 45, no. 6 (2020): 472–83.

Goudie, Andrew, and Heather Viles. *Geomorphology in the Anthropocene*. Cambridge: Cambridge University Press, 2016.

Gould, Deborah B. *Moving Politics: Emotion and ACT UP's Fight against AIDS*. Chicago: University of Chicago Press, 2009.

Grau, Oliver. *Virtual Art: From Illusion to Immersion*. Cambridge, MA: MIT Press, 2003.

Gray, Dylan Mohan, and Ashutosh Phatak, dirs. *Fire in the Blood*. Mumbai: Sparkwater Productions, 2012.

Grove, Jairus Victor. *Savage Ecology: War and Geopolitics at the End of the World*. Durham, NC: Duke University Press, 2019.

Guattari, Félix. *The Three Ecologies*. Translated by Ian Pindar and Paul Sutton. London: Bloomsbury Academic, 2014.

Gupta, Akhil. *Red Tape: Bureaucracy, Structural Violence, and Poverty in India*. Durham, NC: Duke University Press, 2012.

Hamilton, Douglas H. "The Epidemic Intelligence Service." *Virtual Mentor* 8, no. 4 (2006): 261–64. https://journalofethics.ama-assn.org/article/epidemic-intelligence-service-centers-disease-control-and-preventions-disease-detectives/2006-04.

Haraway, Donna J. *Primate Visions: Gender, Race, and Nature in the World of Modern Science*. New York: Routledge, 1990.

Haraway, Donna J. *Staying with the Trouble: Making Kin in the Chthulucene*. Durham, NC: Duke University Press, 2016.

Harrison, Stephen C. "Whither Structural Biology?" *Nature Structural and Molecular Biology* 11, no. 1 (2004): 12–15. https://doi.org/10.1038/nsmb0104-12.

Harrison, Stephen C., Arthur J. Olson, Clarence E. Schutt, Fritz K. Winkler, and Gérard Bricogne. "Tomato Bushy Stunt Virus at 2.9 Å Resolution." *Nature* 276 (November 23, 1978): 368–73.

Heimer, Carol A. "Conceiving Children: How Documents Support Case versus Biographical Analysis. " In *Documents: Modern Artifacts of Knowledge*, edited by Annelise Riles, 95–126. Ann Arbor: University of Michigan Press, 2006.

Heise, Ursula K. *Imagining Extinction: The Cultural Meanings of Endangered Species*. Chicago: University of Chicago Press, 2016.

Helmreich, Stefan. *Alien Ocean: Anthropological Voyages in Microbial Seas*. Berkeley: University of California Press, 2008.

Helmreich, Stefan. "*Homo microbis*: The Human Microbiome, Figural, Literal, Political." *Thresholds*, no. 42 (2014): 52–59. https://doi.org/10.1162/thld_a_00076.

Helmreich, Stefan. *Sounding the Limits of Life: Essays in the Anthropology of Biology and Beyond*. Princeton, NJ: Princeton University Press, 2016.

Helmreich, Stefan, and Heather Paxson. "The Perils and Promises of Microbial Abundance: Novel Natures and Model Ecosystems, from Artisanal Cheese to Alien Seas." *Social Studies of Science* 44, no. 2 (2014): 165–93. https://doi.org/10.1177/0306312713505003.

Hicks, T. C., H. S. Kühl, C. Boesch, P. Dieguez, A. E. Ayimisin, R. M. Fernandez, D. B. Zungawa, et al. "Bili-Uéré: A Chimpanzee Behavioural Realm in Northern Democratic Republic of Congo." *Folio Primatologica* 90, no. 3 (2019): 3–64. https://doi.org/10.1159/000492998.

Hodes, Rebecca. "HIV on Documentary Television in Post-apartheid South Africa." In *A Companion to Contemporary Documentary*, edited by Alexandra Juhasz and Alisa Lebow, 298–313. Hoboken, NJ: Wiley-Blackwell, 2014.

Horton, Richard, and Selina Lo. "Planetary Health: A New Science for Exceptional Action." *Lancet* 386, no. 10007 (2015): 1921–22. https://doi.org/10.1016/S0140-6736(15)61038-8.

Hubbard, Jim, dir. *United in Anger: A History of ACT UP*. New York: Jim Hubbard and Sarah Schulman, 2012.

Husserl, Edmund. *The Crisis of the European Sciences and Transcendental Phenomenology.* Translated by David Carr. 1936. Evanston, IL: Northwestern University Press, 1970.

Iliffe, John. *The African AIDS Epidemic: A History.* Columbus: Ohio University Press, 2005.

Isenmen, Lois. "Toward an Understanding of Intuition and Its Importance in the Scientific Endeavor." *Perspectives in Biology and Medicine* 40, no. 3 (1997): 395–403. https://doi.org/10.1353/pbm.1997.0018.

Islam, Ariful, Mohammed Enayet Hossain, Najmul Haider, Melinda K. Rostal, Sanjoy Kumar Mukharjee, Jinnat Ferdous, Mojnu Miah, et al. "Molecular Characterization of Group A Rotavirus from Rhesus Macaques (*Macaca mulatta*) at Human-Wildlife Interfaces in Bangladesh." *Transboundary and Emerging Infectious Diseases* 67, no. 2 (2020): 956–66. https://doi.org/10.1111/tbed.13431.

Iterson, Gerrit. *Martinus Willem Beijerinck: His Life and Work.* Madison, WI: Science Tech, 1983.

Ivakhiv, Adrian. *Shadowing the Anthropocene: Eco-realism for Turbulent Times.* Santa Barbara, CA: Punctum, 2018.

Ivanovsky, Dmitri I. "On Two Diseases of Tobacco." *Sel'skoe khozyaistvo i lesovodstvo* 169, no. 2 (1892): 108–21.

Iwasa, Janet. "Animating the Model Figure." *Trends in Cell Biology* 20, no. 12 (2010): 699–704. https://doi.org/10.1016/j.tcb.2010.08.005.

Iwasa, Janet. "Crafting a Career in Molecular Animation." *Molecular Biology of the Cell* 25, no. 19 (2014): 2891–93. https://doi.org/10.1091/mbc.E14-01-0699.

Iwasa, Janet. *HIV Life Cycle.* Science of HIV, accessed June 14, 2020. https://scienceofhiv.org/wp/life-cycle/.

Jansen, Patrick A., Ben T. Hirsch, Willem-Jan Emsens, Veronica Zamora-Gutierrez, Martin Wikelski, and Roland Kays. "Thieving Rodents as Substitute Dispersers of Megafaunal Seeds." *Proceedings of the National Academy of the Sciences* 109, no. 31 (2012): 12610–15. https://doi.org/10.1073/pnas.1205184109.

Johnson, Graham T., Ludovic Autin, Mostafa Al-Alusi, David S. Goodsell, Michael F. Sanner, and Arthur J. Olson. "cellPACK: A Virtual Mesoscape to Model and Visualize Structural Systems Biology." *Nature Methods* 12, no. 1 (2015): 85–91. https://doi.org/10.1038/nmeth.3204.

Johnson, Graham T., David S. Goodsell, Ludovic Autin, Stefano Forli, Michael F. Sanner, and Arthur J. Olson. "3D Molecular Models of Whole HIV-1 Virions Generated with cellPACK." *Faraday Discussions* 169 (2014): 23–44. https://www.ncbi.nlm.nih.gov/pmc/articles/PMC4569901/.

Jonas, Olga, and Richard Seifman. "Do We Need a Global Virome Project?" *Lancet Global Health* 7, no. 10 (2019): e1314–16. https://doi.org/10.1016/S2214-109X(19)30335-3.

Jones, Kate E., Nikkita G. Patel, Marc A. Levy, Adam Storeygard, Deborah Balk, John L. Gittleman, and Peter Daszak. "Global Trends in Emerging Infectious Diseases." *Nature* 451 (2008): 990–93. https://doi.org/10.1038/nature06536.

Jones, Therese, Delese Wear, and Lester D. Friedman, eds. *The Health Humanities Reader.* New Brunswick, NJ: Rutgers University Press, 2014.

Jue, Melody. *Wild Blue Media: Thinking through Seawater.* Durham, NC: Duke University Press, 2020.

Juhasz, Alexandra, and Theodore Kerr. *We Are Having This Conversation Now: The Times of AIDS Cultural Production*. Durham, NC: Duke University Press, 2022.

Kavey, Allison B. "A Brief History of Love: A Rationale for the History of Epidemics." In Jones, Wear, and Friedman, *Health Humanities Reader*, 430–41.

Kays, Roland. *Candid Creatures: How Camera Traps Reveal the Mysteries of Nature*. Baltimore, MD: Johns Hopkins University Press, 2016.

Kays, Roland, Brian S. Arbogast, Megan Baker-Whatton, Chris Berne, Hailey M. Boone, Mark Bowler, Santiago F. Burneo, et al. "An Empirical Evaluation of Camera Trap Study Design: How Many, How Long and When?" *Methods in Ecology and Evolution* 11, no. 6 (2020): 700–713. https://doi.org/10.1111/2041-210X.13370.

Kays, Roland, Margaret C. Crofoot, Walter Jetz, and Martin Wikelski. "Terrestrial Animal Tracking as an Eye on Life and Planet." *Science* 348, no. 6240 (2015): aaa2478.

Kays, Roland, William J. McShea, and Martin Wikelski. "Born-Digital Biodiversity Data: Millions and Billions." *Diversity and Distributions* 26, no. 5 (2020): 644–48. https://doi.org/10.1111/ddi.12993.

Kays, Roland, James Sheppard, Kevin Mclean, Charlie Welch, Cris Paunescu, Victor Wang, Greg Kravit, and Meg Crofoot. "Hot Monkey, Cold Reality: Surveying Rainforest Canopy Mammals Using Drone-Mounted Thermal Infrared Sensors." *International Journal of Remote Sensing* 40, no. 2 (2019): 407–19. https://doi.org/10.1080/01431161.2018.1523580.

Kays, Roland, Sameer Tilak, Margaret C. Crofoot, Tony Fountain, Daniela Obando, Alejandro Ortega, Franz Kuemmeth, et al. "Tracking Animal Location and Activity with an Automated Radio Telemetry System in a Tropical Rainforest." *Computer Journal* 54, no. 12 (2011): 1931–48. https://doi.org/10.1093/COMJNL/BXR072.

Keck, Frédéric. *Avian Reservoirs: Virus Hunters and Birdwatchers in Chinese Sentinel Posts*. Durham, NC: Duke University Press, 2020.

Keller, Evelyn Fox. *Making Sense of Life: Explaining Biological Development with Models, Metaphors, and Machines*. Cambridge, MA: Harvard University Press, 2002.

Kember, Sarah, and Joanna Zylinska. *Life after New Media: Mediation as a Vital Process*. Cambridge, MA: MIT Press, 2012.

King, Brian. *States of Disease: Political Environments and Human Health*. Berkeley: University of California Press, 2017.

Kinkela, David. *DDT and the American Century: Global Health, Environmental Politics, and the Pesticide That Changed the World*. Chapel Hill: University of North Carolina Press, 2011.

Kirksey, Eben. *Emergent Ecologies*. Durham, NC: Duke University Press, 2015.

Kirksey, Eben, ed. *The Multispecies Salon*. Durham, NC: Duke University Press, 2014.

Kirksey, Eben, Nick Shapiro, and Maria Brodine. "Hope in Blasted Landscapes." In Kirksey, *Multispecies Salon*, 29–63.

Knorr Cetina, Karin. *Epistemic Cultures: How the Sciences Make Knowledge*. Cambridge, MA: Harvard University Press, 1999.

Koch, Robert. "The Etiology of Anthrax, Founded on the Course of Development of *Bacillus anthracis*." In *Essays of Robert Koch*, translated and edited by Kay Codell Carter, 1–17. Westport, CT: Greenwood, 1987.

Kohler, Robert E. *Lords of the Fly: Drosophila Genetics and Experimental Life*. Chicago: University of Chicago Press, 1994.

Koselleck, Reinhart. *Futures Past: On the Semantics of Historical Time*. Translated by Keith Tribe. 1979. New York: Columbia University Press, 2004.

Kuhn, Thomas S. *The Structure of Scientific Revolutions*. 1962. Chicago: University of Chicago Press, 1996.

Kuklick, Henrika, and Robert E. Kohler. Introduction to *Science in the Field*, edited by Henrika Kuklick and Robert E. Kohler, 1–14. Chicago: University of Chicago Press, 1996.

LaBonte, Jason A., Gregory J. Babcock, Trushar Patel, and Joseph Sodroski. "Blockade of HIV-1 Infection of New World Monkey Cells Occurs Primarily at the Stage of Virus Entry." *Journal of Experimental Medicine* 196, no. 4 (2002): 431–45. https://doi.org/10.1084/jem.20020468.

Lakoff, Andrew. *Unprepared: Global Health in a Time of Emergency*. Berkeley: University of California Press, 2017.

Landecker, Hannah. *Culturing Life: How Cells Became Technologies*. Cambridge, MA: Harvard University Press, 2007.

Landecker, Hannah. "A Metabolic History of Manufacturing Waste: Food Commodities and Their Outsides." *Food, Culture, and Society* 22, no. 5 (2019): 530–47. https://doi.org/10.1080/15528014.2019.1638110.

Landecker, Hannah. "Metabolism, Reproduction, and the Aftermath of Categories." *Scholar and Feminist Online* 11, no. 3 (Summer 2013). http://sfonline.barnard.edu/life-un-ltd-feminism-bioscience-race/metabolism-reproduction-and-the-aftermath-of-categories/0/?print=true.

Larkin, Brian. *Signal and Noise: Media, Infrastructure, and Urban Culture in Nigeria*. Durham, NC: Duke University Press, 2008.

Latour, Bruno. "Circulating Reference: Sampling Soil in the Amazon Forest." In Latour, *Pandora's Hope*, 24–79.

Latour, Bruno. *Facing Gaia: Eight Lectures on the New Climatic Regime*. Translated by Catherine Porter. Oxford: Polity, 2019.

Latour, Bruno. "The Historicity of Things: Where Were Microbes before Pasteur." In Latour, *Pandora's Hope*, 145–73.

Latour, Bruno. "On Technical Mediation—Philosophy, Sociology, Genealogy." *Common Knowledge* 3, no. 2 (1994): 29–64. https://pedropeixotoferreira.files.wordpress.com/2011/01/latour_1994_on-technical-mediation-philosophy-sociology-genealogy_commonknowledge.pdf/.

Latour, Bruno. *Pandora's Hope: Essays on the Reality of Science Studies*. Cambridge, MA: Harvard University Press, 1999.

Latour, Bruno. "Visualization and Cognition: Drawing Things Together." In *Knowledge and Society: Studies in the Sociology of the Present and Past*, vol. 6, edited by H. Kuklick, 1–40. Greenwich, CT: JAI Press, 1986.

Latour, Bruno, and Steve Woolgar. *Laboratory Life: The Construction of Scientific Facts*. Princeton, NJ: Princeton University Press, 1986.

Laudisoit, Anne, Pierre Huyghe, Jacob Willie, Bienvenu Ndjoku, Tiffany Scholier, Jérôme Dz'na, Nikki Tagg, et al. "Chimpanzees Surviving in a Fragmented High-Altitude Forest Landscape of the Congolese Albertine Rift." *Conservation Science and Practice* 3, no. 6 (2021): e403. https://doi.org/10.1111/csp2.403.

Laudisoit, Anne, and Caroline Thirion. *MBudha: In the Chimpanzees' Footsteps*. Gedeon Programmes/Clair-obscur Productions/Ushuaïa TV (France), 2018. Video, 52:00.

Lederberg, Joshua, Robert E. Shope, and Stanley C. Oaks Jr., eds. *Emerging Infections: Microbial Threats to Health in the United States*. Washington, DC: National Academies Press, 1992.

Ledford, Heidi. "Caution Urged over Editing DNA in Wildlife (Intentionally or Not)." *Nature* 524 (2015): 16. https://doi.org/10.1038/524016a.

Leroi-Gourhan, André. *Gesture and Speech*. Translated by Anna Bostock Berger. Cambridge, MA: MIT Press, 1993.

Levinthal, Cyrus. "Molecular Model-Building by Computer." *Scientific American*, June 1966, 42–52. https://doi.org/10.1038/scientificamerican0666-42.

Levinthal, Cyrus, et al., and Massachusetts Institute of Technology. *Proteins*. History of Visualization of Biological Macromolecules Online Museum, Early Interactive Molecular Graphics Movie Gallery, ca. 1966. 16mm film, 06:03. http://www.umass.edu/molvis/francoeur/movgallery/moviegallery.html#proteins.

LeWinter, Renee, and Cynthia Baron. "Bold Statements: The SIGGRAPH '90 Art Show Reflects a New Relationship between the Artist and the Computer." *Computer Graphics World* 13, no. 8 (1990): 74–81.

Linnaeus, Carolus. *Bibliotheca Botanica*. 1736. Port Jervis, NY: Lubrecht and Cramer, 1968.

Lippit, Akira Mizuta. *Atomic Light (Shadow Optics)*. Minneapolis: University of Minnesota Press, 2005.

Loeb, Jacques. *Die chemische Entwicklungserregung des tierischen Eies*. 1909. London: Forgotten Books, 2018.

Lockhart, James, ed. and trans. *We People Here: Nahuatl Accounts of the Conquest of Mexico*. Berkeley: University of California Press, 1993.

Lorimer, Jamie. "Parasites, Ghosts, and Mutualists: A Relational Geography for Microbes for Global Health." *Transactions of the Institute of British Geographers* 42, no. 4 (2017): 544–58. https://doi.org/10.1111/tran.12189.

Lovelock, James. *Gaia: A New Look at Life on Earth*. Oxford: Oxford University Press, 1979.

Lowe, Celia. "Infection." *Environmental Humanities* 5, no. 1 (2014): 301–5. https://doi.org/10.1215/22011919-3615559.

Lustig, Alice, and Arnold J. Levine. "One Hundred Years of Virology." *Journal of Virology* 66, no. 8 (1992): 4629–31. https://doi.org/10.1128/JVI.66.8.4629-4631.1992.

Mann, Jonathan. "AIDS, Health, and Human Rights." *RSA Journal* 143, no. 5462 (1995): 40–48.

Manovich, Lev. *The Language of New Media*. Cambridge, MA: MIT Press, 2001.

Margulis, Lynn, and Dorion Sagan. *Microcosmos: Four Billion Years of Evolution from Our Microbial Ancestors*. New York: Summit Books, 1986.

Margulis, Lynn, and Dorion Sagan. *What Is Life?* New York: Simon and Schuster, 1995.

Martin, Paul M. V., and Estelle Martin-Granel. "2,500-Year Evolution of the Term Epidemic." *Emerging Infectious Diseases* 12, no. 6 (2006): 976–80.

Maturana, Humberto, and Francisco Varela. *Autopoiesis and Cognition: The Realization of the Living*. Dordrecht: D. Reidel, 1980.

Mayr, Ernst. *Systematics and the Origin of Species from the Viewpoint of a Zoologist*. New York: Columbia University Press, 1942.

McCaa, Robert. "Spanish and Nahuatl Views on Smallpox and Demographic Catastrophe in Mexico." *Journal of Interdisciplinary History* 25, no. 3 (1995): 397–431. https://www.jstor.org/stable/205693.

McCormick, Joseph B., and Susan Fisher-Hoch. *Level 4: Virus Hunters of the CDC*. With Leslie Alan Horvitz. New York: Fall River, 1999.

Médecins Sans Frontières. "Undetectable: How Viral Load Monitoring Can Improve HIV Treatment in Developing Countries." Médecins Sans Frontières Access Campaign, July 22, 2012. https://www.msfaccess.org/content/undetectable-how-viral-load-monitoring-can-improve-hiv-treatment-developing-countries.

Metzl, Jonathan M., and Anna Kirkland, eds. *Against Health: How Health Became the New Morality*. New York: New York University Press, 2010.

Milburn, Colin. *Mondo Nano: Fun and Games in the World of Digital Matter*. Durham, NC: Duke University Press, 2015.

Milburn, Colin. *Nanovision: Engineering the Future*. Durham, NC: Duke University Press, 2008.

Mol, Annemarie. *The Body Multiple: Ontology in Medical Practice*. Durham, NC: Duke University Press, 2003.

Montagnier, Luc. "25 Years after HIV Discovery: Prospects for Cure and Vaccine." Nobel Lecture, December 8, 2008. https://www.nobelprize.org/prizes/medicine/2008/montagnier/lecture/.

Moore, Jason, ed. *Anthropocene or Capitalocene? Nature, History, and the Crisis of Capitalism*. Oakland, CA: PM Press, 2016.

Moore, Patrick S., and Yuan Chang. "Why Do Viruses Cause Cancer? Highlights of the First Century of Human Tumour Virology." *Nature Reviews Cancer* 10, no. 12 (2010): 878–89. https://doi.org/10.1038/nrc2961.

Morens, David M., Gregory K. Folkers, and Anthony S. Fauci. "What Is a Pandemic?" *Journal of Infectious Diseases* 200, no. 7 (2009): 1018–21. https://doi.org/10.1086/644537.

Morse, Stephen. *Emerging Viruses*. New York: Oxford University Press, 1993.

Mukharji, Projit Bihari. "Cat and Mouse: Animal Technologies, Trans-imperial Networks, and Public Health from Below, British India, c. 1907–1918." *Social History of Medicine* 31, no. 3 (2018): 510–32. https://doi.org/10.1093/shm/hkx024.

Mukherjee, Rahul. *Radiant Infrastructures: Media, Environment, and Cultures of Uncertainty*. Durham, NC: Duke University Press, 2020.

Murphy, Michelle. "Alterlife and the Decolonial Chemical Relations." *Cultural Anthropology* 32, no. 4 (2017): 494–503. https://doi.org/10.14506/ca32.4.02.

Myers, Natasha. *Rendering Life Molecular: Models, Modelers, and Excitable Matter*. Durham, NC: Duke University Press, 2015.

Nading, Alec. *Mosquito Trails: Ecology, Health, and the Politics of Entanglement*. Berkeley: University of California Press, 2014.

Narat, Victor, Mamadou Kampo, Thibaut Heyer, Stephanie Rupp, Philippe Ambata, Richard Njouom, and Tamara Giles-Vernick. "Using Physical Contact Heterogeneity and Frequency to Characterize Dynamics of Human Exposure to Nonhuman Primate Bodily Fluids in Central Africa." *PLoS Neglected Tropical Diseases* 12, no. 12 (2018): e0006976. https://doi.org/10.1371/journal.pntd.0006976.

Natarajan, Aravind. "Standardized Preservation, Extraction, and Quantification Techniques for the Detection of Fecal SARS-CoV-2 RNA." *Nature Communications* 12 (2021): 5753. https://doi.org/10.1038/s41467-021-25576-6.

Nattrass, Nicoli. *The AIDS Conspiracy: Science Fights Back*. New York: Columbia University Press, 2012.

Neff, Gina, and Dawn Nafus. *Self-Tracking*. Cambridge, MA: MIT Press, 2016.

Neubauer, Cajetan, and Hannah Landecker. "A Planetary Health Perspective on Synthetic Methionine." *Lancet Planetary Health* 5, no. 8 (2021): e560–69. https://doi.org/10.1016/S2542-5196(21)00138-8.

Nguyen, Vinh Kim. *The Republic of Therapy: Triage and Sovereignty in West Africa's Time of AIDS*. Durham, NC: Duke University Press, 2010.

Nobert, Stefan, Andreas L. Birkenfeld, and Matthias B. Schulze. "Global Pandemics Interconnected—Obesity, Impaired Metabolic Health and COVID-19." *Nature Reviews Endocrinology* 17, no. 3 (2021): 135–49. https://doi.org/10.1038/s41574-020-00462-1.

Nocek, Adam. *Molecular Capture: The Animation of Biology*. Minneapolis: University of Minnesota Press, 2021.

North Carolina Museum of Natural Sciences. "Can Drones Help Count Rainforest Animals?" YouTube, November 13, 2018. https://www.youtube.com/watch?v=4PvsI_NTu2A.

Oldstone, Michael B. *Viruses, Plagues, and History: Past, Present, and Future.* New York: Oxford University Press, 2020.

Olival, Kevin, Parviez R. Hosseini, Carlos Zambrana-Torrelio, Noam Ross, Tiffany L. Bogich, and Peter Daszak. "Host and Viral Traits Predict Zoonotic Spillover from Mammals." *Nature* 546 (2017): 646–50. https://doi.org/10.1038/nature22975.

Olson, Arthur J. "Perspectives on Structural Molecular Biology Visualization: From Past to Present." *Journal of Molecular Biology* 430, no. 21 (2018): 3997–4012. https://doi.org/10.1016/j.jmb.2018.07.009.

Olson, Arthur J. "Self-Assembly Gets Physical." *Nature Nanotechnology* 10 (2015): 728. https://doi.org/10.1038/nnano.2015.172.

Osterholm, Michael T., and Mark Olshaker. *Deadliest Enemy: Our War against Killer Germs*. New York: Little, Brown Spark, 2017.

Ostherr, Kirsten. "Animating Informatics: Scientific Discover through Documentary Film." In *A Companion to Contemporary Documentary Film*, edited by Alexandra Juhasz and Alisa Lebow, 280–97. Hoboken, NJ: Wiley, 2015.

Ostherr, Kirsten. "Risk Media in Medicine: The Rise of the MetaClinical Health App Ecosystem." In *The Routledge Companion to Media and Risk*, edited by Bishnupriya Ghosh and Bhaskar Sarkar, 107–17. New York: Routledge, 2020.

Paracer, Surindar, and Vernon Ahmadjian. *Symbiosis: An Introduction to Biological Associations*. New York: Oxford University Press, 2000.

Parikka, Jussi. *Digital Contagions: A Media Archaeology of Computer Viruses*. New York: Peter Lang, 2007.

Parikka, Jussi. *A Geology of Media*. Minneapolis: University of Minnesota Press, 2015.

Parks, Lisa. *Cultures in Orbit: Satellites and the Televisual*. Durham, NC: Duke University Press, 2005.

Parks, Lisa, and Nicole Starosielski. "Introduction." *Signal Traffic: Critical Studies of Media Infrastructures*, edited by Lisa Parks and Nicole Starosielski, 1–27. Champaign: University of Illinois Press, 2015.

Parks, Lisa, and Janet Walker. "Disaster Media: Bending the Curve of Ecological Disruption and Moving toward Social Justice." *Media+Environment* 2, no. 1 (2020). https://mediaenviron.org/article/13474-disaster-media-bending-the-curve-of-ecological-disruption-and-moving-toward-social-justice.

Patton, Cindy. *Inventing AIDS*. New York: Routledge, 1990.

Patton, Cindy. "Mobile Knowledge: HIV Patient Encounters with Endocrinology." *Canadian Journal of Communication* 32 (2007): 335–55. https://cjc-online.ca/index.php/journal/article/view/1878/3148.

Paxson, Heather. "Microbiopolitics." In Kirksey, *Multispecies Salon*, 115–21.

Paxson, Heather. "Post-Pasteurian Cultures: The Microbiopolitics of Raw-Milk Cheese in the United States." *Cultural Anthropology* 23, no. 1 (2008): 15–47. https://doi.org/10.1111/j.1548-1360.2008.00002.x.

Pépin, Jacques. *The Origins of AIDS*. Cambridge: Cambridge University Press, 2011.

Peters, John Durham. *The Marvelous Clouds: Toward a Philosophy of Elemental Media*. Chicago: University of Chicago Press, 2015.

Petersen, Wolfgang, dir. *Outbreak*. Burbank, CA: Warner Bros., 1995.

Piña, Chris, Alpana Dange, Shruta Rawat, Urmi Jadhav, Julia H. Arnsten, Rosie Chhabra, and Viraj V. Patel. "Antiretroviral Treatment Uptake and Adherence among Men Who Have Sex with Men and Transgender Women with HIV in Mumbai, India: A Cross-Sectional Study." *Journal of the Association of Nurses in AIDS Care* 29, no. 2 (2018): 310–16. https://doi.org/10.1016/j.jana.2017.10.001.

Pollmann, Inga. *Cinematic Vitalism: Film Theory and the Question of Life*. Amsterdam: Amsterdam University Press, 2017.

Povinelli, Elizabeth. *Between Gaia and Ground: Four Axioms of Existence and the Ancestral Catastrophe of Late Liberalism*. Durham, NC: Duke University Press, 2021.

Povinelli, Elizabeth A. *Geontologies: A Requiem to Late Liberalism*. Durham, NC: Duke University Press, 2016.

Preston, Richard. "Crisis in the Hot Zone: Lessons from an Outbreak of Ebola." *New Yorker*, October 18, 1992. https://www.newyorker.com/magazine/1992/10/26/crisis-in-the-hot-zone.

Preston, Richard. *The Hot Zone*. New York: Random House, 1994.

Pulendran, Bali, Shuzhao Li, and Helder Nakaya. "Systems Vaccinology." *Immunity* 33, no. 4 (2010): 516–29. https://doi.org/10.1016/j.immuni.2010.10.006.

Pyne, Michael T., Eric Q. Konnick, Amit Phansalkar, and David R. Hillyard. "Evaluation of the Abbott Investigational Use Only Real-Time HIV-1 Assay and Comparison to the Roche Amplicor HIV-1 Monitor Test, Version 1.5." *Journal of Molecular Diagnostics* 11, no. 4 (July 2009): 374–54. http://doi.org/10.2353/jmoldx.2009.080166.

Qiu, Jane. "Chasing Plagues." *Scientific American* (June 2020): 24–32.

Quammen, David. *Spillover: Animal Infections and the Next Human Pandemic*. New York: Norton, 2012.

Rancière, Jacques. *The Politics of Aesthetics*. Translated by Gabriel Rockhill. 2004. London: Bloomsbury Academic, 2013.

Rancière, Jacques. "What a Medium Can Mean." *Parrahesia* 11 (2011): 35–43.

Rasmussen, Nicolas. *Picture Control: The Electron Microscope and the Transformation of Biology in America, 1940–1960*. Stanford: Stanford University Press, 1997.

Redvers, Nicole, Michael Yellow Bird, Diana Quinn, Tyson Yunkaporta, and Kerry Arabena. "Molecular Decolonization: An Indigenous Microcosm Perspective of Planetary Health." *International Journal of Environmental Research and Public Health* 17, no. 12 (2020): 4586. https://doi.org/10.3390/ijerph17124586.

Rheinberger, Hans-Jörg. *An Epistemology of the Concrete: Twentieth-Century Histories of Life*. Durham, NC: Duke University Press, 2010.

Richardson, Eugene T. *Epidemic Illusions: On the Coloniality of Global Public Health*. Cambridge, MA: MIT Press, 2020.

Rivers, Thomas M, ed. *Filterable Viruses*. London: Bailliere Tindell, 1928.

Robertson, James. "The Humsafar Trust, Mumbai, India: Empowering Communities of Men Who Have Sex with Men to Prevent HIV." USAID, AIDSTAR-One, Case Study Series, May 2010. https://humsafar.org/wp-content/uploads/2018/03/pdf_10_AIDSTAR-Case-Study-Series.pdf.

Rodolfo, Kelvin. "What Is Homeostasis?" *Scientific American*, January 3, 2000. https://www.scientificamerican.com/article/what-is-homeostasis/.

Rodrigues, Rashmi, Anita Shet, Jimmy Antony, Kristi Sidney, Karthika Arumugam, Shubha Krishnamurthy, George D'Souza, and Ayesha DeCosta. "Supporting Adherence to Antiretroviral Therapy with Mobile Phone Reminders: Results from a Cohort in South India." *PLOS ONE* 7, no. 8 (2012): e40723. https://doi.org/10.1371/journal.pone.0040723.

Roitman, Janet L. *Anti-crisis*. Durham, NC: Duke University Press, 2014.

Roosth, Sophia. *Synthetic: How Life Got Made*. Chicago: University of Chicago Press, 2017.

Rose, Deborah Bird. "Multispecies Knots of Ethical Time." *Environmental Philosophy* 9, no. 1 (2012): 127–40.

Rose, Deborah Bird, *Wild Dog Dreaming: Love and Extinction*. Charlottesville: University of Virginia Press, 2013.

Rosengarten, Marsha. *HIV Interventions: Biomedicine and the Traffic between Information and Flesh*. Seattle: University of Washington Press, 2009.

Rostal, Melinda, Janice E. Liang, David Zimmermann, Roy Bengis, Janusz Paweska, and William B. Karesh. "Rift Valley Fever: Does Wildlife Play a Role?" *Institute for Laboratory Animal Research Journal* 15, no. 58 (2017): 359–70.

Rostal, Melinda, Janice Liang, Claudia Cordel, William Karesh, Janusz Paweska, and Pamela Oberem. "Understanding Rift Valley Fever." *Wild Ranching* 3 (June 2017): 153–57.

Rous, Peyton. "A Sarcoma of the Fowl Transmissible by an Agent Separable from the Tumor Cells." *Journal of Experimental Medicine* 13, no. 4 (1911): 397–411. http://dx.doi.org/10.1084/ jem.13.4.397.

Rous, Peyton. "A Transmissible Avian Neoplasm (Sarcoma of the Common Fowl)." *Journal of Experimental Medicine* 12, no. 5 (1910): 696–705. https://doi.org/10.1084/jem.12.5.696.

Rous, Peyton. "Transmission of a Malignant New Growth by Means of a Cell-Free Filtrate." *Journal of the American Medical Association* 250, no. 11 (1983): 1445–46. https://doi.org/10.1001/jama.1983.03340110059037.

Ruddiman, W. F. *Plows, Plagues, and Petroleum: How Humans Took Control of Climate*. Princeton, NJ: Princeton University Press, 2005.

Rupp, Stephanie, Philippe Ambata, Victor Narat, and Tamara Giles-Vernick. "Beyond the Cut Hunter: The Historical Epidemiology of HIV Beginnings in Central Africa." *EcoHealth* 13, no. 4 (2016): 661–71. https://doi.org/10.1007/s10393-016-1189-6.

Ruska, Helmut, Bodo von Borries, and Ernst Ruska. "Die Bedeutung der Übermikroskopie für die Virusforschung." *Archiv für die gesamte Virusforschung* 1, no. 1 (1939): 155–69. https://doi.org/10.1007/BF01243399.

Ryan, Morgan. "Molecular Movie Stars." *American Scientist* 7, no. 5 (2009). Accessed July 1, 2022. https://www.americanscientist.org/article/molecular-movie-stars.

Sagan, Dorion. *The Cosmic Apprentice: Dispatches from the Edge of Science.* Minneapolis: University of Minnesota Press, 2013.

Sampson, Tony D. *Virality: Contagion Theory in the Age of Networks*. Minneapolis: University of Minnesota Press, 2012.

Sampson, Tony D., and Jussi Parikka. "The Operational Loops of a Pandemic." *Cultural Politics* 17, no. 1 (2021): 55–68. https://doi.org/10.1215/17432197-8797529.

Sarkar, Bhaskar, and Bishnupriya Ghosh. "Media and Risk: An Introduction." In *The Routledge Companion to Media and Risk*, edited by Bishnupriya Ghosh and Bhaskar Sarkar, 1–24. New York: Routledge, 2020.

Saussure, Ferdinand de. *Course in General Linguistics*. Edited by Charles Bally and Albert Sechehaye. Translated by Wade Baskin. 1916. New York: Philosophical Society, 1959.

Schrödinger, Erwin. *What Is Life? The Physical Aspect of the Living Cell*. Cambridge: Cambridge University Press, 1944.

Seed Movement Fireworks. Supporting Information (Movie S1) for Jansen et al., "Thieving Rodents," 2012. YouTube, accessed July 20, 2021. https://www.youtube.com/watch?v=JebSa7d1e1M.

Shah, Sonia. "Could Monkeypox Take Over Where Smallpox Left Off?" *Scientific American*, March 2013, 66–71. https://doi.org/10.1038/scientificamerican0313-66.

Shah, Sonia. *Pandemic: Tracking Contagions, from Cholera to Ebola and Beyond*. New York: Farrar, Straus and Giroux, 2016.

Shapiro, Nicholas, and Eben Kirksey. "Chemo-Ethnography: An Introduction." *Cultural Anthropology* 32, no. 4 (2017): 481–93. https://doi.org/10.14506/ca32.4.01.

Sharp, Paul M., George M. Shaw, and Beatrice H. Hahn. "Simian Immunodeficiency Virus Infection of Chimpanzees." *Journal of Virology* 79, no. 7 (2005): 3891–902. https://doi.org/10.1128/JVI.79.7.3891-3902.2005.

Shelley, Mary. *Frankenstein: 1818 text*. Oxford: Oxford University Press, 2009.

Sherer, Robert. *The Blood Works: The Sanguineous Art of Robert Sherer*. Atlanta: Kennesaw State University Legacy Project 6, 2012. https://digitalcommons.kennesaw.edu/cgi/viewcontent.cgi?referer=&httpsredir=1&article=1005&context=ksupresslegacy.

Shilt, Randy. *And the Band Played On: Politics, People, and the AIDS Epidemic.* New York: St. Martin's Griffin, 2007.

Siegel, Greg. *Forensic Media: Reconstructing Accidents in Accelerated Modernity*. Durham, NC: Duke University Press, 2014.

Slater, Leo B. *War and Disease: Biomedical Research on Malaria in the Twentieth Century*. New Brunswick, NJ: Rutgers University Press, 2014.

Smith, D. C., and A. E. Douglas. *The Biology of Symbiosis*. London: Hodder Arnold, 1987.

Smithsonian Tropical Research Institute in Panama. *Barro Colorado Island: BCI–Official Video*. YouTube, 2010. https://www.youtube.com/watch?v=tRGG-XmNMhk.

Specter, Michael. "Rewriting the Code of Life." *New Yorker*, December 25, 2016. https://www.newyorker.com/magazine/2017/01/02/rewriting-the-code-of-life.

Soderbergh, Steven, dir. *Contagion*. Burbank, CA: Warner Bros., 1995.

Stanford University Graphic Novel Project. *Virunga: Africa's Oldest National Park*. Palo Alto, CA: Stanford University Press, 2009.

Starosielski, Nicole. *The Undersea Network*. Durham, NC: Duke University Press, 2015.

Stengers, Isabelle. "The Challenge of Ontological Politics." In *A World of Many Worlds*, edited by Marisol de la Cadena and Mario Blaser, 83–111. Durham, NC: Duke University Press, 2018.

Stengers, Isabelle. *Cosmopolitics I*. Minneapolis: University of Minnesota Press, 2010.

Stengers, Isabelle. *Cosmopolitics II*. Minneapolis: University of Minnesota Press, 2011.

Stengers, Isabelle. *Thinking with Whitehead: A Free and Wild Creation of Concepts*. Cambridge, MA: Harvard University Press, 2011.

Stintson, Kathryn et al. "Cohort Profile: The Khayelitsha Antiretroviral Programme, Cape Town, South Africa." *International Journal of Epidemiology* 46, no. 2 (2017): e21.

Subbaraman, Nidhi. "'Heinous!': Coronavirus Researcher Shut Down for Wuhan-Lab Link Slams New Funding Restrictions." *Nature*, August 21, 2020. https://www.nature.com/articles/d41586-020-02473-4.

Sunder Rajan, Kaushik. *Pharmocracy: Value, Politics, and Knowledge in the Global Biomedicine Economy*. Durham, NC: Duke University Press, 2017.

TallBear, Kim, and Angela Willey. "Critical Relationality: Queer, Indigenous, and Multispecies Belonging beyond Settler Sex and Nature." *Imaginations* 10, no. 1 (2019). https://doi.org/10.17742/IMAGE.CR.10.1.1.

Thacker, Eugene. *Biomedia*. Minneapolis: University of Minnesota Press, 2004.

Thacker, Eugene. *The Global Genome: Biotechnology, Politics, and Culture*. Cambridge, MA: MIT Press, 2005.

Thomas, Lindsay. "Pandemics of the Future: Disease Surveillance in Real Time." *Surveillance and Society* 12, no. 2 (2014): 287–300. https://doi.org/10.24908/ss.v12i2.4735.

Thurtle, Philip. *Biology in the Grid: Graphic Design and the Envisioning of Life*. Minneapolis: University of Minnesota Press, 2016.

Timberg, Craig, and Daniel Halperin. *Tinderbox: How the West Sparked the AIDS Epidemic and How the World Can Finally Overcome It*. New York: Penguin, 2012.

Titmuss, Richard Morris. *The Gift Relationship: From Human Blood to Social Policy*. Bristol, UK: Polity, 2018.

Treichler, Paula. *How to Have Theory in an Epidemic: Cultural Chronicles of AIDS*. Durham, NC: Duke University Press, 1999.

Tsing, Anna Lowenhaupt. "Blasted Landscapes (and the Gentle Arts of Mushroom Picking)." In Kirksey, *Multispecies Salon*, 87–110.
Tsing, Anna Lowenhaupt. *The Mushroom at the End of the World: On the Possibility of Life in Capitalist Ruins*. Princeton, NJ: Princeton University Press, 2015.
Tsing, Anna L., Jennifer Deger, Alder Keleman Saxena, and Feifei Zhou, eds. *Feral Atlas: The More-Than-Human Anthropocene*. Online. Redwood City, CA: Stanford University Press, 2021. https://doi.org/10.21627/2020fa.
Tsing, Anna Lowenhaupt, Andrew S. Mathews, and Nils Bubandt. "Patchy Anthropocene: Landscape Structure, Multispecies History, and the Retooling of Anthropology; An Introduction to Supplement 20." *Cultural Anthropology* 60, no. S20 (2019): S186–97. https://doi.org/10.1086/703391.
Tucker, Marlee A., Katrin Böhning-Gaese, William F. Fagan, John M. Fryxell, Bram Van Moorter, Susan C. Alberts, Abdullahi H. Ali, et al. "Moving in the Anthropocene: Global Reductions in Terrestrial Mammalian Movements." *Science* 359, no. 6374 (2018): 466–69. https://doi.org/10.1126/science.aam9712.
Tufte, Edward R. *Envisioning Information*. Cheshire, CT: Graphics Press, 1990.
Uexküll, Jakob von. "A Stroll through the Worlds of Animals and Men: A Picture Book of Invisible Worlds." In *Instinctive Behavior: The Development of a Modern Concept*, edited and translated by Claire H. Schiller, 5–80. 1934. New York: International Universities Press, 1957.
Uncertain Commons. *Speculate This!* Durham, NC: Duke University Press, 2013.
Usher, Anne Danaiya. "South Africa and India Push for COVID-19 Patents Ban." *Lancet World Report* 396, no. 10265 (2020): 1790–91. https://doi.org/10.1016/S0140-6736(20)32581-2.
Vale, Beth Nosizwe, Rebecca J. Hodes, Lucie Cluver, and Mildred Thabeng. "Bureaucracies of Blood and Belonging: Documents, HIV-Positive Youth and the State in South Africa. " *Development and Change* 48, no. 6 (2017): 1287–309. https://doi.org/10.1111/dech.12341.
Van Dooren, Thom. *The World in a Shell: Snail Stories for a Time of Extinction*. Cambridge, MA: MIT Press, 2022.
Van Dooren, Thom, and Matthew Chrulew. *Kin: Thinking with Deborah Bird Rose*. Durham, NC: Duke University Press, 2022.
Vijayakumar, Gowri. *At Risk: Indian Sexual Politics and the Global AIDS Crisis*. Palo Alto, CA: Stanford University Press, 2021.
Vismann, Cornelia. *Files: Law and Media Technology*. Translated by Geoffrey Winthrop-Young. Stanford, CA: Stanford University Press, 2008.
Wald, Priscilla. *Contagious: Cultures, Carriers, and the Outbreak Narrative*. Durham, NC: Duke University Press, 2008.
Wald, Priscilla, and Kym Weed. "COVID-19 and the Outbreak Narrative." *Southern Cultures*, April 2, 2020. https://www.youtube.com/watch?v=aXTzmxc5qhY.
Waldby, Catherine, and Robert Mitchell. *Tissue Economies: Blood, Organs, and Cell Lines in Late Capitalism*. Durham, NC: Duke University Press, 2006.
Walker, Faith M., Charles H. D. Williamson, Daniel E. Sanchez, Colin J. Sobek, and Carol L. Chambers. "Species from Feces: Order-Wide Identification of Chiroptera

from Guano and Other Non-invasive Genetic Samples." *PLOS ONE* 11, no. 9 (2016): e0162342. https://doi.org/10.1371/journal.pone.0162342.

Wallace, Robert G., Luke Bergmann, Richard Kock, Marius Gilbert, Lenny Hogerwerf, Rodrick Wallace, and Mollie Holmberg. "The Dawn of Structural One Health: A New Science Tracking Disease Emergence along Circuits of Capital." *Social Science and Medicine* 129 (2015): 68–77. https://doi.org/10.1016/j.socscimed.2014.09.047.

Wang, Chia C., Kimberly A. Prather, Josué Sznitman, Jose L. Jimenez, Seema S. Lakdawala, Zeynep Tufekci, and Linsey C. Marr. "Airborne Transmission of Respiratory Viruses." *Science* 373, no. 6558 (2021). https://doi.org/10.1126/science.abd9149.

Watney, Simon. *Policing Desire: Pornography, AIDS, and the Media*. Minneapolis: University of Minnesota Press, 1987.

Whiteside, Alan. *HIV and AIDS: A Very Short Introduction*. Oxford: Oxford University Press, 2016.

Winegard, Timothy C. *The Mosquito: A Human History of Our Deadliest Predator*. New York: Dutton, 2019.

Wolfe, Nathan D. *The Viral Storm: The Dawn of a New Pandemic Age*. New York: Times Books, 2011.

Wolfe, Nathan D., Claire Panosian Dunavan, and Jared Diamond. "Origins of Major Human Infectious Diseases." *Nature* 447 (2007): 279–83. https://doi.org/10.1038/nature05775.

Wolfe, Nathan D., Ananias A. Escalante, William B. Karesh, Annelisa Kilbourn, Andrew Spielman, and Altaf A. Lal. "Wild Primate Populations in Emerging Infectious Disease Research: The Missing Link?" *Emerging Infectious Disease* 4, no. 2 (1998): 149–58.

World Bank. *1993 World Development Report: Invest in Health*. Washington, DC: World Bank, June 1993.

World Health Organization (Department of HIV/AIDS) and UNAIDS. "The Treatment 2.0 Framework for Action: Catalysing the Next Phase of Treatment, Care and Support." Geneva: World Health Organization, 2011. http://apps.who.int/iris/bitstream/handle/10665/44640/9789241501934_eng.pdf;jsessionid=F447171D31827D8CBDFAA178F3A5A162?sequence=1.

Worobey, Michael, Thomas D. Watts, Richard A. McKay, Marc A. Suchard, Timothy Granade, Dirk E. Teuwen, Beryl A. Koblin, Walid Heneine, Philippe Lemey, and Harold W. Jaffe. "1970s and 'Patient 0' HIV-1 Genomes Illuminate Early HIV/AIDS History in North America." *Nature* 539 (2016): 98–101. https://doi.org/10.1038/nature19827.

Xia, Shuai, Qiaoshuai Lan, Shan Su, Xinling Wang, Wei Xu, Zezhong Liu, Yun Zhu, Qian Wang, Lu Lu, and Shibo Jiang. "The Role of Furin Cleavage Site in SARS-CoV-2 Spike Protein-Mediated Membrane Fusion in the Presence or Absence of Trypsin." *Signal Transduction and Targeted Therapy* 5 (2020). https://www.nature.com/articles/s41392-020-0184-0.

Yong, Ed. *I Contain Multitudes: The Microbes within Us and a Grander View of Life*. New York: Vintage, 2017.

Yong, Ed. "Microbiome Sequencing Offers Hope for Diagnostics." *Nature*, March 23, 2012. https://www.nature.com/news/microbiome-sequencing-offers-hope-for-diagnostics-1.10299.

Yong, Ed. "The Next Chapter in a Viral Arms Race." *Atlantic*, August 4, 2017. https://www.theatlantic.com/science/archive/2017/08/rabbit-virus-arms-race/536796/.

Youde, Jeremy R. *AIDS, South Africa, and the Politics of Knowledge*. Farnham, UK: Ashgate, 2013.

Youde, Jeremy R. *Global Health Governance*. New York: Polity Books, 2012.

Yousif, Hayder. "Deep Neural Networks for Animal Object Detection and Recognition in the Wild." PhD dissertation, University of Missouri–Columbia, 2019.

Yousif, Hayder, Jianhe Yuan, Roland Kays, and Zhihai He. "Animal Scanner: Software for Classifying Humans, Animals, and Empty Frames in Camera Trap Images." *Ecology and Evolution* 9, no. 4 (2019): 1578–89. https://doi.org/10.1002/ece3.4747.

Index

Note: Page numbers in italics indicate figures; *pl.* refers to the color plates.